**Keep this book. You will
need it and use it throughout
your career.**

About the American Hotel & Motel Association (AH&MA)

Founded in 1910, AH&MA is the trade association representing the lodging industry in the United States. AH&MA is a federation of state lodging associations throughout the United States with 11,000 lodging properties worldwide as members. The association offers its members assistance with governmental affairs representation, communications, marketing, hospitality operations, training and education, technology issues, and more. For information, call 202-289-3100.

LODGING, the management magazine of AH&MA, is a "living textbook" for hospitality students that provides timely features, industry news, and vital lodging information. For information on subscriptions and student rates, call 202-289-3113.

About the Educational Institute of AH&MA (EI)

An affiliate of AH&MA, the Educational Institute is the world's largest source of quality training and educational materials for the lodging industry. EI develops textbooks and courses that are used in more than 1,200 colleges and universities worldwide, and also offers courses to individuals through its Distance Learning program. Hotels worldwide rely on EI for training resources that focus on every aspect of lodging operations. Industry-tested videos, CD-ROMs, seminars, and skills guides prepare employees at every skill level. EI also offers professional certification for the industry's top performers. For information about EI's products and services, call 800-349-0299 or 407-999-8100.

About the American Hotel Foundation (AHF)

An affiliate of AH&MA, the American Hotel Foundation provides financial support that enhances the stability, prosperity, and growth of the lodging industry through educational and research programs. AHF has awarded hundreds of thousands of dollars in scholarship funds for students pursuing higher education in hospitality management. AHF has also funded research projects on topics important to the industry, including occupational safety and health, turnover and diversity, and best practices in the U.S. lodging industry. For information, call 202-289-3100.

INTERNATIONAL HUMAN RESOURCE MANAGEMENT
in the
HOSPITALITY INDUSTRY

Educational Institute Courses

Introductory

INTRODUCTION TO THE HOSPITALITY INDUSTRY
Fourth Edition
Gerald W. Lattin

AN INTRODUCTION TO HOSPITALITY TODAY
Third Edition
Rocco M. Angelo, Andrew N. Vladimir

TOURISM AND THE HOSPITALITY INDUSTRY
Joseph D. Fridgen

Rooms Division

FRONT OFFICE PROCEDURES
Fifth Edition
Michael L. Kasavana, Richard M. Brooks

HOUSEKEEPING MANAGEMENT
Second Edition
Margaret M. Kappa, Aleta Nitschke, Patricia B. Schappert

Human Resources

HOSPITALITY SUPERVISION
Second Edition
Raphael R. Kavanaugh, Jack D. Ninemeier

HOSPITALITY INDUSTRY TRAINING
Second Edition
Lewis C. Forrest, Jr.

HUMAN RESOURCES MANAGEMENT
Second Edition
Robert H. Woods

**INTERNATIONAL HUMAN RESOURCE MANAGEMENT
IN THE HOSPITALITY INDUSTRY**
Edited by Sybil M. Hofmann, Colin Johnson, and Michael M. Lefever

Marketing and Sales

MARKETING OF HOSPITALITY SERVICES
William Lazer, Roger Layton

HOSPITALITY SALES AND MARKETING
Third Edition
James R. Abbey

CONVENTION MANAGEMENT AND SERVICE
Fifth Edition
Milton T. Astroff, James R. Abbey

MARKETING IN THE HOSPITALITY INDUSTRY
Third Edition
Ronald A. Nykiel

Accounting

UNDERSTANDING HOSPITALITY ACCOUNTING I
Fourth Edition
Raymond Cote

UNDERSTANDING HOSPITALITY ACCOUNTING II
Third Edition
Raymond Cote

**BASIC FINANCIAL ACCOUNTING FOR THE
HOSPITALITY INDUSTRY**
Second Edition
Raymond S. Schmidgall, James W. Damitio

**MANAGERIAL ACCOUNTING FOR THE HOSPITALITY
INDUSTRY**
Fourth Edition
Raymond S. Schmidgall

Food and Beverage

FOOD AND BEVERAGE MANAGEMENT
Third Edition
Jack D. Ninemeier

QUALITY SANITATION MANAGEMENT
Ronald F. Cichy

FOOD PRODUCTION PRINCIPLES
Jerald W. Chesser

FOOD AND BEVERAGE SERVICE
Second Edition
Ronald F. Cichy, Paul E. Wise

HOSPITALITY PURCHASING MANAGEMENT
William P. Virts

BAR AND BEVERAGE MANAGEMENT
Lendal H. Kotschevar, Mary L. Tanke

FOOD AND BEVERAGE CONTROLS
Fourth Edition
Jack D. Ninemeier

General Hospitality Management

HOTEL/MOTEL SECURITY MANAGEMENT
Second Edition
Raymond C. Ellis, Jr., David M. Stipanuk

HOSPITALITY LAW
Third Edition
Jack P. Jefferies

RESORT MANAGEMENT
Second Edition
Chuck Y. Gee

INTERNATIONAL HOTEL MANAGEMENT
Chuck Y. Gee

HOSPITALITY INDUSTRY COMPUTER SYSTEMS
Third Edition
Michael L. Kasavana, John J. Cahill

**MANAGING FOR QUALITY IN THE HOSPITALITY
INDUSTRY**
Robert H. Woods, Judy Z. King

CONTEMPORARY CLUB MANAGEMENT
Edited by Joe Perdue for the Club Managers Association of America

Engineering and Facilities Management

FACILITIES MANAGEMENT
David M. Stipanuk, Harold Roffman

HOSPITALITY INDUSTRY ENGINEERING SYSTEMS
Michael H. Redlin, David M. Stipanuk

HOSPITALITY ENERGY AND WATER MANAGEMENT
Second Edition
Robert E. Aulbach

INTERNATIONAL HUMAN RESOURCE MANAGEMENT in the HOSPITALITY INDUSTRY

Edited by Sybil M. Hofmann,
Colin Johnson, and Michael M. Lefever

EDUCATIONAL INSTITUTE
American Hotel & Motel Association

Disclaimer

This publication is designed to provide accurate and authoritative information in regard to the subject matter covered. It is sold with the understanding that the publisher is not engaged in rendering legal, accounting, or other professional service. If legal advice or other expert assistance is required, the services of a competent professional person should be sought.
—*From the Declaration of Principles jointly adopted by the American Bar Association and a Committee of Publishers and Associations*

The author or authors of each chapter are solely responsible for its content. All views expressed herein are solely those of the authors and do not necessarily reflect the views of the Educational Institute of the American Hotel & Motel Association (the Institute) or the American Hotel & Motel Association (AH&MA).

Nothing contained in this publication shall constitute a standard, an endorsement, or a recommendation of the Institute or AH&MA. The Institute and AH&MA disclaim any liability with respect to the use of any information, procedure, or product, or reliance thereon by any member of the hospitality industry.

Project Editors: Tim Eaton
Robert Bittner
Jennifer Smith
Jim Purvis

Contents

viii *Contents*

Congratulations. . .

You have a running start on a fast-track career!

Developed through the input of industry and academic experts, this course gives you the know-how hospitality employers demand. Upon course completion, you will earn the respected American Hotel & Motel Association certificate that ensures instant recognition worldwide. It is your link with the global hospitality industry.

You can use your AH&MA certificate to show that your learning experiences have bridged the gap between industry and academia. You will have proof that you have industry-driven competencies and that you know how to apply your knowledge to actual hospitality work situations.

By earning your course certificate, you also take a step toward completing the highly respected learning programs—Certificates of Specialization, the Hospitality Operations Certificate, and the Hospitality Management Diploma—that raise your professional development to a higher level. Certificates from these programs greatly enhance your credentials, and a permanent record of your course and program completion is maintained by the Educational Institute.

We commend you for taking this important step. Turn to the Educational Institute for additional resources that will help you stay ahead of your competition.

Preface

Most major hotel chains and leading food service companies operate internationally. From a Morton's of Chicago in Singapore to a Popeye's Chicken and Biscuits in Korea, a Westin hotel in Hanoi, a Swisshôtel in Atlanta, a Nikko hotel in New York, a Bass hotel (Inter-Continental) in Athens, or a Sandals-owned resort in Cuba, international operations in the hospitality industry are not a new phenomenon. The accelerating expansion of international brand names and hospitality corporations into new markets throughout the world adds an interesting dimension to this industry's already global presence. Bass Hotels & Resorts (U.K.-based owners of the Holiday Inn and Inter-Continental brands) is in 95 countries, Nikko (Japan) in nearly 20 countries, and Marriott (United States) in more than 50. The question facing all international hospitality companies now is how to select and train employees for this environment.

With the rapidly expanding international focus of so many hospitality companies, it is surprising to find that the topic of global human resource management has been all but ignored in hospitality textbooks. A review of the top U.S. hospitality human resource texts finds little, if any, attention given to global issues. The hospitality industry can no longer afford to operate from an ethnocentric perspective. Each country is unique in terms of a number of factors that will affect a company's HR function and, therefore, potentially the organization's success. Multinational organizations cannot ignore that many human resource processes, developed typically in the company's headquarters, do not assimilate with other countries' differing social and cultural norms and traditions, languages, religions, and legal/political environments.

International Human Resource Management in the Hospitality Industry addresses the totality of the human resources function from the unique perspective of individual countries that have a major hospitality industry presence. An overarching principle of this text is to present the human resource issues and sentiments of each country openly, honestly, and without censor. The text provides a descriptive function in explaining aspects such as cultural distinctions, societal work values, labor market issues, and the legal environment as related to hospitality businesses. The role of the female manager, performance evaluation practices, and training and development are also discussed in many chapters. Beyond simple description, however, each chapter contains prescriptive information to help maximize a hospitality company's success in developing the most effective human resource processes for the specific country. Each chapter presents a range of helpful study aids such as definitions of key terms, discussion questions, and a list of pertinent and useful Internet sites. In addition, many chapters feature a case study illustrating a typical employee scenario and specific approaches reflective of actual HR processes for that country. These cases can be used in a number of interactive, knowledge-enhancing, and skill-building teaching approaches.

As students prepare for the hospitality industry, they need to realize that, whether they are studying in Ireland, France, Lebanon, or Mexico, their careers will very probably contain international experiences. For the future leaders of the industry, as well as current hospitality managers, *International Human Resource Management in the Hospitality Industry* provides a foundation of international human resource knowledge and perspectives in countries as varied as China, Mauritius, Turkey, and Jamaica. With globalization clearly emerging as the trend of the new millennium, *International Human Resource Management in the Hospitality Industry* will be a most valuable tool not only to educators, but also to corporations and hospitality enterprises with operations around the world.

The concept, cultivation, and creation of this book were themselves an international human resource adventure. The idea for the text originated in the summer of 1998 in Lausanne, Switzerland. It was clear that most, if not all, current texts on human resource management were written by either American or British authors. Consequently, they were limited to mostly American and British history, issues, laws, practices, and trends. The text began to take shape in the fall of 1998 in Athens, Greece, when a proposal was drafted and a team of HR experts/authors from 20 countries was recruited. The text became "official" in the spring of 1999 in Atlanta, United States, when a contract was signed, author guidelines established, and deadlines set. The text then took shape over the next 12 months as authors in these 20 countries worked closely with editors in Lansing, United States; Glyfada, Greece; Lausanne, Switzerland; and Atlanta, United States. Finally, *International Human Resource Management in the Hospitality Industry* made its debut in the summer of 2000 at the Annual CHRIE Conference in New Orleans.

This text would not have become a reality without the dedication and hard work of many people. We are deeply indebted to our authors, who have made it possible to view and respect human resource management as a global system of distinct cultural issues and practices that are nonetheless all part of an interdependent discipline and profession, growing closer every day. We also pay tribute to many fine professional associations such as HCIMA, EuroCHRIE, CHRIE, and EUHOFA for providing excellent forums and networks allowing us to find and recruit the most qualified and talented authors.

We also want to thank the untiring assistance of the professional staff of the Educational Institute of the American Hotel & Motel Association. Our deepest gratitude goes to Bob Bittner, Jennifer Smith, Jim Purvis, and especially Tim Eaton. Their patience, skill, and inspiration made it possible to create a focused, balanced, and unique text from a huge diversity of cultural differences, issues, and styles. Very special thanks go to Désirée Baroudy in Athens and Ann Gagnier in Atlanta for their skill in keeping communication flowing freely and frequently among all the authors and editors from around the globe during this international adventure. Bravo to our team. Bravo to our new family.

Sybil Hofmann, Glyfada, Greece

Colin Johnson, Lausanne, Switzerland

Michael Lefever, Atlanta, United States

Introduction

The world has become extremely small within the last decade. In a nanosecond, a new hospitality graduate can submit a résumé via the Internet for an exciting career position on the other side of the globe. The newly constructed hotel or growing restaurant chain can electronically recruit employees from many nations simultaneously. The work forces of many countries have become more culturally diverse. Competition and lucrative investment returns have spurred the expansion of major hospitality players into international markets. Many countries with once limited hospitality interests are now "hot spots" for travel and tourism. From Vietnam to the remotest jungles of South America, opportunities for hospitality development and growth are expanding beyond what could have been even imagined just a few years ago. The role of the human resources function as a strategic business partner has never been more important.

As newly graduated hospitality majors begin their careers, the world truly does await them. Chances are excellent that an international work opportunity will loom in the future. Can managers be effective in any country regardless of their backgrounds? What skills and knowledge will be necessary for their success?

The internationalization of business operations has held a number of surprises for the hospitality industry, as has been the case for many other industries. These international learning experiences have involved even well-known, highly successful companies. For example, after McDonald's opened restaurants in India, it took the company thirteen months to realize that Hindus do not eat beef; sales in India flourished when it started making hamburgers out of lamb. McDonald's had to make similar adjustments as it expanded to other countries; McDonald's restaurants serve beer in Germany, wine in France, and kosher beef in Israel, for example. KFC, the popular U.S.-based quick-service chain featuring fried chicken, did not initially realize that its slogan, "Finger-lickin' good," became "Eat your fingers off" in Chinese.[1] These examples are not presented to make fun of these companies but to illustrate that global expansion, even for leading corporations, can be extremely challenging.

As we look at the most important and vital role of hospitality managers— working with employees to meet and exceed the expectations of guests—the complexities of international management increase exponentially. As the authors of one study of hospitality companies in the international marketplace put it, "expatriate managers' failure to deliver consistently high-quality products, services, and management processes throughout the world can put a company's reputation and long-term competitiveness at risk."[2] As companies enter totally new territory, there are often no precedents and no prior experiences to go on, yet there is no time for a lengthy learning curve.

In a survey of 52 managers from Asia, Canada, Central America, South America, Europe, Australia, and Africa, interpersonal skills were rated as extremely important, with "cultural sensitivity" receiving the highest average rating in importance. "Managerial flexibility" and "adaptive leadership" were also rated highly; these categories incorporated the management abilities of being open to new ideas and being able to overcome cultural differences. Being able to overcome or adjust to cultural differences is very important, since what works in one culture may or may not work in another. For example, while employee empowerment and participatory management styles have been quite effective and popular in American and Western European companies for several years, workers in some cultures are not prepared for this managerial approach. In fact, in some cultures the establishment of informal and egalitarian work relationships between supervisors and workers would result in chaos and discomfort.[3] Other managerial traits found important in the survey included "intercultural competence" and "international etiquette." Whether verbal or nonverbal, a faux pas can alienate employees, guests, and purveyors alike and yet too often the offending manager is totally unaware of the problem.

As an increasing number of managers relocate around the world in pursuit of global opportunities, they are realizing that more is involved in a successful move to another country than simply making travel arrangements and getting all of their household goods shipped there. The number of U.S. expatriate managers that prematurely end their work assignments abroad ranges from 16 to 50 percent. European and Japanese expatriate managers, studied in the same research, reported lower failure rates but still acknowledged the problem of expatriate failure.[4]

In a joint study by Berlitz International and the Institute for International Human Resources, it was found that 77 percent of international transferees, from a variety of businesses, received no career counseling from their employers upon their return from abroad and only 6 percent were offered re-entry training. In light of this, perhaps it is not surprising that about 50 percent of repatriates leave their companies within two years of their return to their home countries.[5]

Peter Drucker, considered by many to be one of the most important management theorists of our time, believes that—despite the many difficulties—all organizations must compete globally:

> All institutions have to make global competitiveness a strategic goal. No institution ... can hope to survive, let alone succeed, unless it measures up to the standards set by the leaders in its field, anyplace in the world.... Strategy, therefore, has to accept a new fundamental. Any institution— and not just businesses—has to measure itself against the standards set by each industry's leaders anyplace in the world.[6]

Obviously, human resource issues are complicated for companies attempting to compete globally. Addressing diverse environments and work forces must be an ongoing management endeavor for international companies. International hospitality companies are no exception.

The complexities of dealing with international human resource issues accentuate the importance of *International Human Resource Management in the Hospitality Industry*. From dealing with expatriation to effective multi-cultural management to repatriation, successful hospitality managers will have to consistently work toward heightened awareness and higher skill and knowledge levels.

Hospitality graduates entering the competitive international hospitality environment must be able to demonstrate the ability to adopt a culturally aware and flexible management style. As this book clearly shows, hospitality businesses in each country have unique concerns specific to their own locale in addition to the challenges they share with other hospitality businesses around the world in our labor-intensive, quality-driven service profession.

International Human Resource Management in the Hospitality Industry provides much-needed information to current hospitality managers and those who aspire to be one someday. It presents the unique perspectives of 20 countries, written by authors that live and work in their respective nations (or have in the recent past). The authors have direct contact with their country's hospitality and tourism businesses and know firsthand the opportunities and challenges involving human resources in these countries.

As you visit each of the featured countries, the numerous common threads that unite the hospitality and tourism industry worldwide become evident. Each country, although in different and varied ways, has societal issues that affect the labor market as well as legal and governmental factors that affect business operations. Much can be learned by viewing this tapestry of human resource influences from a multicultural perspective.

And so we are off for an around-the-world adventure, as each chapter presents a comprehensive view of its country's societal issues, governmental and legal influences, and labor market challenges. Of course, the multi-faceted roles and responsibilities of hospitality human resource managers are also explored—from employee recruitment and selection to training and development of employees in achieving organizational goals. Zhao Liangqing from China provides an insightful description of the impact on hospitality human resources of his country's "reform and opening" policy. From Mauritius, Margaret Boullé and Marc Boullé delineate the strengths and weaknesses of that country's tourism policies. Mwakai Sio describes the labor environment in Kenya. Romania, a country that in the past undervalued service enterprises, has experienced dynamic growth in the tourism industry, and Ray Iunius and Colin Johnson describe the changing opportunities in hospitality and tourism there. Mark Patton portrays the development of the hospitality industry in South Korea and gives readers a glimpse into that country's interesting Confucian culture and its impact on human resource management.

As you read this book, you will gain a comprehensive view of how legalities, clearly a major part of human resource management in any country, can vary around the globe. Margaret Boullé and Claude Reithler describe the implications of the French legal system for hospitality employers, while Said Ladki explains the major legal issues in Lebanon concerning employment. From another part of the world, Marijke Dieleman and Paul Leenders describe human resources in the Netherlands and the implications of the Dutch legal and political environment on hospitality businesses. Armando Sanchez Soto updates the reader on employment legalities in Mexico. The added dimension of labor unions is particularly prevalent in several countries. Arie Reichel and Sharon Amit, for example, explain Israel's "Collective Agreement" and its role in regulating the hospitality and tourism industry's labor relations in that country.

Labor market concerns also seem to be universal and are explored from the unique perspectives of the featured nations. Finding employees and keeping them is certainly a challenge in the United States, even though hospitality employers are engaging in creative recruiting and retention approaches. Marié Connolly investi gates Ireland's labor market issues, as the hospitality and tourism industry experiences tremendous growth there. Hanan Kattara, in Egypt, discusses the changing role of women working in hospitality and tourism, which certainly affects the present labor force as well as that of the future. Teoman Alemdar also discusses human resource concerns for women working in the hospitality industry in Turkey; he summarizes expatriate-manager issues as well. Chandana Jayawardena and Anne Crick describe the attitudes of Jamaican workers toward jobs in the hospitality and tourism sector, while Vladimir Belyansky, Mikhail Laiko, Elena Ilyina, and Dmitri Chtykhno explore recruitment issues in Russia. Reinhard Kunz and Colin Johnson identify some of the challenges faced by Swiss managers in maintaining the quality and image of the Swiss hospitality industry in the face of increased globalization.

The importance of education and training is also keenly felt around the globe. Scotland's Tom Baum and Lois Farquharson discuss the education and training processes in that country as well as their effectiveness in preparing employees for the hospitality and tourism sector. Career development programs utilized in Malta are described by Godfrey Baldacchino; the chapter outlines how the hospitality and tourism industry contributes to the professional growth of the work force. Nikos Skoulas illustrates how the responsibilities of human resource professionals have grown in Greece and emphasizes the importance of human resources as a vital partner in an organization's strategic planning. If the stories told in this book are any indication, the human resources function will continue to expand in importance to hospitality and tourism organizations worldwide.

Take advantage of each "insider's view" in this panorama of worldwide human resource perspectives applied to the hospitality profession. Imagine yourself, whatever your nationality and background, being relocated to each of the 20 countries described in this book and what you would do to maximize your company's success in each of them. Fasten your seat belt and enjoy the trip!

Debra F. Cannon, Ph.D., CHE
Associate Professor
Cecil B. Day School of Hospitality
Georgia State University

---

[1] Robert Rosen and Patricia Digh, "Cutural Illiteracies," *Mosaics—SHRM Focuses on Workplace Diversity* 6, no. 1 (January 2000): 6.

[2] Ursula Kriegl, "International Hospitality Management," *Cornell Hotel and Restaurant Administration Quarterly* 41, no. 2 (April 2000): 64.

[3] Kriegl, 64–71.

[4] Garry Dessler, *Human Resource Management,* Eighth Edition (Upper Saddle River, N.J.: Prentice-Hall, 2000).

[5] Andrea C. Poe, "Welcome Back," *HR Magazine* 45, no. 3 (March 2000): 94–105.

[6] Peter F. Drucker, *Management Challenges for the 21st Century* (New York: HarperCollins, 1999), 61, 63.

About the Editors

Sybil M. Hofmann

Colin Johnson

Michael M. Lefever

Sybil M. Hofmann is the Founder and President of the Alpine Center for Hotel and Tourism Management Studies in Athens, Greece, now entering its fourteenth year of operation as an associate institute of IHTTI—International Hotel & Tourism Training Institutes, Switzerland.

Born in Lebanon, educated in England, married in Switzerland, and now residing in Greece, she is truly a citizen of the world. With a background in business administration, journalism, and public relations, she has worked in England, Switzerland, and Iraq, where she and her husband spent four years employed in the investment industry before they moved to Greece in 1985. Identifying the need for a hotel school in a country where tourism is so important to the economy, Hofmann entered into a partnership with IHTTI, a subsidiary of TOURISTCONSULT, and launched the Alpine Center, which has established itself as the leading hotel and tourism management school in southern Europe.

She acts as the global coordinator for the IHTTI associate institutes located in Australia, New Zealand, Switzerland, and Greece. She is a Fellow of HCIMA—the Hotel, Catering and International Management Association of the United Kingdom, for which she acts as Ambassador for Europe. She serves on the board of EUHOFA—the International Association of Hotel School Directors, where she is the chairperson of the Education Committee. For two years she served as the president of Euro-CHRIE, the European Federation of CHRIE International (CHRIE is the Council on Hotel, Restaurant and Institutional Education). She is now responsible for Euro-CHRIE's administrative office. She is co-founder of the Global Alliance of Hospitality and Tourism Partners, which was launched in 1998 with Georgia State University's School of Hospitality to assist schools and businesses worldwide in establishing international partnerships.

Colin Johnson is Director of the Lausanne Institute for Hospitality Research at the Ecole hôtelière de Lausanne, Switzerland, an accredited Centre of Excellence for applied research for the hospitality and tourism industries.

He serves on the editorial boards of the *International Journal of Tourism and Hospitality Research* and *Praxis: The Journal of Applied Hospitality Management.* He has contributed articles to various hospitality and tourism journals and has research interests in the globalization of service industries, the development of hospitality and tourism in transition economies, and environmental responsibility.

Johnson has more than 20 years of experience in hospitality management and education, having worked for employers such as Compass, Thistle, and Forte, and in various sectors of the hospitality industry, including hotels, restaurants, airline and contract catering, and sports and social clubs. He has worked on business and educational projects in Poland, Kenya, the United States, Russia, China, Hungary, Greece, Switzerland, and the United Kingdom.

He holds a bachelor's degree in History, a Master of Business Administration from the Manchester Business School, and is completing his doctorate at the University of Fribourg, the focus of which is locational strategies of international hotel operators entering central Eastern Europe.

Michael M. Lefever is currently a Professor and Director of the Cecil B. Day School of Hospitality Administration at Georgia State University. He attended the University of California and has a Ph.D. in psychology. He has received numerous teaching awards and has been designated a Distinguished Professor.

Before coming to Atlanta, he was the department head in Hotel, Restaurant and Travel Administration at the University of Massachusetts, Amherst. He also served as Director of Hospitality Management at San Jose State University; Associate Dean of the College of Hotel and Restaurant Management at the University of Houston; and Assistant Department Head of Restaurant, Hotel and Institutional Management at Purdue University.

Lefever has more than 25 years of hospitality management experience. Starting out in a dishwashing job as a teenager, he worked his way up to manager of a full-service Italian restaurant in Lake Tahoe, California. He later was a manager and manager-trainer for Foodmaker, Inc. of San Diego, California; a district manager for Arctic Circle Restaurants in Salt Lake City, Utah; and regional vice president of Shari's Restaurant in Portland, Oregon. More recently, he was the president and chief executive officer of three restaurants and one catering firm headquartered in Sacramento, California.

Lefever has published four books and nearly 100 articles, and served as executive editor and publisher of two top-ranked academic journals for hospitality and tourism research. In a recent nationwide poll, he was ranked first among the 81 most prolific authors in the field of hotel and restaurant management. He serves on numerous boards worldwide and is a Fellow of the Hotel Catering and Institutional Management Association, based in the United Kingdom.

Study Tips for Users of Educational Institute Courses

Learning is a skill, like many other activities. Although you may be familiar with many of the following study tips, we want to reinforce their usefulness.

Your Attitude Makes a Difference

If you want to learn, you will: it's as simple as that. Your attitude will go a long way in determining whether or not you do well in this course. We want to help you succeed.

Plan and Organize to Learn

- Set up a regular time and place for study. Make sure you won't be disturbed or distracted.
- Decide ahead of time how much you want to accomplish during each study session. Remember to keep your study sessions brief; don't try to do too much at one time.

Read the Course Text to Learn

- *Before* you read each chapter, read the chapter outline and the competencies. If there is a summary at the end of the chapter, you should read it to get a feel for what the chapter is about.
- Then, go back to the beginning of the chapter and *carefully* read, focusing on the material included in the competencies and asking yourself such questions as:

  —Do I understand the material?

  —How can I use this information now or in the future?

- Make notes in margins and highlight or underline important sections to help you as you study. Read a section first, then go back over it to mark important points.
- Keep a dictionary handy. If you come across an unfamiliar word that is not included in the chapter's key terms, look it up in the dictionary.
- Read as much as you can. The more you read, the better you read.

Testing Your Knowledge

- Test questions developed by the Educational Institute for this course are designed to measure your knowledge of the material.

- Prepare for tests by reviewing:

  —competencies

  —notes

  —outlines

  —questions at the end of each assignment

- As you begin to take any test, read the test instructions *carefully* and look over the questions.

We hope your experiences in this course will prompt you to undertake other training and educational activities in a planned, career-long program of professional growth and development.

Chapter 1 Outline

China's Tourism and Hospitality Industry
    Expansion
    Opening Wider to the World
    Sunrise Industry
China's Labor Market
    Employment Pressure
    The Service Sector
    Educational Background
    Traditional Culture and the Chinese
       People
    A New Philosophy About Life and
       Work
Human Resource Management
    Employee Recruitment and Selection
    Promotion and Motivation
    Managers' and Employees' Education
    Employee Participation in
       Management
    The Role of Trade Unions
The Role of Government
    Reforming Politics
    Building the Legal System
    Guaranteeing the Rights of Laborers
    Supporting the Tourism and
       Hospitality Industry
    Speeding Up Management Reform
Conclusion

Competencies

1. Describe China's tourism and
   hospitality industry and the impact
   that China's "reform and opening"
   policy has had on it. (pp. 3–7)

2. Describe China's labor market.
   (pp. 7–13)

3. Summarize human resource
   management issues in China.
   (pp. 13–17)

4. Explain the role of China's
   government in supporting the tourism
   and hospitality industry in China.
   (pp. 17–20)

Human Resource Management in China

Zhao Liangqing

Zhao Liangqing *is Vice President, Anhui Institution of Economic Management, People's Republic of China. He is a member of the China Industry Research & Development Council (CIRD). He has worked in the Anhui Management Development Center as Deputy Director, responsible for business executive training and consulting. He has also worked as a Visiting Professor at the Business School, Simon Fraser University, and at the Foundation for International Training (FIT) in Canada.*

TOURISM IS PLAYING a leading role in the economic development of China. The Chinese tourism and hospitality industry has undergone tremendous changes during China's economic transition. It is one of the fastest growing sectors of the national economy, serving as an important source of non-trade foreign exchange revenue. In this chapter, we will introduce China's tourism and hospitality industry, discuss China's labor market, and explore human resource management issues in China. The chapter concludes with a discussion of the role of the Chinese government in supporting the tourism and hospitality industry.

China's Tourism and Hospitality Industry

In 1978, with unusual courage and daring, the late veteran leader Deng Xiaoping designed a significant blueprint for reforming China and opening it to the outside world. Since then, this "reform and opening" national policy has given great impetus to economic development. In the past 20 years, China has maintained rapid economic progress: Gross Domestic Product (GDP) has registered an average annual growth of 9.9 percent, the "consumption level" (that is, the family income level) has increased by 7.4 percent annually, and living standards have improved considerably. Economic reform has expanded significantly, spreading from the coastal areas to the hinterland and including agriculture, basic industries, and infrastructure facilities—as well as the tourism and hospitality industry.

Exhibit 1   China's Tourism Ranking in the World

Year	Foreign Exchange Earnings/World Rank	Number of Visitors/World Rank
1978	41	51
1991	21	12
1994	10	6
1996	9	6
1997	8	5

Source: *China Tourism Review,* 1998.

Expansion

China's tourism and hospitality industry was extremely backward in the 1970s. A foreign traveler would find it hard to get a place to lodge in most Chinese cities. Things have changed dramatically after more than 20 years of development. Modern hotels have been constructed to meet increasing demand. Restaurants and department stores have mushroomed in large and medium-size cities. In 1978, there were no Western-style fast-food restaurants like McDonald's or KFC in China, but now you see them in almost every city.

The past two decades have seen the tourism and hospitality industry become one of the fastest growing sectors of the national economy, and the most vigorous in the service industry. China's foreign exchange earnings from tourism and hospitality elevated the country to eighth in the world in 1997, compared to 41st in 1978 (see Exhibit 1). In 1997, the industry had 152.775 billion RMB yuan of net fixed assets and the industry's total income accounted for 4.16 percent of the country's GDP. The number of tourists from overseas was 31.8 times greater than in 1978, while foreign exchange earnings were 45.9 times larger. Domestic tourism also developed very quickly in the 1990s.

China's hotel industry has also grown dramatically. By the end of 1997, China had 5,201 hotels with 701,700 rooms accommodating foreign tourists; in 1980 there were only 203 such hotels with 32,000 rooms. The 1997 figure includes 2,724 star-rated hotels.

According to the Regulations Concerning Management Over Travel Agencies, in 1997 there were 4,333 domestic and 1,163 international travel agencies, totaling 5,496, compared to 1,573 in 1988. In 1978, the country had only two travel services (China International Travel Service and China Travel Service) with approximately 100 branches.

There is a rich supply of traditional sightseeing opportunities and special tourist sites in China. Theme parks have made remarkable headway in meeting market demands and coping with the needs of the international market. Travel options for tourists have been improved and expanded each year. In addition to the development of 12 state-level tourist and holiday resorts, China also offers tours involving boating, exploring, hunting, and dozens of other specialized tour packages.

With the improvement in tourist transportation, tourist destinations throughout the country have become more accessible. Aviation companies have increased their capacity, adding domestic and international routes. To match this growth, airport construction has picked up pace. Railways, highways, and waterway transportation also have greatly improved. Catering, recreational, and souvenir businesses have grown in number.

Opening Wider to the World

Thanks to China's reform and opening policy, overseas investors are permitted to build, revamp, and/or operate hotels, restaurants, and travel services in China through the form of joint investment or cooperation. Foreign investment should exceed 25 percent of the total registered capital in such ventures. Foreign managers, senior administrative staff, and experts who have signed contracts with such joint ventures are permitted to enter China to provide management services.

Today, there are more than 290,000 approved foreign-funded enterprises in China. Their total employees number more than 17 million, their tax payments account for more than one-tenth of China's total industrial and commercial tax revenues, and their export value amounts to around 40 percent of the nation's total. China's current foreign investment accounts for around 17 percent of the nation's total investment. The amount of foreign funds China absorbed ranked second in the world just behind the United States.

Since the 1980s, the numerous success stories of foreign capital in China have inspired foreign businesspeople to carry out further business undertakings in China. The effort to "invest in China" has grown in momentum over the past few years. The involvement of foreign capital in catering businesses, hotels, and other service operations was regarded as a test in the early period of China's reform and opening policy.

Because it was one of the first business sectors in China to open itself to the outside world, the tourism and hospitality industry has made impressive advancements. Early in 1979, the first group of tourist hotels was set up by means of foreign investment; now there are 498 foreign-investment star-rated hotels in China. From 1979 to the end of 1996, China's tourism and hospitality industry saw $20 billion in foreign investment, making up seven percent of the total amount of foreign capital China allowed in during this period. Foreign investors have brought to China their advanced managerial expertise; more than 30 overseas hotel management groups are involved in managing Chinese hotels, helping China build a tourism and hospitality industry in line with international standards. With the creation in early 1999 of the Provisional Methods for the Trial Establishment of Sino-Foreign Joint-Venture Travel Agencies, China's tourist industry has opened wide to the outside world. An Interim Method on Sino-Foreign Jointly Funded Pilot Travel Services was also introduced with the approval of the State Council. This move will enhance the ability of the domestic tourist sector to compete internationally. Joint ventures will make better use of marketing channels and networks of overseas tourist sources. Having a foreign travel agency as a cooperative partner will also help China's domestic agencies enhance their strength, introduce advanced foreign management and technology into the country, and improve service quality, which will bring about a new competitiveness in the domestic travel market.

In China's 12 state-level tourist and holiday resorts, foreign businesses are permitted to develop tourism facilities and pool funds jointly with Chinese partners to set up travel agencies and operate bus-tour companies. The 12 state-level tourist and holiday resorts are: Golden Pebble Beach in Dalian, Old Stone Man in Qingdao, Taihu Lake in Wuxi, Taihu Lake in Suzhou, Zhejiang River in Hangzhou, Hengsha Island in Shanghai, Wuyi Mountain in Fujian, Meizhou Bay in Fujian, Nahu Lake in Guangzhou, Silver Beach in Beihai, Dianchi Lake in Kunming, and Yalong Bay in Sanya.

Sunrise Industry

Tourism is playing a leading role in the economic development of China. It has become an important source of non-trade foreign exchange revenue. Domestic tourism rose in the early 1980s and continued to grow throughout the 1990s, contributing greatly to the development of China's tourism and hospitality industry. This period also saw a steady increase in the number of Chinese visiting the border or traveling overseas. In 1997, the number of domestic travelers rose to 644 million, producing an income of 211.27 billion RMB yuan; 5.32 million Chinese went overseas as tourists. Also in 1997, China received 57.59 million foreign tourists, taking fifth place in the world. China made $12.07 billion from the tourism industry in 1997.

The booming tourism and hospitality industry has created many jobs. In 1997, the tourist sector alone employed 1.5 million Chinese, plus 7.5 million who worked for the industry indirectly. The tourism and hospitality industry has spurred the development of transportation, telecommunications, and art and craft production, and has given birth to many new industrial sectors. Throughout the country, some 3 million people—4.29 percent of the 70 million poverty-stricken Chinese—have said good-bye to poverty through involvement in tourism and hospitality businesses.

Looking to the future, China's tourism and hospitality development targets for 2010 are:

- Visitors from overseas (including Hong Kong and Macau) touring China are expected to number 64 to 71 million.

- Domestic tourists should reach 2 to 2.5 billion (this is possible because it is expected that many Chinese will take two or three trips, since holiday time is increasing and traveling has become popular in China).

- Foreign exchange earnings from international tourism should come to $38 to $43 billion.

- Home tourism income will reach 1,000 to 1,050 billion RMB yuan, accounting for 8 percent of GDP in 2010.

China's tourism and hospitality industry will strive to further improve and expand lodging alternatives through the building of youth hostels. The tourism

Exhibit 2   China's Working Age Population, 1995–2050 (in Millions)

Year	Laboring Population	Men Age 16–59	Women Age 16–54
1995	731.12	387.55	343.57
2000*	775.10	410.10	365.00
2010*	851.85	456.92	394.93
2020*	859.81	464.72	395.09
2030*	807.52	439.21	368.31
2040*	784.20	422.58	361.62
2050*	729.72	394.25	335.47
*Projected totals			

Source: China Statistics, 1998.

sector will also make an effort to open up the big tourism markets across the country and raise domestic tourism to a new level.

China's Labor Market

The quality, quantity, and composition of the available labor force are considerations of great importance to an employer. This is particularly true if the employer is required to be efficient, competitive, and profitable. China is a huge market not only in terms of consumers but also in terms of labor resources. Social, cultural, attitudinal, and other forces determine many of the labor conditions in China. In this section, we shall discuss the Chinese labor market and Chinese people in general terms.

Employment Pressure

China has the largest population of any country in the world, with more than 1.2 billion people. At present, China has a population of 775 million people in the prime labor pool of 16- to 59-year-old males and 16- to 54-year-old females. By 2016, China will see this population peak at 870 million, but it will stay above 800 million for another 14 years (see Exhibit 2).

In 1998, approximately 870 million Chinese—or about 70 percent of the population—still lived in the countryside, compared to 380 million in the cities. Since 1992, the urban population has been growing by 10 million a year. However, if the 50 to 80 million farmers working in cities or towns are counted as part of the urban population, then the urban population accounts for 33 to 36 percent of China's overall population. If their children are also taken into account, the percentage is even higher. Because more and more laborers from the countryside are moving to cities to look for jobs, China's urban unemployment rate is rising (see Exhibit 3).

Exhibit 3   China's Urban Unemployment Rate

Year	Registered Jobless Urban Population (in millions)	Registered Unemployment Rate (%)
1992	3.934	2.3
1993	4.201	2.5
1994	4.764	2.8
1995	5.196	2.9
1996	5.528	3.0
1997	5.576	3.1

Source: China Statistics, 1998.

The rising jobless rate is the grim side of China's employment situation. Even though the unemployment rate in developed countries is sometimes much higher than three percent, their absolute jobless population is much less than that of China; China's current three percent unemployment rate translates to more than five million jobless workers. Moreover, this is only the registered figure; undoubtedly, many unemployed Chinese go uncounted. Another fact adding to the gravity of the unemployment situation is that, since 1993, the number of workers laid off from state enterprises has been increasing each year—from three million in 1993 to 12 million in 1997, according to 1998's *China Industry Review.* In the next 20 years, China will have to create job opportunities for the existing jobless population as well as for another 120 million young people who will be entering the labor pool for the first time.

The Service Sector

Labor is China's richest resource, but figuring out how to make the best use of it is the key to sustained economic growth. China needs to develop labor-intensive industries and save capital while employing more workers. Enlarging the service sector is one of a number of ways to reduce unemployment. The tourism and hospitality industry is a labor-intensive industry. In addition, according to China's research, when the tourism and hospitality industry creates one job, it creates another five in related industries.

In developed countries, people employed by the service industry usually account for more than 60 percent of the working population. In the case of developing countries, the rate is only around 30 percent. At present, about 26 percent of China's total employees are employed in China's service industry. More than 100 million jobs have been created over the past ten years through the development of the service industry. In order to reduce unemployment and create more jobs, China must step up the development of its service industry, including the tourism and hospitality sector, in the next 5 to 15 years.

Exhibit 4   Changes in School-Age Population, 1995–2050 (in Millions)

Year	Primary	Junior & Senior	University
1995	130.12	117.03	106.24
2000*	132.99	127.16	97.47
2010*	113.38	122.85	111.50
2020*	112.48	107.82	94.68
2030*	106.59	112.30	92.96
2040*	96.35	100.83	88.92
2050*	94.69	96.27	79.88
*Projected totals			

Source: China Statistics, 1998.

Under China's reform and opening policy, the employment and management of workers—even **state-employed workers**—have been freed from direct government intervention. Those who have special skills can change to different trades, departments, or geographic regions. This freedom has encouraged more people to move to the service industry, especially to the tourism and hospitality sector.

Educational Background

There were 120 million Chinese children of primary school age (6 to 12 years) on average between 1991 and 1995, but this figure will increase to approximately 133 million in 2000, according to the Population and Employment Department (see Exhibit 4). This is the largest population group in China today. The population of junior and senior middle school students (ages 13 to 18) will reach 127 million in 2000. The population of university students (ages 18 to 22) is decreasing—from 106 million in 1995 to about 97 million in 2000. However, it is projected to grow to 116 million from 2001 to 2008, and should remain at more than 100 million until 2017, followed by a gradual decline that should level off at about 80 million by the year 2050.

The number of school-age children unable to go to school is declining. A survey shows that 18.36 million children between 6 and 14 years old failed to attend school for various reasons in 1995. Compared to the 1990 number (32.87), this figure dropped by 14.51 million. Statistics show that in 1990 there were 6.34 million illiterates in China between 15 and 19 years old; by 1995, that figure had dropped to 2.51 million. Today there are more than 200 million primary and high school students in China.

Education is one of many areas that has benefited from China's reform and opening policies. High school students now have more opportunities to go to college. In fact, China had 6.3 million college students in 1997, a big increase over the

Exhibit 5   Income and Educational Levels

	Per Capita Income (Yuan)	Taking the Average Income of Those with a Primary School Education as 1	Benefit Rate from Education (%)
At or Above Graduate Level	10,743.98	1.65	8.1
College Level	9,237.45	1.42	8.9
Secondary Vocational School Level	8,393.46	1.29	6.1
High Middle School Level	7,566.06	1.16	5.7
Junior Middle School Level	7,233.60	1.11	4.5
Primary School Level	6,510.87	1.00	—

1.2 million 20 years ago. In 1998, over 34 percent of high school graduates went on to a college or university. The overall educational and technical qualifications of China's employees have grown; today, the average amount of education for China's workers in state-owned and other enterprises is 12.19 years. (In contrast, the average years of education for the Chinese population as a whole are only 5.24.) The number of employees receiving senior middle school or vocational school education is rising; so is the number of workers with a college or university background.

The typically low income of Chinese workers used to make many Chinese wonder how much they would benefit from making an investment in education. A survey by experts of the State Statistical Bureau, however, showed that better-educated employees receive higher salaries. In 1997, the per-capita income of university graduates and post-graduates averaged 10,744 RMB yuan; the income of those with a three-year college education reached 9,237 RMB yuan, up 65 percent and 42 percent respectively over those with a primary school education (see Exhibit 5).

In terms of economic returns from an investment in education, the annual rate of return on a four-year university education or above is 8.1 percent, while the return on a three-year college education is higher at 8.9 percent. This can be explained by the fact that, in recent years, many people with established careers have participated in self-taught or adult education; this group receives what amounts to a three-year college education at a lower cost, which makes their economic return rate higher than for those with a graduate or post-graduate education. The economic return rate for employees with a secondary vocational education or under is reduced in proportion to their educational level. Generally speaking, higher education brings higher economic returns. This trend is expected to become even stronger in the future.

Exhibit 6   Rural and Urban Educational Levels

People Aged 15 or Above	Rural	Urban
With primary school education	28.3%	38%
With junior middle school education	26.6	29.7
With senior school education	4.5	20.7
With college degree and above	0.3	7.6

Source: *China Education*, 1997.

The state of education in China is still far from satisfactory, however, especially in the countryside (see Exhibit 6). China is trying in every way to speed up the country's educational development. The central government will increase state funding for basic, vocational, and high-education projects one percent each year for the next ten years. The state will increase the promotion of vocational and adult education programs, pre-employment and on-the-job training initiatives, and specialized training courses for laid-off workers. Long-distance education will be enhanced through Internet-based educational networks and educational programs delivered via satellite TV. This will ensure that people all across China have educational opportunities.

Traditional Culture and the Chinese People

China is an ancient civilization. There are three major philosophical influences affecting Chinese thought: the ideas of Confucius; Taoism; and the legalist philosophy.

Confucius taught that China must return to the peace and tranquility of the golden age that was supposed to have existed in the far past. Confucianism teaches returning good for good, and justice for evil, and emphasizes devotion to parents, family, and friends; expansion and training of the mind; self-control; and fairness to others. For a time, Confucianism became the state ideology of China, and it remains a dominant influence in the life and history of the people.

Taoism was the second major philosophical influence. The Taoists stressed man's relationship not to society but to nature and the environment around him. Taoism promotes living simply and in harmony with nature; by pursuing a strict diet and meditation regime and not struggling with their lot, people can achieve an inner calm and improved health.

A third major school of philosophy was the **legalist philosophy**, which argued that man is essentially evil by nature and therefore should be controlled by a totalitarian government that rules by a system of rewards and punishments. However, this proved to be too harsh a system for people to accept. Of these three influences, Confucianism, with its encouragement of conformity, proved to be the most viable.

Because of China's traditional culture, the Chinese have a strong sense of family, emphasizing family hierarchy and obligations. The Chinese are a hard-working, practical, and industrious people, concerned with the productivity and the betterment of the lives of the group of persons with which they are working. These characteristics are due in part to an ancient tradition of pride and self-respect and to the state's encouragement of efficiency. There is a difference between honor and face for the Chinese. Honor is real, a matter of conscience; face is concerned with reputation and appearance. The Chinese person not only thinks of his own face, but also of the face of others, as he would not like to make anyone look like a fool in public.

A New Philosophy About Life and Work

From 1949 to the 1970s, the Chinese government tried to build a new social structure. The individual Chinese was to have a new kind of relationship with his fellow man, called "comradeship." Comradeship was a kind of new morality. It called for friendliness and helpfulness between all people of the state, and was widely accepted by most of the Chinese people during this time. This system required that individuals not permit any personal relationship to interfere in any way with the collective goal of the community or the state. To accomplish this, every person was required to participate in self-criticism, as well as the criticism of others.

In China today, people have a more open mind than in the past. They tend to exchange ideas with one another and like listening to other people's opinions before making a final decision. While doing business, they consider their own rights and interests more than in the past, and try to fulfill their own aspirations. Those in the younger generation, in particular, hope they can get faster promotions, earn more money, and enjoy themselves. They have a way of thinking similar to citizens of market-driven countries, which means today's China bears more similarities with these countries.

Even ten years ago, although employees worked earnestly, they lacked the courage to outdo others. This might be attributed to the influence of the traditional Chinese doctrine of egalitarianism. But today, employees are bold in facing challenges and eager to beat the competition.

In 1997, the Gallup Organization conducted a survey in China that asked respondents about basic attitudes toward life and work. One of the survey questions asked respondents to indicate which of the following best represented their philosophy of living:

A. Getting rich through hard work

B. Rising to fame through diligent study

C. Maintaining one's own way of life, without bothering about money and reputation

D. Spending each day without sorrow and anxiety

E. Living a clean and honest life so as to resist the evils existing in the world

F. Selflessly devoting one's all to society, without any thought of self

Choice A was the most frequently selected response (56 percent of all respondents). In rural areas, 69 percent of the people made this choice.

The Chinese Social Investigation Office conducted a survey in 1997 on the theme "the Condition of Present-Day Chinese Youth." With the establishment of the market economy in China and the reform of the personnel system, present-day youths show a high level of confidence in their ability to control their own futures. They consider the following factors to influence their prospects: personal ability (43.9 percent), favorable opportunities (31.3 percent), family background (11.8 percent), and leaders' impressions of them (8.6 percent). In selecting occupations, they first consider what jobs will suit their strong points and then what will get them high incomes. In terms of outlook on morality, young people consider that the most important qualities are honesty (56.7 percent), self-confidence (38.4 percent), being law-abiding (34.4 percent), self-respect (34.3 percent), kindheartedness (27.7 percent), tolerance (24.3 percent), modesty (8.9 percent), and selflessness (1.3 percent). This suggests that young people in China like a flexible morality that is suited to market competition, and are de-emphasizing China's traditional values, which inhibit individual interests and limit individual freedom.

Human Resource Management

There have been many changes in human resource management practices in China over the past few decades. This section will focus on human resource management practices unique to China.

Employee Recruitment and Selection

In 1956, China adopted an employment system whereby the State Labor Department in the various towns and cities assumed responsibility for the recruitment and placement of all workers in state-owned enterprises. This practice applied to the collective enterprises as well. The whole recruitment and selection process was usually less formal than today. Less testing was done, and when it was, the results were likely to be used somewhat superficially. Family ties, social status, and friendships were more likely to be factors in hiring decisions. Under this system, workers had no right to change jobs on their own.

In 1979, the state began using examinations when recruiting employees in the various trades and professions. Applicants were examined both in general and specialized subjects to determine their suitability for the particular trade or industry for which they were applying. This ensured a better fit between the requirements of industry and the interests and aspirations of the applicants. This policy is conducive to industrial growth because it ensures that employees working in a particular enterprise possess the minimal qualifications for performing their jobs satisfactorily.

The introduction of a market economy in China has led to frequent job changes on the part of workers. Workers have been freed from direct government intervention, even if they are state-employed. Those who have special skills can move to different trades, departments, or regions, either in the cities or countryside. This freedom has encouraged more people to enter the service industry, which accounted for 26 percent of the work force in 1996.

Today, all enterprises are free to recruit their workers from anywhere. In order to help businesses as well as job-hunters, the state has energetically promoted employment by developing employment agencies, providing employment guidance and services, and developing professional training. By the end of 1996, the country had 31,000 employment agencies, 2,716 employment service centers, and more than 200,000 labor employment service enterprises involving more than nine million employees. Between 1983 and 1996, the employment agencies had recommended jobs for 70 million people, including 30 million unemployed personnel.

Most enterprises in China now employ workers based on the contract system, which differs from the fixed lifetime employment under the planned economic system of the past. No one now thinks the work he or she is doing is a lifetime job, as every Chinese worker firmly believed some 20 years ago. Workers now have more freedom in choosing jobs and the **work units** (businesses) they wish to work in. A recent survey jointly made by the All-China Youth Federation and the *China Youth Daily* newspaper showed that 37 percent of respondents had changed jobs; each respondent had shifted work units three times on average. In addition, half of the respondents said they were considering changing jobs in the near future.

Promotion and Motivation

In the past, managerial personnel were appointed or selected from those employees who were considered both "red" (that is, politically sound) and "expert" (that is, technically competent) by the government. Party Committee members chose these managers—called "cadres"—through recommendation and discussion.

With the current emphasis on technical competence and leadership abilities as two important qualifications for managerial positions, reforms in the cadre system are being conducted throughout the country. Some reforms already introduced include the recruitment of managerial personnel through examinations, the election of cadres by secret ballots, the holding of opinion polls once every year to check and appraise the performance of elected cadres, the demotion of cadres who are technically incompetent, and the provision of continuing education to cadres. For example, Changhong, a TV manufacturer in Sichuan Province, practices an elimination system that results in 30 percent of its medium-level managers losing their jobs annually through performance-based competition.

In China, the Constitution prescribes two types of incentives to motivate employees to heighten their performance: the state applies the policy of combining moral encouragement with material reward, with the stress on the former. China's leaders, both past and present, have emphasized the superiority of nonmaterial incentives. However, they realize that man's desire for material gains and the promotion of self-interest cannot be eliminated all at once. Now material incentives such as wages, subsidies, and bonuses are becoming quite popular in Chinese enterprises. The nonmaterial incentives used in China are somewhat foreign to the Western mentality. For example, in 1991 the Chinese tourism authority developed a working campaign throughout the country's tourism and hospitality industry and selected 91 **labor models,** 201 advanced workers, and 64 advanced work units. (The "labor model" designation is the highest honor a worker in China can

The "Reform and Opening" Policy's Impact on China's Hotels

With determination and confidence, the Chinese can accomplish anything, remarked Vice President John C. H. Young of the Shangri-La Hotel Group. Citing an example, he said that when the first Shangri-La Hotel was established in Beijing in 1985, the city's telecommunications facilities were poor. People had to use rotary-dial telephones, and communicating with Hong Kong was extremely difficult. In less than two years, however, the situation greatly changed. Communication became more convenient as mobile phones appeared and became a daily communication tool for an increasing number of Chinese. Such fast improvement is rare even in many developed countries, said Young.

Today, hotels in China are coming closer to international standards. Young said that the poor hotel management astonished him when he first came to Beijing in the early 1980s. He recalled his first experiences at a four-star hotel. Porters often stood or sat in the lobby, taking no notice of guests passing by them, letting the guests carry their own luggage. At noon each day, the entire hotel staff poured through the lobby, heading outside with lunch-boxes in their hands. After 6 P.M., the hotel stopped serving meals. Today, such poor service in China's deluxe hotels is unknown.

achieve; the "advanced worker" designation is the second highest honor, reserved for top performers in their fields; the "advanced work unit" designation honors organizations that achieve great success or otherwise make great contributions to society.) The outstanding achievements of these labor models, advanced workers, and advanced work units were publicized nationally via radio, television, and newspapers so that workers and units from the whole tourism and hospitality industry could seek to emulate, learn from, and catch up with these advanced units and individuals.

Managers' and Employees' Education

Training programs for Chinese managers generally emphasize the development of business and management skills, which are recognized as keys to the nation's economic development. The Chinese Tourism and Hospitality Industry Association was established in 1980 to further the goal of developing managers for the tourism and hospitality industry. It sponsors workshops, seminars, and vocational training for management personnel. In addition, management-exchange programs were established with foreign partners.

In 1990, China's tourism and hospitality authority began to implement a staff qualification system that requires everyone who works in the industry to pass certain examinations through a training program. In 1996, 180,000 employees received this training. More than 260 universities and colleges in China now provide degree and vocational training programs for tourism and hospitality. The total number of students in these programs is 49,000.

Employee Participation in Management

In China, employees take part in management through the **congress of workers.**
All advanced enterprises have established their own congress of workers, which
are convened annually. At each congress, the enterprise's leading members give a
report on their workers over the past year, listen to criticisms and suggestions from
the representatives, and adopt resolutions on various matters. At each congress, an
inspection group is elected to check, every three months, on the implementation of
the resolutions adopted. Representatives to each enterprise's congress are elected
directly by the workers and staff of that enterprise. All workers and staff members
have the right to vote, and all can stand for election, provided they meet certain
qualifications. When the congress is not in session, the representatives are divided
into several groups on the basis of workshops, sections, or offices. Each group
checks on the implementation of the resolutions adopted by the congress.

Since the 1980s, most Chinese enterprises—including tourism and hospitality
businesses—have adopted the Management Contract and Responsibility System
(MCRS). Many work teams in enterprises have been set up, and everyone has a
responsibility to contribute to management's success.

The Role of Trade Unions

The All-China Federation of Trade Unions, which is the leading body representing
trade unions in the country, was established in 1952. Trade unions have played an
important role in Chinese society. Chinese trade unions are large working-class
organizations formed on a voluntary basis under the leadership of the Chinese
Communist Party. Trade unions are organized by trade and by geographical locations. Each and every work unit has a trade union.

In the trade unions, the spirit of cooperation between employees and management is emphasized. This notion is rather foreign to the Western world, where
trade unions are looked on by employees as citadels from which they can bargain
with management from a position of strength.

The activities performed by China's trade unions are primarily threefold.
Trade unions:

1. *Serve as links between managers and workers.* On the one hand, trade unions
   frequently transmit workers' opinions and needs to management, to provide a
   basis for the latter to formulate or readjust its principles and policies; on the
   other hand, trade unions educate the workers so they can understand and
   properly implement management's policies.

2. *Serve as training schools.* Trade unions conduct ideological, cultural, and technical education programs among the workers. They run spare-time schools,
   cultural palaces, and recreation halls, and help prepare good workers to join
   the management ranks of their work units.

3. *Promote the welfare of workers.* In addition to organizing schools and recreational halls, trade unions also run workers' sanatoriums and help workers
   resolve disputes with their employers over sick pay, discrimination, discipline, and other work issues. Trade unions also try to find jobs for laid-off

workers and contribute modest sums to help support the families of the poorest workers.

In short, the function of a trade union in China is primarily to promote cooperation between labor and management, foster enthusiasm for work, and boost morale among workers.

The Role of Government

Since the beginning of the economic reform movement, the Chinese government has had a direct impact on the tourism and hospitality industry as well as human resource functions through political reform, legislation, and involvement.

Reforming Politics

In China, political considerations have a pervasive influence on all aspects of society. As a ruling party, the Chinese Communist Party (CCP) leads and supports the people in exercising the power of running the state, holding democratic elections, and making policy decisions, including decisions about policies concerning the operation and management of industrial enterprises. Mr. Mao Zedong made contributions to the independence of the semi-feudal and semi-colonial China, but he failed to achieve more in China's subsequent economic construction. Of course, this type of economic failure did not happen only in China; the former Soviet Union and various East European countries also experienced economic difficulties. Mr. Deng Xiaoping realized that the problems lay in the planned economic system and the political emphasis on class struggle. In 1978, he declared that the primary mission for the CCP, and for the country as a whole, was no longer that of class struggle but rather socialist modernization. One of the basic reasons for the achievements of the reform and modernization drive over the past two decades is that the CCP corrected erroneous concepts and policies. Further economic progress depends on the Chinese government's ability to continue to reform China's political structure, strengthen democracy and the legal system, separate government functions from enterprise management, streamline government, and maintain stability and unity.

In China, economic development is closely related to political reform. The present leadership of China is carrying forward the banner of socialism with Chinese characteristics and has accelerated the process of reform and the restructuring of the political system.

Building the Legal System

Although China has shared with most other Southeast Asian countries a traditional distaste for law and legal concepts, the Chinese government has realized that law constitutes an important part of any modern society. Over the past few years, China has achieved significant progress in legislation and the enforcement and popularization of laws, providing effective guarantees for deepening economic reform and establishing a more stable economic order. The National People's Congress and its Standing Committee have put legislation, particularly economic legislation, at the top of their agendas, closely combining legislative decision-making with reform decision-making, thus guiding, promoting, and guaranteeing the smooth progress of the reform movement. The government has enacted laws governing various aspects of societal functioning, including laws concerning the rights of laborers.

The past 20 years have seen a dramatic change in people's minds about law. They used to be completely ignorant about law and how it functions in society. But most ordinary people have learned how important law is and have learned to protect their legal rights and interests according to law. This clearly demonstrates the achievement of the Chinese government's goal of improving the country's legal structure and democracy while properly protecting human rights. It is expected that the Chinese people's awareness of law and the nation's legal structure will be further improved in the next decade.

Guaranteeing the Rights of Laborers

The Chinese government now pays more attention to guaranteeing the rights of laborers. The Labor Law created in 1994 laid down detailed, comprehensive stipulations on the rights of laborers, such as the right to have equal opportunities for, and free choice of, employment; to get pay for labor; to rest and take leave; to receive labor safety and hygienic protection; to receive vocational training; and to enjoy social insurance and welfare. The protection of laborers' rights has begun to be institutionalized:

- The state has adopted measures to guarantee laborers' right to employment. Since the introduction of reform and opening policies, China has pursued an employment policy that combines jobs recommended by state labor departments with a system to help people get organized for work and become self-employed.

- The state guarantees the right of workers to be paid for their work. In China, all employees, regardless of their age, sex, or race, can get equal pay for equal quality and quantity of work. The state created the Regulation on Minimum Wages in Enterprises, which established a minimum wage guarantee system.

- The state guarantees the right of workers to have rest breaks and take leaves. In 1994 and 1995, the state created laws and statutes that twice reduced working hours, moving them from 48 hours per week down to 40. This new working system has been implemented nationwide. By law, laborers enjoy two "public" or nonworking days a week, statutory festival holidays, and annual leave with pay. Childbearing female workers enjoy at least 90 days of maternity leave with pay.

- To guarantee the safety and hygienic rights of laborers, the state has created and implemented numerous special laws, including Regulations on Factory Safety and Hygiene, Regulations on the Scope of Vocational Diseases, and Methods for the Treatment of Patients Contracted with a Vocational Disease.

- To enhance laborers' professional and working abilities, the state has formulated a series of statutes, including the Law on Vocational Education, and created numerous vocational training establishments, including professional technical schools, to give training to first-time job-seekers as well as laid-off personnel and job transferees. The country has approximately 18,000 vocational schools, with an attendance of more than eight million. Programs dealing with tourism and hospitality are available in most of these schools. Also, as mentioned earlier, the country has more than 260 universities and colleges that have degree and vocational-training programs for tourism and hospitality.

- The state has developed the social insurance business, established the social insurance system, and set up social insurance funds to ensure that laborers legally enjoy social insurance treatment during retirement or when they become ill, suffer an injury, become disabled on the job, contract a vocational disease, lose their jobs, or give birth.

Supporting the Tourism and Hospitality Industry

China's tourism and hospitality industry has made great headway since the economic reform movement began in 1978. In 1986, the State Council put tourism into the national economic and social development plan. In 1992, the central government further defined tourism as a key sector in the service industry. In the outline of the Ninth Five-Year Plan for China's National Economic and Social Development and the Long-Term Targets through the Year 2010, tourism is listed as the number-one priority to be actively developed. In 1998, the tourist industry was designated as a new economic growth point in the national economy at the Conference on Economic Work held by the central government. The move promoted the status of the tourist sector in economic and social development, paving the way for the rapid development of the tourist industry in the twenty-first century. Now, more than 20 provinces, autonomous regions, and municipalities have made the tourist sector a key industry for local economic development.

Governments at all levels have rendered active support to tourism by mobilizing government departments to solve key and difficult issues. By the end of 1998, 60 percent of provinces and key tourist cities had made the decision to speed up the development of tourism and had formulated policies to encourage and expand tourism, thus ensuring the increase of various special funds for tourism development. The governments of over half of the provinces and autonomous regions have passed local tourist laws and regulations. These governments have also effectively tackled problems affecting tourist accommodations and transportation.

On the national scene, the National Tourism Administration in China launched the China Friend Tour '92, China Landscape '93, China Heritage '94, China Folklore '95, China Resort '96, Visit China '97, China Urban and Rural '98, The China Ecological Environment Tour '99, China Tourism 2000, and other theme activities. These campaigns have promoted China's tourism development and attracted a large number of tourists, both from within the country and from abroad.

Over the past three years, the Chinese government has established 54 Excellent Tourist Cities—another step in laying a solid foundation to optimize the tourist environment.

Speeding Up Management Reform

In 1982, the China International Travel Service separated from the National Tourism Administration (NTA); this enhanced tourism management by decentralizing authority. From 1982 to 1985, work units within the tourism and hospitality industry in China changed their management structures by granting planning and decision-making power to lower levels of management and encouraging new approaches to managing, such as "management by objectives." From 1986 to 1992, many tourist enterprise groups were set up. These groups have engaged in hotel operations, travel services, taxi services, and catering, as well as real estate development and tourism advertisement. Some groups have also expanded into such areas as air transportation, electronic communication, and finance. Since 1992, great progress has been made in the tourism industry's market-oriented restructuring, and tourist operations and services—and the management of tourism businesses—have remarkably improved.

Institutional restructuring of the NTA in 1998 was carried out smoothly. The NTA reduced the number of its employees by 40 percent, while enhancing its ability to set tourism standards and guide the construction of tourist cities. This restructuring helped straighten out the tourist administrative system that was created under the old, socialist economy.

Conclusion

Major factors behind the tourism and hospitality industry's huge development in China are the introduction and constant strengthening of market mechanisms, along with a series of readjustments of government policies. Because of the accelerated transition of the old economic system to a market economy, China's tourism and hospitality industry will enter a new developmental period in the next century. According to the State Development Planning Commission's prediction, China's service industry will register an average annual growth rate of nine percent in the next ten years. By 2010, the service industry will make up 40 percent of GDP, and service employees will account for about 38 percent of the nation's total employees. As a key sector of the service industry, tourism and hospitality will play a very positive role in China's transition from a planned economic system to a market-driven system.

Key Terms

Confucius—A Chinese philosopher and educator (c. 551–479 B.C.) whose teachings emphasized devotion to parents, family, and friends; expansion and training of the mind; self-control; and fairness to others.

congress of workers—A body of workers in a state-owned enterprise, elected by all of the workers in that enterprise, which gives workers a voice in how the enterprise is managed and how the workers are treated.

labor model—A worker who has been awarded the highest honor a worker can achieve in China. To be designated a "labor model," a worker must be selected by his or her trade union and approved by the Chinese government.

legalist philosophy—A philosophy which argues that man is essentially evil by nature and therefore should be controlled by a totalitarian government that rules by a system of rewards and punishments.

"reform and opening" policy—The movement in China, begun by Deng Xiaoping in 1978, toward a market economy and a greater openness to foreign investment, businesspeople, and tourists.

state-employed worker—A person holding a job in a business owned by the Chinese government or the government of one of China's provinces.

Taoism—A Chinese mystical philosophy, traditionally said to be founded by Lao-tzu in the 6th century B.C., that teaches conformity to the Tao—the creative principle that orders the universe—by unassertive action and simplicity. Taoists stressed man's relationship not to society but to nature and the environment around him. Taoism promotes living simply and in harmony with nature; by pursuing a strict diet and meditation regime and not struggling with their lot, people can achieve an inner calm and improved health.

work unit—Another name for a business organization or institution in China.

 ## Discussion Questions

1. How has China's tourism and hospitality industry grown since China's "reform and opening" policy was begun in 1978?

2. What are some of the general characteristics of the Chinese labor market?

3. What are the differences between traditional Chinese cultural values and the Chinese people's new philosophy of life and work?

4. How are employees recruited and selected in China?

5. How do Chinese employees participate in management?

6. What roles do trade unions play in China?

7. How does the Chinese government support the tourism and hospitality industry?

 ## Internet Sites

For more information, visit the following Internet sites. Remember that Internet addresses can change without notice.

General Sites

Country Profile: China
http://www.abcnews.go.com/
reference/countries/CH.html

China Internet Information Center
http://www.china.org.cn

China Economic Information Network
http://www.cei.gov.cn

Inside China Today
http://www.insidechina.com/

Chinese Culture and People

Chinese Culture Information Net
http://www.ccnt.gov.cn

China Pages
http://china.pages.com.cn

Confucius—MSN Encarta
Learning Zone
http://encarta.msn.com/find/
Concise.asp?ti=0012E000

The Philosopher Confucius
http://www.csun.edu/~hbchm009/
confucius.html

Taoism and the Taoist Arts
http://www.geocities.com/Athens/
Delphi/2883/

The Daily Tao
http://www.nauticom.net/www/
asti/dailytao.htm

Hotels in China

ChinaHotel
http://www.chinahotel.com

ChinaNetHotel
http://www.chinanethotel.com

Hotel Windows
http://www.hotelwindows.com

Traveling in China

China Travel Union Net
http://www.chinatu.com

China Holiday: China Travel
Resources Network
http://www.chinaholiday.com

China Green Channel Travel Network
http://www.chinagc.com

CTN
http://www.ctn.com.cn

Transportation in China

Internet Information of Communications, China
http://www.iicc.ac.cn

TransChina
http://www.ictspc.gov.cn

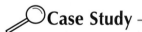

Case Study ——————————————————

The Huizhou Hotel

The Huizhou Hotel is a 200-room, two-restaurant hotel located in Hefei, the capital of the Anhui province. It was built by Anhui's government and is a typical state-owned enterprise. It began operation in 1985, and was the best hotel in the city for many years. The provincial government and local businesses held all kinds of meetings and conferences in the hotel, and businesspeople from outside Hefei always stayed at the Huizhou because it was the only good hotel in town. For over a decade, the hotel enjoyed success.

Over the past several years, however, the Huizhou has operated at a deficit. Now it faces a number of issues and challenges that require attention by its owner, the Anhui provincial government:

1. Slowly but steadily, during the past few years the number of guests staying at the hotel has declined and hotel revenues have fallen, for two main reasons. First, the number of government meetings and conferences held at the hotel has fallen, because China's economy has become more market-driven and less dependent on government intervention. Second, seven joint-venture hotels have begun operating in Hefei during the last several years, so businesspeople and others seeking lodging and meeting rooms in Hefei now have many new hotels to choose from. Born during the era of market reforms in China, the joint-venture hotels from their inception have paid attention to meeting the needs of their customers, because they understood that they must be profitable to survive. In contrast, the staff of the state-owned Huizhou Hotel has not been as sensitive to customer needs.

2. There are 340 employees in the hotel at the moment, but over 40 percent of the staff is made up of administrators—cadres—who were appointed to their jobs by the Anhui government. Most of them have never had any hotel management training, but none of them want to be demoted to a front-line job at the hotel (they would lose face); all want to stay in management positions. Many hotel departments were set up just to provide management jobs for these cadres, so the hotel's management costs are quite high. During the hotel's busy season, it has to hire temporary workers because it doesn't have enough front-line staff, so front-line labor costs are also high, compared to the labor costs for the city's joint-venture hotels.

3. In the last few years, about 20 key young staff members who had hotel and hospitality management educational backgrounds left the hotel to take similar positions in the city's joint-venture hotels. Some of these staff members have already been promoted at their new hotels and have taken on more responsibilities. They are very happy that they made the switch to a joint-venture hotel, not only because they enjoy attractive salary packages but because of the greater personal development opportunities. In the Huizhou Hotel, it usually takes much longer for young staff members to get promoted, so it's likely that more young staff members will leave the Huizhou in the near future to look for better jobs in one of the new joint-venture hotels.

4. At the top management levels of the Huizhou Hotel, five people—including the general manager and four deputy managers—who were appointed by the provincial government will reach retirement age in the next two or three years. Because of this, it is understandable that they have not paid much attention to reforming and developing the hotel.

The administration department of the Anhui government has come to the conclusion that the hotel is in a serious situation and needs to be reformed under strong new leadership. It has decided to find a new general manager for the hotel, but instead of appointing one, as in the past, it has invited applicants from the public at large to apply for the position.

After intensive competition among 12 candidates, Mr. Li Yongshen was chosen to be the Huizhou Hotel's new general manager. Li is a university graduate with a master's degree in business administration. He worked as an assistant manager in a joint-venture hotel in Shanghai for three years, and also served in the military for four years. He is an aggressive, high-energy person who believes in creativity and being pro-active, not just reactive.

Discussion Questions

1. How can Li be creative about reorganizing the hotel and making it competitive in terms of human resource management?

2. What kind of employee motivation system should be set up in this state-owned enterprise?

Chapter 2 Outline

An Overview of the Egyptian Hospitality
    Labor Market
        Industry Labor Problems
        The Role of Females in the Industry
        Legal and Political Environment
        Cultural, Economic, and Social Work
          Values
Labor Relations
        Recruitment and Selection
        Training and Development
        Performance Evaluation Practices
        Motivational Practices
        Career Development Programs
        Disciplining
Human Resources in the Future

Competencies

1. Discuss the main characteristics of the Egyptian hospitality labor market, including labor problems, the role of females, the legal environment, and values. (pp. 27–33)

2. Outline the recruitment, selection, training, evaluation, motivation, career development, and disciplining processes in the Egyptian hospitality industry. (pp. 33–38)

3. Discuss the future of the Egyptian hospitality industry and its potential growth in the 21st century. (p. 38)

2

Egypt: An Attempt to Improve Human Resources Practices

Hanan Saad Kattara

Hanan Saad Kattara
B.S., M.S., Ph.D.
Senior lecturer and researcher,
Hotel Management Department,
Faculty of Tourism and Hotel Management,
Alexandria University, Egypt

EGYPT, OR THE Arab Republic of Egypt, is centrally located between northeastern Africa and southwestern Asia. It is bounded by the Mediterranean Sea on the north, Palestine and the Red Sea on the east, Sudan on the south, and Libya on the west. The population of Egypt (1998 estimate) is 64,824,466. Almost 99 percent of the population live within the Nile Valley and Delta, which constitutes four percent of Egypt's total area. Its climate is characterized by a warm to hot season from May to September, and a cool season from November to March.

The major exports of Egypt are petroleum, petroleum products, cotton and fabrics, vegetables and fruits, clothing and accessories, and aluminum products. The major sources of foreign currency are oil, cotton, Suez Canal revenues, tourism, foreign investments, and remittances of Egyptians working outside Egypt.[1] In recent years, a special concern was given to both oil production and tourism. Tourism is presently on the top of the list of foreign currency earners, helping overcome economic shortages.

An Overview of the Egyptian Hospitality Labor Market

Tourism has grown rapidly to be an industry of countrywide importance; it is no longer an ignored industry. Tourism helps increase the Egyptian gross national product, which in turn leads to national economic development and thus helps to solve the country's economic problems. Therefore, the country saves no efforts to promote tourism in niche overseas markets to enhance the inbound tourist traffic year after year with a reasonable growth rate. The 1998 tourist movement to Egypt

Exhibit 1   Tourist Arrivals from Different Geographical Areas (1997–1998)

Geographical Area	Number of arrivals January–June 1998		Number of arrivals January–June 1997	
	Number	%	Number	%
Middle East	377,090	28.1	327,544	17.2
Africa	55,647	4.2	56,800	3
North America	87,024	6.5	104,219	5.5
Latin America	13,627	1	23,659	1.2
East Europe	79,301	5.9	83,115	4.4
West South Europe	660,010	49.2	1,139,634	59.8
East Asia and Pacific	30,348	2.3	96,871	5.1
South Asia	36,327	2.7	38,666	2
Others	679	0.1	35,079	1.8
Total	**1,340,053**	**100**	**1,905,587**	**100**

Geographical Area	Number of arrivals July–December 1998		Number of arrivals July–December 1997	
	Number	%	Number	%
Middle East	608,857	28.8	565,807	27.5
Africa	75,024	3.6	63,345	3.1
North America	94,806	4.5	102,347	5
Latin America	21,946	1	26,443	1.3
East Europe	108,511	5.1	108,809	5.3
West South Europe	1,109,011	52.5	1,062,856	51.7
East Asia and Pacific	41,009	1.9	70,473	3.4
South Asia	53,344	2.5	54,308	2.6
Others	1,305	0.1	1,441	0.1
Total	**2,113,813**	**100**	**2,055,829**	**100**

Source: Egyptian Hotel Association, *Tourist Arrivals and Nights Report* (Cairo: Egyptian Hotel Association Information Center, September 1999).

reached 3.5 million tourist arrivals and 20 million tourist nights. Statistics showing the number of tourist arrivals and tourist nights in 1997 and 1998, coming from different geographical areas, are illustrated in Exhibits 1 and 2.

In order for tourism to be used as a tool of development, all sub-tourism industries should be wisely developed. The hospitality industry is one of the main sub-industries playing a vital role in tourism development. Economic statistics prove its crucial role; the latest statistics show an accelerated growth in the number of hotel rooms and beds. In seven years, from 1985 to 1992, Egypt's tourist accommodation grew from under 25,000 to 55,000 rooms.[2] The number of rooms reached 71,620 in 1997,[3] increased to 85,543 according to an August 1999 estimate, and 20,000 more rooms are under construction.[4] The number of hotel rooms and beds

Exhibit 2 Tourist Nights from Different Geographical Areas (1997–1998)

Geographical Area	Number of nights January–June 1998		Number of nights January–June 1997	
	Number	%	Number	%
Middle East	1,683,258	22.7	1,778,764	14.2
Africa	331,074	4.5	354,732	2.8
North America	537,034	7.3	736,651	5.9
Latin America	73,634	1	121,235	1
East Europe	442,269	6	493,423	4
West South Europe	3,981,643	53.8	8,277,619	66.1
East Asia and Pacific	171,178	2.3	539,233	4.3
South Asia	170,916	2.3	203,219	1.6
Others	7,675	0.1	10,251	0.1
Total	**7,398,681**	**100**	**12,515,127**	**100**

Geographical Area	Number of arrivals July–December 19987		Number of arrivals July–December 1997	
	Number	%	Number	%
Middle East	3,728,906	29.2	3,867,151	27.5
Africa	513,745	4	513,469	3.6
North America	595,124	4.7	700,777	5
Latin America	91,446	0.7	134,960	1
East Europe	520,766	4.1	482,649	3.4
West South Europe	6,785,323	53.2	7,573,568	53.9
East Asia and Pacific	205,858	1.6	410,246	2.9
South Asia	302,014	2.4	370,920	2.6
Others	8,657	0.1	9,963	0.1
Total	**12,751,839**	**100**	**14,063,703**	**100**

Source: Egyptian Hotel Association, *Tourist Arrivals and Nights Report* (Cairo: Egyptian Hotel Association Information Center, September 1999).

in different geographical regions are illustrated in Exhibit 3. The accelerated expansion in the number of hotel rooms has resulted in an acute shortage in skilled hotel personnel.

Regardless of the existence of the Central Agency for mobilization and statistics (the agency responsible for gathering information and statistics in all industries), the actual size of the hospitality labor force is not well ascertained. It is agreed that the recent growth in the hospitality industry was not accompanied by the same rate of growth in the number of skilled employees.

In the last decade, in an attempt to satisfy the industry needs of labor, the Ministry of Higher Education set plans to increase hotel management faculties and schools. Until 1983, there were only two faculties—Helwan University and

Exhibit 3:   Egyptian Hotel Capacity in Different Tourist Regions

Tourist Region	Number of hotels	Number of rooms	Number of beds
Cairo	146	20,134	41,092
El Canal (Ein el sokhna– Suez– Fayed– Esmailia– Port Said)	42	3,221	6,538
Delta (Al Bagor– Damieta–Mahala Kobra– Mansoura–Shebin Kom– Tanta)	14	534	1,014
North East Coast (Baltim– Gamassa–Ras El Bar)	24	1,055	2,180
North West Coast (Alexandria–Alamein– Behera–Matrouh– Sewa)	85	6,490	13,371
North Oasis	2	42	84
New Valley	6	238	485
Red Sea (Gouna– Hurghada–Marsa Allam– ElQoseir– Safaga– Zafarana)	122	20,045	38,947
Sinai (El Arish– Dahab–Nowebaa– Ras Sedr– Shram El Sheik–Saint Caterine Taba– Tor Sinai)	112	14,363	29,009
South Region (Abu Simbel– Assiout– Asswan– Beni Suef–Fayoum– Luxor– Kena–Menya–Souhag)	91	7,764	15,449
Floating Hotels	227	11,657	23,340
TOTALS	**871**	**85,543**	**171,509**

Alexandria University, each graduating about 70 students per year from the hotel management department—in addition to two hotel schools in Alexandria and Luxor, graduating an average of almost 200 students from both schools.[5]

Presently, there are eight universities offering hotel management studies: Helwan, Alexandria, Cairo (Fayoum campus), Suez Canal, Assiout, Menoufia, Menya, and Southern Valley. In addition to these eight university faculties, nine private sector institutes of higher learning are already operational. At a lower level, more than 30 hotel schools in secondary and post secondary levels are available.

Industry Labor Problems

The growth of the hospitality industry did not happen overnight as it was expected. Many problems arose, on top of which were the industry labor problems, the most flagrant of which are:

- The Egyptian hospitality industry suffers from a high turnover rate. No statistics are available on actual rates, but several interviews with hotel managers project this rate at about 130 percent. This problem is the complaint of all hotels, both chain and independent. The problem is more harmful in independent hotels, which represent 85 percent of the total number of hotels.[6] These independent hotels do not have strong human resource policies that chain hotels have, and thus face greater difficulties in replacing the employees lost to turnover. The problem is much more acute in newly developed tourist regions such as Hurghada, Sharm El Sheikh, and Al Arish. This is due to the fact that employees working in these regions are not usually locals, but come from other, more populated cities. As they work away from their normal place of residence, they do not hesitate to quit whenever any chance for work arises in their city of origin.

* In comparison with many other industries, entry-level employees in the hospitality industry receive a low level of income. Although they gain monthly bonuses from profit sharing and tips, this extra income is unstable due to the seasonality in the volume of business. In addition to other industry job constraints such as long hours of work, changing work shifts, split shifts, and duty during national holidays, these constraints cause a high percentage of hotel employees to transfer to other industries.

* One of the major problems confronting the hospitality industry is the poor labor statistics available. There are no statistics concerning the hospitality industry as an independent sector, with the same labor characteristics and problems. No real labor improvement can be achieved without accurate, updated labor statistics.

* The hotel guests in the Egyptian hotel market are becoming much more sophisticated, with a variety of needs and satisfaction levels. The Egyptian hotel market serves various market segments each with its own needs and requirements. Therefore, hotel managers find themselves facing a multitude of guest needs which they have to cater to. Consequently, hospitality management is confronted with the issue of realizing and understanding guests' varying and changing needs, which is not easy to achieve.

The Role of Females in the Industry

In first-line positions, females are a very strong competitor to males. They succeed in many positions such as receptionists, guest relations, sales representatives, reservation clerks, sales coordinators, waitresses, cashiers, and room maids. They are less apparent in the kitchen, engineering, and maintenance departments. Although the hospitality industry is an attractive sector for females in their early job years, only a small number of them continue their careers in the hospitality industry. This is referred to as **female burnout**. Unfortunately, many of them leave their hospitality careers for other more flexible and less stressful jobs, especially after getting married. However, those who do continue their careers may be seen in top managerial positions in some departments such as marketing and sales, public relations, human resources, and housekeeping.

Legal and Political Environment

The Egyptian hospitality industry suffered for many years from poor image. It was looked at as being the career of less educated people and a transitory industry for temporary job seekers. Thirty years ago, with the allure of hotel chain management, the image changed and the hospitality industry has become the career of highly educated people. Unfortunately, with the shortage of well-trained hospitality labor and the difficulty in filling a vacant position, hotel management of new hotels sometimes must accept poorly qualified applicants. More earnest efforts are needed to refine and boost the industry image. Accepting non-skilled and poorly educated people may be an easy way to fill a vacant position, but of course it has its drawbacks on the industry image and improvement.

Unstable Middle East Political Environment. At present, tourism is the world's largest service sector activity and is, for many countries, of growing economic significance: it is a source of foreign exchange earnings, income generation, and employment.[7] The Middle East is expected to grow the most—forecast at 4.6 percent average a year overall growth between 1995 and 2000. On this basis, the volume of international tourist arrivals is expected to reach 17 million in the year 2000 and 39 million by the year 2010.

The future of tourism in the Middle East confronts a number of constraints. On top of the list are education and training programs for tourism.[8] Therefore, upgrading education and training programs to improve skills, productivity, and service quality, with public/private sector partnerships to enhance standards, structures, and systems, is an essential procedure that should be implemented.[9]

Unfortunately, all efforts of the Egyptian hospitality industry to improve its labor market are confronted with the unstable political environment in the Middle East. Wars, terrorism, and bad publicity are some of the reasons for the shrinkage in the growth of tourism in general, and the hospitality industry in particular.

Employment Legislation. In Egypt, the hospitality industry is subject to labor regulations and laws as in the other industries. Social security entitles employees to pension rights after retirement or disabling labor accidents. Normally, the insurance fees are shared among the hotel and the employee, at 26 percent and 14 percent (respectively) for the fixed salary, and 24 percent and 16 percent for the variable salary. Moreover, laws commit hotels (and other business entities) to appoint handicapped personnel within a percentage of five percent of the total labor force of the hotel, but in non-direct guest contact positions.[10]

It is worth noting that both males and females have the same rights, salaries, working hours (48 hours/week), and holidays, but females are not allowed to work night shifts. Each employee has a 15-day vacation for the first year of employment and a 21-day vacation for the subsequent years until the age of 50, when the annual vacation amounts to one month. Females working in private sector properties have the right for a three-month non-paid delivery holiday, while those in public sector properties have the advantage of a child-care holiday of up to six years.

Work Policies. By law, all Egyptian hotels are charter members in the **Egyptian Hotel Association (EHA)**. The EHA sets the rules that pertain to the proper performance of the hotel industry and keeps records of all hotel facilities in the country, including occupancy statistics. Unfortunately, there is no set of service standards for hotels to abide by. Each hotel has its standard of performance. The EHA only assures that the final image is commensurate with the hotel level.

Cultural, Economic, and Social Work Values

Tourism development in general, and the hospitality industry in particular, falls under general government responsibility. The government used to take the role of providing each tourist region with the main infrastructure, including electric power, a fresh water supply, a road network, and a sewage system. In recent years, tourism development projects were charged with the responsibility of providing their projects in remote areas with electric power and fresh water supply as well as sewage. Airports, which have been and still are a government responsibility, are becoming a possible agreement between government and entrepreneurs through the **BOT system**.[11] Under this system, an investor has the right to *build* an airport, *operate* it for a certain period (maybe 20 years), and then *transfer* it to the government.

Means of transport have become a private sector concern. Tourism superstructures, such as various forms of accommodation and other support industries (restaurants, retail shops, recreation facilities, etc.), are in the hands of the private sector. Therefore, the Tourism Development Authority plans and studies new tourist regions, sets the prospected development parameters, identifies environmental protection issues, and then invites investors to assume their role in developing accommodation and recreational projects within the established strategy.

Seasonality Trends. Seasonality trends are one of the main problems of the Egyptian hospitality industry. Hotel occupancy in different regions illustrates the fluctuation in the volume of business among different seasons. Hotels try to overcome the problem by reducing rates during low season.

Due to the seasonality, labor market demand is unstable; the curve goes up during peak period and dips down in low season. Therefore, hotel management depends to a great extent on seasonal labor during high periods. This, of course, has its impact on the labor that finds the hospitality market an unsecured job market. Moreover, seasonality causes fluctuation in the level of hotel services, as many employees join the hotel at the beginning of the high season without sufficient training. All these factors have great influence on the growth and improvement of the hospitality industry service level.

Labor Relations

Recruitment and Selection

Recruitment is a continuous process in the Egyptian hospitality industry. Due to the high employee turnover, hotels are in a permanent search for capable employees. Both internal and external recruitment channels are used. Although internal channels help in stimulating the preparation for possible transfer and promotion—improving the level of morale and reducing cost and time of recruitment—they are not widely used. Their use is limited to succession planning and cross training. In using external channels, the majority of hotels depend on advertising as a fundamental source for recruitment, although the drawbacks are large pools of applicants and a high consumption of time and money. Unscheduled interviews, internship programs, networking, and positive press are not widely used. Employment agencies represent a new resource for recruiting employees; although not widespread, it will be a promising channel in the future.

In chain-managed hotels, internal channels gain the priority in searching for new candidates, while external channels are more important in individually-managed hotels. In fact, chain-managed hotels are more aware of the importance of internal channels as a fast and easy source for filling vacant positions and promoting existing employees, in addition to guaranteeing consistency in the level of services offered. On the other side, in individually-managed hotels, employees are less stable and have a shorter work lifespan in comparison to hotel chain employees; therefore, these hotels depend on external recruitment channels to fill in vacant positions.

A study conducted to determine the most popular recruitment channels in Egyptian hotels revealed that five-star hotels use internal channels (87.5 percent) and advertising (12.5 percent); four-star hotels use walk-ins (27 percent), existing employees (55 percent), and internships (18 percent); and three-star hotels use existing employees (40 percent), walk-ins (20 percent), advertising (20 percent), and educational institutions (20 percent).[12] It is essential for hotel management to use a variety of recruitment channels in order to enlarge the pool of applicants.

Interview Approaches. Employment interviews, as the heart of the employment process, are very important in the selection process. In Egyptian hotels, many screening approaches are used that are fundamentally based on the personal interview. Personal interviews are the first and the final tool to select an applicant. Some hotel managers find these interviews sufficient to decide whether to accept or reject an applicant, while others use them as a starting point for successive interviews, patterned interviews, behavioral interviews, and testing. Interactive computer interviews are rarely used. The multitude of the interview approaches that the applicant should pass depends to a large extent on the sophistication of the vacant position.

Special Considerations in Evaluating Applicants. Since the hospitality industry suffers from an acute labor shortage and a high turnover rate, the applicant interview process gains a great importance; the top reasons for employees leaving their new job are due to poor selection and interviewing. Only those with high skills and high desire to join the industry should be selected—the hospitality industry should no longer be a waiting station until an opportunity arises in another field. No real improvement in quality and service standards can be achieved without employees' remaining in the industry. Hotel management should use the **WAB (weighted application blank)**, which helps in selecting more stable employees, and discovering the particular data that denote stability.[13] This could be a successful way to select long tenured employees.

Training and Development

Training should be regarded as one of the most effective remedies for improving the hospitality industry. Training can help in responding to new technology, improving performance, satisfying guests, reducing labor costs and turnover rates, and improving employees' morale—in addition to overcoming the shortage of skilled labor.

The Orientation Process. Although the orientation process helps new applicants to cope more quickly with the job and to commit to hotel policies, it is not a successful process in many Egyptian hotels. As long as many hotels accept employees with no previous experience, there will always be a high percentage of employment lost during the orientation process. Moreover, the quality of the orientation influences employee performance: during the first days of work, lasting employee attitudes and habits are born. Therefore, it is necessary to improve the orientation process in order to obtain a well-trained employee and to decrease the number of employees lost during that period.

Egyptians are, by nature, very familiar, with a high sense of hospitality and a positive service attitude, which is to be considered a strong advantage in the Egyptian domain of hospitality. On the negative side, although the Egyptian hospitality evolution is dated to the last two decades, the industry labor has not witnessed the same level of improvement. Hospitality labor needs to be trained on many aspects—the consistency of the service standards, quality control, and satisfying the varied guest needs.

Training, a basic process in human resources management, is a cornerstone in the effectiveness of any hotel operation. This is particularly true in the labor-intensive hospitality industry, where practically all hotels have a continuous need for efficient and productive managers and supervisors in order to guarantee good service quality.[14] Despite this importance, many hotels in Egypt do not have serious training programs. A study revealed that almost 55 percent of four-star hotels and 40 percent of three-star hotels forego training programs.[15] While hotels with a training process use both individual and training programs, learner controlled instruction methods (videos, computer software, books, and manuals) are rarely used.

Performance Evaluation Practices

Success in the hospitality industry depends on the performance of its employees. A set of performance standards is the first step for a high quality of services. Performance dimensions are not standard in all hotel organizations, but they should lead, in any case, to a satisfied guest.

In the last decade, the Egyptian hospitality industry has witnessed a large boom in its service standards and the diversity of its guests' needs. Today, a multitude of guest types exist including affluent businessmen, leisure travelers, conference and meeting planners, and cultural tourists. Each guest has a different set of needs and expectations; this variation requires a more sophisticated performance level in order to meet their individual needs. Therefore, the role of hotel management to define its performance dimensions on the light of consumer needs is not an easy process.

Neither is the implementation of a performance standard system, although it is extremely necessary for a standardized quality of services. Only 27 percent of four-star hotels and 60 percent of three-star hotels apply this system.[16] Even the applied systems are only performed once or twice a year. Thus, a serious look at the performance standard systems in hotels is essential if improvement in services is desired. The following barriers may keep management from implementing successful systems.

- *Evolution of the hospitality industry.* As discussed earlier, the evolution in the Egyptian hospitality industry is dated only to the last two decades. In addition, the industry is witnessing a large expansion of hotels and a continuous shortage of skilled labor. Therefore, hotel managers cannot find the quality of skilled labor that may help in implementing a successful performance standard system.

- *High turnover rate.* A high turnover rate influences the possibility of implementing a successful system. Turnover in entry-level positions brings about the failure of the system. Turnover in managerial positions results in the lack of consistency in the approved performance standard and continuous follow up.

- *Unskilled and transitory employees.* As some employees are either unskilled or uninterested in the hospitality field and merely working until a better opportunity arises, these employees would not be psychologically satisfied and therefore would not be rendering quality service.

- *Periodic review.* Reviewing the system every six months or once a year cannot guarantee continuous follow up and may cause the system to fail.

- *Fluctuation in occupancy.* Hotel managers may be too busy to run the system or may not have enough business to try the effectiveness of the system. Moreover, the fluctuation in the volume of business influences the employee standard of performance, as those who perform perfectly during low period may not perform the same as in high periods.

- *Other barriers.* Services are very hard to standardize; management may react negatively to the system and consider it a waste of time and money; some managers and employees do not believe in this type of system.

Today, the hospitality industry is more concerned with quality control, quality management, quality awareness, and guest satisfaction. An effective tool to achieve the "quality" aim is to run a successful performance evaluation system. Because many Egyptian hotels do not have a performance evaluation system, it is time to let ISO certification enter the hospitality industry. The concern of many industries in Egypt, this certificate will bring forth quality competition in the industry, which in turn will produce a boom in hospitality quality improvement.

Motivational Practices

It is believed that each employee has his or her own set of needs, which may differ from one to another, and from these needs individual motivators could be predicted. Although these motivators are individually based, they are to a great extent derived from and influenced by the surrounding environment. In Egypt, due to the country's economic problems and the low average income, money plays an integral role in motivating employees. Therefore, monetary motivators are important tools—especially among youth starting their work life. A few years later, other human needs may arise, such as social needs or ego needs. In other words, the Egyptian hospitality labor may require a new edition of Maslow's hierarchy of needs—possibly called the Egyptian Maslow's Pyramid. The primary needs include physiological and safety needs, and the secondary needs include monetary needs, social needs, and ego needs successively.

Career Development Programs

Career development programs are essential in the Egyptian hospitality market as it tries to ensure that hotels have enough trained managers to meet present and future needs—in addition to guaranteeing consistent success for hotel management suffering from shortage of highly experienced middle and top managers.

Management Training Programs. A management development program is the-process by which a hotel ensures that it has effective management to meet its present and future needs. Until 30 years ago, apprenticeship was the only way to obtain hotel managers. Management training programs, therefore, did not require a formal structure; the best trainees would, in due time, rise to the top. This "survival of the fittest" philosophy has lost ground. Now, most successful hotels support some formal approach to management training programs.[17]

A study conducted to determine the number of Egyptian hotels running management training programs indicated that only 22 percent of the chain-managed hotels and none of either independent or affiliated hotels apply such a program.[18]

Promotion Policies. Adequate job promotion policies are essential for healthy growth for the whole organization. Because the hospitality industry suffers from a labor shortage in some management levels, a new employee could reach the managerial level in a few years. This is not a rare feature in the Egyptian hotel market—especially in new tourist regions. In fact, fast promotion is just as bad for the hotel operation as slow promotion, and maybe more harmful. Excessively slow promotions may cause the employee to quit or lose enthusiasm for the job, but excessively fast promotions will directly affect not only the job performance but also the overall performance of the hotel—unqualified employees are often promoted only because qualified persons cannot be found.

Sound promotional policies should be set by hotel operations, and management training programs should be developed. All hotels in the Egyptian market should plan and execute management training programs in their properties. Moreover, the international hotel management chains could serve as a breeding ground for individual hotels. The hotel management chains need to continuously monitor training results and develop their management training programs accordingly. Hotel schools and universities should also play an active role in training.

Disciplining

Disciplining employees is an important process for the reinforcement of the quality of services provided by employees. As discussed before, the Egyptian hospitality industry does not have strong performance evaluation systems. This in turn influences the discipline process as there is no clear set of rules and performance standards for the employee to follow.

It is essential to build up a positive disciplining process; the aim should be to improve the employee's performance and protect the employee from quitting. Therefore, employees have to be provided with a complete set of rules and policies, expected consequences in case of failure to follow the rules, consistent follow up, and reinforcement in success.

Human Resources in the Future

As the growth of tourism in general—and the hospitality industry in particular—gains priority in Egypt's development plans, it is essential to find a way to make the industry more competitive. One of the ways is to provide the industry with skilled and trained employees; this will help the industry improve its operational effectiveness and its competitive performance, including its ability to cope with future challenges. As a first step to achieve this aim, it is necessary to study and analyze labor needs in each tourist region to provide a scheme of the required number and skills for the coming years.

With a quick investigation of hospitality industry growth plans, it will be obvious that no success could be achieved without a parallel growth in the industry labor, and this growth should be in terms of number and quality.

It is obvious that the contribution of government, formal organizations, and hospitality institutions to training is extremely important for developing and training hospitality staff. Failure to take a macro or coordinated view of human resource planning and development can lead to neglect and duplication and can possibly have major business impacts on tourism within a region, country, locality, or company.[19]

The Egyptian government should introduce a training scheme that encourages hospitality institutions and schools to produce the desired type of highly skilled employees. Otherwise, there will be a profound gap between educational institutions and the industry. Moreover, training and educational councils should be developed and be a combination of industry leaders and educators, aiming at meeting regional training needs.

All efforts should be geared toward empowering the newly privatized hotel management to conduct their own training. Here, the role of the government should enable the operation between the industry leaders and the national hotel institutions to provide traveling training programs. These **itinerant training programs** should provide mobile training teams to conduct regional training sessions. These training sessions should be mainly addressed to experienced supervisors in order to produce a qualified trainer who, in a short time, will be a trainer in his region and will produce other trainers and trained employees. With the advantages of the multiplier effect of training, it will be possible to provide the hospitality industry with a great number of trainers and trained employees, in order to cope with the future expansions of the industry. In conclusion, all efforts should be directed toward improving the level of performance for a successful hotel industry in Egypt.

Endnotes

1. Ministry of Economics, Information Center Annual Report, 1998.

2. World Tourism Organization, "Global Tourism Forecasts to the Year 2000 and Beyond" 6:ix (Middle East, 1994), pp. 23, 27 , 49–56.

3. Salah A. Wahah, "Tourism Statistics: Report" (August 1997), pp. 5–6.

4. Egyptian Hotel Association, *Hotel Capacity Statistics Report* (Cairo: Egyptian Hotel Association Information Center, 1999).

5. Egyptian General Organization for Hotels and Tourism, *Annual Graduates Statistical Report*, 1998.

6. Egyptian Hotel Association, *Egyptian Hotel Guide* (Cairo: Egyptian Hotel Association, 1999).

7. J. Fletcher and J. Latham, "International Tourism Training," *Tourism Management* 10, no. 2. (June 1989), 164–166.

8. "Vision 2020," World Tourism Organization, 1998.

9. "Travel and Tourism: Jobs for the Millennium," World Travel and Tourism Council (January 1997), pp. 2, 6, 12.

10. Law 137, Ministry of Labor, 1981.

11. Salah A. Wahah, interview on August 31, 1999.

12. Hanan Kattara, "Upgrading the Skills of Hospitality Industry Personnel in Egypt" (master's thesis, Alexandria University, 1992), pp. 187, 202, 219.

13. Brooks Mitchell, "Bio Data: Using Employment Applications to Screen New Hires," *The Cornell Hotel and Restaurant Administration Quarterly,* February 1989, pp. 56–61.

14. David Wheelhouse, *Managing Human Resources in the Hospitality Industry* (East Lansing, Mich.: Educational Institute of the American Hotel & Motel Association, 1989), pp. 146–147, 193–196.

15. Kattara, "Upgrading the Skills."

16. Kattara, "Upgrading the Skills."

17. Lewis C. Forrest, *Training for the Hospitality Industry,* 2d ed. (East Lansing, Mich: Educational Institute of the American Hotel & Motel Association, 1990), pp.191–200.

18. Hanan Kattara, "Management Training Programs in the Egyptian Hospitality Industry" (paper presented at EuroCRIE Conferences, Lausanne, Switzerland, November 1998), 7.

19. "World Travel and Tourism Council Concerns," *World and Travel Review,* vol.1 (World Travel and Tourism Council, 1991), pp. 206–209, 231–234.

Key Terms

BOT system—Under this system, an investor has the right to *build* an airport, *operate* it for a certain period (maybe 20 years), and then *transfer* it to the government.

Egyptian Hotel Association (EHA)—Sets the rules that pertain to the proper performance of the hotel industry and keeps records of all hotel facilities in the country, including occupancy statistics.

female burnout—When females leave their career for other industries after many years of experience.

itinerant training programs—Mobile training teams that conduct regional training sessions; addressed primarily to experienced supervisors in order to produce a qualified trainer who will produce other trainers and trained employees.

WAB (weighted application blank)—A recruitment process that uses key questions to help select the applicant who is most likely to stay in the hotel.

Discussion Questions

1. What are the main characteristics of the Egyptian hospitality labor market?

2. What are the problems confronting the Egyptian hospitality labor?

3. How does the Egyptian hospitality industry contribute to national and regional economic and socio-cultural development?

4. What kind of improvements could be achieved in the process of recruitment, selection, training, evaluation, motivation, career development, and disciplining in the Egyptian hospitality industry?

5. What recommendations does the author suggest to improve the Egyptian hospitality industry labor? What are your own recommendations?

Internet Sites

For more information, visit the following Internet sites. Remember that Internet addresses can change without notice.

Egypt Information Search
http://www.egyptsearch.com

Egypt State Information Service
http://www.us.sis.gov.eg

Egypt Tourism Authority (ETA)
http://www.tourism.egnet.net

Governments on the WWW (Egypt)
http://www.gksoft.com/govt/en/eg.html

Chapter 3 Outline

The Most Popular Destination in
the World
    Tradition, Innovation, and
      Individualism
The Development of Tourism
The Hospitality Industry Today
    Tourist Flow and Occupancy
    Hotel Industry Structure
    Implications for Human Resources
The Legal Context
    Working Hours
    Job Security
    Social Charges
    Hospitality Regulation
Labor Market Issues
    The Changing Image of Hospitality
Industrial Relations
    Collective Bargaining
    Staff Representation
    Strikes
Cultural and Societal Distinctions
    Individualism vs. Authority
    A Hierarchical Society
    Cross–Cultural Relations
The Changing Role of Human Resource
    Management
    Recruitment and Selection
    Training, Development, and
      Evaluation
    Human Resource Challenges Today
Conclusion

Competencies

1. Identify the main forces that have
   contributed to the development of the
   French hospitality industry.
   (pp. 43–49)

2. Describe the implications of the French
   legal system for hospitality employers
   and employees. (pp. 49–52)

3. Assess the ways in which the unique
   aspects of French culture and
   traditions affect organizational culture
   and labor relations in France.
   (pp. 52–56)

4. Identify the changing needs of the
   hospitality industry in terms of
   employee qualifications and skills and
   the resulting new patterns of
   recruitment and retention. (pp. 57–59)

5. Describe the different factors that need
   to be taken into account in human
   resource management in a context of
   increasing globalization. (pp. 59–60)

3

France: Maintaining French Identity in the Face of Globalization

Margaret Boullé and *Claude Reithler*

Margaret Boullé *holds a Doctorat d'Université from the Sorbonne, Paris, a master's degree from the University of Aix-en-Provence, and B.A. Hons from the University of Melbourne, Australia. She has taught at Monash University (Australia), the Institute of Education (Mauritius), and New York University (U.S.A.), and has also been a consultant for United Nations organizations in New York and Geneva. She is currently Executive Admission Counsellor at the Ecole Hôtelière de Lausanne, Switzerland.*

Claude Reithler *was formerly Regional Director of Human Resources for Hilton International and General Manager of the Paris Hilton. She is an experienced seminar leader in management and human resources, and she is currently working in the Middle East with Megicon Contracting and Development, Cairo.*

The Most Popular Destination in the World

France is the most popular tourist destination in the world, with consistently more tourist arrivals every year than any other country. Despite the development of new world markets and the changing patterns of tourist flow brought about by globalization, France maintained its position over the ten years from 1988 to 1997, showing an average growth of 5.1 percent in tourist arrivals, compared with the already strong increase of 4.6 percent for Europe as a whole. Recent years have shown particularly significant growth, from more than 60 million tourists in 1995 to 71 million in 1998. At the start of the new millennium, France maintains its leading position as a destination for ten percent of world travelers.[1]

For many, France is first and foremost Paris, which has been a magnet ever since the days of the European "grand tour" of the eighteenth and nineteenth centuries. Paris, with its museums and art galleries, its great boulevards and small cafés and bistros, has drawn intellectuals, writers, and artists from all over the world, and has always been a haven for exiles or those misunderstood and unappreciated in their own countries. It is impossible to wander through Paris's streets without seeing the city through the prism of all those who have loved it before. "Tear out my heart and you will see Paris in it," said French writer Louis Aragon.

Of course, France is not only Paris. Part of the reason for the country's popularity is its central location in Europe, as well as its exceptional geographical position: the diversity of its landscape, its mild climate, and the numerous recreational activities it can therefore offer. France's landscapes range from the beaches of the Mediterranean coastline, the lavender and olive groves of Provence, and the salt marshes and white horses of the Camargue, through Alsace in the northeast with its gabled wooden houses and nesting storks, to the cathedrals of Chartres and Rheims in the grayer north, or the towers and turrets of the Châteaux de la Loire reflected in the tranquil waters of the Loire River. Mountains, which cover a fifth of French territory, are also popular destinations.

Every region in France has its own long tradition of food and wine, protected by **appellations** that guarantee the character and authenticity not only of the great wines, but also of cheeses such as Roquefort—which is made in one small region of the world, with one particular type of ewe's milk, injected with special mold spores, and slowly ripened in limestone caves. This is the country in which the maître d'hôtel Vatel committed suicide when the fish he needed for a dinner to be prepared for Louis XIV did not arrive on time, and in which the restaurant ratings of each new *Michelin Guide* are awaited with anguish.

The attraction of France is that of a legend: a dream of fine living, connoisseurship, good taste, sophistication, and traditional excellence. Paradoxically, its reputation is also one of inventiveness and style: from the first motion picture made by the Lumière brothers, through the zipper and the non-stick pan, to the TGV high-speed train or the Franco-British *Concorde*. The mixture of tradition and bold innovation may be found in every aspect of French life, not least in its urban landscape—from I. M. Pei's daring transparent glass triangle in the courtyard of the Louvre to the Beaubourg Art Center, with its provocative factory-like tubes set in the midst of traditional Parisian cafés.

If the magic is so potent, it is in part because the French themselves believe in it so utterly. Their concept of France as a country set apart—with the high moral mission to spread its ideal of humanism, justice, and culture through the world—is summed up by the expression so frequently heard: *l'exception française*. France thinks of itself as the arbiter and the guardian of human rights and civilized values.

The need to proclaim and defend their individuality, coupled with a supreme disregard toward what others think of them, are essential aspects of the French character that have had profound implications for France's relations with the rest of the world. They have certainly helped to shape the tourist industry and are likely to determine, at least in part, its future development.

Tradition, Innovation, and Individualism

The main characteristics of the French—a love of tradition, a gift for innovation, and a strong sense of individual identity—also characterize the hospitality industry in France.

First, tradition is revered. Much of the hospitality market today continues to be made up of small, family-owned enterprises, reflecting a deeply traditional attachment to property handed down from generation to generation, and all very different from each other. As a result, there is no uniform standard.

Yet the French continue to innovate. At the time of its introduction, Club Méditerranée featured a highly original concept: the all-inclusive destination resort. At another level, the Formule I budget chain launched by Accor shows characteristic innovation and commercial daring and has been tremendously successful in France, with a 95 percent yearly occupancy rate. However, it is doubtful, for cultural reasons, whether the chain's advanced technological concept (four rooms grouped around common bathroom facilities that are automatically cleaned and disinfected) and its marketing concept (one rock-bottom non-negotiable room rate) can be exported to other developed countries in which in-suite bathrooms are the norm.

The strong sense of individualism among the French is reflected in a generally wary attitude toward globalization and anxiety about the place of France in an increasingly American-led industry. The demonstrations led by French farmers against McDonald's restaurants during September 1999 are highly symbolic: the groups who lured customers away from McDonald's with "hamburgers" made of Roquefort and foie gras were standing up for the values of individualism, culture, and tradition against the steamroller of uniformity represented by the ubiquitous Big Mac.

However, in a world in which globalization appears inevitable and in which France, like most other countries, continues in the direction of consolidation, this defiant David-and-Goliath stance may not be sufficient to maintain viability. Responding to internationalization does not necessarily mean uniformity; it also means becoming attentive to the needs of new and different clients and making them feel well-received and welcome. Human resource management has an important role to play in encouraging awareness of client needs and in trying to modify the "take us as we are" attitude that is all too common in France.

The Development of Tourism

The development of tourism in France over the last 50 years has largely been a success story. In 1945, the sector was fragmented and anarchic. It consisted of a large number of small family businesses scattered across the country. Such establishments were often highly seasonal in nature, and they offered a wide diversity of products and limited services.

To a certain extent, this pattern continues today, reflecting the French desire not to be herded into package holidays but to organize individual vacations without recourse to tour operators or travel agencies. At the same time, there has been a growing move toward concentration with the development of a limited number of large enterprises, and the beginnings of more horizontal integration (for example, acquiring ownership of other hotels) as well as vertical integration (buying into tour operator or transport companies).

The growth of the industry in recent times began with the post–World War II reconstruction period. During the 1950s, at a time when the market was still largely internal, hotels belonged to two main categories: the hotels de luxe and the others. The luxury European hotel had a reputation for service and quality; this concept of high-quality service was in direct contrast to the burgeoning U.S. hospitality industry of the time, in which comfort was predominant and service rudimentary. Today, the trend seems to be reversed, with a growth in service quality being more characteristic of the U.S. market and of international chains.

The 1960s were characterized by rising living standards, more leisure time, and increased international travel. With the new influx of international visitors, particularly Americans, chain development made its timid beginnings. In 1967, Novotel was launched, based on the Holiday Inn concept. As a three-star hotel, it appeared luxurious compared to the independent hotels of the time, with large guestrooms and bathrooms, and in-room televisions. The concept flourished and became the first successful venture of what was to become the powerful Accor Group. In the 1990s, with more favorable economic trends, budget expansion slowed and upper-level market segments gained share again. Today, integrated chains at all levels are part of the landscape and growth continues consistently but reasonably—four to six percent a year, as against seven to eight percent worldwide.[2]

Figures do not, however, adequately represent the growing importance of the chains. For instance, although they represent only about 14 percent of the hotel stock in France (compared with 72 percent in the United States), one tourist night out of two is spent in a chain property. Similarly, restaurant chains represent less than three percent of food and beverage establishments but 19 percent of the guest turnover for the sector.[3] This may be explained in part, however, by the larger size of restaurant chain units, which have many more seats and faster turnover as compared to the smaller size and still-sacred longer meal times of the traditional French restaurants.

Since the mid-1990s, the French economy, which is fourth in the world, has been booming. Unemployment, which has always been high in France, fell to less than ten percent in May 2000, after steadily dropping over the previous six years from a postwar high of 12.6 percent. The projected growth rate for the economy is 2.8 percent.[4]

Tourism, as an important part of the economy, seems set to benefit from the general upward trend, and recent growth has been particularly encouraging. The most recent figures show an increase for both European and overseas tourists—from five percent to ten percent for Northern Europe and the United States and a significant upswing of 10–20 percent for Asia.[5] In terms of occupancy and revenue, a recent report from KPMG shows steadily increasing occupancy rates across all categories. This increase, in conjunction with rising average daily rates, is reflected in the general increase in RevPAR, from 7.8 percent to 19.9 percent according to category.[6]

As a note of caution, however, it should be remembered that part of the upswing has been due to various one-time sponsored events, such as soccer's World Cup in 1998. It remains to be seen whether the momentum achieved is sufficient to carry the French hotel industry through to a new period of sustained growth.

The Hospitality Industry Today

While France's position as the first tourist destination is undisputed, the situation is different with regard to earnings from tourism. In 1995, for example, France was in second position after the United States; in 1998, Italy surpassed France, with receipts of $30.4 billion compared to France's $29.7 billion—both figures well behind the United States with $74.2 billion.[7]

Although France does not figure on the list of the top 50 countries for expenditure per individual tourist, tourist expenditure does make significant contribution to the French balance of payments, which has averaged about 7.5 percent over the past few years. However, the disparity between tourist arrivals and tourist receipts is surprising.

Tourist Flow and Occupancy

Recent figures show that 87 percent of tourist arrivals in France originated from Europe, of which 53 percent came from Western Europe (Austria, Germany, Netherlands, Switzerland, Belgium, Luxemburg). Visitors from the Americas came to about 4 million, of which 2.3 million were U.S. citizens. The East Asia and Pacific regions provided a total of 2.4 million tourists, including more than 600,000 Japanese; Africa and the Middle East accounted for about 1.2 million visitors.[8]

It is clear that one way to increase tourist receipts is to increase overseas arrivals. Occupancy rates show that tourists from Asia and the Americas tend to stay in hotels rather than in private houses, youth hostels, etc. They also stay longer than European tourists. Currently, tourist nights in hotels and similar establishments represent only about 11 percent of all tourist nights in France—and the vast majority of tourists who spend nights in this category come from Europe. This pattern of accommodation results in a much lower level of tourist receipts.

Hotel Industry Structure

A system of classifying hotels has been developed by the Ministry of Tourism, which awards a number of stars to an establishment based on criteria such as room size, number of bathrooms, and other amenities. Not all enterprises are classified by the ministry, however; for instance, many smaller, lower-priced hotels are under local administrative authority, particularly in rural areas. The number of classified hotels has remained stable for the last few years, at about 20,000 establishments. Of these, there are about 17,000 independent hotels. In addition to these, unclassified hotels represent a huge group that has never been adequately assessed; estimates vary from 11,000 to 17,000.[9]

Coach Omnium reports the following distribution of classified hotels as of January 1, 1999: 14.1 percent integrated chains, 29.1 percent voluntary chains (consortia, franchises, management contracts), and 56.8 percent independent establishments. In terms of rooms, however, figures are as follows: 36.1 percent integrated chains, 23 percent consortia, and 40.4 percent independent establishments.[10]

Integrated Hotel Chains. The figures given above help to explain why, although chains occupy a minority position in France, they record a disproportionately high number of tourist nights, and their market share is 45 percent of the 19,700 classified hotels in France.[11] But the number of rooms is only one factor. Chains have been successful because customers like them; they represent a guarantee of comfort and quality not always matched by the independents. Although, as elsewhere, it is often business customers who express preference for a chain (60 percent), clients traveling for other reasons also often choose chains—41 percent, as against 31 percent who prefer an independent hotel and 28 percent who do not state a preference.[12]

Two groups control 71 percent of chains, under 30 different brands: Accor and the Société du Louvre / Envergure. Most other chains do not reach critical mass for brand recognition.

Accor is now the fourth group in the world in terms of the number of hotels, with 2,481 hotels in 76 countries. This is a considerable achievement in a market in which seven of the ten leading chains are American. Unlike most other groups, Accor is extremely diversified in terms of market segmentation, ranging from super-economy to upper-market brands, including Novotel, Sofitel, Ibis, Formule I, Etap, and Mercure.

For a home-grown product, Accor has a surprising global presence. Among major international chains, only seven companies, including Accor, have properties in 50 or more countries. Many international companies concentrate to a large extent on their home market; thus, room share for such brands as Hilton and Cendant in the Americas is 95.8 percent and 94.6 percent, respectively. By contrast, room share for Accor in France is 33.7 percent.[13]

Accor has become a growing empire, with its increasing vertical and horizontal integration, including Europcar and the travel agency Carlson Wagonlit. Its success is acknowledged by the profession, although there is some anxiety about its dominant position.

Consortia and Independents. Among consortia, growth is slower than among the integrated chains. Responding to the perceived French need for individuality and lack of uniformity, the voluntary chains seem to be emphasizing quality rather than quantity, with more attentiveness to client needs. Logis de France is the largest group by far, and most recent growth in France has taken place within this group. Two other well-established groups, Relais & Châteaux and Relais du Silence, are now focusing primarily on expansion outside of France.

Restaurants. Chains represent only three percent of restaurants in France, and traditional French cuisine continues to flourish. However, perhaps because brand recognition is so high and they appear so visible, fast-food chains in particular generate resentment within the profession, as well as being denigrated as an American import by the general public. McDonald's is the leading restaurant chain in France, with 800 restaurants and 4.1 percent of restaurant clientele; as the ultimate symbol of Americanization, it tends to receive the most abuse.

Interestingly, McDonald's has been successful in France partly because it has adapted to the special needs and expectations of the French. In France, 90 percent of McDonald's restaurants are franchised, with special attention given to implantation in the local community. It has also toned down its visual impact, and has avoided locations that are nationally symbolic and, therefore, "too emotional." These include monuments, museums, or memorials that are closely linked to French history and traditions, where the presence of a nearby McDonald's would seem to indicate a cultural takeover and would be resented. Other chains that have not made the effort to adapt their product have not managed to penetrate the French market.

Implications for Human Resources

In a rapidly evolving market with ever-increasing chain penetration, one of the main issues is that of the match between employee skills and experience and changing industry requirements. Until recently, most employees have learned on the job, gradually working their way up to senior positions. The increasing complexity of the industry and rapid technological advances require very different qualities and qualifications at both operational and managerial levels than those needed previously. Education and training have become important issues.

Another important issue is employee motivation. The hospitality industry has recently gone through hard times, resulting in lower salaries and increasing job uncertainty. Attracting motivated staff while ensuring profitability is increasingly challenging for those in charge of human resources.

Finally, increasing global competition needs to be acknowledged by human resources departments if quality service is to be assured.

The Legal Context

France is one of the most highly centralized and highly regulated countries in the world, with comprehensive, often arcane, rigid labor laws concerning both conditions of employment and remuneration of employees. The labor law (*Code du Travail*) is constantly expanding. The system results in a heavy administrative burden that is particularly daunting for the small and medium-size enterprises that make up the bulk of the hospitality industry.

The fundamental intention behind the proliferation of rules has been social protection and justice. France has historically been years ahead of most other countries in social reform. However, the resulting industry costs and constraints restrict entrepreneurship and often discourage foreign investment.

Working Hours

One example of progressive social policy is the regular reduction in working hours. In 1936, the Popular Front government voted a 40-hour work week and two weeks' paid leave annually; a third week was added in 1956, a fourth in 1969, and a fifth in 1982, when the legal working week was further reduced to 39 hours. In 1999, a 35-hour week was voted and is gradually being implemented. France today is among the industrialized countries with the fewest working hours.

It does need to be noted, however, that the hospitality industry has often been treated as a special case because of the type of work involved. The industry is particularly affected by the prospect of the 35-hour week. Many hoteliers and restaurateurs are worried about how they can function and about how costs can be absorbed. Two possible solutions involve increasing the number of employees and increasing productivity.

Job Security

The labor code ensures a high level of job security, with comprehensive employment contracts. The two main types of contract are permanent and fixed-term, including seasonal contracts, which are regulated in detail. There is also a system of overtime for certain jobs, including many in hospitality and catering.

The terms of employment contracts have allowed very little flexibility, although in recent years there have been some legislative changes that open up more possibilities. **Annualized contracts** were first authorized by the 1993 employment law, and these can now be used to counterbalance staffing problems by allowing longer working hours at peak periods. Annualized contracts permit work hours to be spread out over the whole year, allowing for variation in work hours to balance peak times and off times, so that overtime does not have to be paid. However, annualized contracts can be implemented only if negotiated with and agreed to by the unions. Otherwise, employers have to juggle the legal possibilities offered by the various employment contracts. This is not easy because of rigid definitions. In big cities, for example, labor inspectors do not accept seasonal contracts because they consider the city's occupancy to be stable, due to year-round events that ensure a fairly regular flow of visitors. (This is in contrast to ski resorts, for example, which may operate only part of the year or may make very little money in the off-season.) One possibility is increasing part-time work; recent legislation gives employers the possibility of paying reduced social contributions for certain part-time workers. However, unions are wary because of the increased danger of exploitation.

It is very difficult for an employer to dismiss an employee; only reasons involving serious lack of competency or professional fault or misconduct are acceptable. A lengthy legal procedure is usually necessary in order to terminate employment, together with adequate prior notice and generous severance allowances, both linked to the duration of employment. Employees must always be interviewed in person before they are served with a notice for dismissal and must be accompanied by an **employee representative**, an employee elected by other employees to be their representative vis-à-vis management. (There is a legal obligation in France for all enterprises of more than 50 employees to elect such representatives.) All legal procedures must be followed with great care; otherwise, employees may take their employers to court.

Annual negotiations are mandatory between management and unions. If there is no official union represented in the enterprise, negotiations then occur between management and employee representatives. Negotiations concern salaries, working conditions, working time, training, and the right of expression. The negotiation process is mandatory, but, legally, it does not have to lead to an agreement. If it does not, however, management risks a strike.

Social Charges

France is an advanced welfare state with a comprehensive social security system that is financed through a complex system of contributions from firms and employees; it is one of the most expensive in the world and is becoming increasingly difficult to maintain. *La sécu* includes coverage for generous old-age pensions, family allowances, and basic medical coverage of about 80 percent, often supplemented by semi-private insurance. Basically, it ensures decent minimum living conditions and medical coverage for the whole of France's population.

Not surprisingly, social charges for French enterprises are among the highest in the world. In 1999, compulsory deductions came to 45 percent of the GDP.[14] It is clear that social costs are a determining factor in the dynamism and profitability of the economy as a whole and of the hospitality industry, as a labor-intensive sector, in particular. Social costs are often cited as a major cause of the high unemployment rate, as employers are reluctant to take on new employees both because of the high cost of social charges and because of the difficulty and expense involved in terminating employment. The social cost of salaries has continually to be weighed against turnover.

Hospitality Regulation

The hospitality sector has traditionally been difficult to regulate. At the time of the Popular Front government in the 1930s, much of the industry operated outside the minimal regulatory framework in place for other sectors, with something of an "outlaw" mentality, a perception of itself as different and beholden to none. Some of the laws passed since that time have been designed to bring the sector into the fold and especially to generate revenue for the State; others are designed to protect working conditions and wages in a context of high casual employment, or temporary jobs.

One of the most important laws relating to the hospitality industry is the landmark **Godard Law** (*Loi Godard*) of 1934, which remains in force today (new operations have the legal right to decide whether to implement it or not). The original aim of the law was to allow the Ministry of Finance better control of hotel revenue and salary mass. It was also designed to ensure that workers received a minimum salary that would allow them not to depend on tips. The law authorized a rise of 15 percent in the price of hotels and services, including also the price of tipping. This 15 percent was to be redistributed among different categories of hotel personnel, allotting tips to those who were in direct contact with guests.

The provisions of the Godard Law were enacted in accordance with the labor patterns of the Thirties. With the evolution of the industry, these categories rapidly became obsolete for all but smaller hospitality enterprises. For example, the typical concierge's job of the 1930s has been broken up into many more highly differentiated jobs, many of which are not covered by the law, resulting in curious anomalies. In today's context, housekeepers and bellstaff receive the 15 percent; employees who work in reception or reservations do not.

The fact that this law and others have not been adequately updated to keep pace with the evolving industry has had far-reaching consequences in such areas as salary growth and distribution, hiring and job patterns, and the complex relationship with the trade unions. Many larger enterprises have had constant recourse to legal advisors to help them avoid some of the difficulties entailed.

Labor Market Issues

In 1998 France reported a working population of 22.7 million. Two million people earn their living directly or indirectly from tourism, including 612,000 in the hotel and restaurant business.[15] As a labor-intensive industry, the hotel and restaurant sector has a large number of operative or line-level workers and proportionately fewer employees in management. The sector is one in which most workers earn the basic wage. There is also, as in other countries, high turnover and a high proportion of temporary and seasonal jobs. In addition, there is considerable clandestine employment, mostly of foreign workers who are illegal residents in France.[16]

The labor market seems to be approaching a crisis. In an area that traditionally generates jobs, there is a paradoxically high unemployment rate of 16 percent for the hospitality industry, compared with less than 12 percent for the general population. As well, there seems to be a lack of qualified workers. The industry no longer appears to have the attraction that it did only a few years ago, when it seemed to offer not only a certain glamour but also the opportunity to rise fairly rapidly in the profession.

The change seems to be due to two factors. First, with competition from the chains and an increasing financial burden, many small enterprises have been struggling. In hard times, enterprises tend to dismiss workers, and the owners take on most of the tasks themselves. During the recession in 1991, 27 percent of French hotels and 47 percent of restaurant owners did not employ any wage earners at all.[17] The hard work does not attract the younger generation and they see few prospects of advancement. Family-owned establishments, which traditionally handed their businesses down to the next generation, are finding more and more that their children do not wish to continue the tradition.

In the chains themselves, career prospects no longer seem as inviting as they did a few years ago. This is part of a general management problem that has existed in larger enterprises in the industry since the 1990s. In order to motivate employees, the promise of rapid promotion is held out, resulting in a top-heavy structure with too many employees clustered at a "glass ceiling" of mid-level supervisory responsibility. The problem is increased with shift work, which increases the number of "chiefs" and has resulted in a situation where there can be, for example, one maître d'hôtel for every five to ten employees, resulting both in lower productivity and higher salary mass. With the recession of the mid-1990s, general managers reacted to this blocked hierarchy by attempting to reduce staff, managing to do so with some success despite union opposition.

There is another problem at the management level: The young employees hired in the early 1990s have since reached management level and are now blocking advancement for those behind them.

The Changing Image of Hospitality

The hospitality industry is having difficulty today attracting motivated and dynamic employees because of its image as primarily offering unskilled, low-status positions with long working hours and difficult conditions.

Salaries have fallen over the last 15 years. Reacting to increased social charges, increasing competition, and the recession, managers trying to balance total salary mass against turnover in order to ensure profitability have had to reduce the number of employees while simultaneously building a strategy for planned turnover of staff through short-term contracts. Fifteen years ago, a rate of 1.5 to 2 employees per room in luxury hotels was the norm; today, the range is from 0.8 to 1.1. There is little attempt to encourage employee loyalty, both because of added social costs and because it is much more difficult to fire long-term employees in times of financial difficulty. Salaries therefore stay low, and there is increasing job precariousness and little possibility of promotion.

The sector is also increasingly seen to be low-status. According to official statistics, 48 percent of hospitality occupations are classified in the category "domestic workers" and 40 percent in the category "independent workers and employers with 0 to 2 employees," which, according to the International Labour Organization, "traditionally comprises the largest share of untrained persons."[18]

Hospitality jobs are likely to be more demanding today, with employees working longer hours. The reduction in staff means that remaining employees have to be multi-skilled. Part of this evolution has been due to the development of the chains, which have had a profound impact on the profession and revolutionized the labor market. Often they have been more socially advanced than independent enterprises, reducing working hours, setting up programs to integrate new employees, and developing staff training. However, chains are still considered relatively conservative employers. They have been able to impose lower salaries, and they are often more demanding in terms of skills and efficiency required.

Industrial Relations

Trade unions are a particularly important force in France in all sectors of the economy. Freedom to join a trade union is a constitutional right and is also provided for in the Labor Code (Article L411-5). Surprisingly, membership in unions is low; today, only ten percent of employees are unionized, the lowest figure in Western Europe.[19] However, the influence of the unions is much more important than this figure suggests, resulting from alliances among the various unions themselves as well as from links between unions and other employee representatives.

Collective Bargaining

In common with most Western European countries, industrial relations in France are based on collective bargaining, resulting in agreements in which employees may receive more advantages than those guaranteed by law. Collective bargaining takes place either between management and trade unions, who designate their members within a company, or between management and other employee organizations.

There are five major unions representing five different political trends: the CGT, which is close to the Communist Party; the FO, which has socialist sympathies; the CFDT, also pro-socialist but more moderate; the CFTC or Christian socialists; and the CGC, which represents white-collar employees and is more right-wing. Unlike unions in many other countries, unions in France are not specific to any one industry or category of workers. Union representatives within a particular company are designated by the union itself; they are not elected by the staff.

The relationship between unions, companies, and the government depends upon a complex and delicate balance of power. The collective bargaining structure exists within a political web in which unions participate at a high level in national discussion, and union leaders have direct access to ministries, as does senior management.

Staff Representation

Staff representation is extremely complex, and the legal and technical aspects need to be understood by all human resources managers. Trade unions and other employee organizations such as the employees' council (*comité d'entreprise*) play a key role in the collective bargaining process. The *comité d'entreprise* is a legal obligation in all enterprises of more than 50 employees, whether there is a union or not. Unlike union members, *comité* members or employee representatives are elected by the staff. The *comité* may exist instead of, or in addition to, a trade union; the *comité* itself may be either unionized or non-unionized.

Several other forms of staff representation exist. Many employees do not want to belong to a union because of the link between unions and political ideologies; however, they are very conscious of the need to fight for social rights. They may therefore create "house unions" or may simply represent themselves individually or as the voice for an informal group of employees.

Strikes

One particularly visible aspect of labor relations in France is the frequency of strikes. The need to go on strike and to demonstrate, often violently, in the streets seems to be a national characteristic. Strikes concern every economic sector and practically every category of job, including transportation workers, electricity and gas workers, teachers and students, truck drivers and the post office, doctors, journalists, radio stations and the weather report bureau—even the ten bird chasers (*effaroucheurs d'oiseaux*) at Orly Airport.

Strikes are not as much of a headache for employers as one might think, and strikes in hotels cause less disruption for guests, perhaps, than lost luggage, overbooked flights, and transportation delays. In addition, strikes in France do not have the negative emotional connotations that they may have in other countries. Strikes are a normal and even expected part of the bargaining process. They are usually looked upon relatively indulgently by the French themselves, who are often in basic sympathy with the strikers.

In general, striking in France is simply part of the "rules of the game" in negotiations between employers and employees, governed by many unwritten rules. Each side has an assigned role to play. If employers, for example, are too readily forthcoming and perceived as too ready to fall in with the workers' point of view, they are viewed with suspicion by unions and the effect may be negative rather than positive. Employer/employee relations are usually perceived as basically adversarial.

Cultural and Societal Distinctions

As already seen, the distinctive French culture permeates all aspects of business life. Although characteristics and trends may superficially seem the same as those in other countries, a closer examination shows that very different forces are often at play beneath the surface, with profound consequences for future development.

Individualism vs. Authority

The strongly individualistic nature of the French and their simultaneous need for authority can be understood through the insights offered by cross-cultural analysis. Geert Hofstede, a sociologist who specializes in intercultural analysis, has shown, for example, that France is high on the "uncertainty avoidance" scale; that is, it is a culture in which the members "feel threatened by uncertain or unknown situations" and seek to avoid ambiguity. People look for a structure in their lives that makes events clearly interpretable and predictable—hence, the need for guidance in the form of a large number of written and unwritten rules.

Interestingly, France also ranks high on the "individualism index," and the combination of these two measures goes a long way in explaining the "French paradox." French society is highly dependent on rules; at the same time, it is strongly individualistic, so that people continually try to defend the individual against the system and to fight against authority even as they acknowledge it. The need for rules is "not based on formal logic but on psycho-logic."[20]

This analysis can help in understanding the effect of the regulatory environment on French industry and labor relations, in an area where too hasty judgments are sometimes made by outsiders. From the Anglo-Saxon viewpoint, the rigidity of the French system may seem to be simply an unfortunate detail—a brake on the dynamism of economic development that the French would be well advised to do something about. However, the situation is much more complex than this.

Author John Ardagh's comment is typical: "The French have had a long love-hate relationship with the State. They resent it, yet cling to its apron-strings and expect it endlessly to provide."[21] There is a basic contradiction between the belief in France as enshrined in the French system and the equally strong need to rail against it. Grousing (*râler*) is a national characteristic.

Even though the system is accepted, a large amount of energy goes into challenging it and trying to find ways around it. One prime example: tax evasion, which has been described as practically a national pastime, was officially reported in 1996 as being equal to two-thirds of the revenue from income tax.[22] The different forms of contestation within the system become a series of unwritten rules in themselves and are implicitly accepted by all those involved.

A Hierarchical Society

It is important to understand the hierarchical nature of French society—a pyramid structure in which those at the top are not only a social elite but also a product of the extremely selective French educational system. Nearly all senior managers in France have graduated from the small number of highly prestigious *grandes écoles,* which train them for future high posts both in the civil service and in state and private industry. The importance of the school attended, and of the degree obtained, creates a huge power gap between top management and the rest of the employees.

Until now, the hospitality industry did not fit into this pattern. Managers rose through the ranks and did not constitute an elite imported from the outside. However, with the recent creation of MBAs in hotel administration, the industry has been tending to imitate other sectors, with important implications for human resources management.

Cross-Cultural Relations

The play between employees, unions, and management depends in part on the diversity of cultural and ethnic groups in the hospitality industry. Broadly, three different cultures characterize the hospitality industry in France: Anglo-Saxon, Latin, and Muslim.

At the top management level, there is a mix of nationalities, predominantly from European countries rather than from the United States, due to working permit regulations. Another very important factor of influence is the Muslim culture, represented by people from many different countries worldwide, who occupy mostly unskilled jobs. Social advancement for this group is a major aim for the government and is taken into account in all kinds of training programs. As in other countries, the presence of diverse ethnic groups can lead to tension in the workplace.

With globalization, Anglo-Saxon management practices have become a pervasive influence throughout the industry. These practices are often in an uneasy relationship with the Latin temperament and behavior patterns. For example, the Anglo-Saxon approach is results-oriented and based on customer satisfaction; in France, management tends to focus more on who is responsible for getting things done. One American who knows both sides has summed up the situation as follows: "In France, they count on very sophisticated people; in the United States, the sophistication is in the system of organization."[23]

Another aspect of the difference between French and Anglo-Saxon management styles is a result of the French preoccupation with written rules and contracts, which contrasts with the more informal Anglo-Saxon approach. Ardagh describes the difficulties of managers who try to introduce American techniques into the workplace: "It can drive them mad, for although attitudes may have changed, the official regulations that govern working life have not been properly updated."[24]

The Changing Role of Human Resource Management

Traditionally, employees have been hired by the director of a hotel or restaurant, who has usually had the experience of working gradually up the career ladder, acquiring a thorough knowledge of every aspect of the industry while doing so. In the 1970s and early 1980s, the royal path was first to become food and beverage manager, at a time when most hotels still had their own restaurants. In the mid-1980s, marketing became increasingly important and many marketing managers went on to become directors. In recent years, financial and legal knowledge has become so essential that many general managers come from a finance background. Today, human resources management covers so many complex, interrelated issues that it has often become a key post requiring highly specialized knowledge and skills covering many different areas. Although it is common in smaller enterprises for the director to continue having the responsibility of recruiting and managing employees, many larger independent enterprises and chains now have a human resources manager.

Today, it is difficult to find the right candidate for the post of human resource manager from within; this is perhaps why chains in particular have tended to appoint human resource experts from outside the industry. However, these appointments have usually been unsuccessful. In the absence of an inside, intimate knowledge of the many facets of the industry, these managers have tended to make mistakes regarding job profiles and the qualifications needed, and have not been able to conduct job interviews with the skill required to hire the right candidate.[25]

The qualities needed for a human resource manager in France today (or for a GM, if there is no specialist in the management team) are a reflection of the evolution of the industry. Essential qualities include:

- A strong legal and financial background, as well as a thorough knowledge of politics and labor laws.

- Familiarity with the work organization of a hotel as well as with the communication styles characteristic of the industry. It has to be remembered that most hospitality products are consumed as soon as they are bought, and that there are often strong immediate reactions on the part of the client that must be dealt with appropriately.

- An intuitive knowledge of, and sensitivity to, cultural elements within the hospitality labor force, to be applied in everything related to selection and recruitment as well as staff social relations.

- The ability to keep abreast of shifts in motivation and the changing labor scene—in terms of career development, salary, and quality of life—at every level of the hierarchy.

- The ability to keep abreast of the latest technological developments in the industry and to undertake needs assessment and training as necessary.

Recruitment and Selection

Recently there has been a proliferation of schools offering hospitality courses, and more and more candidates with hotel school diplomas are applying for jobs. However, their increasing number poses a problem. Most diplomas provide two-year professional qualifications, training students for operations responsibilities at the mid-management level. Graduates do not want to begin on the lowest rung and often disdain what is perceived as manual work. One human resource director for a low-budget hotel chain stated that budget hotels did not seem to interest graduates, even at the management level, as the type of work involved too much hands-on labor and too little sitting in an office giving orders.[26]

Chains and even small hotels are reluctant to hire hotel school graduates who bring with them higher salary expectations, preferring to hire less-qualified people at a lower salary. Hotel school graduates are usually taken on at a level that is lower than could be expected for their qualifications, resulting in employee frustration and resentment. It is significant that today only one hospitality graduate out of five is still in the profession five years after starting work.[27]

Some French universities have begun to offer management degrees in hospitality, including the prestigious post-graduate program in international hospitality management administered jointly by Cornell and Essec. Otherwise, candidates have tended to study elsewhere; in Switzerland, at the Ecole Hôtelière de Lausanne, French students regularly account for a third or more of the student population.

In contrast to the qualities needed for a human resource manager, hotel managers need to have general managerial skills and usually a good commercial background. Hotels are therefore tending to hire graduates from management or commercial schools, with generally successful results. Nevertheless, the hotel industry does not offer highly paid positions; even if candidates have an MBA, they are often discouraged by the financial package they are offered.

Training, Development, and Evaluation

Training is considered important, and the French government has initiated progressive policies in this area. Training programs are designed to help the unemployed develop the qualifications necessary to re-enter the job market and to enable those who are employed to update their skills.

A 1971 law made it obligatory for all employees to be able to benefit from time off in order to pursue further training, over and above any in-house training provided by the company. Within the hospitality industry, all enterprises pay a special tax (about 1.5 percent of their gross payroll) that is remitted to an official association in charge of continued training in the industry, the FAFIH (*Fonds d'assurance formation pour l'industrie hôtelière*). The FAFIH is in charge of providing information about and financing for many different types of training: internships, ongoing refresher courses, training in new technologies. On condition that the employer effectively spends the money, the 1.5 percent can be used to organize internal programs, with or without FAFIH. However, in many small enterprises, these opportunities are not taken advantage of, and there is no systematic assessment of needs or follow-up.

Many chains have extensive in-house courses designed for the special needs of their employees. Accor's "Académie Accor" is particularly well known. It has a purpose-designed company campus and proposes customized training programs and coaching. Accor also has a comprehensive program for needs assessment. Once a year, all the operational units (hotels, travel agencies, etc.) draw up a list of their training needs, and appropriate courses are then planned by the various training committees. Accor has also developed a system for optimal follow-up: evaluation is done through questionnaires that employees fill in after each training course—once on completion of the course and then again a month later—to monitor whether objectives have been reached and whether there has been improvement in employee performance.

Human Resource Challenges Today

As has been seen, it is often difficult to implement human resources "best practices" in France because of the constraints encountered at all levels: legal, political, and social. In the light of the government's social strategy to provide benefits and security to all, and to help the most disadvantaged sections of the population, managers have a choice of strategy.

One choice is to develop a human resource management strategy focusing mainly on unskilled people. In this case, managers can take advantage of the many government subsidies, training contracts, and fiscal advantages available. They can then better control their payroll and the rate of career development; however, they take a risk concerning the quality of the operation.

The other option is to decide to hire graduates, choosing among various categories of diplomas and degrees offered in France. In this case, managers have to offer higher salaries and cope with the eagerness of qualified young people who want a fast career track. The cost of human resources management may become higher—the payroll will be less easy to control—but the quality of operations will be superior.

Conclusion

Although France is in a strong position in the context of world tourism, there are several warning signs on the horizon. With globalization, the pattern of international tourism is changing and so are client wants and needs. The challenge for France is to find how to maintain its distinctive character and yet remain competitive in the face of increasing internationalization.

However, these two different aims may not be as incompatible as the French tend to believe. Trends today seem to be away from uniformity, as customers increasingly seek value that comes from the quality of the welcome offered, personalized service, and a different kind of travel experience. Even the chains are tending increasingly to adapt to local settings and cultures. The battle may not be one of France against the rest of the world at all. It should not be forgotten that when French farmers took up arms against the Big Mac and uniformity in the name of Roquefort and individuality, it was American Roquefort lovers who created an Internet site in order to put pressure on their government to reverse its decision to tax imports of the French cheese.

The hospitality sector is becoming more complex and is not always sufficiently aware of new developments in other industries. In the scramble to attract and maintain customers, efforts are often centered on upgrading physical plants and modernizing the hotel stock to international standards. While this may be important, many believe that the main emphasis should now be on identifying and responding to customer trends and needs, and investing in improving service quality in order to attract clients and build loyalty. Paying greater attention to service quality in relation to client needs at every point of contact implies a major rethinking of labor and human resources issues and a redefinition of the role of human resources management in an increasingly international context.

A human resources manager today has to be able to reconcile very different needs in order for a hotel or restaurant to become not only a profitable business, but an enterprise that consistently offers high service quality in response to changing market trends. This involves a delicate balancing act. Efficient staff planning has to be undertaken in the context of strict regulations concerning seasonal work and short-term contracts. A payroll level that allows the profitability of the operation to be maintained also has to offer salaries and benefits at a level sufficient to attract and retain high-quality, dedicated staff. Pressure imposed by unions and employee representatives needs to be responded to while respecting the law and also maintaining harmonious staff relations.

Motivating employees becomes a key factor, both at the entry level and in terms of possible promotion. While juggling staff turnover, personnel budgets, and union requirements, a human resources manager must be able to use training programs to ensure that staff are able to upgrade their professional skills and also as a motivational tool for career development. The pressure to improve efficiency and productivity needs to be balanced with the need for quality of life.

In the past, France's solutions to human resources problems have tended to be innovative and socially advanced. They have often been taken as a source of inspiration for other countries. In the future, France will need to continue building on its strength as a socially progressive state, while seeking innovative solutions to the complex new problems brought about by globalization, thus corresponding to its sense of mission and remaining true to *l'exception française.*

Endnotes

1. *Le Monde,* 15 September 1999.

2. *L'Hôtellerie,* 12 March 1999.

3. *L'Hôtellerie,* 12 March 1999.

4. *Le Monde,* 16 September and 19 September 1999.

5. *Le Monde,* 18 September 1999.

6. *The French Hotel Industry 1999* (Paris: KPMG—Axe Consultants, 1999).

7. World Tourism Organization, *Yearbook of Tourism Statistics, Vol. II, 51st ed.* (Madrid: WTO, 1999).

8. World Tourism Organization.

9. Mark Watkins, *Restaurateurs, Hôteliers: si vous saviez ce que vos clients pensent de vous…* (Paris: Editions BPI, 1999), pp. 60, 88.

10. *L'Hôtellerie,* 15 March 1999.

11. *L'Hôtellerie,* 15 March 1999.

12. Watkins, p. 41.

13. Murray Bailey, *The International Hotel Industry: Corporate Strategies and Global Opportunities,* 2d ed. (London: Travel and Tourism Intelligence, 1998), p. 98.

14. *Le Monde,* 18 September 1999.

15. *Le Monde,* 18 September 1999.

16. *Le Monde diplomatique,* January 1997, p. 18.

17. International Labour Organisation, *New Technologies and Working Conditions in the Hotel, Catering, and Tourism Sector* (Geneva: ILO Sectoral Activities Programme, 1997), p. 26.

18. International Labour Organisation, *New Technologies,* p. 30.

19. John Ardagh, *France in the New Century: Portrait of a Changing Society* (London: Viking, 1999), p. 163.

20. Geert Hofstede, *Software of the Mind: Intercultural Cooperation and Its Importance for Survival* (London: McGraw-Hill, 1991), pp. 120–121.

21. Ardagh, p. 9.

22. Ardagh, pp. 194–195.

23. Quoted by Joseph Fitchett in the *International Herald Tribune,* 13 October 1999.

24. Ardagh, p. 727.

25. *L'Hôtellerie,* 1 July 1999, p. 15.

26. *L'Hôtellerie* 14 May 1998, p. 15.

27. Watkins, p. 68.

Key Terms

annualized contracts—In contrast to short-term contracts, which provide for a certain number of hours per week during which an employee can legally work, annualized contracts allow work hours to be spread out over the whole year, allowing for variation in work hours to balance peak times and off times, so that overtime does not have to be paid.

appellations—Stringent French laws that control every factor contributing to the unique characteristics of a wine or cheese.

comité d'entreprise—An employees' council that is legally mandated for all businesses of more than 50 employees. Also known as employee representatives, *comité* members are elected by staff and may work alongside of or instead of trade union representatives. The *comité* itself may be unionized or non-unionized.

employee representative—An employee elected by other employees to be their representative to management.

Godard Law—Passed in 1934 and still in effect, this law authorized a 15 percent increase in the price of hotels and services, which would be redistributed to those employees who were in direct contact with guests. The law was intended to reduce dependence on tip income and to allow the Ministry of Finance better control of hotel revenue and salary mass. However, it has not been updated to keep pace with the changing nature of hospitality businesses.

 Discussion Questions ———————————————————————

1. One of the ways in which the French "take us as we are" attitude is most noticeable is in guest contact at the front desk and elsewhere. How can staff be helped to see things from the customer's point of view?

2. What kind of benefits/compensation package could be offered to attract well-qualified candidates to positions at the middle- and upper-management levels in French properties?

3. In what ways could the small enterprises that make up the bulk of the French hospitality industry attract a more international clientele without losing their character and individuality?

4. What are the main qualities needed by a general manager to cope with the extremely organized nature of personnel representation and to be able to negotiate with union and/or employee representatives?

 Internet Sites ———————————————————————

For more information, visit the following Internet sites. Remember that Internet addresses can change without notice.

The Accor Group
http://www.accor.com/sa/
default.asp

Essec Business School—
Cornell/Essec's Masters Program in
International Hospitality Management
http://www.essec.fr/imhi/
index.html

European Union
http://www.europa.eu.int

FAFIH (French)
http://www.fafih.com

French Embassy (Washington, DC)
http://www.info-france-usa.org

L'Hôtellerie (French)
http://www.lhotellerie.fr

International Hotel & Restaurant
Association (Paris)
http://www.ih-ra.com

International Labour Organisation
http://www.ilo.org

McDonald's Restaurants
http://www.mcdonalds.com/
countries/france/index.html

National Institute of Statistics (French)
http://www.insee.fr

UNIFHORT (French)
http://www.unifhort.asso.fr

Case Study ⎯⎯⎯⎯⎯⎯⎯⎯⎯⎯⎯⎯⎯⎯⎯⎯⎯⎯

Rumors on the Right Bank

Le Talleyrand is a three-star hotel on Paris's Right Bank, close to the Place Vendôme in a deluxe shopping area. This beautiful and popular property has 120 rooms, including three suites and 15 singles, full room service, one bar, one 80-seat restaurant that serves breakfast and dinner only, and three connecting banquet rooms with 50 seats each. The hotel experiences an annual occupancy rate of 83 percent. Occupancy is high from April to September, lower in October and November, and at its peak during the first half of December. Average daily rate is about FF1,000. The food and beverage department represents 38 percent of the total annual revenue.

The hotel employs 57 permanent workers. In times of seasonal occupancy and banquet activities, the hotel uses temporary and part-time contracts.

General Manager Claire Gambini, a 34-year-old woman, and Gerard Duquesne, a 29-year-old executive assistant in charge of food and beverage, manage the hotel. Both are fairly new to their jobs.

In addition, Front Office Manager Robert Lamy is dynamic and very professional; General Housekeeper Adrienne Lecoq is hard-working, suspicious of foreigners, very quiet, unassertive, and frightened by conflicts; and Maître d' René Santini efficiently coordinates the various food and beverage outlets. The three of them have been working for the hotel for the last seven years. There is no human resources manager.

At this property, unions are very strong, particularly the CGT (*Confédération Générale du Travail,* a union that is close to the Communist Party). One of its main representatives, 36-year-old M. Ibrahim Bouchachi, is a native of Algeria who has been living in France for the past 25 years. He has been working for Le Talleyrand for the last 15 years and has a permanent working permit. Currently, he is a waiter assigned to the bar/room service areas.

The labor inspector controlling the hotel is 34-year-old Martine Dupasquier. She is known to favor the unions.

Room service is combined with the hotel's bar. Room service is open from 6 A.M. to 10:30 A.M., and the bar is open from 11 A.M. to 2 P.M. and from 5 P.M. to 11 P.M. M. Bouchachi works in this department as a chef de rang and serves breakfast to the clients who want it delivered to their rooms. After that, he goes to the bar. His work schedule is from 6 A.M. to 2 P.M. A colleague is responsible for the bar service in the evening.

Management has decided to reorganize this service, canceling the room service activity but reinforcing the bar during the evening. These two changes correspond to guest comments, and represent a revenue increase and productivity savings.

Therefore, M. Bouchachi's schedule has to be changed. Management proposes to him that he should work a split shift, from 10:30 A.M. to 2 P.M. and from 5 P.M. to 10 P.M., with 45 minutes for dinner. Executive Assistant Gérard Duquesne calls him for a meeting on a Friday, explains the situation, and tells M. Bouchachi that the change will take place the following week.

M. Bouchachi does not say anything during the meeting with M. Duquesne. However, he does not change his schedule and continues to work his usual hours. M. Duquesne summons him to his office and informs him that he must change his schedule. Since M. Bouchachi still does not comply with instructions, M. Duquesne sends him a written warning.

The management is not aware that M. Bouchachi is very reluctant to work in the evening. Nobody knows about it, but he has, in fact, got an undeclared evening job elsewhere, for which he is well paid. Unable to speak of his problem directly, M. Bouchachi goes to his union in order to enlist its support. He tells the union that this change in the organization of the hotel is simply an excuse and that the management wants to get rid of him. As a matter of fact, he says, he has overheard the general housekeeper criticizing his work and his role as an employee representative. M. Bouchachi then calls a meeting with the staff, describes his problems, and tells them that management is on the brink of implementing many other changes that will affect them all as well.

The atmosphere in the hotel is rapidly deteriorating and rumors start spreading. There is even a rumor about a possible strike. At this point, the labor inspector calls the GM, Claire Gambini (who has just come back from a week-long business trip), and informs her that she has received an official complaint from the CGT and that Mme Gambini is required to call an urgent meeting of the employees' council (*Comité d'entreprise*).

Mme Gambini meets with Gérard Duquesne to learn all the details of the story and to decide on the best course of action.

Discussion Question

1. What should the general manager of the Talleyrand do to solve the conflict?

Chapter 4 Outline

The Changing Role of the Greek
    Hospitality Industry
      The New Value of Tourism
      Challenges to Greece's
        Competitiveness
      Future Development
The Hospitality Labor Force
      Labor Relations
      Education and Training
The Human Resource Department
      Recruitment, Selection, and Hiring
      Orientation
      Training Concerns
Strategic Planning
      The Inventory and Development Plan
Looking into the Future

Competencies

1. Describe the hospitality industry in Greece, including the important role of the human resources department. (pp. 67–71)

2. List the social and legal issues concerning the Greek hospitality labor force. (pp. 71–74)

3. Discuss the many responsibilities of human resource professionals in Greece. (pp. 74–77)

4. Explain the value of strategic planning, as well as the steps involved in developing an inventory and development plan. (pp. 77–80)

4

Greece: The Hospitality Industry in Transition

Nikos V. Skoulas

Nikos V. Skoulas *is the managing director of Nikos Skoulas and Associates, S.A., an international business consulting and training services firm based in Athens, Greece. In addition, he has devoted a substantial part of the past 35 years to tourism, both in government service and the private sector, serving as president and chief executive officer of Royal Olympic Cruises, chairman of the board of ASTIR Hotels, secretary general of the Hellenic Tourism Organization, and minister of tourism for Greece.*

The Changing Role of the Greek Hospitality Industry

After several unsuccessful attempts to industrialize, Greece came to realize that its future growth and development should be based on those elements that offer unparalleled competitive advantages—namely Greek culture, natural beauty, exquisite island complexes, and the hospitable nature of the Greeks. As a result, Greece began to restructure its economy toward tourism development in the 1970s.

Due to inexperience, the burgeoning industry depended on major European tour operators for know-how, transportation, and marketing access to tourist markets. The result was a mass model of leisure tourism with heavy concentrations of hotel beds only in certain areas of Greece, causing an imbalance in regional development patterns. This imbalance had an additional negative effect on the other sectors of the economy—including agricultural production and processing, and light manufacturing—as well as corresponding negative effects on labor market composition.

Policy makers and hospitality industry practitioners realized that tourism and the other economic sectors are interdependent. Soon, a new economic development policy was in place. Based on this policy, the hospitality industry should make maximum use of local production—especially in fresh and processed food items, where Greece holds a decisive comparative advantage.

There were additional challenges as well. In the early stages of tourism development, the prevailing assumption was that, in order for Greece to enjoy the benefits of economic growth, there must be trade-offs in the form of damage to the environment. Experience has shown, however, that economic growth and environmental protection are not mutually exclusive; in fact, they are in a state of synergy. As a result, economists and social planners now treat culture and environment as resources upon which tourism—as an economic activity—depends for its long-term survival. The beneficial effects of this policy are quite evident today.

The New Value of Tourism

Over the past 30 or so years, Greece has done well at selling a leisure product at attractive prices while building on its unique position in the Eastern Mediterranean area.

Today, Greece's geography, climate, history, and cultural characteristics consistently attract large and ever-increasing numbers of international tourists, and the Greek economy is energized by active consumer demand for goods and services. Tourism represents one of the most dynamic branches of the Greek economy and has a profound impact on the gross domestic product, investments, employment, the environment, and society as a whole. Exhibit 1 shows the recent effect of travel and tourism on the Greek economy in comparison with other European countries.

Annual international tourist arrivals exceed 12 million. According to the Hellenic Tourism Organization, international and domestic night stays exceeded 100 million in 1999, including an estimated 43 million unrecorded night stays in rooms-to-let, villas, apartments, and other supplementary hospitality facilities. Foreign exchange receipts in 1999 were US$5.186 billion.

Because of inadequate reporting methods, these figures do not reflect the true significance of the hospitality industry. The only way to assess its true value to Greece's economy is to measure production aimed at satisfying tourist demand.

Challenges to Greece's Competitiveness

Two critical factors have a negative impact on Greece's ability to stay competitive: seasonality and accessibility.

From the beginning, Greek tourism has been based on providing summer leisure vacations. Consequently, many tourist resorts literally shut down for five months each year. As Exhibit 2 shows, approximately 83 percent of tourist arrivals happen during the period from May to September. As a result, billions of dollars' worth of investments remain dormant and hundreds of thousands of workers walk to the unemployment office. These wasted resources, together with the need to write off fixed assets and allocate fixed expenses over seven months instead of twelve, weaken the country's competitive standing.

Greece's geographical position in relation to the countries of origin of its tourists means that the country depends on air transport for almost four out of five tourist arrivals, three quarters of which fly by charter carriers (see Exhibit 3). This

Exhibit 1   Economic Impact of Travel and Tourism in Europe

	Gross Domestic Product	Employment	Capital Investment
	% of Total	% of Total	% of Total
European Union	14.1	14.5	15.8
Austria	17.6	17.2	20.1
Belgium	13.8	14.2	21.7
Denmark	15.1	15.3	17.1
Finland	15.5	15.2	17.2
France	14.8	14.7	16.6
Germany	10.8	8.9	11.4
Greece	**18.3**	**16.3**	**22.3**
Ireland	16.5	18.8	19.9
Italy	16.1	18.4	18.2
Luxembourg	10.4	10.4	14.1
Netherlands	13.2	12.7	13.6
Portugal	19.4	19.5	20.1
Spain	22.7	24.3	27.5
Sweden	11.7	12.0	16.7
United Kingdom	12.3	12.6	10.7

Source: World Travel & Tourism Council, 1999

adds to the cost of tour packages and reduces the country's ability to be competitive. The situation with some southern European competitors is just the opposite: two out of three visitors to Spain arrive by surface transport.

In order to deal with this situation, Greece needs a strong presence in the air transport arena, both in terms of charter and regular airline fields; unfortunately, there is only Olympic Airways, which, in spite of its good efforts, cannot provide adequate support. A hopeful sign is the emergence of three small air carriers that provide coverage for domestic routes and are expanding beyond the Greek frontiers.

Future Development

Notwithstanding these and other structural problems, the Greek tourism industry has experienced satisfactory growth in terms of both international arrivals and night stays. There is, however, reason for concern about its future development and competitiveness.

Exhibit 2 The Seasonality of Greek Tourism

Night Stays by International Tourists, by Month			
MONTH	**% OF TOTAL**	**MONTH**	**% OF TOTAL**
April	4.26	January	.63
May	12.30	February	.69
June	15.01	March	1.47
July	18.01	November	.91
August	20.73	December	.70
September	16.46	Winter Season Total	4.40
October	8.83		
Tourism Season Total	95.60		

Source: National Statistical Office and Hellenic Tourism Organization

Exhibit 3 International Arrivals by Air and Charter

Year	Percent of Total by Air	Percent of Air by Charter
1981	60.70	62.45
1985	68.89	67.21
1989	66.26	74.44
1991	69.79	76.93
1993	75.62	76.49
1995	79.16	80.37
1997	76.95	76.62
1998	79.20	76.36

Source: National Statistical Office and Hellenic Tourism Organization

In recent years, several new competitors—including Turkey, Tunisia, Malta, Morocco, and Syria—have entered the tourism arena, offering similar mass-leisure product at lower prices due to lower labor costs. The price/value relationship of Greece's product has now been visibly challenged. As a result, most tour operators demanded and received from hoteliers and travel agents prices in drachmas that were equal to or lower than those of the preceding year.

While one cannot deny business operators their right to negotiate for lower prices, such practices have led to a vicious circle of ever-lower prices and quality. If this trend continues much further into the future, it will have direct negative implications for tour operators and guests alike. Mere price competition is not a viable practice for any business, especially the service industry. There are other, more desirable and more effective alternatives.

New Market Positioning. Government, business, and labor leaders have agreed that Greece should attempt a transition to quality, activity-oriented tourism—for example, thematic holidays that can satisfy varied interests for cultural activities, sports, conferences, business and incentive travel, sailing and cruise vacations, gastronomic experiences, adventure tours, health and beauty regimens, religious tours, and ecotourism.

This move toward enriching Greece's product mix with programs for more eclectic, more demanding, and more affluent target groups is already meeting with apparent success. This success, in turn, has spurred interest in new, upscale hospitality facilities (four- and five-star hotels), supplementary tourism infrastructure (golf courses and other sports facilities, conference facilities, marinas, spas) and new, general infrastructure projects (airports, public transportation, highways, ports). There is also a discernible new emphasis on the importance of professional training for the hospitality industry.

The Hospitality Labor Force

During the late 1960s and early 1970s, demand for leisure holidays in the southeast Mediterranean and Greece grew substantially.

Tour operators sought hospitality facilities suitable for beach holidays but were unwilling to take the investment risk in a new destination. So, they encouraged Greek entrepreneurs to invest while the tour operators supplied the technical expertise.

As a result, financially successful people such as landowners, engineers, and physicians—people hitherto unrelated to the hospitality industry—took on the development process. Typically, farm workers, after completing the winter olive harvest and the spring fruit and vegetable chores, became hotel staff for a rather short summer season. They learned by doing and by making mistakes.

As tour operators and guests began to demand a higher level of service, it became apparent that schools for hospitality professionals, continuing-education programs, and on-the-job training were an essential part of tourism development. Hospitality schools were created in all major tourist regions. Subsequently, hospitality staff and services took on a more professional character.

In the 1980s and 1990s, significant progress was achieved. At the turn of the century, the tourism economy is providing employment to at least 630,000 workers (16.3 percent of the total labor force), and the education levels of tourism and other service workers have risen: 28 percent have completed only primary and junior high school, 49 percent have finished only high school, and 23 percent have graduated from college.

Over the next few years, a number of factors should work toward creating a high level of employment and a corresponding decline in the rate of unemployment, which now stands at about 11 percent (lower in the tourism sector), close to the average of the European Union countries.

Positive economic factors include a high rate of growth in the GDP, a significant increase in investment, an improvement in competitiveness, and a stable monetary environment—all leading to an inflation factor of less than two percent. Forecasts for growth in the Greek economy after 1999 are particularly encouraging.

Labor Relations

Greece is an extremely democratic country. Workers' rights are strictly protected by the Ministry of Labor and Social Affairs as well as by trade unions. However, it is precisely because employers and HR managers do understand the trade unions and labor laws that a positive work climate exists.

In fact, hotels, restaurants, and travel agencies have enjoyed a very long period of industrial peace. Collaboration among employers, employees, and the state has been ongoing, resulting in a positive work climate that helps to avert work stoppages, especially during the sensitive high season. Unfortunately, this has not been the case in the transportation sector, where disruptions have occurred as a result of unsettled industrial disputes. Tourist coaches, inter-city buses, trains, and especially Olympic Airways have been the main culprits. Understandably, such interruptions have a negative impact on travel and tourism. The new climate created by the apparent success of the privatization process and the euphoria of better economic performance is bringing about a new positive reality with a dramatic decline in work days lost.

Even so, continuing business restructuring, technological modernization in all sectors of the Greek economy, and **rationalization of recruitment** in the public sector all help to explain the rise in unemployment in recent years.

Two Weaknesses. In spite of the robust growth in the private sector and great improvements in the management of the public sector, two clearly identifiable weaknesses have had a negative impact on the hospitality industry: an inflexible and poorly organized public administration and a poor linkage of the educational and vocational systems with the needs of the labor market. However, progress is being made on both of these points, especially on the latter.

The National Action Plan for Employment, developed by the Ministry of Labor and Social Affairs in 1999, is a comprehensive and ambitious program aimed at linking vigorous long-term development performance with increased employment, greater social development, cohesion, and integration. The total cost of this plan—co-funded by the European Union and the Greek government—exceeds US$3 billion for the entire economy. The plan contains 22 guidelines in support of—among other things—lifelong learning, linking educational and vocational training systems to labor market demand, reinforcing opportunities for women through affirmative action, facilitating worker reintegration into the labor market after a long absence, and addressing the major problem of undeclared work.

Undeclared Workers. The problem of undeclared work has been aggravated in the recent past as a result of the conflicts in the Balkan region. According to 1999 data provided by the National Employment Agency, 352,637 aliens have applied for a temporary stay permit, while it is estimated by the Ministry of Public Order that at least 700,000 mostly illegal economic immigrants reside in Greece. This, by any standard, represents an enormous number for a country with a population of just over 10,500,000 people. While these economic immigrants provide some advantages to the economy, the jobs they can perform typically require few skills. The sheer magnitude of their numbers presents major problems for the integration process and has led to cultural, economic, and social tensions.

Women in the Labor Force. As a result of changes in the family law in response to emerging social trends, more and more women are entering the labor force. Still, according to Eurostat data, 42 percent of Greek women in the age group of 25–42 state "homemaker" as their profession in comparison to the European Union average of 32 percent.

Fifty-one percent of university students are women, and it is worth noting that the percentage of women holding managerial positions is rising sharply in the tourism professions, which offer career opportunities for women. Although the percentage of women who hold executive positions—i.e., hotel managers—is still relatively small, women have a very visible presence in department management positions in hotels and travel agencies.

Education and Training

A number of institutions are providing a variety of educational and vocational training programs ranging from purely academic content to applied on-the-job training.

The Ministry of Tourism runs nine Schools for Tourism Professions: two college-level schools for hotel managers and seven technical, quasi-vocational schools for entry-level prospective employees. In addition, the ministry operates a college-level school for tour guides, maintaining the highest standards in all of Europe.

Out of 18 universities in Greece, five—Athens, Piraeus, Aegean, Patras, and Macedonia—provide undergraduate programs in business administration with an emphasis on hospitality subjects. Seven of the 16 technological educational institutions maintain degree programs in tourism management. The newly founded Open University for distance learning also offers courses in hospitality. In 1999, the University of the Aegean initiated the first accredited postgraduate program on tourism planning, management, and policy. The University of Piraeus is in the process of accreditation for a master's program in hotel management.

A number of private colleges associated with foreign universities provide general management and tourism training. Among them is The Alpine Center, an associate institute of IHTTI in Switzerland, which has an outstanding record of quality education in hospitality and a perfect record in placing its graduates.

In addition, substantial funds are expended by the national government on continuing education for working tourism professionals, through the National Employment Agency. These programs are generously co-funded by the European Union's Social Fund. However, as a result of inexperience and inadequate control mechanisms, much of this effort has proved ineffective and wasteful in the past; today, the programs are gradually becoming modernized and are administered with increased integrity and effectiveness.

Vocational Training. In the past, the hospitality industry has been extremely weak in one critical area: vocational training designed to prepare prospective entry-level workers for a career in this increasingly demanding and fast-growing industry. Perhaps the most significant development in this long-neglected area has been the new initiative by the Organization for Vocational Education and Training to create 32 job classifications for the tourism and transport industries. The initiative is funded by the European Union and the Ministry of Education, with the active participation of the business and academic communities.

The basic concept of this initiative is for high school graduates to attend theoretical and practical classes at one of 220 institutions of vocational training across the country. After two years of classes, these young people can take entry-level jobs as waiters, cooks, receptionists, travel agency clerks, airline clerks, conference and seminar support staff, tour leaders, mountain and ecological tour guides, marina administrators, **agrotourism** unit managers, taxi and tourist bus drivers, as well as 20 more hospitality jobs.

With this extensive educational and training infrastructure, the Greek hospitality industry can face the future with confidence and optimism.

The Human Resource Department

The vast majority of Greek hospitality businesses are small-to-medium in size. Historically, these businesses began as and have remained family enterprises.

In these privately held companies, all authority was concentrated in the hands of the owner, with only bits delegated to members of the family or trusted employees, usually accountants. Management styles ranged from entirely autocratic to paternalistic and, occasionally, idiosyncratic. Not surprisingly, the so-called personnel manager was relegated to filling out employment and social security papers and handling the payroll. All decisions concerning hiring, firing, compensation, or promotions were made by the owner-boss.

Happily, however, the past few years have seen the adoption of more modern and effective styles of management. Technocrats, team builders, and professional managers, who delegate responsibility and authority to trained and experienced staff, are now very much in demand.

An increasing number of hospitality companies are boasting human resource management departments. Most of them provide basic services such as hiring and training; a few have established a full complement of sub-departments capable of supporting all necessary human resource functions (see Exhibit 4). The new HR manager is an experienced and sensitive professional who brings a university education in both the hospitality industry and the field of human resource administration and development.

The new organizational culture encourages the active involvement of all line managers in all personnel functions. This includes personnel selection, training and development, performance evaluation, motivation, and the development of a strategic plan that can meet the needs of the enterprise now and into the future. In this context, the role of the human resource manager is not autonomous and isolated from the operational functions of the company, but rather is especially strategic, coordinating and supporting operational management at all levels.

Exhibit 4 Organization Chart for the Human Resource Department (Large Company)

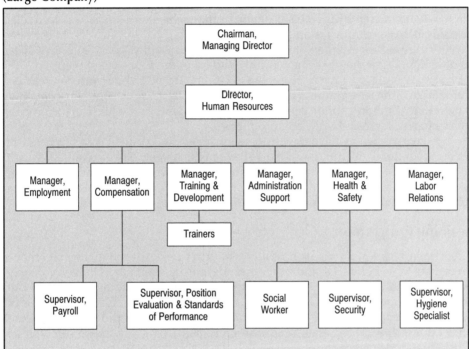

Through coaching and an emphasis on lateral communication and teamwork, the human resources manager supports operating managers in their key functions, which include position descriptions, performance standards, personnel selection, training, performance appraisal, compensation, and decisions about promotions.

Recruitment, Selection, and Hiring

Until recently, recruitment and selection in the hospitality industry were done haphazardly. This was due to the seasonal nature of the industry, inexperienced managers, and the inability of the hospitality industry to attract promising candidates as a result of the sector's poor image as a career provider.

Recruitment, selection, and hiring for the industry are gradually taking a more rational and systematic approach. Instruments such as extensive curricula vitae, résumés, and applications for employment constitute the basis for in-depth interviews and background checks. Suitable candidates are proactively pursued, based on well-documented position descriptions that identify the essential responsibilities of each position. The new procedures help to eliminate the arbitrary exercise of authority, pin down reporting relationships, and become the basis for developing standards of performance for each specific responsibility.

Orientation

The new management culture recognizes the importance of thorough orientation for newly hired employees. This is a process that helps build a positive work relationship between employee and employer. Providing full information to the new hire concerning the mission, beliefs, operating philosophy, goals and objectives, and work practices helps the new member adapt in the new environment.

For an industry in which human relations are of paramount importance, familiarizing the new entrant with all he or she needs to know about the company, its working conditions, and its people is an especially important task in the process of making newcomers happy and productive.

A few companies have begun to use audio-visual presentations that reflect their corporate identity and vision and have published employee manuals, which often include a full explanation of wages, benefits, work rules, and procedures. Many such documents state the company position on employee behavior on the job, confidentiality, sexual harassment, punctuality, and other related matters.

Training Concerns

After three decades, the Greek hospitality industry has matured to the point that a large pool of experienced and trained candidates is available. These are people who have graduated from the various hospitality schools and have acquired on-the-job experience both in Greece and abroad. (Expatriate Greeks who studied in foreign universities, colleges, or vocational schools and who acquired work experience both in the United States and Europe represent a great source of potential workers and managers.)

Given the multinational and multilingual origin of Greece's tourist arrivals, knowledge of foreign languages is a prerequisite. Greek hospitality training programs have given adequate recognition to the need for learning foreign languages. The focus is primarily on English and German, but education also includes French, Russian, Japanese, and many other languages.

Other programs provide skills training for all employees in **green duties**, health and safety practices, and total quality management. The realization that the client of the future will make his or her decision to book in a particular facility based on whether that facility has acquired certification for health and safety or certification for quality assurance has given great impetus to this kind of training.

In some instances, employers lay out on-the-job training programs for new employees as part of the orientation process. This enables the employer to quickly ascertain any job-specific training gaps so it can fast-track the new employee into an easier adjustment and full integration into the new environment.

Ongoing Training. Some companies have realized that there is no better way to tell an employee that they care about the employee's future than by involving him or her in continuous training. These companies have hired professional training managers, with senior management providing full support to the training department. They adopt the principle that all line managers in the organization should treat training as an essential part of their job; their performance is measured by how well they train and develop their employees.

A few employers maintain ongoing skills training and management development programs that promote synergy and teamwork. Additionally, they offer specialized training programs for such things as personal computers, sanitation, work safety, quality assurance, and so on. These few employers believe that staff who are offered training and development programs on a continuing basis feel more committed, more loyal, and more secure—and are consequently more productive. This trend seems to be spreading. One can only hope that it will become the universal culture in dealing with human resources in the hospitality industry.

Performance Appraisal. One area in which little progress has been achieved is the appraisal of employee performance based on measurable results rather than behavioral characteristics. Compensation, salary increases, promotions, and other means of performance recognition—all of which are important motivational tools—are often governed by subjective considerations. A great deal needs to be done toward establishing a more rational and objective system of position benchmarking, compensation, and promotions.

Strategic Planning

In the new, fast-changing economic, sociopolitical, and cultural environment, Greek hospitality enterprises are hard at work developing strategic plans that will allow them to compete effectively now and in the future.

These strategic plans assess the competitive position of hotel companies and their relative strengths and weaknesses, define their medium- and long-term objectives, and contain specific programs in order to achieve those objectives. For the larger and more successful companies, this takes the form of elaborate, fully integrated plans that are spelled out in detail, usually accompanied by business and action plans expressed in budgeted financial results. For smaller operations, this often takes the form of a brief statement spelling out the company's identity, market positioning, and basic objectives, based on empirical data and little or no formal research. In other instances, strategic planning—if it can indeed be called strategic—is no more than verbal references in meetings among the members of the small management group.

One development that helps this process is the emergence of a new class of entrepreneurs, the sons and daughters of the pioneers who funded and founded the Greek hospitality industry. After receiving the benefit of growing up in their parents' businesses and acquiring a hospitality culture, they have had the opportunity to study at some of the best hotel and catering schools in the world. They have brought back with them a high degree of specialization in hotel operations, culinary arts, international marketing, and finance. These are the young professionals who now lead the process of modern strategic planning.

Unlike the traditional passive routine of yesteryear, the new entrepreneurs formulate organizational structures capable of supporting the strategic plan. In addition to refining the managerial and functional structure within their companies, they design methods, financial reports, and management information systems essential for the implementation of the strategic plan. However, the strategic plan and the organizational structure that will support it are not sufficient in themselves to secure the future of hospitality enterprises. Hospitality businesses still must have the right people who will, at the right time, fill the necessary jobs in support of the business objectives.

The Inventory and Development Plan

Every development plan contains a variety of programs and actions, which will probably require new departments and professionals to staff them. Even without new initiatives, certain positions naturally become vacant as a result of retirement, resignation, dismissal, or death, and they must be filled. Although these staffing requirements are not always predictable, depending on the size and complexity of the business, some companies have understood the need to create and maintain a plan for human resource inventory and development as the basis to support their strategic plan.

The human resource managers with specialized knowledge and experience are asked to design and maintain the plan with the full involvement of the operational managers. Where full collaboration and teamwork (not typically considered to be virtues in Greece) are practiced, the results are impressive. More forward-looking companies have organized "visioning" and training sessions for all members of middle and senior management, where the value of collaboration is underlined and implementation tools are taught and practiced.

A human resource inventory and development plan is a major component of the total program for the organization and development of the business. It is non-bureaucratic and requires minimal time and written procedures. The plan's main objectives are:

- To reflect the human resource inventory with the greatest possible accuracy

- To identify existing and future staffing needs for the implementation of the strategic plan

- To help in the design and implementation of the necessary training programs for preparing the staff to meet the development needs of the enterprise

- To provide opportunities for personal growth for staff with knowledge, ability, and ambition

To meet these objectives, inventory and development plans typically contain at least four distinct stages.

Stage One. The first stage involves a performance evaluation for each employee, an assessment of his or her capability for future development and readiness for promotion. An integral part of this stage is the completion of a **career record**, which should be updated each year accompanied by a performance evaluation conducted by the immediate supervisor. A career record, also called a career path, shows the positions held by the employee and future positions for which he or she is being trained. It is a map of where the employee has been and may go in the future, rather than an evaluation of performance.

Stage Two. The second stage deals with the organizational analysis of the company and takes into consideration estimated future needs for new positions at all levels of management—positions that will be abolished, as well as positions that will become vacant as a result of promotions, transfers, retirement, or unsatisfactory performance.

Stage Three. At stage three, the results of the work at stages one and two are recorded in a way that "marries" the personnel inventory with management succession. For each new position and for each position that is likely to become vacant, two or three prospective candidates for replacement are identified. The estimated time frame for management succession is also usually spelled out.

Stage Four. The fourth and most important stage involves designing a personal career development plan for each employee with growth potential, in order to make them capable of supporting the company's goals and objectives. Such plans are based on the employee's current level of knowledge, experience, and management ability, as well as the availability of appropriate training and development programs.

In all cases, the human resource director and the training manager coordinate and monitor the plan in close collaboration with the line managers and external resources.

Looking into the Future

Greece has decided to protect and make more competitive its core tourism assets: sun, beaches, and culture. At the same time, the new hospitality industry development strategy rests on two pillars: a fast transition to activity-oriented, thematic tourism throughout the year and high-quality service offered by fully trained, sensitive, and motivated professionals.

In pursuing this course of action, it is necessary to consider the forces that shape the world around us and bring about changes in our lives and businesses at unbelievably rapid rates. The economies and hospitality enterprises likely to survive and prosper in the future are those that recognize these forces and the changes they bring—including the growth of multinational corporations and transnational financial institutions, the globalization of the travel and tourism industry, the consolidation of tourist activity, the elimination of trade barriers, developments in the former Soviet Union, and regional conflicts in the Balkans and elsewhere.

At the micro level, businesses have to deal with more informed and demanding customers, who insist on value for money, superior quality, and details on the products and services they can expect at a given property. Today's guests want to know what tourism entrepreneurs, manufacturers, and retailers are doing to protect the environment and the resources upon which they, their children, and their grandchildren will base their survival.

But perhaps the most profound of all changes is the shift from an industrial society to an information society. In the post-industrial society, most people spend their time creating, processing, or distributing information—and that, of course, means relying heavily on electronic technology. In this new, knowledge-based global order, the competitive advantage is no longer found in capital, land, machines, or other traditional factors of production but rather in the correct use of human resources and technological development. At center stage are the modern workers who bring change and who define, produce, and control the new technologies.

The money we spend for training and development of our human resources is the best investment we can make in the long term. Our people are an asset that appreciates in value. The most promising development in the Greek hospitality industry is the realization by all concerned that placing our human resources at the center of our development strategy is the most productive investment we can make for the new millennium.

Key Terms

agrotourism—Tourist activities that involve direct contact with the rural world and nature. Also known as farm tourism.

career record—A document indicating the positions held in the past by an employee and future positions for which the employee is being trained.

green duties—Practices related to environmental protection and preservation— for example, a hotel's practices regarding water recycling and conservation.

rationalization of recruitment—New hiring practices that seek to address prior problems with overstaffing and inefficiencies. Current practices require that a job opening must exist and that it be filled based on the results of written examinations and qualifications.

Discussion Questions

1. What prompted the Greek hospitality industry to attempt a relatively fast transition from mass-leisure tourism to activity-oriented tourism?

2. What are the two most serious structural problems having an adverse effect on the Greek hospitality industry and its ability to compete? What are the reasons for the effects of these structural problems?

3. What is the role of human resources in Greece's efforts to upgrade the quality of service in the hospitality industry?

4. Should hospitality operations in Greece treat funds allocated for human resource training and development as an expense or an investment? Explain your viewpoint.

Internet Sites

For more information, visit the following Internet sites. Remember that Internet addresses can change without notice.

Association of Greek Tourist
Enterprises
http://www.travelling.gr/sete

Eurostat
http://europa.eu.int/comm/
eurostat/

Greek National Tourism Organization
http://www.gnto.gr

Greek Travel Pages
http://www.gtpnet.com

Hellenic Chamber of Hotels
http://users.otenet.gr/~grhotels/

Hellenic Ministry of Labor and Social
Affairs
http://www.labor-ministry.gr

National Statistical Service of Greece
http://www.statistics.gr

Statistical Office of the European
Communities
http://europa.eu.int

World Tourism Organization
http://www.world-tourism.org/

World Travel and Tourism Council
http://www.wttc.org/

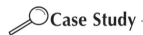 ## Case Study

Building on Past Success

In the early 1970s, a successful civil engineer who owned and operated a construction company decided to join the move toward tourism development. He built a 300-room, "A"-category (approximating four stars) resort hotel, taking advantage of rather generous investment incentives. Despite his lack of experience in the hospitality business, he showed remarkable entrepreneurial traits and a high degree of sensitivity for quality facilities and services, considering the prevailing standards at that time. He hired experienced executives and staff, who became personally loyal to him and made a financial success of the venture.

Over the years, he managed to develop his company into a hotel chain, comprising four resort complexes that included both new construction and acquisitions. Two of the hotels are of the "Deluxe" category (approximating five stars). Today, Alpha Holiday Resorts offers accommodation in 2,900 beds and employs 1,215 people, and the Alpha Holiday Resorts brand enjoys international recognition for upscale facilities. The company has enjoyed high occupancy rates (91 percent last year) and impressive profitability. Sales last year exceeded US$41.5 million and the pretax profit amounted to US$4.65 million.

The style of management has been clearly paternalistic, with the owner having the last word in all facets of the business. However, some capable department managers negotiate with tour operators and manage day-to-day operations. The staff is personally dedicated to the owner and respect him in return for the respect he accords each of them. They are also loyal to his inner group of trusted department managers. Additionally, the vast majority of employees are proud to belong to the organization and are pleased to work for its success.

However, most employees are confused regarding the lines of authority, their specific responsibilities, how salaries and promotions are determined, and how each staff member fits into the total picture. Professional development has been limited to on-the-job training and mentoring by more senior employees, but there are no systematic and comprehensive procedures in place.

The owner's son and daughter, who both received master's degrees in hospitality and finance from European universities, are actively involved in the business as executive vice presidents. The owner seems to have done a good job of mentoring them and has been gradually delegating responsibilities to them.

This company recently acquired two more hotel complexes (of the "Deluxe" and "A" categories). Both units are located in cities and will operate year-round as business hotels with some resort features. The planned investment for upgrading and expanding these properties to 1,750 beds will require more than US$30 million. An additional staff of 750 year-round employees will be required.

The owner and his son and daughter are now concerned that what has worked so successfully in the past may not be appropriate for the new properties. Specifically, they want to:

- Increase bed capacity by about 50 percent.

- Add new staff proportionately.

- Commit to significant new investment, 50 percent of which will come from bank financing.

- Run two city hotels with year-round operations, representing diversification into an operational model for which the company has no experience.

Discussion Questions

1. Based on the information provided here, what recommendations would you make to the principals of Alpha Holiday Resorts concerning the following two points?

    - Implementation of investment plans and operational and marketing initiatives

    - Organizational structures, management style, and human resource administration and development

2. What specific additional types of information would you require in order to develop and submit a thorough plan that, if implemented, would help the company to meet the challenges of the enterprise (old and new)?

Chapter 5 Outline

Ireland and Its Hospitality Industry
  Tourism Industry
  Hospitality Industry
  Employment Statistics
Hospitality Labor Market Issues
  Careers in Hospitality
  Recruitment and Selection
  Training and Development

Competencies

1. Discuss the Irish tourism industry, including recent changes and their impact on the hospitality sector. (pp. 85–87)

2. Identify Ireland's employment statistics and labor market issues. (pp. 87–89)

3. Discuss recruitment and selection techniques including the role of government, training and development, educational institutions, and trade union membership. (pp. 89–92)

5

Human Resource Management in Ireland: Industry's Challenge During a Period of Unprecedented Growth

Marié Connolly

***Marié Connolly** is lecturer in Hotel Administration at Dundalk Institute of Technology in Ireland. Her wide and varied hospitality career includes 16 years teaching Hotel and Tourism operations and management when she held posts within the Further and Higher Education system in Britain, the Swiss Hotel School System in Greece, and more recently, continuing her teaching career in Ireland, her country of birth. Her 12-year career in industry includes London hotels, where she worked in front office and training, and in Greece where she was Assistant Rooms Division Manager in a luxury beach resort hotel. Marie has taken two career breaks, one to take her Certificate in Education (University of London) and more recently to take her MSc in Hotel and Catering Management (University of Ulster).*

Т HE RECENT UNPRECEDENTED success of the tourism industry in Ireland, along with the growth in the Irish economy, has brought Ireland to the fore—having made positive strides within the past 10 years. This chapter aims to give the reader an insight into some of these recent developments, the challenges that have been created for the industry, and steps that are being taken to respond to these challenges.

Ireland and Its Hospitality Industry

An island on the northwestern edge of Europe, Ireland is 302 miles (486 km) long and 171 miles (275 km) wide. The Republic of Ireland consists of 26 counties; its capital, Dublin, is situated on the eastern side of the island. The population, recorded in the 1996 census as 3,626,087, is projected to reach four million by 2006. Statistics show that 44 percent of the population is based in the largest cities and towns.

The rugged Atlantic coastline to the west has created spectacular coastal scenery and the gentler Irish Sea coastline to the east provides beautiful scenery of a softer nature. In between these coastlines, the mountains, rivers, lakes, and numerous shades of green have come together to create a beautiful tapestry of nature at her finest. This is maintained by the mild temperate climate influenced by the gulf stream flowing off the west coast.

Ireland has a rich and varied culture, contributed to by a number of incursions over the centuries, with an abundance of castles, houses, and monuments—including some that pre-date the pyramids. Its cities and towns are as diverse in character as its countryside—from the sophistication of Dublin, the city of famous writers, theaters, pubs, and Georgian elegance, to remote villages in the far west where the Irish language and old traditions remain intact. Ireland's culture cannot be separated from its musical heritage, with modern, classical, and traditional music being made and enjoyed by all.

One of the most rapidly growing economies in the **European Union (EU)**, Ireland's traditional agriculture-based economy has experienced many changes recently. Developments in computer technology, the service sector, and the tourism industry have led to the emergence of the **Celtic Tiger** phenomenon. This unprecedented economic growth has led to a surge in employment opportunities resulting in close to a 50 percent increase in employment over the past 10 years.

The repositioning of the agricultural base of the Irish economy has led the government to encourage the agricultural community to diversify, encouraged by programs that are in place to develop the rural tourism potential of the countryside—an asset highly valued by visitors.

Tourism Industry

Ireland's prime tourism markets have traditionally centered on the United Kingdom and North America, but more recent developments have led to the growth of the European market—especially in the business and short break sectors. The majority of tourists visiting Ireland (65 percent) tend to do so on an independent basis, while the rest (35 percent) travel with tour operators.

Over the past 10 years, visitor numbers have more than doubled and foreign revenue earnings have almost trebled.[1] Now one of Ireland's largest industries, tourism's contribution to the gross national product has grown from 5.4 percent in 1988 to 6.2 percent in 1996. Evidence of this growth is further supported by World Tourism Organization research which shows that tourism grew faster in Ireland than in any other European country in 1995.

The main sectors of the industry in Ireland can be identified as: Hotels, Restaurant, Licensed Trade, Catering, Approved Accommodation, Travel and Transport, Heritage and Cultural Centers, Tourist Information Services, Visitor Attractions, and Leisure and Recreation. The promotion and monitoring of these main sectors is currently being carried out domestically and internationally by two separate tourism authorities—the Northern Ireland Tourist Board (responsible for marketing Northern Ireland) and the Bord Fáilte Irish Tourist Board (responsible for marketing the Republic of Ireland). The benefits of joint marketing campaigns for the island of Ireland product has been highlighted by key trade associations; however, the delicate negotiations around a joint venture have not yet been agreed upon by politicians in the North and South. The Northern Ireland Hotel Federation and the Irish Hotel Federation (IHF) are encouraging the politicians to reach an agreement and recognize the genuine needs of the industry as a whole.

Hospitality Industry

Accommodation in Ireland, which is reported to have grown by a remarkable 12 percent in the last two years, is wide and varied. It ranges from unique historic luxury castles and manors in outstanding locations (which provide the visitor with high quality service and facilities) to international style-hotels in the main cities and tourist centers (which provide excellent accommodation and good service) to a superb range of independent family-run quality hotels and guest houses.

Ownership of the accommodation sector is largely held by family-run/managed units (61 percent), with 28 percent being part of a group and 11 percent private company ownership. This highlights the significance of the friendly family-run establishment—and the importance of the warmth and friendliness of the people (rated by visitors as one of Ireland's most valuable assets).

The number of three-star hotels is reported to have increased from 175 in 1992 to 261 in 1998—reflecting an annual average growth of seven percent. The average hotel size has increased from 34 rooms with 71 beds to an average of 40 rooms with 87 beds. The growth in the number of larger properties is putting a strain on the profitability of the smaller traditional units—with a possible over-supply result in some locations.

The emergence of the Celtic Tiger has prompted the arrival of international hotel companies such as Radisson SAS, Conrad International, Forte, Holiday Inn, Ibis, and Stakis. Also, the trade press recently reported the planned opening of a new 161 bed Westin hotel by U.S. group Starwood Hotels & Resorts.

Employment Statistics

The Irish labor force is projected to increase from its 1998 level of 1.62 million to just under two million by 2011, assuming continuing net inward migration. Emigration, a longstanding Irish phenomenon, has been reversed due to the growth and development in the economy. The female contribution to the labor force, currently standing at 40 percent, is projected to increase to 43 percent by 2011.

As a major employer, tourism provided 188,068 jobs in 1996. According to these statistics, the number of people employed in Ireland's tourist industry had grown by 20 percent over the previous four years.[2] Dublin, with its concentration of businesses, is the main employment center. The majority of jobs (77 percent) are considered permanent, with seasonal employment accounting for only 18 percent and occasional employment less than five percent.

Gender composition among permanent employees is 48 percent male and 52 percent female[3]—a shift from the previous composition of 41 percent male and 59 percent female in 1996.[4] This increase in male employment is due to the rising number of permanent posts available. The figures, however, differ within the seasonal and part-time employee groups where females account for 66 percent.

A further survey indicated that the total number of people employed specifically in the Hotel and Guesthouse sector (a combination of the Hotels and Approved Accommodation sectors) amounted to 50,133 in 1998, an increase of 20 percent since 1996.[5]

The reasons for employment increases have been attributed to the number of new establishments (60 percent) and improved trading conditions (40 percent). The total number of firms in the industry has grown by more than 10 percent. The single biggest employer in the industry in 1996 was the Licensed Trade sector, while the second largest employer was the Hotel and Guesthouse sector.

Staff turnover is a problem facing many operators. Statistics relating to staff turnover for permanent full-time positions appears to be variable; however, recent industry research estimated turnover is in excess of 25 percent—a considerable increase on a six percent figure quoted in 1997. Monitoring this movement has revealed that 55 percent of permanent skilled staff within the hotel sector who have ceased employment have remained within the industry, while 31 percent have moved to another industry, and 14 percent have emigrated.

Hospitality Labor Market Issues

Competition for labor has pushed up rates of pay and seen the continued reform of employment practices in the industry

Occasional press reports from the Tourism Minister relating to accounts of low wages and long hours in the industry have been dismissed by the IHF chief, who commented that the industry has to compete in an area of virtually full employment—they have to pay market rates to get the staff they need. Rogue employers in the hotel and catering industry, however, continue to aggravate the industry image problem—some examples cited are not paying overtime, making young people (age 16) work until 3:30 A.M., and exploiting students by paying them only IR£1.50 per hour and making them work excessive hours.

Employees from mainland Europe joining the Irish workforce are probably not attracted by Irish wages, which are, in some cases, much less than they would get in their own country. However, the offer of free accommodation—which is often offered by rural establishments to attract staff where no suitable local workforce is available—is seen as a definite bonus.

Careers in Hospitality

Sustaining quality jobs, career advancement, competitive terms, and conditions of employment against other industries has not been easy, although current legislative changes—such as the introduction of a minimum wage and the Working Time Act—should help overcome problems in the conditions of employment by making the industry a more attractive career option.

Creating an opportunity to promote hospitality as a first choice career, not just a job, should be sought out as a way of recruiting well-motivated, enthusiastic employees. This can be aided by the provision of training and development opportunities for employees, encouraging them to advance within the organization and thus reducing staff turnover.

Career opportunities within the organization should be considered for all staff and not just focused, as it would presently appear, on the young graduate—the wealth of experience and loyalty to be tapped in more mature employees could create an even greater asset.

Jurys Doyle, Ireland's largest hotel company, has recently introduced a formal graduate training program consisting of 18 months in operations where a grounding in basic skills is given. Having achieved satisfactory performance levels, the trainee will progress to a more specialized skills area—human resources or sales and marketing for example.

Recruitment and Selection

Skills shortages, already a problem for the expanding tourism industry, are now an issue for the industry as a whole, so competition is tough. Trade and national press headlines highlighting the acute shortage of skilled staff for the industry are not uncommon ("Industry Reports Difficulty in Recruiting Skilled Staff" and "Celtic Tiger Threatened by Shortages of Skilled Staff"). Even unskilled staff seem to be eluding employers, given the demands on the general labor force in a thriving economy.

A recent survey on industry employment indicated that an estimated 9,827 vacancies in the hotel and restaurant sectors had not been filled.[6] Hoteliers are finding it impossible to recruit Irish staff in sufficient numbers. This labor crisis has led 46 percent of hoteliers and 10 percent of guest house owners to recruit staff from abroad. Apart from the annual influx of students (particularly during the summer), France and Spain are the most common countries of origin for foreign hotel and restaurant workers, followed by Germany and Norway. However, as many of these personnel come to advance their language skills, they tend to move on after a few months.

According to hotel human resource personnel, such traditional recruitment vehicles as newspaper advertisements are getting a zero response. This has caused a swing toward the use of recruitment agencies or/and recruiting staff from the United Kingdom or mainland Europe. In an attempt to deal with Ireland's staffing problem, a few employment agencies are opening branches in Sweden and Finland and have longer-term plans to open offices in Poland, Hungary, and the Czech republic.

Trade Initiatives. Companies have started offering various incentives to reduce turnover and promote employment longevity.

- The Campbell Bewley catering company gave staff who had worked in the company for more than two years 41 shares each—valued up to IR£1,500.

- The Jurys Doyle group will pay its staff a "goodwill bonus" of about IR£160 for each year of service, also guaranteeing that there will be no lay-offs and that their career prospects will be protected.

- A new business venture, facing challenges of open poaching of staff, established an introduction bonus. After a six-month duration, the bonus would be paid to the staff member who made the introduction—providing both were still in employment. Aiming for higher levels of involvement and job satisfaction, staff were also empowered with greater autonomy and responsibility in the workplace.

- Tax allowances on personal income were being sought by the Small Firms Association in a bid to deal with labor shortages. The association said this would make working more attractive to those who are tempted by global operators who can afford to pay more.

The IHF **Quality Employer Program**, conceived in 1996 in response to a study on labor shortage and industry working conditions, is the industry's response to widespread criticism of the industry as an employer and the problems being experienced by hoteliers in recruiting and retaining staff. It is an admission by the IHF that some of its members need to upgrade their employment policies if they are to compete for staff and if the industry is to improve its image among job seekers. Best practice performance standards include such issues as recruitment, induction, contract of employment, working conditions, training, assessments, and exit interviews. A comprehensive statement of current practices must be produced by a participating establishment. Thereafter, a program should be instituted leading to the upgrading of current practices to comply with the standard and pass an audit to achieve the Quality Employer symbol. Regular self assessments will be required to measure compliance, and independent audits and spot checks will be applied.

Government Initiatives. The **minimum wage requirement**, which came into effect in Spring 2000, clearly gives direction to employers by indicating what employees' wage entitlements are. Such clear information might create a more level playing field for employers—with the more successful ones who are investing in training and development coming out ahead. The minimum wage is IR£4.40 on an hourly basis. However, SIPTU (Services, Industrial, Professional, and Technical Union—the largest general union in Ireland and the union under which the hospitality industry is classified) and mandate unions (a small number of unions that operate in some regions) recommended that the rate should be IR£4.80. Bringing pay scales in line with other industries is a big step in rectifying the image problem.

An IHF trade report requested government incentives to increase labor-force participation. The report recommended that an emphasis should be placed on encouraging housewives to return to the workforce (through a new Homemakers Tax Allowance of an additional IR£2,000 per annum) and that procedures needed to be streamlined to allow easily issued work permits for non-EU nationals. If the tax-free incentive is introduced, it would allow an additional 40,000 people (including members of farming families) to re-enter the workforce.

In addition, to meet high demand for consistent high-quality service, increased access to training is needed and should be provided at key centers throughout the country. The training investment, the IHF identified, should be focused at specific needs identified and in areas of regional deficits.[7]

Poor working conditions relating to hours of work might generally be considered as the second most common complaint given by employees in the industry. The **Working Time Act**, which defines normal hours of work, hours of work for young people, breaks, holidays, etc., will bring long-term benefits to the industry by helping improve the industry's poor image. It will be costly, but it could be a great advantage. Given the clear guidelines for employers, it would be hoped that the negative industry image will make some headway in retaining its staff and giving thcm a rewarding career.

Training and Development

Established in 1963, the state tourism training agency, or CERT (Council for Education, Recruitment, and Training), has the responsibility for education, recruitment, and training of personnel for the tourism industry in Ireland.

The wide range of services offered by CERT range from identifying employment and training needs to developing national training structures and programs, and from the recruitment and training of school leavers planning careers in the industry to on-the-job training and business advice.

Working alongside the National Training Certification Board, CERT has designed a range of skills-based courses covering many disciplines. These courses are delivered nationwide through a selection of suitably-resourced third-level education centers.

Only one-third of hotels and three percent of guest houses have an action plan for training—with 20 percent of hotels and two percent of guest houses having a dedicated training budget.[8] This poor training provision may be seen as a product of the independent or small business nature of the hotel sector in Ireland, where management structures may not be so clearly defined and where in many cases training is seen only as an immediate expense without any long-term return.

The Minister of Tourism is looking for IR£350 million to invest in tourism marketing, product development, and training over the next seven years of the new National Development Plan. The partnership of government, state agencies, and the private sector has been seen as one of the keys to the dynamic success of the tourism industry in Ireland.

The European Commission—the body that makes policy and legislation—has recognized the value of the tourism industry and has been instrumental in directing funding to assist in the development of sustainable tourism policies and their implementation.

Educational Institutions. Ireland has a good provision of third-level institutions offering a wide range of skills, operations, and management courses. There are two centers offering higher-level degree programs and two private schools offering management programs; most fall within the state sector.

The range of courses fall within the national qualification band of CERT. Some individual centers, according to regional needs, have established independent institute programs or, in some cases, have franchised established courses from other educational centers. The broad level of skills expertise gained by the students of the institutions is generally considered good by the industry (due in part to the amount of industrial experience considered integral to the courses).

The recruitment of students for courses in hospitality, although variable, remains reasonably healthy. The impact of travel and tourism courses on student applications has been apparent, but an improved industry image would help readjust the balance and reduce the loss of trainees from the industry. Thereafter, it is up to industry to manage their retention.

Trade Union Membership. Ireland has traditionally been characterized by relatively high levels of trade union density.[9] However, trade union membership appears to be more prevalent in the larger hotel groups, which in turn are higher in density in main city locations. The smaller regional establishments, by nature, do not appear to have such active union participation. Changing EU work regulations may well affect the degree of membership, depending on how well these are interpreted by employers.

The continued success of tourism in Ireland will depend on sustaining the industry. Ireland's image as a relaxed, stress-free quality location must be maintained if it is to retain its position in the international marketplace.

The integral role played by staff and their professionalism in delivering this quality product are paramount in this equation. However, this can only be achieved by recruiting adequate numbers of well-trained staff of the right caliber.

Every effort will need to be made by the industry, and its overall support systems, to raise the profile of the hospitality industry to give it a more professional status. Within such an improved structure, employees will be able to establish challenging and rewarding careers that in return will give industry a more professional workforce around which management strategies can be planned.

Endnotes

1. Bord Fáilte Marketing Ireland to the World, Bord Fáilte Irish Tourist Board Annual Review, 1998.
2. From "Ten Facts about Irish Tourism," http://www.cert.ie/S1P04.htm on September 15, 1999.
3. CERT Employment Survey of the Tourism Industry in Ireland (Dublin: CERT, 1998).
4. CERT Employment Survey of the Tourism Industry in Ireland (Dublin: CERT, 1996).
5. CERT Employment Survey of the Tourism Industry in Ireland, 1998.
6. CERT Employment Survey of the Tourism Industry in Ireland, 1998.
7. "Hotel & Catering Review," *IHF Millennium Plan for Tourism,* vol. 32, no. 6 (June 1999), p. 5.
8. CERT Employment Survey of the Tourism Industry in Ireland, 1998.
9. P. Gunnigle, N. Heraty & M. Morley, *Personnel & Human Resource Management—Theory and Practice in Ireland* (Dublin: Gill & Macmillan, 1997).

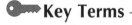# Key Terms

Celtic Tiger—The term which refers to the period of unprecedented economic upturn in the Irish economy.

EU (European Union)—The union of 15 European states for trade and social benefits.

minimum wage requirement—Legislation adopted to raise minimum wage levels to comparative European levels.

Quality Employer Program—A program established (by the IHF) to help the industry create and implement quality human resource practices with the aim to improve its poor employer image and overcome recruitment and retention problems.

Working Time Act—Legislation brought in through membership of the EU defining normal working hours and other conditions of employment relating to hours of work, holidays, breaks, etc.

Discussion Questions

1. What developments have caused the emergence of the Celtic Tiger?
2. What sectors of the tourism market choose Ireland as a destination?
3. What are the special features of hotel ownership in Ireland?
4. What are the reasons for the major surge in employment?
5. What initiatives are being taken by the industry in Ireland with a view to retaining staff?

Internet Sites

For more information, visit the following Internet sites. Remember that Internet addresses can change without notice.

Bord Fáilte Irish Tourist Board
http://www.ireland.travel.ie

Northern Ireland Tourist Board
http://www.ni-tourism.com

Central Statistics Office of Ireland
http://www.cso.ie

State Tourism Training Agency (CERT)
http://www.cert.ie

Hospitality Ireland
http://www.hospitality-ireland.com

Chapter 6 Outline

The Israeli Labor Market
The Hospitality Industry in Israel
Human Resource Management
    Commando 180
    Employee Turnover
    Outsourcing and Employment
      Agencies
Collective Labor Agreement
    The Structure of the Collective
      Agreement
The Academization of the Hospitality
    Manager

Competencies

1. Discuss the unique conditions of the Israeli labor market and its hospitality industry. (pp. 95–98)

2. Explain Israeli human resources management, including the concept and history of "Commando 180," the turnover phenomenon and its causes, and outsourcing and employment agencies. (pp. 98–102)

3. Outline the Collective Agreement and its role in regulating the industry's labor relations. (pp. 102–106)

4. Discuss the academization process in the field of hospitality management and its impact on the industry. (pp. 106–108)

6

Human Resource Management in Israel

Arie Reichel and *Sharon Amit*

Arie Reichel is a Professor, Associate Dean for Academic Affairs of the School of Management, and Chairman of the Department of Hotel and Tourism Management at Ben-Gurion University of the Negev. He founded the only department in an Israeli university that grants a B.A. degree in Hotel and Tourism Management. He has a Ph.D. in Strategic Management from the University of Massachusetts in Amherst, Massachusetts. He has published dozens of scholarly articles and serves as the head of the Israel Ministry of Tourism Human Resource Development Committee.

Sharon Amit completed his B.A. in Hotel and Tourism Management at Ben-Gurion University of the Negev, where he is presently a graduate student and research assistant in The School of Management. He has worked at the Moriah Hotel in Eilat and at The Beersheva Hilton Hotel.

THE STATE OF ISRAEL extends over an area of 22,000 square kilometers (about 8,500 square miles) with a population of six million people.[1] The population is highly diverse, with 80 percent Jews and 20 percent Arabs.[2] Most of the Jewish inhabitants immigrated from numerous nations around the globe. Since its independence in 1948, Israel has been in varying states of conflict and war with its Arab neighbors. The last 20 years have been marked by gradual peace processes, commencing with Egypt in 1978. The country maintains a large military, which constitutes a significant economic and social burden.

During its early years, the State of Israel relied heavily on agriculture. However, major technological improvements and investments have transferred the economy more and more toward service industries and advanced technology. These processes have been accompanied by major liberalization and privatization, exposing the local economy to global competition.

The Israeli Labor Market

The working population in Israel is around two million, of which 43 percent are women. The employees are distributed relative to the various industries. The level of education of the work force is considered high, with 45 percent having completed more than 13 years of schooling.[3] It is commonly believed that the high level of education constitutes one of Israel's competitive advantages.

Most of the wages are determined via a lengthy process of negotiations among the government (the largest employer), the unions (**Histadrut**, which includes most organized labor), and the Manufacturers Association of Israel. The resulting agreements form frameworks for sectorial wages and are adapted to inflation and the cost of living index. Work conditions are set by labor laws, including minimal conditions at work such as the number of vacation days per length of employment. As of June 1999, the average monthly salary in Israel was NIS 6,200 (about US$1,500); the minimum monthly wage is approximately NIS 2,950 (US$715). Clearly, the minimum wage is applicable to the hospitality industry, and, as will be later shown, has a major impact on the cost structure of the hospitality industry.

The Hospitality Industry in Israel

At the beginning of 1999, there were over 41,770 rooms in 318 hotels. This figure represents only government registered institutions, and shows a 40 percent increase since 1992.[4] (There are another 4,000 rooms in hostels and rural tourism establishments that are not registered with the Israel Ministry of Tourism.) The hotels are not ranked using the star system, but rather according to their main function (for example, spa vs. business). According to the Central Bureau of Statistics, 54 percent of the rooms are in categories equivalent to "deluxe."[5]

The demand for Israeli hotels stems from two major sources: domestic and foreign tourists. The average Israeli takes two vacations each year, averaging US$520 per family on each vacation.[6] Close to 50 percent of that budget is spent on accommodations. In 1998, domestic tourists accounted for nine million nights (54 percent of the total). This represented a growth of 74 percent since 1992.[7] In the same year, the total demand for hotel rooms was estimated at 16.7 million nights, which indicated 60 percent growth since 1991.

As of 1998, foreign tourists accounted for 7.7 million nights, which represented a decline since the record year of 1995, when 2.2 million tourists arrived in Israel and accounted for 9.5 million nights. The average foreign tourist stays for 15 days and spends US$1,320.[8] It is estimated that 45 percent of the total expenditure is dedicated to hotel accommodations.

In terms of the profiles of the tourists, close to 28 percent are on religious pilgrimage and 25 percent are travel and leisure; Western Europe and North America are the major points of origin, accounting for 80 percent of tourists. The peak months are March, April, July, August, and October, but the distribution is year-round. Foreign tourism is highly sensitive to geopolitical events in Israel and the Middle East; tension and warfare are highly correlated with quick downturns in tourist arrivals.[9] The relative isolation of Israel has made air arrivals the major form of transportation.

The four major hotel centers are Jerusalem, Eilat (on the Red Sea), Tel-Aviv (Israel's major city), and Tiberias (on the Sea of Galilee). Together, these locations offer 65 percent of all rooms. Between 1989 and 1999, Eilat became the leading resort city in Israel. Another area under fast development is the Dead Sea shore, which caters to both health-seeking and spa tourists. The last decade has also been characterized by the entry of numerous international hotel chains into the Israeli market. Chains such as Holiday Inn, Radisson SAS, Days Inn, Accor, Hilton International, Hyatt International, and Sheraton have significantly expanded their number of hotels in preparation for the anticipated demand derived from both the Millennium and the peace process between Israel and its neighbors.

Foreign tourists account for 50 percent of the hotels' income, while 40 percent is derived from domestic tourists and 10 percent from other sources such as banquets and special events.[10] Labor is the dominant cost (44–46 percent of all costs), followed by operations (38–41.6 percent), management (11 percent), and rent (four to six percent).[11] This cost structure clearly illustrates the dilemma faced by hotel management who must deal with seasonal or geopolitical-driven declines in demand: how to cut costs without sacrificing the level of service or laying off skilled and loyal employees. This dilemma is accentuated by the fact that most employees are tenured, and those that are highly skilled are handsomely paid, including various social benefits (retirement, educational, and savings funds). Consequently, most hotels would avoid laying off their employees even when faced by major crises, such as the case of the Gulf War.

The pressure on profitability is understandable when one considers that the average construction costs of a hotel room are US$100,000 (not including land and pre-opening costs); the investment in a luxurious room can easily approach US$200,000. It should be noted, however, that the government of Israel supplies special grants to hotel investors, depending on location. A high-priority development area would qualify investors for a grant up to 24 percent of their total investment. The grant ratios also vary over the years, but usually stay in the range of 12–24 percent. These investment incentives are also available for upgrades and remodeling. Other types of incentives include tax benefits and the acquisition of relatively inexpensive government land without public bidding. For example, in August 1999, the Four Seasons chain was granted prime land in Jerusalem at nominal costs without an open bid. This case illustrates the importance placed on the development of the hospitality industry in Israel.

The significance of the industry to the economy of the State of Israel is often presented and promoted by the **Israel Hotel Association (IHA)**. This body represents close to 350 hotels, with the mission to protect the interests of its members and present them nationally and internationally. In accordance with its mission, IHA represents the hotels in collective bargaining with employee unions and lobbies the government to promote the hoteliers' causes. Moreover, IHA is engaged in national and international marketing campaigns, and also deals with human resource development. Hotel executives have also formed their own organization, the Israel Hotel Managers Association, whose purpose is to protect and promote the professional level and interests of hotel managers.

Human Resource Management

Human resource managers in Israeli hotels, as in other countries in the world, have to fit the employee mix to changing circumstances. From an economics viewpoint, the hotel is interested in cost cutting and maximum flexibility in the adjustment of the number of employees. On the other hand, a professional, courteous, and loyal workforce cannot be automatically altered according to changing conditions. This dilemma has some unique characteristics for Israeli human resource managers; namely, the availability of high-quality seasonal employees, the status of tenured employees, outsourcing to employment agencies, and the binding industry Collective Agreement. In addition, many managers have to deal with the military reserve duty, which can take up to 30 days a year until an employee is 50 years old.

As of June 1999, more than 30,000 people were directly employed by the hotel industry, 44 percent of whom are women.[12] Between 1992 and 1996, there was a 34 percent growth in the number of employees; however, since 1996, the growth rate has declined by two percent a year. Currently, hospitality employees account for 1.5 percent of all employees in the Israeli economy.[13] According to the Central Bureau of Statistics, employees in the hospitality segment have some characteristics that distinguish them from other workers:

- Only 27 percent have finished more than 13 years of education, as opposed to a 45 percent average of the total Israel labor force. It should be noted, however, that 59 percent of the hospitality employees have had some professional training.

- More than 62 percent are younger than 34 years old. Clearly, it is a "young" industry, with 29 percent in 18–24 age range.

- The average number of hours worked per week is 43, as opposed to an average of 37 hours in other industries.

- More than 98 percent of all employees are salaried (as opposed to self-employed).

- The average monthly salary of hospitality employees (US$1,100) is 38 percent lower than the national average monthly salary (US$1,500) as of June 1999.[14]

- The percentage of non-Jews employed (20 percent) reflects their ratio in the population of Israel.

The city with the highest number of employees is Eilat (6,800), followed by Jerusalem (6,150). Most of the employees (70 percent) are employed by upper-scale hotels. Such hotels also tend to pay their employees more than the lower-level hotels (in 1998, US$1,155 and US$970, respectively).

The supply of employees is determined by several factors. The most significant one is the situation in the country's labor market. Clearly, during recession, more potential employees are available. Another demand factor is related to the employment situation within a given district. For example, there are pools of temporary employees near college campuses. A third factor is government incentive policies. For example, the government views tourism and hospitality as high-priority occupations. Soldiers who have completed their compulsory military service who then engage in six months of hospitality employment following their discharge are awarded a cash incentive.

Commando 180

One cannot fully understand human resource management in Israel and the issue of turnover without referring to the unique phenomenon known as **Commando 180**. In 1991, the Israeli Knesset (parliament) passed the Discharged Soldiers Law which contains a provision for a special cash incentive from the government for any discharged soldier who completes 180 working days in a national priority occupation. The high-priority occupations include agriculture, construction, and tourism. As of June 1999, the incentive was NIS 6,400 (US$1,560). Commando employees are housed with other hotel employees in a hotel-supplied apartment. The hotels also supply free transportation and free meals in the employee cafeteria.

Most Jewish Israeli youths are required to join the army immediately after high school. Men serve for three years, while young women serve for 20 months. Druze men (a unique ethnic Arab group) are also drafted. Arab youths are usually exempted from army service, but they may join the National Service Voluntary Forces, which focuses on hospitals and social welfare programs, or an elite regular Army unit of Bedouin-Arab trackers. The Discharged Soldiers Law has had a significant effect on the hospitality industry. Thousands of young, talented, and energetic employees join the industry. They are attracted especially to remote, high demand sites, and immediately add to the quality of the workforce: upper middle-class youth are found in most of the high employment demand hotels. However, in most cases, their tenure is just long enough for them to save money for the almost socio-culturally-required "passage of adulthood": a year long "walk-about" to the Far East or South America.

A close examination of the phenomenon reveals that it is a mixed blessing for the hospitality industry. On one hand, highly intelligent young people are joining the industry; but on the other, they add considerably to the high turnover problem. Moreover, the abundance of such a resource pushes down the basic wages. The cash incentive is considered by management as an additional US$260 a month above minimum wage. Clearly, the majority of the "Commandos" would not consider working for minimum wage (i.e., without the added incentive package). The main objective of these youths is to reap the benefits—often working around the clock to save as much money as possible. Most do not stay more than the required six months, although a few are absorbed by the industry and soon start their ascent to junior managerial positions. It is estimated that less than 15 percent stay beyond six months, and less than five percent see their future with the industry. The short employment period encourages human resource managers to channel Commando

180 employees to the food and beverage department, security, or other occupations that require very short training. Departments that require more training employ fewer incentive employees.

In sum, the Discharged Soldier Law has had a profound effect on the hospitality industry. Both hoteliers and the youths usually praise the mutual benefits. Mr. Raffi Sadeh, Chief Executive Officer for the large Isrotel chain, explains, "Even if the waiter spills coffee, or the waitress mixes up the silverware, they are so nice and attractive that our guests are thrilled to have them." It is not clear, however, what the long-term effect of Commando 180 is on the industry, especially from the viewpoint of tenured employees.

Employee Turnover

Worldwide, the hospitality industry is noted for high turnover rates. According to estimates, the average turnover rate in Israel is 150 percent, with the bulk of employees leaving within the first four months of employment.[15] Analyzing turnover statistics reveals variability according to hotel departments and geographic location. The department most affected by turnover is food and beverage, followed by housekeeping. Respondents of a national survey ranked lack of suitability for the job due to difficult conditions as the major reason.[16] The unusual work hours, the physical burden, as well as the supervisory obedience requirement were among factors most contributing to the perception of "difficult" conditions. Note also that these two departments are often occupied by youth who come to work for short periods of time (Commando 180). Since entry requirements are very low, it is extremely easy to replace employees.

Another turnover pattern is found in hotel kitchens. Some hoteliers have adopted a tactic of firing cooks after a three-year period in order to avoid their accumulation of very high benefits. Again, there is an ample supply of new cooks to replace the "old" ones.

Turnover rates are the highest in more remote tourist areas such as Eilat and the Dead Sea. One study revealed that this is probably not caused by the relatively long distances traveled to and from work or by seasonal layoffs, but rather by employee dissatisfaction caused mainly by perceived low pay, their need to adapt to the ever-changing requirements of the hotels (such as periods of high and low demands with different types of tourists), and by physical difficulties (such as traveling in high-temperature desert areas).[17]

It should be noted that turnover also prevails among the "hard core" hospitality employees. These employees see the industry as their "home," but they often do not exhibit high commitment and loyalty to a particular hotel. This problem is accentuated by the rapid development of new hotels, which attract employees away from their competitors and which, after a short period, also become "victims" of newer hotels offering jobs.

This lack of organizational commitment has become a crucial challenge for human resource managers, especially in high growth areas. Clearly, from the viewpoint of the hotel, high turnover is a burden—in addition to the constant need to recruit new employees and complete their orientation and training, certain employees exhibit a lax attitude toward obedience to superiors. In response to this problem, human resource managers have been devising various plans for the welfare of their employees that are designed to enhance their commitment to their employers. Among these plans, the most notable are career plans, where the employee is consulted about a preferred, realistic organizational progress plan and openings in training and development programs, either through the Center for Professional Development or other organizations.

Some human resource managers, such as those in the Hilton chain, decided that the issue of organizational commitment can be identified at the employee selection stage. Thus, they attempt to predict an orientation toward organizational loyalty during the initial interview process with departmental managers. Workshops are offered for executives to train them about how to assess and detect commitment orientation. The results of these efforts are not yet available.

Some of the major tasks of the human resource manager are listed below, highlighting the specific conditions in Israel:

- *Recruitment.* There are several ways to recruit employees. The prevailing one is through friends (estimated by industry experts to account for at least 30 percent of new employees), followed by word-of-mouth (20 percent), initiatives of job seekers (15 percent), placing ads in newspapers (10 percent), and through employment agencies (six percent). Other sources include transfers within a chain and Israel Ministry of Labor referrals.

- *Selection.* Investment in a systematic process of selection is usually reserved for employees who are candidates for career paths and show managerial potential.

- *Trial Period.* According to the Collective Agreement (discussed later in the chapter),there is a six-month trial period. This is considered a very long period for an industry that requires very limited training for numerous positions. The long trial period is viewed as a "victory" for the hoteliers in the collective bargaining process because during this period, the employees hardly have any rights (i.e., they are expendable).

- *Training.* Most training programs within the hotel are labeled "horizontal" (i.e., training employees in various tasks within the same organizational hierarchy). This facilitates a smooth transition for employees from job to job, according to emerging needs.

    In addition, however, the penetration of international chains into the Israeli hospitality industry has triggered the establishment of management development programs: employees who possess the requisite ability and motivation enter a specified career path that includes training in the various departments, as well as attending courses offered by the headquarters of the chain. Similar training and career paths are offered by some chains to graduates of hotel degree–granting institutes.

- *Evaluation.* Even hotels that have lax selection criteria tend to pay special attention to the evaluation of all employees. At lower levels, department heads fill out a standard evaluation form, which is submitted to the human resource manager every six months. At the managerial level, the evaluation process involves both a detailed evaluation form and a verbal feedback session.

- *Promotion.* Promotion in the hospitality industry in Israel is considered very quick (see Exhibit 1). The high turnover at both the employee and managerial levels creates numerous advancement opportunities. The progress rate varies among departments and hotel locations; the fastest track is found in food and beverage departments. Hotels located in remote resorts offer faster tracks than those located in the center of Israel (where turnover rates are relatively low).

Outsourcing and Employment Agencies

The need for a flexible workforce has recently pushed many hotels toward outsourcing employment. The use of employment agencies for outsourcing has been viewed in the industry as a panacea for fluctuations in the demand for employees, and also as an indirect way to limit the number of tenured employees. Housekeeping, food and beverage, catering and events, and security are the areas most utilizing outsourcing. There are not yet available statistics about the magnitude of this phenomenon, but, according to industry experts, it is more prevalent among the "less sophisticated" hotels. Upper-scale or foreign chain hotels tend to refrain from outsourcing, since they prefer to develop their own workforce and to avoid the risk of guest contacts with non-committed employees. However, when it comes to menial, low-level, back-of-the-house tasks, many hotels employ temporary employees via employment agencies that rely on foreign workers, mostly from Africa. In remote sites like Eilat, foreign workers prefer to be employed in two hotels simultaneously, completing two shifts in 24 hours. This way, they can earn more money in a short time period and return to their countries of origin, usually to higher-level "white collar" jobs that pay very little in comparison to their gains in Israel. It should be noted that these employees are not considered hotel-employed, but agency-employed workers who do not benefit from hotel incentives such as gifts, holidays, and—most importantly—termination compensation.

Collective Labor Agreement

A crucial aspect in human resource management in Israeli hotels is the **Collective Agreement**. This Agreement is a framework of rules encompassing almost any formal interaction between the employee and the hotel management; it includes general items that reflect Israeli labor laws, as well as those items unique to the hospitality industry. As noted earlier, the Agreement is a product of a collective bargaining process between the Histadrut unions and the IHA. Factors such as the situation of the industry (decline vs. growth), demand for labor, and political climate affect the results of the negotiations.

The first Collective Agreement was signed in 1972, and it established a pattern by being in effect for two-and-a-half years. However, an Agreement does not expire unless a new one is signed. Each Agreement is based on the previous one, and is the product of negotiations and bargaining points of the unions and the

Exhibit 1   Examples of Promotion Paths

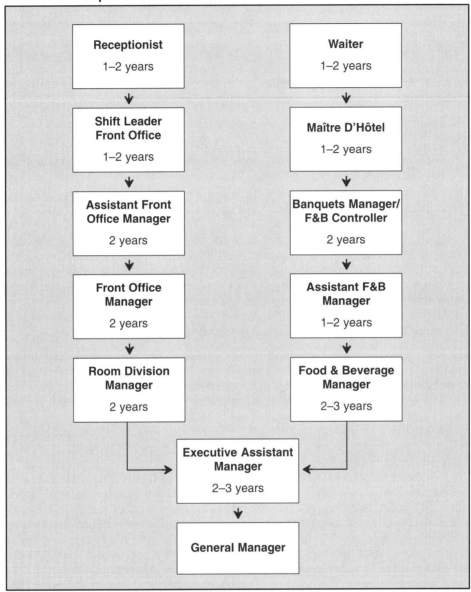

IHA. In addition, items reflecting the current social, economic, and legal conditions are added to the Agreement.

Examining the contents of the Agreements throughout the years indicates that the power of the unions is declining. This trend is evident in other sectors as well; the Histadrut is losing both its power and an increasing number of members because many organizations prefer to sign personal contracts with their employees. At the same time, the power of the IHA is rising. According to industry experts, the strengthened position of the IHA is not only the result of crises in tourism demand caused by geopolitical upheavals—which have enabled hoteliers to present inflexible demands to their workers—but also because it managed to form a firm and steady front. Moreover, it can be argued that the declining power of the union reflects the general transition of Israel into a capitalist economy. Over the years, there seems to have been three major issues of concern from the standpoint of the IHA:

1. Labor flexibility according to the special circumstances of the industry.

2. The problem of "obedience." It is argued that many employees are confronted with numerous "temptations" or situations to pilfer hotel goods such as towels, dishes, cutlery, and food.

3. Harmonious labor relations. The union sees as its major task the protection of the rights of tenured (but *not* non-tenured or seasonal) employees.

Each Agreement serves as the basis for the next one, often reflecting new trends in labor relations. For example, the 1999 Collective Agreement includes a section that deals with sexual harassment on the job. In addition, the Agreement includes a clause that entails bonuses for employees in case the high occupancy expectations for the millennium are met.

The Structure of the Collective Agreement

The first chapter includes terminology and explanations; for example, the difference between tenured and seasonal employees, the time frame, and the types of businesses that are included under the Agreement.

The second chapter deals with the employee on-the-job trial period. A trial period of six months enables management to terminate an employee with a day's notice without a formal explanation. The chapter also explains the tenure process in detail, and assigns priority in promotion to junior managerial positions according to length of employment within the hotel.

The third chapter deals with working hours. As of June 1999, the Histadrut of Hospitality Employees has managed to achieve a shorter definition of a "work week" (40 hours over 5 days) than the one prevailing in other sectors (42.5 to 45 hours usually over six days).[18] On the other hand, the IHA insisted on dividing or adding the hours of work to fit the unique conditions of operating the hotels, and it is their prerogative to determine the days off. This chapter also specifies the bonuses granted on extra work hours or working during holidays.

The fourth chapter deals with wages. It should be noted that, in addition to the basic salary, there are components such as tenure with the organization and the number of children that affect total wages. The average addition amounts to three percent. Moreover, the Agreement entitles the employees to a one percent bonus for having passed Ministry of Labor professional certificate programs.[19] For the year 2000, employees will get a special bonus, pending specified occupancy rates: a 70 percent occupancy rate earns a 10 percent bonus on basic pay, 72 percent earns a 12.5 percent bonus, and a 75 percent occupancy rates raises the bonus to 15 percent.

The fifth chapter of the Agreement deals with benefits. Major benefits for tenured employees include 10 days of holidays in accordance with the employee's religion, 190 percent pay on Saturdays, and a range of 200–212 percent pay on various important religious Holy Days. Paid vacation days vary according to tenure in the organization; it ranges from 12 days during the first year to 23 days a year from the ninth year on. The employee is also entitled to annual vacation expenses, varying with tenure. Additional benefits include:

- A contribution equal to 12 percent of the employee's salary paid by the employing hotel to the employee's pension fund (the employee pays 5.5 percent).

- Employer-paid transportation expenses to and from work and arranged transportation when necessary.

- Payment of a 0.25 percent fee to the Center for Professional Advancement in Hospitality, a joint venture of the IHA and the Histadrut that offers numerous courses each month for all kinds and levels of hotel tasks. The employee adds another 0.25 percent of total salaries to the Center.

- A tax-free savings fund (originally conceived for various professional studies) that enables the employee to discharge the money accumulated after six years tax-free. The employer pays 7.5 percent, while the employee pays 2.5 percent.[20]

- Meals supplied at very low prices in an employee cafeteria.

All these benefits are described in detail in order to illustrate the huge gap between employee salaries and employer costs. Clearly, this cost structure contributes to the aforementioned problem of cost reduction in periods of crises and decline.

The sixth chapter of the Collective Agreement deals with termination and compensation. The initiating party, the employer or the tenured employee, is required to submit notice of termination a month in advance. Termination compensation is paid to employees whose departure is not their fault (for example, retiring employees, or specific cases when the employee moves to another city). The compensation is calculated as the last month's salary multiplied by the number of years with the organization. It should be noted that the compensation is taken from a special fund toward which the hotel pays six percent of all employee salaries every month. If the employee is not entitled to compensation, as in cases of voluntary leave or dishonorable termination, the hotel may retrieve the money paid to the fund.

The seventh chapter deals with mutual commitments. There is a detailed description of the task of the employees' union representation in each hotel. The framework for handling labor disputes is also presented. Included is a statement that both parties are committed to harmonious labor relations while the Agreement is in effect. This statement constitutes a crucial requirement from the standpoint of the IHA, since one of the major threats to the industry would be a strike in the midst of the peak season.

The appendix to the Agreement includes a special section on employee discipline. It states the "dos" and "do nots," and the accompanying sanctions. Subjects vary from absenteeism and lack of obedience to regulations and superiors. Other subjects include the right of top management to move employees from department to department and disciplinary rules related to appropriate behavior on premises. Sanctions vary from warnings filed in the employee's personal file, to temporary suspension, termination, and termination without compensation (the most severe sanction). As noted earlier, the subject of sexual harassment has been recently added to the Agreement.

Another section of the appendix deals with modifications that are based on the geographic location of the hotel. For example, in remote resorts such as Eilat or the Dead Sea, employees are entitled to special compensation and additional benefits such as five domestic flights a year within Israel. Yet another section deals with determining the minimum salary for each junior position (up to the position of department head). These "steps" are not significantly different from the legal minimum wage, but they serve as a platform for all the benefits and compensation that are detailed in the Agreement.

It is interesting to note that, in spite of the Agreement that enables the formation of unions at the hotel level, there are very few such local unions. Those that exist are usually at a chain-headquarters level only. The following reasons explain this phenomenon:

- The employees have their own powerful representatives in the Histradrut who make up for the lack of a local union.

- The Collective Agreement covers most of the dilemmas that could arise in the work place.

- Heterogeneity of hotel jobs means that hotels include a large range of occupations in areas that have relatively low commonality. Sometimes employees do not see reasons to form a union with presumably non-related occupations.

- A relatively large number of employees do not see their future in the hospitality industry. Some spend only six months as discharged soldiers (Commando 180).

- A certain percentage of the employees have expectations of quick promotion to managerial positions.

- Some employees have a very high level of involvement and identity with the hotel and do not see any reason to question management decisions and the current situation.

Consequently, local unions are rare and labor relations are stable.

The Academization of the Hospitality Manager

One cannot fully understand current human resource management in the hospitality industry in Israel without acknowledging the academization of the hospitality management profession. Until 1994, university graduate managers or employees were a rare phenomenon. Since priority was given to promotion from within, the career paths were very clear: from bellboy to general manager. One could not become a manager unless he or she started in the lowest level job and then worked up the organizational hierarchy. Not only that, the industry did not attract college graduates, since it supplied no incentives to educated people. This clearly promoted the poor image of the industry and its employees.

For decades the paths were set: employees were supplied either by relatively low level professional schools or "off the street" without training and education. During their years with the organization, they would be trained both on the job and in various professional-technical courses such as cooking. Those who aspired to managerial positions had to face a major barrier: a government license. One could not become a general manager without passing a government test that included written and oral sections. The committee that prepared the test and examined the candidates comprised mainly senior managers who reflected the experience, values, and attitudes of the tradition of the industry. Candidates had to complete a two-year diploma, but not an academic degree program. The diploma courses were offered mainly by one organization, which became a monopoly and often employed instructors from the industry. All the above created a relatively traditional, insulated, self-perpetuating industry that developed its own culture, body of knowledge, hierarchy, and procedures, and was protected by the government (which also ran the main technical training center for the industry).

In the lead up to the millennium, the industry has gone through several revolutions:

1. The government (Ministry of Tourism) had to cancel the executive license requirements as part of the privatization and liberalization processes in the Israeli economy. This means that it is now the sole responsibility of the owner to decide who should be the general manager.

2. Industry leaders realized the importance of higher education, and started to promote programs where liberal arts university graduates would join the industry. Many of such "conversion" programs failed, since their graduates did not stay in the industry.

3. At the same time, a college degree in Israel has become a common "commodity." Numerous positions that required high school diplomas 20 years ago have begun to require a degree from an academic institution.

4. The penetration of foreign chains into Israel has raised the need for educated employees and managers. The first major endeavor by the industry to promote academic training in Israel was attempted by a foreign general manager of an international chain; he founded a not-for-profit organization aimed to encourage "academization" in the hospitality industry but, despite all efforts, the attempt failed. International chains raised the level of sophistication in hospitality management and emphasized profit orientation.

5. Tourism was declared an important industry and one of the means of enhancing the peace process in the Middle East. More and more talented youths were interested in education and careers in the various tourism segments.

6. Israeli universities established hospitality and tourism management departments (Ben-Gurion University and The Hebrew University of Jerusalem). The high demand for these institutions encouraged local entrepreneurs to

establish branches of American and British universities of varying quality. Within three years, nine degree-granting programs were operating in a country of six million.

These trends shook up the industry, which has not yet managed to fully adapt. For example, many student interns complain of poor attitude from managers without formal training. Moreover, while university graduates expect to get appropriate wages reflecting their status and investment, it seems that most hotels refuse to adjust wages. The result is often mutual disappointment. However, some graduates are fully committed to the industry and are ready to conform to the traditional career paths, given the promise that the advancement will be much quicker than it has been in the past.

The academization process triggered requests from veteran executives to get university degrees in order to maintain their status and competitive advantage. As of the summer of 1999, the industry was still bewildered and not able to distinguish between the different degree programs, while attempts are made to rank the various academic programs in terms of quality and orientation. Many executives prefer not to hire university graduates because of their wage and career expectations. Moreover, they are threatened by the young, energetic, and ambitious youth. At the same time, the organization has to adopt sophisticated accounting, finance, and marketing techniques, and the need for highly educated managers is apparent. This results in a "mixed feeling" approach that still has to be resolved.

Endnotes

1. State of Israel, *Facts about Israel* (Jerusalem: Prime Minister's Office, 1998).

2. Central Bureau of Statistics, *Tourism and Hotel Services Statistics Quarterly* (Jerusalem: Ministry of Tourism, 1998).

3. Central Bureau of Statistics, *Tourism and Hotel Services Statistics Quarterly* (Jerusalem: Ministry of Tourism, 1997).

4. Israel Hotel Association, "The Hospitality and Tourism Industry in Israel" (in Hebrew) (Tel-Aviv: Israel Hotel Association, 1999).

5. Central Bureau of Statistics, 1998.

6. "Analysis of the Tourism and Hospitality Industry," *Globes* (in Hebrew) (1998).

7. Israel Hotel Association, "Tayaroot A Special Issue" (in Hebrew) (August 1999).

8. Central Bureau of Statistics, 1998.

9. R. Bar-On, "Measuring the Effect on Tourism of Violence and the Promotion Following Violent Acts," in A. Pizam and Y. Mansfeld (eds), *Tourism, Crime and International Security Issues* (New York: Wiley, 1996).

10. "Analysis of the Tourism and Hospitality Industry."

11. Central Bureau of Statistics, 1998.

12. D. Yarden, "A Note on the Industry" (in Hebrew) (Tel-Aviv: Israel Hotel Association, 1999).

13. Central Bureau of Statistics, 1998.

14. "The Collective Agreement in the Hospitality Industry," *Heshev* (in Hebrew) June 1999.

15. BDI Consulting, *Operational Recommendations for Human Resource Development* (in Hebrew) (Jerusalem: Israel Ministry of Tourism, 1998).

16. BDI Consulting, *Operational Recommendations*.

17. BDI Consulting, *Operational Recommendations*.

18. "The Collective Agreement in the Hospitality Industry."

19. Israel Hotel Association and the Histradrut, *General Collective Agreement for the Hospitality Industry* (in Hebrew) (Tel-Aviv: 1999).

20. Israel Hotel Association and the Histradrut, *General Collective Agreement for the Hospitality Industry* (in Hebrew) (Tel-Aviv: 1994).

Key Terms

Collective Agreement—A framework of rules encompassing almost any formal interaction between the employee and the hotel management; it includes general items that reflect Israeli labor laws, as well as those items unique to the hospitality industry. The Agreement is the outcome of negotiations between the representatives of the Hospitality Employee Union and the representatives of the Israel Hotel Association.

Commando 180—A term used to describe the phenomenon of young men and women, recently discharged from the military, who work in the hospitality industry for 180 days, entitling them to a special monetary benefit added to their salary. The benefit is given only to people who, after their military discharge, join industries which are considered national high-priority fields.

Histradrut—The name of the central organization of Israel's trade unions.

Israel Hotel Association (IHA)—This body represents close to 350 hotels in collective bargaining with employee unions and lobbies the government to promote the hoteliers' causes. IHA is also engaged in national and international marketing campaigns and deals with human resource development.

Discussion Questions

1. How would you describe the unique situation of tourism in Israel? Explain and specify the reasons for this situation.

2. What is the impact of the Collective Agreement on the hospitality industry? In your opinion, does the Agreement have any bearing on the quality of service in the industry?

3. What effects might the "academization" process have in the Israeli hospitality industry?

4. What is the role of "Commando 180" in the Israeli industry? Do you think it has a positive or a negative effect on human resource management?

5. What factors contribute to the turnover issue of Israeli hotel employees? In your opinion, what policies can be implemented in order to mitigate the magnitude of the turnover problem?

 **Internet Sites** ———————————————————————————

For more information, visit the following Internet sites. Remember that Internet addresses can change without notice.

Eilat.com
http://www.eilat.com/

IsraelVisit
http://israelvisit.co.il/

Israel Hotel Association
http://www.israelhotels.org.il/

National Committee for Labor Israel
http://www.laborisrael.org/

Israel's Tourism Guide
http://www.inisrael.com/

WebGuide Israel
http://www.webguideisrael.com/

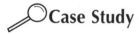 **Case Study** ———————————————————————————

University Students and the Moriah Hotel

Mr. Ohad Hadari has served as the Human Resources Manager for the Moriah Hotel in Eilat for the past eleven years. This 296 room and suite hotel has a core of loyal employees who have resisted temptation to move to newer hotels on the nearby promenade. In addition to these employees, Mr. Hadari hires temporary employees in accordance with high demand periods—usually around Christmas, when many Europeans flock to the sun-drenched city of Eilat. The other peak season is during July–August, when thousands of Israeli families fly or drive down to Eilat and populate the full range of hotels, from the most modest motels to the deluxe hotels.

Some of the temporary employees work for only six months. These are men and women freshly discharged from the military who benefit from a special incentive if they work six months in a government priority sector (in this case, hospitality). These employees are considered very bright, able, and energetic, but most do not see their future with either the Moriah or the hospitality industry in general.

Early one morning in June, Mr. Hadari sat in his office bewildered. "What shall I do with these applications?" he asked his administrative assistant, Jill Ben-Dor. "There are 15 applications from first and second year students from Ben-Gurion University who would like to pursue their practical training with us."

"What's the problem?" answered Ms. Ben-Dor. "Aren't they like the regular trainees we have been getting for the last 20 years?"

"No," said Mr. Hadari. "These are college students and we are expected to treat them like our own employees."

"Oh, that's a different story," said Ms. Ben-Dor. "What shall we do?"

"Let me think about it," answered Mr. Hadari. "I will try to make a list of the pros and cons of employing these kids so it will be easier for us to make up our minds."

He then closed the door to his office, disconnected the telephone, and started preparing the list.

Discussion Questions

1. What are the pros of hiring university hospitality students?
2. What are the cons of hiring university hospitality students?

Chapter 7 Outline

"Out of Many, One People"
  Social and Economic Indicators
  The Development of Jamaica's
    Tourism
  The Hospitality Sector
Labor Demographics and Labor Market
  Issues
  Education
  Women at Work
  The Labor Pool
The Legal and Political Environment
  Labor Laws
  Industrial Relations
Cultural Distinctions and Societal Work
  Values
Recruitment and Selection
  Recruitment Sources
  Selection Methods
Training and Development Practices
Performance Measures and Evaluation
  Guest Feedback
  Employee Recognition
The Place of the Human Resource
  Department
Conclusion

Competencies

1. Identify the unique aspects of
   Jamaica's population that positively
   and negatively affect the hospitality
   industry. (pp. 113–116)

2. Identify significant features of
   Jamaica's labor laws that affect hotel
   operations. (pp. 116–120)

3. Describe the attitudes of Jamaican
   workers toward tourism and their jobs.
   (pp. 120–121)

4. Identify important sources and
   methods of recruitment and selection,
   and discuss major hotel training
   practices and institutions.
   (pp. 121–124)

5. Discuss the role of the human
   resources department in the Jamaican
   hospitality industry. (pp. 124–125)

7

Human Resource Management in Jamaica: Responding to Challenging Times

Chandana Jayawardena and *Anne P. Crick*

Chandana Jayawardena is an international hotelier with 28 years of experience in Asia, Europe, the Middle East, South America, and the Caribbean. He is the chairman of the Hotel & Catering International Management Association (HCIMA) for Jamaica, HCIMA Ambassador for the Caribbean and South America, and associate professor of hospitality management for International Management Centres. Currently, he serves as academic director and program leader in tourism and hospitality management at the University of the West Indies, Jamaica.

Anne P. Crick currently lectures in organizational management and human resource management at the University of the West Indies. In addition, she has worked extensively in training and food and beverage management in several Jamaican hotels. Her current research interests include personalized service in the hotel sector and emerging trends in the workplace.

"Out of Many, One People"

Jamaica is the third largest Caribbean island and the largest in the English-speaking Caribbean. The island is 146 miles long and varied geographically, ranging from the Blue Mountain peaks to the plains and coastal areas. The first Jamaicans were the Arawak Indians, whom Christopher Columbus found inhabiting the island when he arrived in 1492. The island was then occupied by the Spaniards, who have left their legacy in the names of many of the towns and rivers across the islands. In 1655 the island was captured by the British and remained in their possession until it was made independent in 1962.

The English used the island to grow sugar for export to Europe and imported Africans to work as slaves on the sugar plantations. As a result, over 90 percent of the Jamaican population is of African descent. Indentured laborers from China and India after the abolition of slavery added to the mix, helping to form a rich melting pot of races, cultures, and religions.

Social and Economic Indicators

Jamaica is heavily dependent on foreign exchange for its survival, and the government has therefore encouraged any industry that produces or attracts foreign exchange. Tourism, with its potential to attract large sums of foreign money, has received much government attention and support.

Up until the 1980s, Jamaica's major foreign exchange earnings were derived from its traditional exports of bauxite (used to produce alumina) and agricultural products. With the fall of world prices for these products in the 1980s, tourism fast became the country's major foreign exchange earner. In addition, the shift in recent years toward globalization and trade liberalization has brought increasing dependence on tourism for foreign exchange earnings and employment opportunities.

Currently the hotel sector directly employs over 30,000 workers. Many others are employed indirectly in support industries and in the restaurants, stores, and attractions in and near the tourist areas.[1]

The Development of Jamaica's Tourism

As perhaps the best known of the Caribbean islands, Jamaica enjoys a good reputation not only for its climate and beaches but also for its famous Blue Mountain coffee, reggae music, and excellence in athletics. It is also a picturesque and charming tourist destination, attracting over one million visitors per year, primarily to large resort hotels on the north coast. Part of Jamaica's charm is that it offers visitors a variety of attractions to meet different preferences, requirements, and tastes, perhaps reflecting the evolution of the island's tourism.

Tourists first started coming to the island in the early part of the twentieth century. The first tourists came from Europe by ship and stayed for weeks or months at a time to take advantage of the warm climate and reputed curative waters. To meet their needs, a number of small hotels and guest houses sprung up in the coastal areas and near the mineral baths. The long stays—as well as repeat visits by many of these guests—meant that hotel employees became accustomed to delivering friendly and personalized service, features that hoteliers continue to provide today.

The advent of mass tourism during the 1950s was fueled by both the availability of relatively cheap and fast airline travel, as well as a growing recognition by the Jamaican government of tourism as a vital foreign exchange earner and significant employer. This period started the growth of the large hotel and a primary focus on **"sun-lust" tourism**. Hotels therefore faced the challenge of maintaining

Exhibit 1   Visitor Arrivals by Source

Countries	Stopovers (in Thousands)	% Share
USA	829.3	67.7
Europe	212.7	17.4
Canada	109.8	9.0
Caribbean	36.8	3.0
Japan	10.8	0.9
TOTAL	1,225.3	100.0

Source: *Annual Travel Statistics,* 1998, Jamaica Tourist Board

the personalization of the small hotel while maximizing the efficiencies of much larger properties.

The third major phase of Jamaica's tourism began in 1976 with the advent of the first **all-inclusive** hotel. Most of the all-inclusives tend to be large, and they often struggle not to lose the personal touch. Moreover, the all-inclusive is not merely an accommodation, it is a destination. The all-inclusive provides the visitor with a carefree vacation of sand, sea, and sun, enjoyable within the confines of that particular venue.

With the development of Jamaica's tourism industry, the type of tourist has also changed. As shown in Exhibit 1, most visitors now come from North America rather than from Europe. The more recent visitors also come for a shorter period of time, with the average stay for North Americans being seven nights. Visitors from Europe stay longer—for example, 13.2 nights in 1998, with visitors from the United Kingdom staying an average of 20.3 nights. Jamaica is therefore attempting to diversify its market in order to attract more of these long-staying guests.[2]

The Jamaica Tourist Board is seeking to develop tourism as a year-round activity. There are therefore many promotions—such as an annual reggae festival and film festival—intended to attract visitors to the island during traditionally "soft" periods. The tourist board is also targeting special types of groups with different needs. In the past three years, for example, Negril, a major resort city, has been host to students on spring vacation and has attracted hundreds of young people to the country. There have also been efforts to promote and expand the island's ecotourism. These strategies bring increased diversity to the tourist sector. They also increase the demands made on the hotel staff.

The Hospitality Sector

As Exhibit 2 shows, Jamaica's tourism is concentrated on the North Coast towns of Montego Bay, Ocho Rios, and Negril, where some of the best beaches are found. There are, however, many small hotels located on the South Coast for those tourists who prefer a quieter and less structured vacation. The interior, because of its lush

116   *Chapter 7*

Exhibit 2   Capacity and Occupancy by Region

Region	Hotel Rooms	% Occupancy
Montego Bay	4,153	59.6
Ocho Rios	3,859	63.5
Negril	2,928	63.1
Port Antonio	313	25.4
Kingston & St. Andrew	1,537	47.1
Mandeville & South Coast	303	37.8

Source: *Annual Travel Statistics*, 1998, Jamaica Tourist Board

vegetation and mountainous terrain, is ideal for "green travelers." Kingston, the capital, caters primarily to business travelers.

Jamaica's hotel sector now bases its product on three factors: high-quality service, product variety, and personalization. All of these factors are highly dependent on the ability of hospitality staff to be professional, skilled, efficient, and flexible—and, at the same time, friendly and hospitable. Hotels are also in a mode of continuous improvement in order to remain competitive and to meet the demands of the **"new tourist."** This requires personnel who are not only focused on delivering quality service in the present, but who are sensitive enough to realize what changes are needed for the future and creative enough to deliver them.[3]

Jamaican hoteliers and the Jamaican government realized early on the importance of training and developing their employees as a way of remaining competitive. The industry today is moving toward an era of professionalism, characterized by highly trained and educated employees and continuous improvement.

Labor Demographics and Labor Market Issues

A critical factor in the movement toward professionalism is the labor pool from which the hotel can draw. Three major factors affect the Jamaican labor force: the quality and type of education, the emergence of professional women, and the unemployment rate.

Education

The quality of the education system directly affects the quality of the labor force available to a hotel. Jamaica's education system is modeled on the British system, and education is mandatory up to the primary level (Grade Six). Almost two-thirds of the students go on to secondary high or vocational schools, which prepare them for entry-level positions in tourism. Many also go on to one of Jamaica's many degree-granting colleges and universities that prepare them for supervisory and management positions in the industry.

While the Jamaican education system is a good and well-rounded one, there are pockets of poor performance that may affect a future employer. The most serious of these are weaknesses in English and mathematics. These pose a challenge to the tourism industry as literacy and, increasingly, mathematical ability are critical to effective performance. Hotel managers have to be particularly concerned about the fact that, while most high-school graduates understand English very well, many are more comfortable communicating in Jamaican patois. Managers have to constantly sensitize employees to the need to communicate in standard English.

Many students leave school without having acquired any fluency in a foreign language. Spanish is taught in most schools, and French and German are taught in several high schools. But unless students choose to major in languages, they will not develop the fluency required for interacting with tourists from all over the world. Most hotels requiring fluency in a foreign language must therefore provide on-site training for their employees. This has not yet become a major problem, since over 85 percent of the island's visitors are English speakers, but it could become an important consideration as the island continues to diversify its tourism.[4]

Women at Work

Jamaica has been described as a matriarchal society due to its many female-headed households and the active role that Jamaican women play in society. For decades, Jamaican women have worked outside of the home, sometimes out of necessity but also because of a desire for an independent income. In recent years, they have channeled their energies into more than simply acquiring jobs; they are developing the requisite qualifications that will equip them for top positions in organizations. Today, Jamaican women are graduating from high schools, colleges, and universities in greater numbers and with better qualifications than their male counterparts. For example, 1998 statistics indicate that 72 percent of graduates from the University of the West Indies, the island's major university, were female. This provides a large pool of highly qualified women from which the hotel industry can draw.

The increase of women in the work force, however, has implications for the structure of work and work relations. Men and women have worked side by side for decades. Now, for the first time, women may dominate the supervisory and managerial levels. This may become a source of conflict, particularly in those departments that traditionally employ a large number of men. The industry must ensure that both women and men are exposed to the issues surrounding their new roles and that, when necessary, training and counseling take place.

The hotel industry will also have to ensure that it does not lose qualified and experienced women because of an unwillingness to give them the top posts in the organization. Jamaican law has for many years given men and women equal rights; yet, while there are many women who manage departments in hotels, there have been only two female general managers of major hotels. Some women perceive a glass ceiling. As a result, they may leave the hotel, depriving it of a valuable resource.

The increase in the number of women at the supervisory and management levels also requires provision for their special needs. Many women believe, for example, that a promotion forces them to choose between their career and their family. This is particularly the case in the hotel industry, where working hours tend to be long and irregular. The challenge is for the hotel to devise flexible schedules that allow employees to successfully manage both aspects of their lives.

The Labor Pool

The most recent labor statistics indicate a rate of 16 percent unemployment, with four percent being chronically unemployed (that is, unemployed for more than a year). With new strategies such as re-engineering and restructuring, which often reduce a company's labor force, more workers may be laid off in the near future. Unemployment is particularly high in the rural areas close to hotels because of a decline in traditional agricultural pursuits. This provides the hotel industry with a large pool of employees from which to draw; recruitment efforts are likely to be very successful, increasing the likelihood of finding qualified personnel. The high unemployment level also means that, once employed, personnel are unlikely to leave a job unless they have a secure job offer. They may also fear being terminated and are therefore likely to be highly committed to their jobs and responsive to training and development efforts.

The major danger to tourism from this high unemployment level is a large group of unemployed people who see the tourist as their only source of income. Tourist harassment is an issue that the government and hotels must confront. Within hotels, human resource departments often become involved in this effort through educational programs that stress the hazards of tourist harassment. Most recently, these efforts have been extended to the schools by a government program called "Infusion Tourism," which is intended to develop positive values and attitudes toward tourism and to alert young minds to the importance of the industry to the country. Some hotels also co-opt the wider community by involving some community members in hotel activities. For example, a seller of straw hats or baskets may conduct a basket-weaving class for guests at the hotel for which she is paid and gains exposure and, hopefully, sales.

The labor market in Jamaica poses both an opportunity and a challenge for hoteliers. The industry has an adequate supply of employable and qualified labor, and this increases the likelihood of attracting suitable employees. At the same time, the industry must be aware of the shortfalls of the educational system and create opportunities for these to be overcome on the job. The Jamaican hotel industry is highly proactive in its efforts to ensure that candidates for the job are qualified. However, these efforts are carried out against the backdrop of a very dynamic legal and political environment.

The Legal and Political Environment

Labor Laws

Jamaica is currently dominated by two major political parties that have strong roots in trade unionism. Perhaps as a result of this close relationship, many of Jamaica's labor laws may appear to be more lenient than labor laws in other countries, such as the United States. While some of these provisions may increase the cost of labor, they are also beneficial because they give the worker a greater sense of job security and provide legal recourse for both employee and employer.

Jamaica has a minimum wage under the Minimum Wage Order of 1975. It has limited impact on hotels, however, as most hotels pay significantly above this rate. Hours of work are subject to negotiation, but traditionally there is a 40-hour work week, with time-and-a-half for overtime work and work on public holidays. Other major laws include the Holidays with Pay Law, which entitles all employees to a minimum of two weeks of sick leave with pay. The Maternity Leave Act of 1979 entitles pregnant women to 12 weeks' leave with pay after one year of continuous employment.

Unionism is strong in Jamaica. Under the Labour Relations and Industrial Disputes Act of 1975, workers are provided with a number of important rights, including compulsory reinstatement of wrongfully dismissed workers, compulsory poll taking and recognition of trade unions, and protection against discrimination for trade union membership. The same law also includes the Labour Relations Code, which sets out the responsibilities of employers, workers, and trade unions. Workers are given the right to belong to a union and take industrial action, but all parties are expected to have due regard for the national interest. For example, if the main association of taxi drivers decided to go on strike during the height of the winter (tourist) season, it would make it very hard for tourists to move around—which would be against Jamaica's national interest, since tourism is a major industry.

Other significant parts of the code include guidelines for the settlement of disputes and the procedures for disciplinary measures. These many laws have the effect of reducing the level of conflict over basic issues.

Industrial Relations

Conflict will not disappear, of course, and there have been strikes, "go-slows," sit-ins, and sick-outs that have had a serious impact on the very sensitive tourist industry, particularly within the hotel sector. Hotels have used three basic approaches to dealing with such situations:

- Trying to prevent the formation of a union

- Responding paternalistically

- Collaborating with the union

Trying to prevent the union from coming into the hotel may be beneficial for only a short time, since Jamaican labor laws allow workers the right to form unions and allow unions the right to poll workers. The strategy may therefore backfire and create intense conflict. Operations with a **paternalistic view** attempt to reduce the perceived need for unions by paying generously and providing good benefits and incentives. This approach has been successful for a time, but in most cases, workers eventually want the perceived security that a union will provide.

A third approach is for managers to accept the reality of unions and to work collaboratively with them to achieve mutual gains. This approach is relatively new to Jamaica and is not widespread in the hotel sector. It has been used with great success in the manufacturing and agricultural sectors, however, and it is only a matter of time before it is adopted by hotels. Hotels, in fact, have more to lose from industrial unrest or worker dissatisfaction because the effects are immediately transmitted to guests. Therefore, many hotels try to develop incentives and benefits that meet workers' needs and keep them happy.

Cultural Distinctions and Societal Work Values

Good salary and benefits provide only one source of motivation. Jamaican workers have multiple needs, and there are some unique characteristics that managers need to take into account if they are to create a motivated and committed work force.

One of the primary factors affecting motivation in the Jamaican work force is the relationship between management and workers. The country's institutions and management styles have been greatly influenced by the plantation structure in which European owners, local or localized overseers, and African slaves maintained a tense working relationship.[5] In this structure, the primary means of motivation was coercion, while leadership was authoritarian and communication was top-down. Unwittingly, many hotels replicate this structure by having an expatriate management team that may not be familiar with the customs and value systems of the workers they supervise. The use of local middle management to bridge the gap may not always be successful, as these managers may face the same distrust that is shown to their managers. Hotels in this situation have to make attempts to bridge the gap by understanding Jamaican culture and building upon it rather than trying to replace it with something else or ignoring it. Human resource managers may play a very important role in alerting expatriate managers to sensitive issues and providing opportunities for dialogue.

It is important that managers remove the layers of distrust because recent data collected from the work force suggest that Jamaican workers really enjoy working in tourism. In a nationwide survey conducted between 1977 and 1988, Ken Carter determined that 91 percent of tourism workers felt they were doing something worthwhile, and 90 percent found the job fulfilling.[6] Despite their positive feelings, however, 48 percent of them admitted they were not putting out their best efforts, indicating a vast amount of untapped potential and lost productivity. Carter's study found that most tourism workers believed that management did not care about them or consider them as equals. They also felt left out of important decisions and that they were not given an adequate share of the profits. Addressing these issues may be very useful, as 54 percent of those surveyed stated that they were willing to do more but felt they were prevented by bad conditions at the hotel. There is therefore both the need for human resource managers to address the needs of workers and a great opportunity if they do so. Human resource managers may take heart from the fact that these areas of dissatisfaction were substantially lower than those of employees in non-tourism jobs.

Human resource managers may also be heartened by the fact that, according to Carter's study, most tourism workers do not resent serving people of other nationalities and races. This may be because of Jamaica's plantation past, which has provided it with a great mixture of races, nationalities, and religions. Today, Jamaica's motto—"Out of many, one people"—reflects the harmony in which these different groups work. Managers from different cultures often encounter wide acceptance. The challenge to human resource managers is not so much to build an appreciation of others, but rather to explain some of the cultural differences and their implications.

Jamaica's success in tourism to date is therefore partially reflective of a government and people dedicated to tourism, as well as certain natural conditions that make Jamaicans very accepting and hospitable to others. Human resource managers must, however, ensure that they do a good job of selecting those employees who have shown the commitment and ability to work in tourism. The next section examines these critical issues.

Recruitment and Selection

As the previous section indicated, tourism is a desirable occupation and recruiting willing employees is not usually difficult. In fact, managers often have had the opposite problem and have discovered the importance of targeting their recruitment very narrowly to avoid receiving too many applications.

One recent strategy, adopted primarily by all-inclusive hotels, is to target those employees who see themselves as having a career with the hotel, rather than just a job. Associated with this trend is the move toward recruiting employees who have superior educational qualifications or who wish to receive further training in the industry. Hotels are mindful of the fact that they need more qualified employees in order to meet the requirements of the more demanding and diverse tourist population. At the same time, hotels recognize that they must provide more avenues for the growth and development of these employees. The result is a strategy that attracts the right type of employee while it helps to keep employees loyal and committed to the organization.

There are, however, three disadvantages related to promising employees a career within the hotel rather than just a job:

- Employees who are promised a career may expect regular promotions and may become dissatisfied if the hotel does not promote them as quickly as they expected.

- Long-term employees may become stuck in a particular routine and way of doing things even if they are promoted regularly. This may reduce their ability to be creative and to take risks—two factors that are important in providing effective personalized service.

- The cost may be prohibitive and may never be recouped. Hotels may spend heavily on providing an employee with local and foreign training; this may be more expensive than selecting an employee who has received training before coming to the hotel. The employee may also leave before the hotel has recouped its investment.

Human resource managers must therefore carefully weigh the advantages and disadvantages of this approach based on their unique requirements.

Recruitment Sources

Human resource managers may recruit directly from vocational and secondary schools. The premier vocational school in Jamaica is a government-sponsored academy that provides training in food and beverage service, front office operations, maintenance, and housekeeping. The goal is to prepare trainees for entry-level positions in hotels, yet many trainees have quickly moved up the ladder to the supervisory and management levels. In addition, many secondary schools train students in the culinary arts and in housekeeping, and these students are also suitable for entry-level positions. Finally, the University of the West Indies and the University of Technology both offer degrees in catering, hotel management, and tourism; graduates are usually suitable for junior management, supervisory positions, or management trainee positions. In all cases, organizations may host students for an internship period varying from two weeks to three months. In this period, they may determine the suitability of the applicant for future full-time employment.

Selection Methods

Selection is usually done by the hiring department and the human resource department. Human resources will typically conduct the initial screening and general tests for literacy and mathematical aptitude. The department will also try to determine technical suitability. Some hotels also involve the general manager, who attempts to determine whether or not the employee is a good fit with the culture of the hotel. This multiple screening ensures that only the best candidates get through and reduces the possibility of personal bias from any single individual. It also sends a signal to the candidate that the hotel takes the exercise very seriously.

A weakness of the selection system is the over-reliance on interviews. While they are highly suitable for assessing a candidate's ability to communicate effectively, they often fail to measure other important aspects, such as the abilities to work autonomously and to make good decisions. One of the problems that human resource managers face in this regard is the shortage of personality tests designed specifically for the Caribbean. They must therefore either use tests that may have a built-in cultural bias or substitute some other, more-subjective measures of personality.

Mistakes in selection may be costly for the organization. Once a mistake is recognized, there are two choices: terminate the employee (ideally, before the end of the probationary period) or train the employee. Termination is usually a last resort, and most organizations opt to work with the employee to correct any problems. Training is therefore an integral part of the hospitality industry and is used as a remedial tool as well as a developmental one.

Training and Development Practices

Successive Jamaican governments have placed a lot of emphasis and money on the training of tourism workers and the sensitization of members of surrounding communities to the requirements of tourism. For example, the **Tourism Product**

Development Company conducts various types of training at minimal costs to tourist organizations and hotels, and the Runaway Bay Hotel Academy trains entry-level workers.

All-inclusive hotels lead the way in terms of expenditure on training and depth of training. The Sandals chain, for example, has multiple links with training and educational organizations throughout the world, and employees of their hotels may take courses in what they call the "Sandals University." SuperClubs, the other major all-inclusive chain, has launched a similar thrust. The intent of these hotels is simply to develop the skills of their employees to the highest possible standard. Training is particularly critical for all-inclusives because their guests are likely to have much more contact with hotel staff and to use the hotel facilities more extensively, since all of their needs are met within the confines of the hotel. Quality and quantity of service are therefore important issues for these hotels.

Other hotels may not have the resources of all-inclusives but do form linkages with local and foreign training agencies to ensure that their staff are well-trained. The British-based Hotel and Catering Board has, for example, been associated with the Jamaica Tourist Board for many years and has offered training in various hotels and tourist agencies.

Tourism entities may also seek to influence the training conducted by vocational and training institutions. They may do this by providing direct financial support for specific projects. More often, they work closely with such institutions and provide information about their own needs. In some instances, managers may spend some time teaching in the classroom or providing guidance for students. In these ways, they maintain the dynamism necessary for these institutions to be relevant and useful providers for the industry.

Despite the many training institutions, there are shortages of certain types of employees—particularly, qualified and experienced chefs. One strategy has been to send local chefs overseas for training. Another has been to recruit chefs from abroad and have them work alongside local chefs to provide on-the-job training. The latter is much more cost-effective, and many major hotels have at least one chef from overseas.

Training is an important aspect of the human resource manager's job as it involves conducting training in-house as well as coordinating with other agencies to provide training outside of the organization. Fortunately, the Jamaican government is fully committed to training within the tourism sector and provides significant financial and technical support.

Performance Measures and Evaluation

While training may provide employees with the necessary skills, it does not ensure that they will effectively use these skills and provide good service. Most hotels therefore rely heavily on performance evaluation measures to assess performance.

Guest Feedback

Most employees can get immediate feedback from guests if they are observant and display empathy. Ideally, most performance evaluation and correction will take place at this person-to-person level. This is in fact the thrust of much of the customer service training to which hotel employees are exposed. Most hotels also use guest satisfaction surveys to elicit specific feedback on the performance of individual departments and services. Information from these surveys is compiled on a weekly basis and fed back to department heads and supervisors to use in one of several ways.

Good performance usually leads to praise and recognition of particular employees or departments, while poor performance is used as an indication of where further training is required. The Jamaica Tourist Board also conducts regular visitor-satisfaction surveys that provide general data about how visitors to the island perceive the general standards of service and areas needing improvement. Finally, the tour agencies also conduct their own satisfaction surveys and keep hotels advised of how well they are rated.

All of these types of surveys form part of a wider goal-setting program in which individual departments attempt to attain and maintain a particular satisfaction and quality level. This system provides employees with specific and challenging goals, quick feedback, and an atmosphere of competition and interest. Its success is evident from a Carter survey in which 90 percent of tourism employees stated that they had a clear understanding of what their job was and the quality of performance that was expected of them. Sixty-four percent felt that they were kept advised of their performance levels as well as their strengths and weaknesses.[7]

Employee Recognition

Many human resource departments also use surveys and guest comment cards as part of an employee recognition scheme in which excellent employees are recognized both publicly and privately—by having their pictures prominently posted and by being given an award and a letter of appreciation. Once again, many all-inclusives are foremost in this arena by providing employees with very attractive prizes and incentives for good performance; recently, for example, one of the chains awarded the employee-of-the-year the keys to a house. Cars and trips to other hotels are also frequent prizes.

The Place of the Human Resource Department

The human resource strategies previously discussed all suggest an important role for the human resource department. The department in many situations is an active part of the strategic management team, and its implementation of the strategic decisions will have an important effect on the hotel's profitability and quality of service. Despite the important contribution that this department may make, some hotels do not operate with the services of such a department.

Small hotels are often so limited in resources that they cannot afford a separate human resource department. In this case, the manager and supervisors must do all the recruitment, selection, training, and disciplining of employees. This may be an advantage. In a small hotel, employees and management are in constant interaction, and managers are close enough to the job to know exactly what they are looking for in a potential employee. In rural areas, the hotel manager is also likely to know the applicant or know someone else who does. Recruitment may therefore be as informal as sending a message to someone to come in for an interview. The small size also makes it relatively easy for the manager to assess performance and conduct impromptu training sessions. However, managers and supervisors may lack training skills and other important skills. In this case, small hotels may benefit from the relatively low-cost training offered by government agencies.

At the other end of the hotel spectrum, at least one major hotel chain has decided not to use human resource managers, making managers responsible for overseeing the human resources needs within their own departments. The corporate office assists in recruiting, but department heads must do their own selection, job-specific training, disciplining, and termination. The intention is to make managers as accountable for human resource management as they are for such functions as revenue management and production.

While the intent is good, managers may find it difficult to effectively manage all of the human resource tasks in addition to their substantive posts. Moreover, managers in large hotels often cannot closely monitor the activities of all their employees and may be unable to provide the support that is available from a separate human resource department. Hotel management may obtain the desired result of making managers accountable for their employee-related procedures, such as hiring and disciplining; however, in the absence of effective training in the correct procedures, they may be presenting managers with a responsibility for which they are not equipped.

Conclusion

Human resource managers in Jamaican hotels must focus on creating motivated, committed, and professional employees within the hotel. They must also focus on creating a supportive community outside of the hotel. Human resource managers must therefore be proactive in diagnosing problems and developing quick but effective solutions. The industry is highly organized to do so and draws on a large network within and outside of the country. Substantial government support also helps the industry to achieve its goals of professional and friendly performance.

In this new millennium, however, there are many challenges to the traditional ways of providing service. The "new tourists" require service that is personalized rather than standardized, want to be active in creating the type of environment they desire, are more interested in exploring their destination, and, finally, may be more demanding of and less loyal to a particular product. Jamaican hotels and destinations are positioning themselves to meet the needs of these new tourists, but the industry is constantly evolving. All hotels must continuously review and, where necessary, make changes to their human resource strategies in order to meet guests' changing needs.

Endnotes

1. Jamaica Tourist Board, *Annual Travel Statistics* (1998).

2. Jamaica Tourist Board, *Annual Travel Statistics* (1998).

3. The concept of the "new tourist" is taken from Auliana Poon, *Tourism, Technology and Competitive Strategies* (Wallingford, England: CABI Publishing, 1993).

4. Jamaica Tourist Board, *Annual Travel Statistics* (1998).

5. Locksley Lindo, *Caribbean Organizations* (Mona, Jamaica: University Printery, 1995).

6. Kenneth Carter, *Why Workers Won't Work: The Worker in a Developing Economy: A case study of Jamaica* (London: Macmillan Caribbean, 1997).

7. Carter.

Key Terms

all-inclusive—A property at which all food, beverages, accommodation, laundry, and entertainment are included in one prepaid price.

"new tourist"—Consumers who are flexible, independent, and experienced travelers whose values and lifestyles are different from those of the mass tourists.

paternalistic view—An underlying management belief that employers have superior wisdom and know what is best for employees. Paternalistic employers may attempt to provide workers with benefits under the belief that employees receiving these benefits will be indebted to the employer and realize that unions are unnecessary.

"sun-lust" tourism—When tourists visit a destination primarily for the attractions of beach and climate, in contrast to tourists who come to experience a new destination.

Tourism Product Development Company—An agency established by the Jamaican government under the Ministry of Tourism for the development of standards and the improvement of the tourist product. It offers training and assistance to hotels at substantially reduced rates.

Discussion Questions

1. What worldwide trends have determined the shift in the human resource requirements of Jamaican hotels?

2. Based on your reading of the chapter, what are the important personal characteristics and skills that Jamaican hoteliers seek in their line staff?

3. What are the advantages of having a government agency heavily involved in hotel training? What drawbacks, if any, do you see to this?

4. What are the major differences between the human resource requirements of all-inclusive hotels, standard properties, and small hotels?

5. What are the strengths and weaknesses of the Jamaican labor force, and what are the implications for human resource management?

6. Identify three advantages and three disadvantages of hotels promising a career rather than a job. How does this fit in with the current world trends of contract employment?

7. The chapter suggests that the international hotel chain may replicate plantation-style relationships. How would you prepare an expatriate general manager to deal with some of the issues that would arise out of this, and what advice would you give to him or her about how to motivate and interact with local staff?

Internet Sites

For more information, visit the following Internet sites. Remember that Internet addresses can change without notice.

Embassy of Jamaica
(Washington, D.C.)
http://www.caribbean-online.com/
jamaica/embassy/washdc/

Jamaica—General Information
http://luna.cas.usf.edu/~alaing/
jamaica.html#CONTENTS

Jamaica Tourist Board
http://www.jamaicatravel.com

Sandals Resorts
http://www.sandals.com

Statistical Institute of Jamaica
http://www.statinja.com/

SuperClubs Resorts
http://www.superclubs.com

Case Study

Conflict with the Concierges

At the Montego Bay White Sand Resort, an all-inclusive property on Jamaica's north coast, management has recently decided to increase the level of service that the resort offers its guests. This will require the concierge department to move beyond its traditional role of reconfirming airline tickets and making tour reservations. In fact, these functions will be turned over to other agencies. The new role of the concierge department will be to operate concierge suites that will cater to the needs of individual guests.

Currently there are four staff in the concierge department, but that number will increase to eight. At the regular weekly staff meeting, some members of the management team are discussing who should be hired to fill the new positions.

"I believe that the four current concierge staff members have served us well in the past," said General Manager Delroy Clarke. "But we simply cannot live in the past any longer. Our resort has to take a dramatic step forward, and I'm afraid that these staff will probably be stuck in the old mode. I don't think they will have the flexibility to meet the new requirements of their positions."

"Pardon me, but I disagree," Concierge Supervisor Marcia Jones interjected. "The only thing holding them back from their new roles is training. If we can provide training for all of them, I feel certain that they can all adapt. Don't forget: between them they have some 14 years of experience. They have extensive knowledge about the hotel, and they've made numerous valuable contacts at the various attractions on the island."

Norma Brown, the front office supervisor, spoke up. "Training is great," she said, "but I don't think all of the training in the world is going to give us the personal excitement we need in these positions. As you might remember, last week I argued for keeping the two best performers, moving the other two to other departments, and then advertising for the other six positions. Today, I'm not so sure about that. My concern is whether mixing new staff and old staff might dilute the enthusiasm of the new employees."

"So you're suggesting that we replace the entire team?" Clarke asked.

Brown sighed. "I'm just not sure. Frankly, I'm worried about the message we might be sending to hotel staff if we replace all four of them. I mean, traditionally, the hotel has promised employees a career. We have not terminated anyone except for serious disciplinary breaches."

"Junior," Clarke said, turning to the resort's operation manager, "what are your thoughts?"

"Honestly? I believe that if we truly want to move ahead and make major progress as a hotel, we cannot be locked into the traditions of the past. I understand what Marcia and Norma are saying—and, of course, I sympathize with those folks whose jobs may be affected—but I think it's time the White Sands Resort adjusted to the new economy and set personal feelings aside. We cannot afford to carry employees if they are not really needed."

Discussion Question

1. What steps might General Manager Delroy Clarke recommend taking in order to make the best decision regarding current and future staffing in the concierge department?

Chapter 8 Outline

Hospitality and Human Resources in
  Kenya
    Labor Market Issues
    The Legal and Political Environment
    Cultural Distinctions and Societal
      Work Values
Labor Relations
    Recruitment and Selection
    Training and Development
    Performance Evaluation
    Career Development Programs
    Industrial Relations
Contemporary Issues
    Expatriate Labor
    Equal Employment Opportunities
    Environmental Impact
    Corporate Culture

Competencies

1. Describe the labor environment in
    Kenya. (pp. 131–135)

2. Explain the human resources
    management process as it relates to
    Kenya hospitality operations.
    (pp. 135–139)

3. List the contemporary issues facing
    Kenyan hospitality. (pp. 139–141)

8

Human Resource Management in Kenya

Mwakai K. Sio

Mwakai K. Sio received a Bachelor of Science degree in hotel administration from Cornell University in 1974 and worked briefly with the Ministry of Tourism in Kenya before joining Kenya Utalii College as a lecturer. He now serves as Principal of Kenya Utalii College. In addition, he is a fellow of the Hotel, Catering, and Institutional Management Association, and a member of the American Hotel & Motel Association, the board of the Journal of Travel and Tourism, *and the advisory board of the International Training and Tourism Institute.*

KENYA IS LOCATED on the Indian Ocean coast of Africa. It is bordered by Ethiopia and Sudan to the north, Uganda to the west, Tanzania to the south, and Somalia to the east. The most outstanding features are the Great Rift Valley, Lake Victoria, and Mount Kenya. The country has a coastline with white, sandy beaches, rich in tropical marine life.

The country's marked climatic variations give it stunningly contrasting vegetation, ranging from tropical rain forests, grassy savannas, and alpine deciduous forests to rocky deserts. This diversity has provided conditions that are conducive to a wide range of economic activities. Most of the arable land is under agriculture, which, being the mainstay of the economy, occupies the overwhelming majority of the country's 32 million people. Large areas of the low grasslands where wildlife is in abundance have been preserved in their natural state as parks and game reserves.

Hospitality and Human Resources in Kenya

Tourism is an important component of the country's economy. Until 1997, when it was surpassed by agriculture, it was the leading foreign exchange earner. The main tourist activities range from recreation along the coast to wildlife safaris in the parks. Tourism organizations have developed in line with these activities, with holiday resorts along the coast and game **lodges** and tented camps in the parks. Other hotels are located in towns to cater to businesspeople and tourists. Nairobi, the capital city, is the aviation gateway to the country and the commercial center of the East African region; consequently, most hotel and tour companies have their headquarters and central reservation offices in the city. Mombasa is also host to many hospitality organizations by virtue of being the largest town on the coast, where the majority of Kenya's 232 star-rated hotels are situated.

Labor Market Issues

The hospitality industry directly employs about 150,000 people. A further 300,000 earn their living through tourism-related activities. Despite this seemingly large work force, there are imbalances in the area of labor supply.

Labor Supply Status. The primary labor market for Kenya's hospitality industry has a shortage of properly qualified personnel in the area of food and beverage.[1] The number so far trained in the country is less than the number needed, and the current crop of chefs and cooks is still very young and has yet to gain the requisite experience. This problem is aggravated by a lack of training and application facilities in most training schools. On the other hand, the primary labor market is temporarily over-supplied with waiters, receptionists, and housekeeping supervisors. The secondary labor market is under-supplied with maintenance staff conversant with maintenance of physical plants and equipment.

The above deficiencies are derived from the current education system which, due to economic constraints, is skewed in favor of social sciences at the expense of technical training. Enrollment in science and technical training at the post-secondary level stands at only 23–26 percent. This has resulted in high unemployment for graduates in social sciences and a shortage of technical workers in the secondary market.

The high unemployment level compromises performance standards and productivity. This is because some organizations opt to employ cheap, unskilled labor, which is in plentiful supply.

Labor Turnover. Currently, no national hospitality industry index exists regarding labor turnover. However, labor mobility is more pronounced in the lodges than in urban hotels, due to the lack of basic social amenities in the lodges' isolated surroundings. Those who accept jobs in the lodges remain in such employment only until they can acquire other jobs in urban hotels.

Generally, salary and wage differentials between one hotel and another are not sufficiently wide to warrant substantial labor turnover among senior and middle-level managers. There are, however, substantial differences in management styles practiced in individual hotels, which is a contributing factor to senior and middle-level managers' mobility. As for the junior staff, the need for better pay is the leading factor in turnover.

The Legal and Political Environment

The development of human resources principles and practices in Kenya cannot be divorced from the political evolution of Kenya as a nation. During the colonial era, government policy on labor issues was largely influenced by the demand for cheap labor for European settlements. The policy then was to force black Africans to seek employment in European-owned commercial enterprises by imposing taxes on every adult male black African. (The Resident Native Ordinance of 1902 required all adult male Africans to pay a poll tax and a hut tax for each residential building constructed.) This policy was reinforced by an entrenched system of racial discrimination that placed Africans at the bottom of the ladder in terms of wages and job responsibilities. The settlers further agitated for a freeze on wage increments to ensure that Africans did not become economically independent. It is not surprising, therefore, that labor issues played a very significant part in the clamor for independence in the 1950s.

When the country achieved full independence in 1964, the focus shifted from agitation for human rights to ensuring economic growth and improvement of employment conditions for all, especially the hitherto underprivileged black Africans. In order to ensure fair working conditions for all and to remove the vestiges of racial discrimination in the conditions of employment, the Conditions of Employment and Regulation of Wages Act was passed. This act addresses the plight of unskilled and semi-skilled workers, who also happen to be the most disadvantaged in terms of remuneration, and empowers the Minister of Labour to issue minimum wage guidelines for the lowly paid cadre of employees, such as waiters, stewards, messengers, and gardeners. It also stipulates the working hours for all employees. These conditions are based on the International Labour Organisation's conventions.

After independence, the Kenya government found it necessary to redress the existing racial disparities in the job market. Its stated policy—called **Kenyanization of employment**—was to enable qualified Kenyans to take over jobs held by expatriates. It was effected by strengthening the Immigration Act to ensure rapid upward mobility of African workers to positions of management. The law limits the availability and duration of work permits for expatriate workers and also requires expatriate managers to train Kenyan understudies to take over the positions of departing expatriates. The law further denies work permits to foreigners in areas where qualified Kenyans are available.

Recent liberalization of the political and economic spheres of the country has rendered protectionist policies in the labor market unrealistic. The emphasis has shifted from Kenyanization of jobs and the improvement of the lot of employees to attraction of foreign investment. This policy has necessitated a relaxation of restrictions on expatriate labor to accommodate the insistence by foreign investors to place their own people in key areas of their organizations (especially in senior management positions) to protect their investments. The changing management styles, fueled by the increasing use of computers and information technology, have led to more efficient work practices at the expense of job creation.

Cultural Distinctions and Societal Work Values

The population of Kenya is composed mainly of Africans but includes a small percentage of Asians and Europeans. There are about 42 ethnic groups who are dominant in specific regions of the country. For example, the Somali are found in the northeastern part of the country, the Luhya in the western region, and the Mijikenda in the coastal areas. The urban areas are multi-ethnic.

Due to Kenya's rapid population growth, a lot of strain is put on its economic resources. Consequently, only a small proportion of the population enjoys access to education, adequate health care, and the economic prosperity needed to make choices in their lives. In fact, about 47 percent of the population lives below the poverty line. This has had the adverse effect of creating ethnic tensions with regard to the allocation of national resources and the creation of job opportunities.

Language. Most Kenyans speak at least two languages: their ethnic tongue and Swahili. Swahili is the national language, the common tongue spoken daily in social settings and at mass gatherings. However, by virtue of Kenya having been a British colony, English is the country's official language, used for transacting business and in government.

Chances are that any person a visitor may meet will be able to communicate in English. Although Kenyans have learned the British variety of English in a classroom setting, oral communication in the language is affected by the ethnic backgrounds of the speakers; one would easily notice the different accents from the various regions in Kenya.

Religion. Kenya does not have an official state religion, but about 80 percent of the population professes the Christian faith. Some of the largest Christian groups in Kenya are the Roman Catholics, Anglicans, Methodists, and Baptists. In addition, Muslims, Sikhs, Hindus, and Jews also have a substantial presence in Kenya.

As in many countries, religion is a personal matter. Employers do not insist on knowing one's religious beliefs. The country's constitution provides for freedom of worship, and employers often provide time off to observe religious holidays.

Attitudes. The culture of most Kenyans has generally emphasized interdependence, especially among family members, clan, or community. One belongs to a group and is bound by the expectations of that particular group.

In group activities, one is supposed to consult and build consensus before reaching a decision. Elders are respected in all communities. Younger people who have made achievements in various fields can be accepted as elders despite their age. Such achievements may be in education or business, which provide them with influential positions in their communities.

Kenyans are taught to value courtesy and generosity, respect for others, and obedience to the elders and those in authority. These traits occur naturally in Africans because of the traditional filial bonds that exist in African culture due to the extended family system. The bonds emphasize each person's responsibility in the community. The traits manifest themselves at the place of work through respect for authority, deference to age irrespective of rank, and a spirit of togetherness among the workers.

Personal Appearance and Time. The traditional dress is disappearing with the influence of urbanization and world fashion trends. Most people dress casually in informal settings and in suits or jackets when undertaking some business. In resort hotels and game lodges, which tend to be sited within culturally conservative surroundings, employees in guest contact areas are encouraged by their employers to don traditional attire. This imparts awareness of the local communities' cultures on the guest.

In social settings, Kenyans tend to provide time for the host to be ready before they arrive. This has given the impression that they are too casual about time.

Labor Relations

Recruitment and Selection

In Kenya's hospitality industry, the application of the traditional methods of recruitment depends on the category of staff being recruited. On average, most of the star-rated hotels and other hospitality sectors recruit their senior management—general managers, resident managers, and line managers—through job bureaus, executive search agencies, and advertisements in newspapers. Middle-level managers such as assistant managers, housekeepers, and chefs are recruited through placement offices from colleges, particularly Kenya Utalii College; others, particularly cooks, are poached from other organizations. Lower management and junior levels of staff are recruited internally and from colleges. A combination of recruitment methods is used in the case of **casual employees,** or temporary workers, ranging from recruiting from local communities to referrals from local chiefs and other employees. This practice is common at coastal hotels and game lodges, where the hospitality establishments have cultivated interactions with the homogeneous local communities.

Different selection methods are used to identify the most suitable candidates. The two criteria commonly used in Kenya are qualifications and experience for the job. Both the personnel manager and the relevant departmental manager in most cases do the short listing of the candidates. The most commonly used selection methods are oral interviews and practical and written tests.

Training and Development

Training became a major concern in the early 1960s immediately after Kenya's independence. The government realized that one of the areas crucial to the rapid acceleration of economic development was the exploitation of the tourism potential afforded by the country's beautiful flora, fauna, and beaches. There was already an advanced hotel network in place. So the government began developing human resources for the hospitality industry with the realization that providing quality service and internationally acknowledged tourism products was important for the growth of the industry.

The initial emphasis was on the training of professional personnel to take over key managerial positions in the industry through the policy of Kenyanization of employment. The initial cadre was provided by a hotel training school established at Kenya Polytechnic in 1969. In time, it was realized that, for the training to have the desired effect, it was important to extend the same to the lower cadre. It was for this reason that a larger and better-equipped training institution, Kenya Utalii College, was established in 1975. The college took over the training of managers from Kenya Polytechnic and extended the training in hospitality services to the lower cadre—namely waiters, cooks, receptionists, travel agents, and, later, tour guides. A training tax on hotel services was established in 1971 to finance training for the industry.

The training provided at Kenya Utalii College has had a marked impact on the quality of service provided in the hospitality industry, which compares favorably with international standards. In addition, the number of trained personnel has substantially increased over the years, although it is still a small fraction of what the industry needs.

Efforts have been made to close the training gap through in-service courses and management development programs. The impact of these courses is encouraging. Establishment of private colleges has provided the industry with an additional source of trained personnel. The quality of these colleges' products, however, appears to be compromised by inadequate personnel and training facilities. In order to harmonize the quality of training, there is the need to standardize the curricula of the various hospitality programs offered by private and public colleges in Kenya. It may also be necessary to create a licensing body to monitor the establishment and subsequent operation of these colleges.

The Kenyan hospitality industry has developed to the extent where top managerial jobs require a higher level of training than that offered at local colleges and universities. Training has focused mainly on operational areas of the industry, and this has limited the rise of locally trained personnel to the level of general managers. There is a need, therefore, for executive-level training.

Performance Evaluation

Most organizations recognize the importance of performance evaluation and carry out appraisal activities once or twice in the year.

The emphasis on performance evaluation is different depending on the category of staff being evaluated. For senior staff, the emphasis is on results and the evaluator is interested in the extent to which the objectives of the organization have been met. As for junior staff, the focus is on employees' behavior and their way of working.

Most organizations have developed elaborate forms, detailing the criteria mentioned above. Budgets and reports are very useful for evaluating senior managers. For junior staff, observations by the supervisors constitute the main evaluating method. Guest comment cards perhaps provide the most objective means of evaluating staff performance. Exhibit 1 illustrates some of the criteria used for evaluating staff at the subordinate, supervisory, and managerial levels.

Most organizations plan for appraisals and prepare staff for them. The average notice given to the employee is 14 days. In carrying out the exercise, organizations use job descriptions and appraisal forms. In order to make the appraisal more objective and meaningful, most organizations conduct training on appraisal systems for managers and supervisors.

Exhibit 1   Evaluating Staff Performance

Staff Categories	Evaluation Criteria
Subordinate Staff	Attendance, timekeeping, appearance/personal hygiene, courtesy, product knowledge, and health and safety awareness
Supervisory Staff	Demonstration of product knowledge, health and safety awareness, and leadership skills
Managerial Staff	Ability to set procedures and standards, ability to plan and organize, demonstration of skills related to team building, communication, motivation, appraisals, etc.

Career Development Programs

The approaches to implementing effective career development programs vary among organizations depending mainly on their size. The units within chain hotels, by far, have more clearly thought-out programs than the independent units. This is also true of larger tour companies, since they tend to have well-established human resources systems applied throughout the entire chain.

An examination of the career programs of most hospitality operations will indicate that they primarily address the need for increased skills—mainly in operational areas—and the need for effective management. Few organizations seem to emphasize career development.

There are a number of possible explanations for this seeming lack of emphasis on career development. For one, the human resources function in the hospitality industry in Kenya is lowly placed in the organizational hierarchy. Consequently, the industry emphasizes only one aspect that influences the need for career development, which is organizational effectiveness. The other three aspects to consider—that is, organizational adaptation and improvement, organizational culture and climate, and human resources planning—are generally overlooked. Even organizational effectiveness is not given its due consideration, as most organizations do not emphasize the factors influencing it. Such factors include a clear understanding of available managerial paths that can affect job satisfaction, management turnover, and loyalty to the organization.

The industry does not seem, in general, to be proactive in developing effective career programs. It is forced to institute these as a reactive measure in response to customer demands or events from competitors. For example many organizations were forced to abide by food safety standards only after they were pressured by European tour operators.

The most successful hospitality organizations in the country have invested substantially in developing their staff at all levels. The results can clearly be seen from the quality of service they offer and the customer satisfaction that results from these efforts.

Many organizations use on-the-job training methods such as coaching and job rotation and transfers. However, there seems to be little use of understudy assignments and mentoring. Off-the-job training methods are applied, but mainly in the form of seminars and lectures. There is quite a potential in this area, especially for the supervisory and management staff. Hospitality organizations can also benefit from the increasingly popular outdoor-based training programs that utilize experiential learning.

Industrial Relations

Kenya has fully adopted the International Labour Organisation's conventions in all spheres of labor management. In particular, the right to organize and bargain collectively by forming trade unions is enshrined in the country's constitution. Victimization of trade union officials for their trade union activities, whether by the state or their employers, is specifically prohibited by law. The bulk of the unionized staff is composed of the lower cadre of employees, which accounts for approximately 90 percent of the total number of employees in the industry.

The law encourages resolution of disputes by negotiation rather than litigation, strikes, or lockouts. The underlying philosophy is to encourage harmonious industrial relations, with emphasis on the avoidance of antagonism between organizations and their staff. To this end, the Industrial Relations Charter was formulated in 1962 to provide a procedure for solving disputes, with the sole aim of providing a harmonious relationship between labor and capital in the interests of rapid economic progress of the soon-to-be independent nation.[2] Further, the Trade Disputes Act requires that the settlement of every trade dispute be negotiated through the parties' own free process.

These negotiations usually start at the organization's premises. The Kenya Union of Domestic, Hotels, Educational Institutions, Hospitals, and Allied Workers, the union for personnel in the hospitality industry, is represented in these negotiations by a shop steward. The shop steward is an employee of the same organization, and his knowledge of the organizational set-up and problems makes amicable settlement of the disputes involving that organization relatively easy to achieve. In the event of no agreement being reached, the minister responsible for labor instructs the parties to report a dispute to the Industrial Court. The court's decision is final and binding on both parties.

The Kenya hospitality industry's over-reliance on foreign tourists, who account for about 80 percent of the market, makes it very sensitive to any industrial instability. It is in consideration of this that both the government and hotel operators readily encourage peaceful resolution of trade disputes. The Kenya Hotel Keepers and Caterers Association and the Kenya Union of Domestic, Hotels, Educational Institutions, Hospitals, and Allied Workers have very cordial relations.

This harmony is reflected in the manner in which the two parties handled the employment crises caused by the tourism industry slump that hit the country in 1997 and 1998. In 1997, ethnic tensions at the coast developed into public disturbances that were given wide and sometimes negative coverage in the European press. As a result, European tourists were discouraged by the media reports from traveling to Kenya. This resulted in mass cancellations of hotel bookings by both foreign and local tourists. Business fell so low that some hotels had to close down, resulting in numerous layoffs. The industry had never before faced such a situation. The union and the association devised methods for dealing with the problem without crippling the hotels financially, while at the same time minding the employees' welfare.

In the end, employees made proposals that included voluntary salary cuts, forfeiture of a month's salary, and alternate voluntary unpaid leave for all members of staff, including the management cadre. This kind of arrangement was unprecedented in industrial relations in Kenya. It was a bitter pill to swallow, but the only other alternative for the employees was to join the ever-increasing ranks of the unemployed. These proposals were implemented and industrial stability was maintained for the duration of the crisis.

Contemporary Issues

While the hospitality and tourism industries in Kenya are currently facing a number of important economic and social challenges, four issues should be of particular concern to human resources professionals.

Expatriate Labor

Expatriate labor forms a very significant part of the work force at the management level. This is due to the fact that a large proportion of the hospitality industry in Kenya is foreign-owned. Hotels employ expatriates as chefs and senior/executive management. Tour firms employ expatriates in positions such as finance managers, operations managers, and chief executives.

A survey conducted by Kenya Utalii College found that most Kenyans resent the employment of expatriates and see it as a way of denying them employment opportunities. They cite the fact that the country has a large pool of highly trained and qualified managerial staff to manage the local hospitality industry besides exporting labor to other countries. The proponents of employment of expatriate labor argue that the expatriates possess certain skills that are not available locally, and that they form a necessary bridge for foreign investment.

The issue of expatriate labor is likely to be debated until policy and actual practice are more closely aligned. In the meantime, the major hurdle the expatriate manager must overcome is cultural; he or she must be careful to respect the social practices and religions of the local community.

Equal Employment Opportunities

Although the Kenya constitution outlaws discriminatory practices in all spheres, including employment, there are no affirmative laws on equal employment opportunity. The issues of gender equality and concern for the handicapped have, of late, drawn great attention.

In Kenya, women are not sufficiently represented in managerial positions of the hospitality industry. In traditional African culture, the woman's place is seen as being in the home. For this reason, women prefer to work in jobs that are less strenuous and are performed during normal working hours. This has led to many women being predominantly in positions such as personnel management, guest relations, marketing, and reservations.

The employment of the physically impaired seems to be limited to back-of-the-house areas requiring minimal or no guest contact. At present, there is an association for the physically impaired that strives to address issues affecting its members; however, the movement has not made significant strides.

Environmental Impact

The last decade of the twentieth century witnessed a rapid change in the terrain within which the tourism industry in Kenya operates. The political and socioeconomic changes within and without the country greatly affected the stability of the tourism industry. This changing terrain has affected human resource practices, with organizations aligning their strategies to ensure their survival.

The Kenyan hospitality industry is largely dependent on foreign tourism, and any disturbance in the environment has a major impact on the state of the industry. This was evidenced when hotels experienced sudden cancellations during the disturbances along the Kenyan coast in 1997. Although the situation is normalizing today, the opening up of alternative destinations in the southern African region has slowed the recovery rate.

Economic liberalization has resulted in increased investment in the tourism sector, which has, in turn, increased competition. This has forced organizations to increase efficiency through technological applications in their operations, thereby reducing reliance on human personnel. Organizations have been forced by a combination of technological developments and the poor state of the industry to retrench staff. The country has, as a result, suddenly found itself faced with surplus labor. As temporary as this may be, it has resulted in some people seeking employment in other sectors of the economy or, for those who want to remain in the hospitality industry, employment in other parts of the world, especially in the southern African region.

Corporate Culture

The industry's corporate culture stems from its history and traditions. The industry was developed mainly to serve tourists who came for hunting safaris and the wealthy settler community. Most hospitality establishments were foreign-owned. An official government policy of racial discrimination in all spheres of the economy meant that black Africans could only be employed as menial workers in back-of-the-house areas. Even those black Africans who came in to replace departing white workers on the eve of independence were former domestic employees of the departing foreigners. Although a lot of changes have occurred since the early years of independence, many structures and attitudes have not fully disappeared.

It is apparent, therefore, that the traditional hierarchical structure is the norm within the industry. Most organizations are well structured, and the chain of command must be followed. Orders come from the top and the subordinates are expected to carry out instructions with little or no participation.

Employees are "on their own"—with supervisors having a sink-or-swim attitude toward subordinates. This situation, coupled with little emphasis on training and low or nonexistent training budgets, leaves employees cautious and ill-equipped to take risks. In addition they have little flexibility in developing new systems.

In many cases, employees harbor the suspicion that rewards and punishment are erratic. There is a perceived lack of objective measurement of quantity and quality of work. Mistrust and competitiveness lead to highly politicized organizations.

A number of developments are changing the traditional corporate culture. First, the realization of the contribution of the individual—coupled with the need for enlightened leadership—is forcing organizations to focus on exploring the full potential of the individual worker by providing a facilitating environment. Second, there are highly educated persons at all levels who are challenging the status quo. In line with the changes in the national political arena, employees are demanding more democracy in the workplace. Organizations are also being exposed to these requirements by professional management organizations that are increasingly focusing on proper corporate governance. Third, competition—especially from foreign organizations—has exposed the weaknesses of relying on traditional ways of getting work done.

Organizations that are in the lead in this area are showing higher employee satisfaction and relative industrial peace. Even in the recent past, when the tourism industry has been experiencing low business, these organizations seem to have been faring better in business. This may suggest that their corporate culture has a role in their stability.

A continuing trend by organizations to move toward team-oriented, flexibly structured, participative, open, reward-oriented, and high-standards organizations is clearly discernible. This is due partly to the need to conform to contemporary practices and partly to meet the requirements of the environment. Toward this end, Kenyan operations, in addition to traditional friendliness, are increasingly exhibiting values such as quality consciousness and concern for the local communities, the environment, and professional management.

Endnotes

1. Human resources management practices survey, conducted by Kenya Utalii College, Business Administration Department, 1999.

2. Saeed R. Cockar, *The Kenya Industrial Court* (Nairobi: Longman Kenya, no date), p. 4.

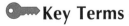 # Key Terms

casual employees—Persons employed on an hourly or daily basis.

Kenyanization of employment—The government policy requiring businesses to give priority to Kenyan citizens over expatriates when hiring.

lodges—Hotels situated in the wilderness.

Discussion Questions —————————————————————

1. How do Kenya's political and legal environments regarding the employment of expatriates compare to those of your country?

2. What limitations do you see in the career development programs that are in wide use in Kenyan hospitality operations?

3. What legal framework exists in Kenya to ensure equal employment opportunities?

4. How can the performance evaluation process be improved in Kenyan hospitality properties?

Internet Sites —————————————————————————

For more information, visit the following Internet sites. Remember that Internet addresses can change without notice.

Africa Online
http://www.africaonline.co.ke/

Coastweek Online
http://www.coastweek.com/

The Daily Nation
http://www.nationaudio.com/

Kenya Travel and Tourism Centre
http://www.thevillage.co.ke/Travel/index.html

Kenyaweb
http://www.kenyaweb.com/

KPMG Peat Marwick—Nairobi, Kenya
http://www.kpmg.co.ke/

Chapter 9 Outline

The Korean Hospitality Industry
    Structure of the Korean Hospitality
    Industry
Labor Demographics and Market Issues
    Working Conditions and
    Characteristics
    Supervisory and Management
    Positions
    Unionization
    Challenges to Overcome
Legal and Political Environment
    Workplace Legal Issues
    Wage Laws
    Political Environment
Cultural Distinctions and Societal Work
    Values
    Language Barrier
    Work Ethic
Labor Relations
    Recruitment and Selection
    Training and Development Practices
    Performance Evaluation Practices
    Career Development Programs
Confucian Ethics in Conflict with Modern
    Market Demands
    The Five Relationships
    Conflict with Modern Market
    Demands
Future of the Hospitality Industry in Korea

Competencies

1. Understand and discuss the history and development of the hospitality industry in Korea and identify the three major stages in its development: pre-liberalization of travel, post-Olympic expansion, and the financial crisis/IMF stage. (pp. 145–149)

2. Describe the forces at work in the Korean labor market and explain how they affect the hospitality industry. (pp. 150–155)

3. Describe the challenges facing human resource managers with respect to Westernization, globalization, and the changing political and economic climate in Korea. (pp. 155–159)

4. Identify recruitment, selection, training, development, and performance evaluation practices, including career development programs. (pp. 159–162)

5. Define the five Confucian relationships and explain their effect on human resource management in Korea. (pp. 162–166)

9

The Republic of Korea: Human Resource Management in a Confucian Society

Mark E. Patton

Mark E. Patton has been a Visiting Assistant Professor in the Tourism Management department at Keimyung University since 1996. He holds a B.A. and M.B.A. from Michigan State University and is currently enrolled in the Ph.D. program in Tourism at Hanyang University in Seoul. He is on the editorial boards of The Asian Journal of Business and Entrepreneurship, Tourism Research, *and the* Hotel Administration Research Journal, *all published in Korea. He has contributed articles to the* Hospitality Research Journal, The Cornell Hotel Restaurant and Administration Quarterly, The FIU Hospitality Review, *and the* Journal of Hospitality and Leisure Marketing. *His teaching and research specialties include service management, hospitality and service marketing, and intercultural interaction.*

THE REPUBLIC OF KOREA (often called South Korea, a descriptive but unofficial name, or simply Korea) occupies the southern portion of the Korean Peninsula, a landmass jutting south–southeast from Manchuria toward the Japanese archipelago. The total area of the peninsula is 221,607 square kilometers (roughly the same size as the United Kingdom), of which South Korea occupies 45 percent (slightly larger than Hungary or Portugal). Mountainous to the north and east, the peninsula slopes down to broad coastal plains in the south and west. To the south and west of the peninsula are some 3,000 small islands. Rocky and mountainous, the Korean peninsula boasts hot, humid summers and cold, often snowy winters.

Founded in 1948 following liberation from 50 years of Japanese colonial rule, the Republic of Korea was soon plunged into a devastating civil war against Communist factions that had seized power in the Soviet-administered northern portion of the peninsula. The war ended in an armistice in 1953, leaving the peninsula divided into two nations: the Republic in the south and the communist People's Republic in the north. The division was not quite equal, however, as the South held two-thirds of the original population but was left with less than half of the land and natural resources. Following the war, the Republic faced a daunting task: rebuilding the war-torn nation with few resources other than a relatively uneducated, poverty-stricken, and war-weary population.[1]

South Korea rose to the challenge, however, and in the short span of 50 years, has grown into one of the economic powerhouses of Asia. Before the financial crisis of 1997, Korea's annual GDP was reported as US$476.6 billion, with a per-capita GNI of US$10,307. The population of 46.9 million (1999) boasts one of the highest literacy rates in the world. Highly urbanized (78.5 percent of Koreans live in cities), the Korean people have transformed themselves from an agrarian society into a highly educated and industrialized one. South Korea excels in the manufacture of computer chips, consumer electronics, automobiles, and ships, having moved away from lower-margin consumer goods such as clothes and shoes. The rapid growth, however, has not been entirely without social cost.

Situated between two powerful and often adversarial neighbors, the Korean people have perhaps more than their share of xenophobia, or fear of anything that is strange or foreign. Throughout its history, Korea has been subject to invasion attempts (some successful, some not) and, as a result, the government—although nominally democratic since the founding of the Republic—still has a very strong streak of authoritarianism. The difficulties brought about by the partitioning of the peninsula and the distrust of the Communist North have resulted in often harsh measures taken against the populace by the government in order to maintain control of the nation. National elections are still often accompanied by student riots, and government crackdowns (such as the 1980 Kwangju incident, in which the army laid siege to the city and thousands of protesters were killed or disappeared) are still fresh in the minds of citizens. Recent changes in the world, however, have brought about gradual reform in Korea: the fall of Communism in Europe and the progressive liberalization of the Chinese economy have prompted the South Korean government to become more open with its policies. The recent Asian financial crisis, necessitating a multibillion-dollar bailout loan from the **International Monetary Fund (IMF)** has also forced the South Korean government to reevaluate its fiscal policies, and the government is disentangling itself gradually from direct involvement with the economy.

The Korean Hospitality Industry

Restrictions on travel have deep roots in Korean society. During the **Chosun** era (1392–1910), travel was something enjoyed by the upper classes only. Ordinary citizens were bound to the land by tradition and it was understood that, by custom, they never strayed far from home. Following the lead of their forebears, the authoritarian regimes of the early Republic put strict controls on international travel. Fearing a **brain drain** to the West, the government restricted foreign travel to students studying abroad, government officials, and business travelers. Overseas travel for tourism purposes was practically unheard of, and travelers had to lodge large sums of money with the government as a deposit against their eventual return to Korea.

As the economy began to prosper, however, and more and more people began to earn disposable income, the urge to travel for recreational purposes began to manifest itself among the populace. The Korean government, acknowledging the desire to spend money on leisure pursuits, determined that *domestic* travel was an economically sound outlet for this desire. Conspicuous consumption of imports, or travel abroad, would only result in an overall trade deficit, and trade surpluses were what the government was counting on for continuing economic growth. Restrictions on imports and international travel were maintained, but the government began investing in transport infrastructure and in facilities to promote domestic tourism. Historically and culturally significant areas were set aside as national and provincial parks, and corporations were encouraged to invest in lodging facilities.

The lodging facilities that began to spring up during the 1960s and 1970s, however, were at opposite ends of the spectrum: in Seoul and Pusan, luxury hotels built by the large *chaebol* such as Hyundai and Daewoo—and run by international hotel companies such as Sheraton and Hilton—catered largely to foreigners, while Korean locals found accommodation in small *yogwans*, which were usually individually-operated small properties with Korean-style *ondol* (heated-floor, bedless) guestrooms. Since most destinations within the Republic can be reached within a day's travel, there was little need for transient lodging facilities. Most of the *yogwans* were built near national parks for sightseers and in the cities to cater to overnight domestic business travelers.

The 1980s brought great changes to the hospitality industry in Korea. The first great leap forward came with the announcement that the 1988 Olympic Games would be held in Seoul. Along with massive infrastructure (roads, subways, and sports venues) development to support the 1988 Olympics and the preceding 1986 Asian Games, many new hotels were built in anticipation of the throngs of spectators who would attend the Games. Not only did the Games themselves bring a wave of spectators, media, and athletes to Korea, but the news that Korea was a worthwhile destination, and no longer the poor, war-torn country made familiar to the Western world through television shows like *M*A*S*H*, spread around the globe. Tourists looking toward Asia began to see past Japan and notice Korea for the first time, and international tourist arrivals began to skyrocket.

At about the same time, the political upheaval surrounding the presidential election of 1987, and continuing pressure both from within the country and from outside sources, led to ever-more-liberal policies. In 1989, the final restrictions on international travel were lifted, and Koreans joined the rest of the world as tourists. This had two major effects.

The first effect of travel liberalization was that the government, seeing large outflows of money following Korean travelers out of the economy into the coffers of other nations, stepped up efforts to promote Korea as a destination to foreigners. The Olympics were the starting point, but the early 1980s saw several campaigns (such as the "Visit Korea Year") that were designed to bring in more international visitors. Investment in upscale hotel development continued, with new resorts being built in areas such as Yongpyong and on Cheju Island. The Korea National

Tourism Organization's role expanded as it began to provide a unified voice for promoting Korea to the world.

The second effect of travel liberalization was the education of the Korean traveler. Having seen the wonders of Bangkok, Paris, London, Rome, and New York, Korean travelers were no longer content to stay in a small *ondol* room in a *yogwan* where they were likely to be required to provide their own towels and soap. The dreaded **amenity creep** set in, and soon Korean hoteliers were building more upscale properties outside of the major cities in order to cater to the increasingly sophisticated palates of their domestic guests. The tourist hotel, a rough equivalent to an upscale motel in the United States, made its advent at this time.[2]

The hospitality industry continued to grow steadily throughout the 1990s as more and more Koreans found the time and money to travel and as more foreigners found Korea an appealing destination. Increasing political stability in Asia resulted in more visitors from other Asian countries, and the general perception of Korea as a newly "safe" destination brought in visitors from the West. However, underlying faults in the overall economy began to show themselves in early 1997, and by the end of the year the entire region was plunged into what is colloquially known as the IMF Era—named after intervention from the International Monetary Fund. Almost overnight, the *won* (the Korean unit of currency) fell in value against major world currencies, and by the middle of 1998 was at half its pre-crisis value. Massive layoffs in Korean industry were planned, and many carried out in the early stages of the crisis. Koreans no longer had the extra money to travel, and the low value of the *won* made international travel, once within easy reach of most Koreans, nearly impossible.

Hotels, supported mostly by discretionary income—whether on the part of the pleasure traveler or on the part of a business traveler supported by his company—found their business suffering. The watchword of the day was "back to basics," and staying in a hotel, or even eating out at a hotel restaurant, was seen as a wasteful excess.

In the years since the crash, though, Korea has undergone stringent economic reform. By the end of 1999, the silver lining of this economic cloud was beginning to show. The drop in the exchange rate made visiting Korea very inexpensive for foreigners, and in the first quarter of 1998 there was a noticeable increase in the number of foreign arrivals. Investment in Korea also became less expensive; as the yen, pound, dollar, and mark could buy more, foreign investment began to flow into the country at increasing rates. Some of this investment went into new hotels, and several foreign chains began exploring the virtually nonexistent mid-price market.

Again recognizing the value of foreign tourism as a means to earn foreign exchange, the government of President Kim Dae Jung declared tourism a "strategic national industry" and the President himself appeared in advertisements for Korean tourism directed at the international market. The government also began to promote the development of the convention and meetings market, which had been previously untapped. Current development strategies include the liberalization of investment rules for foreign companies wishing to build lodging properties in Korea; government-supported development of convention facilities; and the building of the new Inchon International Airport, which will supplant Japan's Narita Airport as the new international hub for northern Asia.

Structure of the Korean Hospitality Industry

Luxury Market. The luxury (designated "super deluxe") market is still dominated by foreign chains. Flags represented in Korea include Hilton, Hyatt, Westin, Sheraton, Radisson, and Ritz Carlton. These hotels are located primarily in Seoul and Pusan, with a few in the resort areas of Kangwon Province and Cheju Island. The two top Korean brands at this level are Lotte, which has super deluxe properties (usually accompanied by a Lotte Department Store) in Seoul and Pusan, and Shilla, which is planning to expand into the mid-price and economy markets with its forthcoming "Geolodge" and "Geoville" concepts to be developed as chain properties.[3]

Deluxe hotels (one step down in price and service level from the super deluxe) are found in Seoul, Pusan, and other major cities throughout Korea. Although a greater proportion of hotels at this level use a private label, many are still under the management of foreign chains. Companies represented among the deluxe hotels include Sofitel, Novitel, Holiday Inn, and Holiday Inn Crowne Plaza. Korean Airlines and Lotte also manage several properties at this level.

Resorts. Korea has primarily two types of resorts: seaside and alpine. The resorts are clustered in mountainous Kangwon province in the northeast and on semi-tropical Cheju Island located in the Korea Strait to the southwest of the peninsula. Although the resorts do not constitute a separate grade of hotels, most of them fall into the super deluxe and deluxe categories.

Tourist Hotels. The greatest number of properties are classified as tourist hotels, which are further divided into first, second, and third class hotels. However, all three classes of tourist hotels combined account for only 14 percent more guest rooms than the super deluxe and deluxe categories (see Exhibit 1). Tourist hotels are distributed throughout the country approximately according to the population: these are the hotels frequented by domestic travelers on either overnight business or short holidays. These hotels also often have a reputation of being "love hotels," which originally became popular in Japan for clandestine assignations.

Kukmin* and Family Hotels.** Responding to the growing demand for lower-priced family accommodations, some 20 ***Kukmin (citizen) and Family hotels have been built, usually near national or provincial parks. These provide similar amenities to a tourist hotel at a better price: they are better equipped than the *yogwans* and also avoid the sometimes seedy reputation of the tourist hotels and *yogwans*.

Yogwans*, Inns, and *Minbak*.** The remainder of the hospitality industry is made up of hundreds of small *yogwans*, inns, and ***minbak (private homes or rooms for let to travelers). These small operations are ubiquitous throughout Korea, are of varying quality and size, but are mostly family-owned-and-operated businesses, offering little more than a bed (or *ondol* floor), a bathroom, and shower.

Exhibit 1   The Breakdown of Korean Hotel Properties and Rooms in each Class of Service

Class	Number of Properties	Number of Rooms	Rooms subtotal
Super Deluxe	27	12,880	22,066
Deluxe	46	9,186	
Tourist 1st Class	166	14,061	24,685
Tourist 2nd Class	125	6,963	
Tourist 3rd Class	79	3,661	
Kukmin	10	1,334	3,095
Family	10	1,761	
Total	**463**	**49,846**	**49,846**

Source: Hotel & Tourism Management in Korea (http://thor.prohosting.com/~tourism/index.htm [Korean]), February 1998.

Labor Demographics and Market Issues

Korea possesses a highly educated and relatively young work force. Men outnumber women greatly in the workforce, but this has begun to change as young women wish to pursue careers in line with their educations, and as women who work as a career (not out of necessity) are beginning to become more socially accepted. Older married women do reenter the workforce as laborers or by working in their own or family businesses, but rarely return to positions in the major companies.

The changing nature of the Korean economy as it evolves from an industrializing nation to a developed, information-based society is evident in the movement of labor out of the agriculture/aquaculture and manufacturing industries. College graduates in Korea, as in other developed nations, see factory work as being unworthy of their skills, and thus are demanding higher salaries. The demand for higher salaries has caused Korean employers, particularly in light and unskilled industries, to either shift production overseas or to bring in **guest workers**.

During the late 1990s, manufacturing employment decreased by over 10 percent per year. Employment in agriculture, aquaculture, forestry, and mining—already depleted by workers shifting to the manufacturing sector in the 1970s and 1980s—is also steadily decreasing by three to five percent per year.

The hospitality industry has benefited from this labor shift, being able to draw experienced workers from manufacturing and other industries.

Working Conditions and Characteristics

Working conditions in the Korean hospitality industry overall resemble those of other nations. For the most part, facilities are quite comparable in size and quality to those found anywhere in the world. Differences exist, of course, in working hours, pay, and other benefits.

Working hours in Korea are longer than in the U.S. or Japan. The legal work week is 44 hours, but companies regularly schedule employees to work up to 74 hours per week. Overtime pay is haphazard. Even if extra time is not explicitly scheduled, employees (especially office employees) are encouraged to stay late and come in early. Anyone who does not comply is socially ostracized from the work group and finds it very difficult to accomplish his tasks.

Scheduled work time is also very different. A typical front desk clerk's shift will have him or her working from noon one day to noon the next, a 24-hour shift, with breaks for meals and short naps amounting to no more than six hours of the 24. The clerk then has 24 hours off work, and works his next shift starting at noon the next day. This schedule continues for up to three or four weeks non-stop, and then the employee is given a break of 48 hours before he must report to work again.

This sort of schedule is very common for customer-contact employees in the hotel: back-of-the-house employees will often find themselves scheduled to work 10- or 12-hour shifts, seven days per week, with only one or two days off per month. This grueling schedule is the primary cause of burnout and turnover in the Korean hotel industry.

Compensation in the hotel industry in Korea, as in other nations, is low compared to more high-tech businesses. The average part-time hourly wage (as of 1999) is W2,000 or the equivalent of US$1.66. Salaries start low but are competitive with those of other entry-level service jobs like bank tellers.

Bonuses, especially for salaried workers, are very high in Korea and usually come at year-end. Given a profitable year, companies pay salaried employees sometimes as much as 150–200 percent of their yearly salary in a lump sum bonus at the end of the year. Hourly employees are often awarded a bonus of the equivalent of one or two month's pay. In economically bad years, such as 1997 and 1998, however, the bonuses shrink almost to nothing, leaving employees in debt if they had depended on this year-end windfall to defray personal expenses.

Other benefits include enrollment in the nationalized health insurance system and in the national Social Security retirement system (both mandatory), and meals, uniforms, transportation to and from work by company bus, lodging facilities for employees who do not have a residence within commuting distance, and company retirement plans (all optional, but usually offered).

Turnover in the hotel industry in Korea is high among part-time employees, but full-time employees show greater loyalty to their employer. Even after the era of lifetime employment, loyalty to one's company is still held as a virtue in Korea. In the current economy, too, having any full-time job is seen by many as a blessing which should not be given up easily. Reasons for high turnover usually involve the work schedule, low pay, the difficulty of the work (especially in the housekeeping and kitchen areas) and the low prestige of hospitality as a career. Part-time employees have further reason to leave the job when they find that there is no guaranteed career path that will lead them into a full-time position.

The 1997 financial crisis saw the end of lifetime employment in Korea as companies sought to improve their financial situation by laying off employees.

Although this affected manufacturing industries much more than hospitality, where lean margins already had the labor force pared to a fairly efficient minimum, the result of the financial crisis was a deep-freeze in hiring. The labor market, long a sellers market, became a buyers market almost overnight, as excess labor was cast off. The unemployment rate, which had previously averaged between two and three percent per year, skyrocketed to around eight percent, where it remained at the end of 1999. This situation has proven to be advantageous to hotel managers, who may now be more selective in choosing employees, and who have a larger pool of unemployed skilled workers from which to choose.

Supervisory and Management Positions

In the case of foreign-managed luxury chain properties, upper management consists primarily of expatriates whose tenure is often as short as one year. Middle management at the foreign-operated luxury properties, as well as most of the management team of the Korean-run luxury and tourist hotels, consists of managers from other industries with little or no hospitality background. A large *chaebol* such as Daewoo, for example, is engaged primarily in manufacturing (originally textiles, now consumer electronics and automobiles). A hotel owned by Daewoo such as the Seoul Hilton will likely have a foreign general manager who presides over an upper management staff comprising managers transplanted from other branches of the Daewoo conglomerate. This combination of management personnel produces interesting conflicts, not just in the usual sense of expatriate versus native, but also in terms of specialized expertise. Upper managers find themselves dealing with not only a culture different from their own, but a middle-management team that may have little or no background in hospitality. Middle managers find themselves operating in an unfamiliar type of business, with subordinates who may be highly skilled in hotel service, but do share their culture, and superiors who are both from a different culture and have hospitality expertise that they themselves lack. This can be very frustrating all around.

The expatriate manager will find it difficult to tell whether claims that "We've always done it this way" means "This is the Korean way to do things" or "This is the way we do things in the semiconductor manufacturing division." In the first case, it may be good for the expatriate manager to incorporate the "Korean way" into his way of operating; however, the second case may not be appropriate in a hospitality setting at all.

The Korean middle manager may find his authority challenged not only by the foreigner, whom he may not respect due to his foreignness, but also by subordinates who know the hospitality business better than he does.

Finally, the employees find their loyalties divided between a general manager who knows the hotel business but is not Korean, and middle managers who are Korean but lack the knowledge and expertise to do the job. The question always remains in their mind, "Do I follow the lead of my fellow Koreans, because we are Korean, or do I follow the lead of the foreigner, because he knows what he is doing?" The answer to this question is highly unpredictable.

Men vs. Women. Although more women than men work in hotels in Korea, most management positions are occupied by men, and for the most part career paths for women are short. Recent legislation abolishes sex discrimination in the workplace, but centuries of tradition are difficult to overcome. Most women in the workforce leave either when they marry, or if they stay on, when they become pregnant for the first time. Returning to the workforce later in life, for a woman, is extremely difficult. Hotel employees are no exception: women employed in hotels leave their positions (or are asked to leave) when they marry or become pregnant. Employers therefore do not value women as much as they do men, whom they see as being more loyal in the long run. Men, not women, are groomed for supervisory and managerial positions. Women are hired primarily for their visual appeal and less for their skill or experience, and are replaced when their appearance starts to deteriorate.

Unionization

The Korean labor force is highly unionized, but in a way that is different from unions in the United States. Unions are formed, not on an industry basis, like the United Auto Workers, but on a company basis. Daewoo, Hyundai, the Seoul Metropolitan Subway Corporation, and other large companies all have their own company unions. Employees of hotels owned or managed by unionized corporations are required to become members of the company union. Union membership, however, in the case of most companies, is dominated by employees of their manufacturing divisions, and so the concerns of union leaders are more likely to reflect those of the manufacturing divisions rather than of the hospitality operations.

A notable exception to this pattern is Samsung, which owns and operates the Shilla hotel. Samsung is not unionized. Other than this one exception, however, nearly all hotels from the tourist level and upwards are unionized. Inns and *yogwans*, of course, are not, being small family businesses. Unions are therefore not highly influential on the hotel operation per se, but rather have indirect influence according to how they affect the parent company of any particular hotel.

Challenges to Overcome

The hotel industry in Korea has several image obstacles to overcome as it becomes a large-scale employer in the Korean economy. These challenges include:

The Common Conception of Hospitality as Being an Undesirable Business. An anecdote that circulates among those connected with the hotel industry in Korea has it that a young man, newly promoted at his job and realizing some financial success, visited the home of his girlfriend's parents to ask her father permission to marry her. The father asked the young man which company he worked for, of course, and he named one of the large *chaebol*s. The father, impressed with having an employee of such a prestigious company as a son-in-law, agreed to the engagement on the spot, and preparations were made. On the day of the wedding, however, the families of the bride and groom were meeting for the first time, and the groom's father happened to mention that his son was the manager of a hotel owned by the *chaebol*. Upon hearing this, the bride's father announced his intention to call off the wedding, claiming that no daughter of his was going to marry a *hotel manager!*

This story may or may not be true, but it does reflect a longstanding traditional distaste for the hospitality business in Korea. Historically, the occupation of most honor was that of a scholar, or government official. Holding land was second to this, and craftsmen of various kinds were also afforded respect, as were farmers. However, engaging in trade was held to be a low-status job, and right above butchery as the lowest sort of occupation one could have was that of a tavern or inn owner. In addition, while the job of innkeeper itself was held in low esteem, it was also customary that inns were usually where the *kisaeng*, or courtesan, would ply her trade if she was freelancing. In other words, before the concept of the brothel came to exist in Korea, an inn was where one could usually obtain the services of a (very high class) prostitute. Tourist hotels and inns today still have this reputation, deserved or not. Whatever the reason, the lodging industry in Korea is still not regarded as a very prestigious place to work, and many families do not want their daughters in particular to seek a career in hospitality.

The Misconception that Hospitality Employees and Managers Require No Special Knowledge. Hospitality and tourism are relatively new fields of study in Korean universities; the oldest programs date back to the late 1970s. Since many of the domestic managers in Korean hotels moved into their positions from other industries, and since much of the actual work done in hotels is comparable to "keeping house" (cooking, cleaning, making beds, etc.,) there is still a feeling among hotel owners and managers that no special training or knowledge is required to work in a hotel. Needless to say, service quality in Korean hotels suffers because of this. The training programs (or lack of them) in Korean hotels also reflect this attitude, as does the historical lack of close cooperation between the hotel industry and hospitality and tourism education programs.

This problem has been mitigated somewhat in recent years, though, as university programs in hotel and tourism have taken the initiative in developing relationships with hotel properties, and have begun to promote their graduates as applicants to the hotels. In addition, there is a new breed of professional hotel manager beginning to surface in Korean hotels, particularly noticeable in the Lotte hotels. Well trained in their specialty, whether it be as sales manager or chief sommelier, and often holding a graduate degree in hotel management from prestigious universities in Korea or overseas, these new managers are making great progress in improving the level of professionalism in the Korean hotel industry.

Turnover, Especially among Part-time Employees. Turnover is a perennial problem for service businesses, particularly hospitality businesses. Because of the image problem and the long working hours, the Korean hotel industry is no exception to this rule. Combating high turnover with better benefits and more reasonable work shifts should improve productivity and service quality, though, and attract more career-minded employees to work in hotels as professionals, rather than as temporary employees seeking stopgap employment while looking for something better. In addition, career paths can be made available to part-time employees that will allow them to move into full-time positions with more responsibility and better pay.

Long Working Hours. Perhaps the major complaint at all levels of the organization is that of the long working hours required of hotel management and employees. Whereas the hotel is unique among businesses in being open 24 hours per day, seven days a week, 52 weeks per year, this does not mean that individual employees must work 70-plus hours per week. Altering the traditional work schedule to better accommodate the employees' needs will surely result in more satisfied, better employees, and make the hotel industry a more attractive employer.

Legal and Political Environment

In moving from third-world underdeveloped nation status in the 1950s to developing industrialized economic power at the new millennium, Korea has skipped over some of the stages of industrialization, one of which was the development of a social safety net such as exists in the United States or more extensively in Europe. Nationalized health insurance became a reality in the 1990s, and a Social Security (retirement insurance) program went into effect nationwide in 1999 after several years of preliminary testing.

Because of the lack of this sort of a security net, Korean citizens have traditionally been great savers, often putting away upwards of 30 percent of their annual income in savings, investments, and insurance policies. Saving at this rate requires (a) earning an income that is substantially higher than is necessary to cover one's basic expenses and (b) severely curtailing one's discretionary spending. The comparatively low wages in the hospitality industry have sustained its reputation as a temporary occupation rather than a career, as employees work long enough to find something better that will enable them to save at a high rate.

The advent of the social security net and the "IMF" economic crisis have taken some wage pressure off of Korean hotel companies. Unable to afford imported goods as before, and not needing to save so much to pay for unexpected medical bills or for their retirement, Koreans are not as demanding when it comes to their salaries as they were a decade ago. Many feel that having any job is a good thing. Since all full-time jobs come with comparable government-sponsored benefits, working in the hotel industry is now more desirable than it once was.

Workplace Legal Issues

Legal issues prevalent in the Korean hospitality industry include: sexual harassment (legislation to combat this was enacted in early 1999); age discrimination (many companies will not hire anyone for a customer-contact position that is over the age of 25, and some companies will actually lay off customer-contact employees or transfer them out of their jobs once they reach the age of 30 or 35); and a high emphasis on physical appearance over actual ability.

Legislation has also been enacted to eliminate sex discrimination in the workplace, but prevailing social attitudes will take some time to change. Korea is working to make the changes effective through social pressure rather than strict interpretation of the law, and so the change is too slow for some, but less disruptive to society in the long run. In many cases, the issues are very new: that is, while the problems have existed for a long time, the recognition of the problem is only recent. For this reason, Korean lawmakers are attempting to educate employers and employees first, before bringing these new laws into full force.

Financial Crisis Driving Labor Strife. One of the first responses to the financial crisis was a series of large layoffs that began in early 1998. Many companies, recognizing that most of their male employees were heads of households and responsible for dependents, while most of their female employees were single women, started the layoffs among their female employees. This naturally raised the issue of sexual discrimination, and the fairness of this policy is still under debate.

Companies such as the Seoul Metropolitan Subway Corporation, which operates the eight subway lines servicing nearly 15 million people who live in and around the capital city, have responded to layoffs by proposing a solution attempted in France. This solution is a shorter work week, along with longer (unpaid) vacations. Under this proposal, instead of laying off any employees, every employee's work week would be cut back and their pay would be cut accordingly, allowing the company to spend less money on labor but retain the same number of employees. So far this proposal has met with opposition from the government, which favors layoffs as a way for companies to reorganize for better efficiency and effectiveness.

Demonstrations are sponsored seasonally in Seoul and other metropolitan areas by company labor unions, and recently these two topics (layoffs and shortening the work week) have been the focus of the demonstrations. It is doubtful that the government will change its position on the work week issue, and the sex discrimination issue is still undecided, so these issues will likely be points of conflict for some time to come.

Wage Laws

There is no minimum wage in Korea. Hotel managers are therefore free to set their own wage levels. That said, it can be observed that most businesses arrive at a standard fair wage for their industry or the type of work they are hiring employees to perform. Most part-time restaurant and hotel employees are paid between W1,800 and W2,500 per hour (US$1.50 and US$2.08, respectively). Part-time employees are not subject to taxation, though, so employees receive the full value of their wage.

Tipping is not customary in Korea, although hotels are allowed to charge a fixed percentage "service charge" above the room rate or price of a meal. This service charge is paid to the employees that were working during that shift regardless of whether they participated directly in the sale that earned the service charge. Since tipping is done in this forced manner (the guest is required to pay the service charge) and distributed evenly among all employees, the value of tipping as an incentive to provide good service is negated.

Political Environment

A recent article in the *Dong-A Ilbo* (a daily newspaper from Korea with an English and Korean version) cited the Korean government as number 12 on the list of most corrupt governments. Graft and kickbacks are par for the course, and this unethical behavior naturally overflows into the corporate sector. Two previous presidents, Chun Doo Hwan and Roh Tae Woo, have both been jailed for accepting illegal contributions and squirreling them away in huge secret slush funds. These scandals, and the 1997 economic crisis, have forced the government to disentangle itself from business.

The advantage to this change is that businesses have much greater freedom to develop and grow. Instead of being forced by the government to undertake new business ventures, companies are free to evaluate the potential profitability of a project and to reject it if it is not profitable. The downside is that the government no longer offers interest-free or low-interest development loans to companies: they must now face the risks and meet the qualifications of the financial markets.

This change has therefore slowed the development of new hotel properties and the expansion of Korean and foreign hotel chains into the family/mid-price market.

Encouragement to Entrepreneurs and Small Businesses. The government still does operate programs to support entrepreneurs and small businesses. The low-interest or interest-free loans of the past are almost gone, but instead entrepreneurs may apply for government grants, especially if they are planning to open a business in an economically depressed area. In addition, many small business consulting and research institutes have been set up on college campuses to provide entrepreneurs with low-cost or free advice on how to best start their business. On some campuses, small business "incubators" have been set up, where entrepreneurs are allowed to actually start their business using school facilities at little or no cost, and then move out once they begin to turn a profit. Many of these entrepreneurs start hospitality businesses, primarily restaurants or inns.

Opening the Hotel Market. A final political change follows the gradual opening of the Korean stock market to foreigners, as well as the lowering of restrictions on foreign capital and the easing of qualifications that foreigners must show in order to purchase real estate. These changes, again stemming from the financial crisis and the need for Korea to acquire foreign exchange, have resulted in the opening of the mid-price hotel market to foreign chains. Many opportunities for prospective hotel managers and employees will exist in the coming years as new hotel development in Korea moves away from single, several-hundred-room deluxe and super deluxe properties to smaller, more evenly distributed and numerous mid-price chain hotels.

Cultural Distinctions and Societal Work Values

One of the most obvious features of Korea is its homogeneous society. While it has influenced and been influenced by the cultures of its nearest neighbors, China and Japan, Korea has kept its culture distinct and unique. In addition, unlike China, which has a proliferation of ethnic groups and several versions of its language, or Japan, which has its Ainu ethnic group on the northern island of Hokkaido and the Okinawans on the island of Okinawa, Korea has only one language and one ethnic group. Diversity is definitely not seen as a virtue in Korea. Although Koreans are very accommodating and friendly, there are still strong barriers to becoming accepted in Korean society if one is a foreigner. This extends to foreign visitors, who often find that the polite service they receive is a result more of grudging tolerance than a sense of heartfelt hospitality.

A monolithic culture usually results in a monolithic mind set, and expatriate managers working in Korea, regardless of how well they understand and adapt to the culture and how well they are accepted by their Korean peers and subordinates, often find that resistance to new ideas or ways of doing things is virtually insurmountable. "That's the way we have always done things" is a catchphrase that is usually sufficient to shoot down any new idea, no matter how sound or well-presented it may be.

Language Barrier

Koreans are proud of their language and of the scientifically designed script that they use to write it. However, justifiably so or not, the language of international business is English. The language spoken by most tourists to Korea is Japanese, and the language of Korea's largest neighbor is Chinese. While most Koreans do have some training in English and at least one other foreign language, language is still a barrier and is always a major issue in hiring and training. Unfortunately, employees are often hired on their English ability alone, and have little ability to perform the task for which they are hired. Conversely, employees who are highly skilled at their job are passed over simply because of poor English proficiency.

Work Ethic

Older Koreans, remembering the years of horror and starvation of the Japanese occupation, and then the Korean war, have a very deep-seated work ethic. They have known sacrifice, and it was on their backs and by their labor that the Republic was built. Perhaps it is because of their strong work ethic that the long work shifts and long work week have not been challenged until recently.

Younger Koreans, starting in particular with those of Generation X (born between 1961 and 1981), lack this strong work ethic. They have no memory of the worst times, and for most of their life they can remember living comfortably, if frugally, with their basic needs adequately met. In addition, the prosperity of the 1980s gave rise to a consumer society in which weekly trips to the movie theater and frequent visits to department stores have become the entertainment of choice of the younger generation. These Koreans do not want to work 74 hours per week, with only one extra day off per month, with little or no vacation time, for years on end. They have the means, and the desire, to have more leisure time, and they do not want to waste their youth working from sunup to sundown.

Middle-aged Koreans, those who were children shortly after the war, and who do remember the hard times but only vaguely, have reached the point where they are ready to trade off some of the extra money and security gained from constant labor in favor of more time to spend with their children (just now entering high school and college) and in pursuit of their own pastimes.

These three generational differences: old-timers who see work as a necessity, youth who really do not want to work that hard, and middle-aged Koreans who are willing to work less if it means more time to enjoy life, produce conflict in the workplace. Upper management expects their subordinates to continue to work as they themselves did, but middle management and new hires are rebelling against this tradition. It will probably take some years before these issues are resolved, and managers who have a more balanced perspective on work and leisure are established in the top ranks of business management.

Manners and Formality. A curious feature of Korean society, and one that is very evident in the hotel industry, is a strong emphasis on manners and formality. This stems partially from **Confucianism**, the philosophy that underlies all social interaction in Korea. Unfortunately, this often comes at the expense of responsiveness and quality service. Foreign visitors to Korea are often pleased at the deference they receive: hotel employees bow in greeting, are dressed very formally, and table service is very formal and proper. However, something as simple as getting honey instead of sugar for one's tea can be a monumental task because "tea is not served with honey." Strict adherence to the rules, however arbitrary, inappropriate, or outdated those rules may be, takes precedence over meeting the guests' needs or finding a more efficient way of performing a task.

Westernization and Globalization. Since the founding of the Republic, Korea has gradually opened to the world and the world has discovered Korea. Westernization has come in the form of obvious product "invasions" such as blue jeans, Hollywood movies, and KFC, and in the form of less obvious concepts such as Christianity, democracy, and capitalism. Adopting these new ideas, products, and ways of thinking while still maintaining a unique society has always been a challenge, and often a topic of heated debate, in Korean society. Korea continues to become more cosmopolitan—more global—with each passing year, but still manages to retain its Koreanness.

Labor Relations

Recruitment and Selection

Hotels in Korea recruit on two levels. Recruitment for part-time and entry-level help, especially customer contact employees, is usually done through word-of-mouth, requests to local universities or junior colleges, notification to other training institutions, and occasionally an ad in the local newspaper.

Recruitment for salaried and/or supervisory positions takes two forms. Line employees usually seek out the hotel on their own initiative and apply directly through the human resources departments. Sometimes word-of-mouth plays a factor, and on rare occasions the human resources department will take out advertisements. These employees often have experience in the hospitality business, and even if they do not, are interested enough in working in a hotel that they seek employment directly.

Most staff employees, on the other hand (in the case of hotels owned by *chaebol*), are assigned to work in the hotel by the hotel's parent company. Most large companies hold employment entrance examinations once or twice each year. These employees are hired *en masse* after passing the entrance examination, and then are assigned to various arms of the company. While they are educated and experienced enough to pass the company entrance examination, they may have no experience or knowledge of the hospitality industry, and more importantly, no interest in working there. This gap in experience and desire between line employees and staff employees creates a great deal of tension, and the social gulf between the two is seen in some organizations as unbreechable.

Selection of line and staff employees also follows different criteria. Line employees, who usually work in the front office, kitchen, and housekeeping, are selected based on their hospitality-related skill and experience, and especially in the case of women, on their personal appearance (height, weight, shape of their face, skin tone, and body shape all are considered). Age also plays a factor for women, as many hotels will not hire a woman over the age of 25. Staff employees, who have little or no contact with guests, and who perform functions that are not entirely unique to the hotel business, are selected based on expertise in their particular area of specialty, whether that be accounting, finance, or human resource management. They also must past the parent company's entrance examination. Staff employees, however, unlike line employees, are eligible to be transferred out of the hotel to other divisions of the parent company after a certain period of time: line employees are considered employees of the hotel, not the parent company, and are rarely transferred to other divisions.

Part-time and entry-level employees are selected on the same basis as the line employees. A pleasant physical appearance and youth are the most important factors. Women who are overweight or short have little chance of working at the front desk or in the dining room of a restaurant. Again, laws have been enacted to change this, but the change is slow, and hotel managers argue that the guests are paying to be served by young, pretty employees, and that choosing guest-contact employees based on these criteria is necessary to maintain the hotel's image and quality of service.

Training and Development Practices

Foreign hotel and restaurant chains have the most developed training programs. Usually these programs consist of transplants of programs developed in their home markets, with appropriate changes made to suit the Korean workforce. Some, like T.G.I. Friday's, have established training institutions in Korea to train their employees. Training in these organizations consists of service skills, task-specific skills, supervisory skills, and personal enrichment training.

Company Training. *Chaebol*-owned hotels require employees to attend a minimum number of hours annually in a company training program. These training programs usually take place off-premises at company-owned training centers, and do not involve job-related skills. Instead, these training sessions focus on **personal enrichment training,** including things like table manners, languages, and personal financial management.

Small and independently owned hotels do not have the resources to support this sort of training program, and instead bring in a training specialist or college professor for a special lecture at regular intervals throughout the year. Like the company training programs, these special lectures usually have little connection to job skills and focus instead on personal enrichment issues.

Internships. Until recently, internships were little more than an opportunity for college students to cut class for a month and hang around in a hotel or travel agency. However, until the financial crisis made a larger labor market available to hotel managers, there was growing concern regarding the availability of appropriately trained labor. Several hotel companies have begun to develop internship programs that have a strong training component, in the desire to identify and attract talented students from various hotel and tourism management programs in Korea. These programs are still few and far between, and the financial crisis has more or less stopped the development of these programs cold.

On-the-Job Training. Job-specific training, except in the foreign chain hotels, is largely restricted to on-the-job training. Korean society already has a very strong tradition of master/apprentice, and new employees usually adopt the role of apprentice to their more experienced colleagues quite easily. Korea, like Japan, is a **high-context society**, in which there is a high level of tacit mutual understanding. This makes on-the-job training fairly efficient, as employees are accustomed to being observed by others as they work, and to observing others to learn a particular skill. The downside to this is that there is very little change over time in the way things are done, and very little critical analysis of the way things are done. Increasing efficiency or effectiveness by introducing new work methods is very difficult.

Performance Evaluation Practices

This area of human resource management is probably the least developed in the Korean hotel industry. Obtaining employment with a company has traditionally been based on a rather objective and strenuous entrance examination, but once hired, the employee was virtually guaranteed a job for life. Promotions, raises, and transfers after being hired are arbitrary and based on the subjective decision of superiors. It is likely that this tradition is what has given rise to the high amount of graft and corruption in the government and in corporations. Since there are no objective performance criteria that must be met in order to gain a raise or promotion, employees curry the favor of their superiors through gifts and contributions (or to put it more bluntly, bribes).

Only the recent financial crisis and exposure of corruption among government officials has brought attention to this problem. Human resources departments in many industries have started to implement objective performance appraisal systems. The hotel industry in Korea is just now beginning to implement merit pay systems and to establish formal annual performance appraisals. These systems are so new (many are still in the planning stage) that there is virtually no information on them, and most companies are still reluctant to talk about how they plan to implement these policies.

While the change from an arbitrary, secretive system of raises and promotions to an objective, open one would seem logical and more fair to all involved, this change is meeting with great resistance throughout the Korean labor force wherever it is being implemented. Under the new system, lifetime employment is no longer guaranteed. Many employees are concerned that they will fail to meet whatever criteria are established for their performance review, and will lose their jobs. Others simply do not want to make the effort to improve their performance, or adhere to performance standards, having become comfortable with buying the favors of their superiors. Middle and upper management are resentful, because they obtained their positions by "buying" the favor of their superiors and have spent a lot of money to get where they are. They feel that it is now their turn to be on the receiving end of the graft, and that if the system changes to a performance appraisal/merit pay system, that they will be unable to recoup the investment they made in their careers from their subordinates, who would otherwise be bribing them for raises and promotions.

Career Development Programs

Career development programs as such exist only in large upscale properties and foreign-based chains: most employees still do not regard hospitality as a true career. *Chaebol*-owned hotels usually have two career paths available: one for the line "hotel" employees, who may continue to work for the hotel management company, and transfer from hotel to hotel; and one for the staff "company" employees, who may transfer to another operating unit within the *chaebol* doing the same basic job they do for the hotel. The greatest obstacle to employees seeking to progress along the former career path is language, as there are usually not more than one or two properties affiliated with any one foreign chain in Korea, and so moving to another hotel means learning another language. Korean employees, however, are steadily improving their ability with both English and Japanese, and the rate at which they qualify for overseas positions in their hotel chain is increasing.

Independently owned hotels have no formal career development program. From the employees' point of view, this is not unusual, because most employees (especially women) do not expect to make a career of their job in the hotel. From the point of view of the hotel, it also makes sense, because it is only rarely that they will need to replace a manager, and since they do not have a chain in which to rotate people from property to property, there are very few opportunities for advancement for which to prepare employees. Since the unemployment rate has increased, too, hotel managers find it easy to recruit replacements for those who leave, and so there is very little perceived need for career development.

Confucian Ethics in Conflict with Modern Market Demands

As mentioned before, Korea has maintained its uniqueness even in the era of globalization. One of the forces that helps to maintain Korean culture is Confucianism, a philosophy that permeates the life of every Korean, regardless of education level, occupation, or religion.

The Five Relationships

Confucianism is more than a set of manners, although formal manners are the most obvious manifestation of the philosophy in daily life. At the core of Confucianism as a way of life are the Five Relationships, which delineate all possible roles one might find oneself in, and how to act accordingly in any one of those roles.[4] The Five Relationships are:

1. Father/son (fidelity) (this can be also seen as parent-child)

2. Ruler/subject (separation) (also superior-subordinate)

3. Husband/wife (distinction) (also man-woman)

4. Elder/younger (order)

5. Friend/friend (trust)

Of course, the English translations of the relationships and their meanings are not sufficient to convey the true essence of the philosophy, but these approximations are adequate for discussion. The relationships that play the biggest role in managing human resources would be the second, third, and fourth: ruler-subject, husband-wife, and elder-younger. The first two, adapted for the modern workplace, are superior-subordinate and man-woman.

Following Korean Confucianism, superiors and subordinates are members of separate classes. This recognition of separate ranks extends beyond the workplace to social situations, and crossing the boundaries dictated by Confucianism results in severe social penalties (ostracization from one's peer group is most common). For example, when going out for drinks after work, the most junior members of the group are expected to pay, and the senior manager in the group never pays. When touching glasses in a toast, the rim of the subordinate's glass must never be elevated above the rim of the superior's glass. In addition, the superior never pours a drink for himself: it is expected that his subordinates will keep his glass full at all times. As another example, a superior may call his subordinates at home at any time of day or night if there is a need to, but a subordinate should never call his superior at home unless there is some sort of grave disaster at the workplace.

Male-female relationships have been alluded to previously in this chapter, when discussing the fact that women in Korea do not usually seek true careers, while men do. The traditional Confucian relationship holds men and women to be completely different from one another, and makes clear distinctions regarding what is an appropriate job or task for a man and what is appropriate for a woman. Confucianism is still used as a reason to confine women to jobs such as waitress, housekeeper, and front desk clerk, while excluding men from those jobs. Conversely, women are often prevented from having supervisory positions, while men are not.

Older-younger is somewhat similar to superior-subordinate. The rule in Korea is that age is always deferred to, even if the actual age difference is a manner of weeks or days. In addition, regardless of the company rank of the two individuals involved, a younger person is expected to defer to the older, even if the younger person is the manager and the older is the subordinate. In this respect, superior-subordinate and older-younger come into conflict, and there is rarely a clear solution to the problem.

To understand the role of these relationships in the workplace, it must be understood that these roles are immutable. In any given situation, one's role is established from the beginning and does not change, *even if the situation itself changes.* For example, suppose that Mr. Kim and Mr. Park both have the same job in a hotel, but Mr. Kim was hired some months before Mr. Park. That initial situation establishes Mr. Kim as Mr. Park's superior *in hiring order*, even though they do the same actual job. Then suppose that Mr. Park is promoted to a supervisory position, and Mr. Kim is not. Even though Mr. Park is now Mr. Kim's superior, Mr. Kim is still Mr. Park's *senior*, simply because he was hired first.

This sort of philosophy makes it extremely difficult for managers to promote and transfer employees based on the employee's individual merit, or even on the needs of the hotel itself. In the above example, while Mr. Park may be more qualified than Mr. Kim, and may very well have earned the promotion, the issue still remains as to whether Mr. Kim will follow Mr. Park's direction, since Mr. Kim *and* Mr. Park still see Mr. Kim as superior to Mr. Park. It is extremely difficult to break the status quo under such a system, and expatriate managers unfamiliar with the long history of Korean employees under their supervision can make disastrous mistakes by promoting the wrong person. Confucianism has been seen by some as a major source of the resistance to performance evaluation programs and merit-based pay systems.

In addition to making it very difficult to meet the needs of the organization, this philosophy serves to limit the growth potential of employees. Instead of moving Mr. Park along in his career path at a speed that is appropriate to his talent and ambition, the hotel manager must wait to promote him *at each level* until Mr. Kim, his senior, has been promoted. Young employees find their career paths blocked by older employees, and women find their career paths blocked or dead-ended simply because they are women.

Conflict with Modern Market Demands

The modern hospitality industry, like other industries, demands a flexible, "flat," adaptable, innovative organizational structure. Confucianism stands in almost direct opposition to this, being (a) very inflexible—relationships are determined from the beginning of one's association with the organization and do not subsequently change; (b) vertical instead of horizontal—with the exception of friend-friend, each of the Five Relationships is a vertical relationship, and all of them describe which party is the deferent one in the relationship; and (c) very non-adaptable to new situations.

In addition, Confucianism comes into conflict with more modern, democratic ideals such as reward for merit. Since one's advancement in the company depends more upon the order in which one was hired, or one's age, or one's gender, there is little motivation to work harder in order to obtain a raise or promotion.

Since reward for merit is not compatible with Confucianism, it is often the case that people occupy positions for which they are not qualified, simply because it was their "turn" to be promoted. This results in poor organizational performance, because vital positions are not occupied by the best employee for the job.

Recently, awareness of the conflict between Confucianism and the demands of modern life has been growing in Korea, and there is considerable debate about the merits of this philosophy and whether it is a help or hindrance to Korea's continued growth and success. The conflicts in the workplace caused by this philosophy are becoming more and more evident, and calls for reform and abandonment of Confucianism are becoming more and more strident.[5]

Future of the Hospitality Industry in Korea

Despite the challenges faced by the hotel industry in Korea, its future is a fairly bright one. Demand is certainly going up, and the reputation of the hotel industry as a challenging and exciting place to work continues to grow. Several opportunities for growth in Korea are evident:

- *Inchon Airport Construction.* Due to be completed shortly after the turn of the millennium, the Inchon International Airport will replace Tokyo's Narita Airport as the main international hub for Northeast Asia. Just over an hour by bus or subway from downtown Seoul, this airport will draw unprecedented numbers of international travelers to Korea, if only to transfer from international to intraregional carriers as they continue their journeys to Japan, China, Taiwan, or Southeast Asia. The airport is expected to generate greater awareness of Korea as a primary destination, as well as generate increased demand for lodging as a secondary destination. Initially there will be a need for new hotel facilities at the airport itself, but the new airport's influence on tourist arrivals, and thus demand for room nights, should spur the construction of new hotels throughout the Republic.

- *Building Bridges to North Korea.* In the late 1990s, the Hyundai Corporation, under the aegis of its chairman emeritus, Jeong Joo Young, opened talks with the government of North Korea with the purpose of developing Mt. Kumgang, just up the eastern coast from the Demilitarized Zone, for South Korean tourists. By 1998, the corporation had begun tours to Mt. Kumgang, which is not only known for its unparalleled scenery but also has a sentimental value to Koreans on both sides of the border. Tourists can now travel to Mt. Kumgang on an overnight cruise from the port of Donghae in South Korea, and hike the region for three days, staying on the cruise ship overnight. Tours to Mt. Kumgang were opened to foreigners in February 2000. Although there have been some difficulties in launching this development, it heralds a new era in South-North relations, and hopes are that further trade links, and tourist development, can be established with the North. South Korean hotel companies will no doubt be the first ones to build and operate modern hotel facilities in the North, and demand will certainly increase as the North opens up more of its tourism destinations to outsiders.

- *Demand for Mid-Price Facilities.* As mentioned earlier in this chapter, there is a serious lack of mid-price accommodations in Korea. Foreign chains have concentrated on building deluxe or super deluxe hotels that cater primarily to business travelers, largely at the insistence of the *chaebol* that own the hotels. Shilla will be the first Korean hotel operation to venture into the mid-price and family markets with its Geolodge and Geoville concepts. *Yogwans*, with their seedy reputation and unpredictable level of quality, will eventually be phased out as mid-price chain hotels grow throughout the country. These new hotels will create further demand for educated and experienced hotel professionals, as they in turn satisfy the demand for affordable, standardized lodging facilities throughout the peninsula.

• *Opportunities for Existing Properties.* While the demand for affordable accommodation will likely result in a large number of *yogwans* being replaced by chain properties, there still exists an opportunity for owners of small inns and *yogwans* to band together in a Best Western–style management association. It would not be difficult for operators of these small hotels in different cities to establish a common brand identity and standardized package of amenities, thus enabling them to compete with chain properties. Bright young hoteliers entering this market may find that the *yogwans* provide them with an opportunity to make their mark on the Korean hotel industry without involvement from foreign chains or the *chaebols*.

In keeping with the spirit of globalization, Korean hospitality leaders recognize the need to develop standardized, high quality lodging facilities at all price levels and that are geographically dispersed throughout the nation, not just clustered in the major metropolitan areas. However, in a spirit of revived nationalism, and a renewed sense of control over their own destiny, these same leaders are seeking to develop the Korean hospitality industry in a uniquely Korean way. Future hotel development in Korea is sure to sustain the flavor of Korea that many foreigners expect to enjoy when visiting the Republic, and will provide many opportunities for prospective hotel employees.

Endnotes

1. Woo-Keun Han, *The History of Korea* (Seoul: Eul-Yoo Publishing, 1970).
2. DeHyun Sohn, *Hanguk Munhwaeui Maeryukgwa Gwangwang Ihae* [The Attractions of Korean Culture and Understanding Tourism] (Seoul: Ilshinsa, 1992).
3. "Shilla Hotel hotel chain saeop bongyuk jinchul" [Hotel Shilla's advancement into genuine chain hotel operations] *International Hotel & Restaurant* (August 1999) pp. 78, 101.
4. Byeong Cheol Choi, *Gongjaga Salaya Naraga Sanda* [Confucius Must Live if Korea Survives] (Seoul: Shi-A Publishing, 1999).
5. Kyong Il Kim, *Gongjaga Jukoya Naraga Sanda* [Confucius Must Die if Korea Survives] (Seoul: Bada Publishing Co., 1999).

Key Terms

amenity creep—The tendency, as the target market becomes more affluent and sophisticated, for a hotel to increase the variety, quality, and cost of amenities offered with the guestroom.

brain drain—A phenomenon observed in developing nations where their smartest citizens flee in significant numbers to developed, more prosperous countries, leaving the developing nations with a shortage of intellectual leaders.

chaebol—The Korean term describing a financial clique consisting of varied corporate enterprises engaged in diverse businesses and typically owned and controlled by one or two interrelated family groups.

Chosun—The last dynasty of Korea, spanning the years 1392 to 1910. The Chosun Dynasty ended with the deposition of Kojong and the onset of Japanese occupation. Also known as the Yi Dynasty. Chosun is also another popular name for all things Korean, including the Korean peninsula and the language.

Confucianism—A philosophy of life originated by the Chinese scholar Confucius (552–479 B.C.), delineating the proper relationships between individuals in society. While Confucianism played a strong role in the development of Chinese, Korean, and Japanese society, it is only in Korea that it still has any significance today.

guest workers—Workers brought in, usually on a temporary basis, from another country to do labor that natives no longer find desirable or when there are no longer enough people in the domestic workforce to fill all available positions.

high-context society—A society in which a great deal of meaning is communicated with a paucity of language, relying more or shared understandings, common learning, tradition, and nonverbal communication.

International Monetary Fund (IMF)—Established in 1944, the IMF is a financial pact between nations; its objectives are to foster orderly foreign exchange arrangements, convertible currencies, and a shorter duration and lesser degree of balance-of-payments disequilibria. The IMF is also empowered to exercise surveillance over the exchange rate policies of members.

kukmin—The literal translation is "citizen"; *Kukmin* hotels are budget hotels built with the average citizen in mind. This category was established to provide an alternative to *yogwans* and appeal to the family travel market.

minbak—The literal translation is "private-lodging"; a private house or room for let to travelers.

ondol—The literal translation is "heat-collides"; believed to be the first known central heating system, this involved heating a living space by venting exhaust from cooking fires through flues built under the floor. Now used to mean any system that heats by convection through the floor.

personal enrichment training—Training intended to develop employees' personal skills such as time management, planning, goal setting, self-awareness, etc. in order to make them more effective in their personal lives. This is assumed to make them more effective on the job as well.

yogwan—Small, usually privately-owned, mid- or low-priced lodging in Korea. Most *yogwans* feature *ondol* rooms and provide few amenities other than telephone, towels, and soap.

Discussion Questions

1. What are the major economic issues facing Korean hotel companies?

2. What are some of the challenges facing Korean hotel managers in employee recruitment and retention?

3. What is the nature of the conflicts arising between different levels of management in Korean hotels?

4. What is the impact of Confucian philosophy on the human resource function of performance evaluation?

5. What sort of challenges must be met in order to reduce age and sex discrimination in Korea?

Internet Sites

For more information, visit the following Internet sites. Remember that Internet addresses can change without notice.

Cheju Grand Hotel
http://www.grand.co.kr/html/eindex.html

Chong Wa Dae (Office of the President)
http://www.bluehouse.go.kr/english/index.php

Government of Korea
http://www.korea.go.kr/ehtm/ushome.html

Grand Hyatt Seoul
http://www.hyatt.com/pages/s/selrsba.html

Hotel & Tourism Management in Korea
http://thor.prohosting.com/~tourism

Hotel Hyundai
http://www.hyundaihotel.com/e_hotel.html

Hotel Inter-Continental Seoul
http://interconti.lg.co.kr

Hotel Lotte
http://hotel.lotte.co.kr

Hotel Shilla
http://www.shilla.samsung.co.kr

Korea National Statistics Office
http://www.nso.go.kr

Korea National Tourism Organization
http://www.knto.or.kr

Korean Embassy
http://www.mofat.go.kr/en_usa.htm

Novotel Ambassador Kangnam
http://ambassadors.co.kr/novotel/korea/main1_.htm

Radisson Seoul Plaza Hotel
http://www.seoulplaza.co.kr/

Ritz-Carlton Seoul
http://www.ritz.co.kr

Sejong Hotel
http://www.sejong.co.kr

Seoul Palace Hotel
http://www.seoulpalace.co.kr

Sheraton Walker Hill
http://www.walkerhill.co.kr/

Sofitel Ambassador
http://ambassadors.co.kr/sofitel/main1.htm

Swiss Grand Hotel Seoul
http://www.swissgrand.co.kr

## Case Study

Seniority vs. Service

The Kumgok Hotel is a 150-room tourist hotel located on the north shore of Cheju Island. The hotel has a full-service restaurant, coffee shop, banquet hall, and room service, and adjoins a department store that has a fast-food court. In the immediate area are some eight other hotels of similar or higher quality, and taken together, the nine hotels represent the bulk of tourist-quality lodgings on the north side of Cheju. Their main competition for overseas and mainland tourists is the resort complex on the south side of the island, and for overseas and mainland business travelers, the *yogwans* located in downtown Cheju City. The airport is located approximately three kilometers away.

Mr. Myongho Choi, the human resources manager, is a native of Cheju island, a former government employee, and a graduate of Hongik University in political science. He has worked at the Kumgok Hotel for the past eight years. Mr. Choi needs to hire a new Front Desk Supervisor immediately, as the young woman who has held the post for the past five years recently married and moved to live with her husband on the mainland. Calls to the two local colleges offering hospitality degrees have turned up a few leads for entry-level and part-time jobs, with no one interested or qualified to take on a full-time supervisory position.

Mr. Choi's friend, Mr. Seungchol Lee, is the catering manager at Kumgok. He is also a former government employee and classmate of Mr. Choi at Hongik University. Mr. Lee is two years older than Mr. Choi and held a higher government post than he did, so he is Mr. Lee's "senior" even though he was only recently hired as catering manager following early retirement from public service. He has no supervisory authority over Mr. Choi.

Over a casual lunch one afternoon, Mr. Choi mentions that he is having a very difficult time finding someone to fill the Front Desk Supervisor position. Mr. Lee responds by mentioning his nephew Seobang, who is looking for work. Mr. Choi is disappointed as Mr. Lee discusses Seobang's qualifications and indicates that he is looking for someone who is properly qualified and has front desk experience. Mr. Lee replies by scoffing that "Seobang has a degree from the best university in Korea—that should be qualification enough for any job. As for experience, anyone can work in a hotel; it doesn't take any special skills. Besides, you need a man in that position. Another girl will just run off to get married like the last one. And remember I'm your senior, you should do what I say. Remember that time we had the demonstration against President Park back in..."

Mr. Choi isn't sure what to say. Seobang is a Seoul native and has just graduated with lackluster marks from Seoul National University (Korea's most prestigious university) with a degree in Mechanical Engineering. His marks have made him unattractive in the job market and he has been unable to find work in his chosen field. He has never been to Cheju and does not speak the local dialect. He also has no work experience outside two years of mandatory military service.

Shortly after this conversation, Mr. Choi receives a very well written letter of introduction and resume from Ms. Yaeni Jo. She is a 25-year-old Cheju native who has recently graduated from a smaller regional university in Hotel and Tourism Management, and who has been working at the front desk of an even larger hotel for the past two years—a 200-room hotel that caters to tourists. She speaks and understands the native dialect well, which will make it easy for her to communicate with her subordinates, but she also speaks flawless standard Korean and is competent in English and Japanese.

As he is looking over the resume, about to pick up the phone to call and offer Ms. Jo a ticket to fly down for an interview, the phone rings and it's Mr. Lee. "My nephew is coming down on the first plane tomorrow. I told him you had a job for him."

The only thing Mr. Choi can say is, "I understand," before he hangs up the phone and puts the resume down on his desk.

Discussion Questions

1. What risks does Mr. Choi take in hiring Seobang over Yaeni? And vice-versa?

2. According to modern recruitment criteria—and what would be best for the hotel as a business—which candidate should be hired as the Front Desk Supervisor? Why?

3. If you were Mr. Choi and decided to hire Yaeni, how would you deal with Mr. Lee?

4. As a manager, how do you prioritize between the needs of the business and cultural traditions when they come into conflict with one another?

5. How would this situation be different if there were not a shortage of qualified labor on Cheju Island?

6. To what extent does the common perception in Korea of hospitality as "not really a business" have an effect on this case?

Chapter 10 Outline

A Post-War Plan for Growth
Cultural Differences
    Gender Discrimination
    Religion
    Societal Attitudes toward Hospitality
    The Legal and Political Environment
Labor Market Analysis
Conclusion

Competencies

1. Explain the challenges facing
    Lebanon's hospitality human
    resources. (pp. 173–174)

2. Identify cultural differences and
    societal work values as they affect
    employment in hospitality.
    (pp. 174–176)

3. Describe legal issues pertaining to
    employment, age, racial tension, and
    safety and health. (pp. 176–177)

4. Discuss the labor market and the
    availability of a qualified work force.
    (pp. 177–179)

10

Human Resource Challenges Facing the Lebanese Hospitality Industry

Said M. Ladki

Said M. Ladki, *Ph.D., is associate professor of hospitality management at the Lebanese American University. Previously, he served on the faculty of West Virginia University and Georgia Southern University. A native of Lebanon, he has published more than 32 scholarly papers, focusing on research in the areas of food service, hospitality, tourism, lodging, marketing, industrial catering, and strategic management in the hospitality industry.*

A Post-War Plan for Growth

Blessed with a distinguished location and favorable climate, Lebanon was once regarded as the most attractive tourist destination in the Middle East. Before the beginning of the civil conflict in 1975, the contribution of tourism to Lebanon's gross national product was 20 percent. But by 1977, it had declined to 7.4 percent. It bottomed to zero throughout the 1980s.[1] Since the end of the civil conflict in 1992, the Lebanese government has been actively involved in rebuilding the country's infrastructure and reviving the tourism industry to regain its pre-war eminence.

Currently, Lebanon is witnessing a significant increase in the number of tourist arrivals. According to statistics released in 1998 by the Ministry of Transportation, the number of tourists arriving in Lebanon increased from 425,000 in 1992 to 963,000 in 1997. The constant rise in the number of arrivals has been accompanied by a sharp increase in the number of international hospitality firms that are rushing to the lucrative Lebanese market.[2] Firms such as Holiday Inn, Marriott, Howard Johnson, The Accor Group, Quality International, TGI Friday's, Hard Rock Cafe, McDonald's, Pizza Hut, Domino's Pizza, Subway, and Hardee's have all entered the market since 1995.

In its attempt to reposition the country, the Lebanese government, along with the World Tourism Organization, has developed a national tourism plan for the period of 1996–2010.[3] The plan projects that about 3.2 million tourists will visit Lebanon by the year 2010, representing an average growth of nine percent annually. It also projects about eight million tourist nights, with an average annual growth rate of 10.2 percent during the period of 1995–2010. To achieve these targets, the plan calls for an increase in the number of hotel rooms from 18,660 in 1995 to 63,820 in 2010. Additionally, the plan calls for the reorganization of the tourism sector, reform of laws and regulations governing hospitality firms, development of a national tourism data center, and development of Lebanon's human resources to meet the expected demand for hospitality professionals. As hospitality developers and investments continue to pour in—and as the number of hotel rooms and arrivals continues to increase—employment in the hospitality and tourism sector will grow.

During the war years, Lebanon witnessed a sharp increase in the migration of its skilled labor. Technically competent Lebanese hospitality professionals relocated to more prosperous tourist destinations in the region, creating a vacuum in the marketplace. Local hospitality operators were not able to retain their experienced staff or hire new skilled staff. As departing employees left, new recruits received training to bring their skills up to acceptable standards. However, once the new recruits developed a sense of mastery of the job, they had little difficulty finding better employment elsewhere. Lebanese hospitality managers felt as if their operations were becoming training grounds for people to acquire basic skills, then move on. As a result, hospitality operations in Lebanon are seen as having a low-skilled work force characterized by high turnover, lack of adequate training, and frail management and supervisory skills.

Lebanon has not yet developed a human resource strategy to support the future growth of tourism in the country. According to some estimates, total employment in the tourism sector must reach 76,670 employees by 2010.[4] That represents an average growth of 5.8 percent annually. Despite such a projected increase in employment, the government has not addressed this issue. A work force preparedness report evaluating tourism development in Lebanon stated, "Already, Lebanon is faced with a shortage of workers in the skilled and semi-skilled positions. Not only the industry workers are few, but training new workers in many cases is proving to be difficult. Some international hotels find that training costs in Lebanon and ratio of staff to rooms are among the highest in their systems (for example, 3 employees per room in some places, compared to the industry ratio of 1 or 1.5)."[5] If no immediate actions are taken to remedy the situation, it appears that within the coming few years Lebanon's hospitality industry will face a human resource crisis.

Cultural Differences

Even though many aspects of the Lebanese lifestyle have been westernized, culture and tradition still have significant impact on one's practices. The eastern concept of a male-dominated society still influences the lives of most people. Gender discrimination is present in our patriarchal society, and men are favored over women in several positions. Religion also guides the lives of many people. Finally, the not-so-positive attitude that Lebanese citizens hold toward employment in hospitality is also a result of our culture. These factors and many others contribute to the shortage of labor supply in our society.

Gender Discrimination

Although the positions occupied by women are currently much better than 10 years ago, women are still not allowed to occupy many of the jobs men can hold, despite Lebanese labor laws that prohibit gender discrimination. Our employment practices reflect the perception of women as housewives or, at most, secretaries. As a result, women represent a minority in the hospitality business, making up only 27 percent of the work force. Lebanese women in hospitality are mostly house-keepers, receptionists, or secretaries.

It is not acceptable for women to work late or travel alone for work purposes. Hospitality employers do not welcome the idea of hiring female individuals for the night shifts. The older generations of hospitality recruiters are even less likely to hire women than their younger counterparts.

As of this writing, only two women have attained upper-level managerial positions in Lebanon. In mid-level management positions, female managers represent 33 percent of the labor force. Some men cannot accept the idea of a woman superior to them. Others do not think a woman is capable of holding high manage-rial positions.

Religion

Religious values directly influence the lives of many people in our society. Religion, to many Lebanese, is a way of life, a direction to higher values, and a guide for proper social and human behavior. Many people believe that a hotel, with its perceived free-spirited living and atmosphere of amusement and nightlife, may alter human behavior or encourage the younger generation to drift away from mainstream societal values. As a consequence, lots of parents do not like to see their children (especially their daughters) work in hotels or serve the night shift for fear of moral or behavioral change. Moreover, having contact with liquor and pork products makes conservative Muslims avoid working in hospitality.

Societal Attitudes toward Hospitality

One of the challenges facing human resources development in the Lebanese hos-pitality and tourism industry is the negative cultural perception associated with the business. Lots of people associate the hospitality industry with nightlife, gambling, low wages, limited career opportunities, and moral or behavioral corruption.

To recruit workers, the industry must enhance its image by informing poten-tial employees that a hospitality career is morally sound, decent, and able to pro-vide good living standards. There are a number of strategies for doing this. Hospitality organizations can invite the public and concerned parents to look behind the scenes at various hotel operations. Le Vendôme Inter-Continental Beirut, for example, has developed videotapes that show potential employees the realities of work in hospitality.[6] The video is used as a recruitment tool and is made available to the public.

Another aspect that gives the industry its negative image is rooted in Lebanese society. Most Lebanese refuse to learn back-of-the-house skills such as cooking or housekeeping because they are not prestigious. This creates a shortage in back-of-the-house positions. If one were to analyze the personnel composition of Lebanese hotels, one would notice that most of the back-of-the-house posts are occupied by foreign staff. For example, when the prestigious Regency Hotel was not able to find a local chief steward, the hotel recruited an Indian national for that post.

Other people may prefer not to choose careers in hospitality because advancement opportunities are limited. This was the case during the war years when job mobility was restricted. An employee would stay in the same position forever. The introduction of new international chains such as Marriott, Holiday Inn, Best Western, and Inter-Continental has made job advancement opportunities more likely. These hotels have established career paths and usually offer people the opportunity to develop within their systems. However, these hotels prefer to hire foreign-trained managers with extensive background and experience in managing hotels according to corporate standards. Unfortunately, most privately owned Lebanese hotels do not offer career development programs. The absence of such programs negatively affects recruitment possibilities and the number of new entrants into the work force.

Lebanese hospitality operators must establish career development programs to develop and motivate their employees. Career development is at the core of human resource development. Any organization that takes staff training and development seriously is indirectly encouraging employees to take part in planning their own career in relation to organizational goals—and that increases the probability that the right people will be available to meet the organization's changing staff needs. Additionally, if hospitality operators support career development programs, employees may exhibit greater loyalty and commitment to the organization, which results in lower turnover.

The Legal and Political Environment

A variety of legal and political restrictions and practices affect the Lebanese hospitality industry.

Foreign Labor. Ninety percent of the employees needed in hospitality are in unskilled service areas such as food and beverage and housekeeping.[7] The shortage of labor in the semi-skilled and unskilled categories has compelled local hospitality operators to hire foreign labor. It is not surprising to find a hotel or restaurant in Lebanon at which the kitchen and service staff are from Syria or Egypt, housekeeping staff are from Sri Lanka or the Philippines, and laundry, valet parking, and other service personnel come from Sudan, Nigeria, Kenya, or Ethiopia. These legal employees enter the country with a valid work permit made possible by the Lebanese Ministry of Labor. Their selection is based on previous work history and accomplishments, work-related experience, and education as related to the job.

Hospitality employers who want to hire foreign employees must first verify the identity, residence permit, length of stay, and eligibility of work for all individuals. Afterward, a legal work permit will be issued. Lebanese law stipulates that a company can hire one foreign laborer for every four local employees. The government does not allow a hospitality firm to hire foreign labor until it has advertised the position in local papers and found that there are no applicants for the advertised position. Consequently, many hotels are employing foreigners without notifying the government. They register them as trainees from other countries in order to avoid the long and cumbersome paperwork process; to maintain their residency, foreign employees register as trainees at the Department of Labor and with immigration authorities.

There are certain front desk and food and beverage positions for which the Lebanese Ministry of Labor strongly recommends the hiring of Lebanese nationals. However, many hotels find themselves forced to hire foreign executive chefs or front desk managers due to the unavailability of skilled indigenous staff. Hotels that hire foreign individuals fear not knowing what to do if their executive chef or front office manager were to depart, since there are no qualified local staff to hold these posts. There is a consensus among most hotels and restaurant managers that fresh hospitality vocational school graduates are not technically competent. Even at the middle- and upper-management levels one will find American, British, German, and French personnel. Nonetheless, there are certain hotels that refuse to employ foreigners and prefer to hire locals.

Age. For employees under the age of 16 (and under 18 for certain jobs), there are special employment laws restricting maximum working hours, night work, jobs involving certain hazardous equipment or chemicals, and the serving of alcoholic beverages. To avoid the restrictions associated with this issue, most hospitality employers prefer not to hire minors. The decision not to hire minors has reduced the size of the labor pool and discriminated against a group of young individuals who are capable of working and who might later choose hospitality as a career.

Safety and Health. Lebanese labor laws mandate that all hospitality service firms must provide a safe working environment for their employees. Employers are required to set mandatory job safety and health standards, conduct inspections, and keep records of injuries, illnesses, and fatalities. Though it may not sound economically cost effective, Le Vendôme Inter-Continental Beirut's safety measures require all housekeeping and room service personnel to render their services in teams; working in teams, a female room service employee, for example, would not feel embarrassed or unsafe when delivering an order to a room occupied by a male guest.

Labor Market Analysis

Though hotels recruit applicants for particular jobs, candidates first make an occupational choice that defines the kind of job they will pursue. It appears that the

Lebanese hospitality and tourism industry has failed to influence occupational choice factors in its favor. For example, the high literacy rate in Lebanon, the mastery of several foreign languages by most citizens, and investment growth in hospitality should all have been translated into positive actions to recruit more people. The industry's lack of action to influence occupational choice factors lies behind the current labor shortage crisis.

A relatively low number of women work in our society. However, women constitute 27 percent of the hospitality labor force, and that number is expected to grow due to the increased demand for hospitality professionals and the willingness of women to enter the hospitality domain.[8] As in the western world, the hospitality industry in Lebanon relies on young individuals to fill many of its entry-level positions. Young people from 15 to 25 represent 19 percent of the population and are a potential labor source that can learn fast, adopt new skills, and achieve high positions.[9] To cope with labor shortages, concepts like part-time employment and employee leasing—the hiring of employees for a specific task or a specific time period—have just been introduced into the hiring/recruitment circles.

The country's literacy rate is 95 percent and most citizens are trilingual, speaking English, French, and Arabic. The high literacy rate leads most new entrants to the work force to apply for supervisory or managerial positions. Very few individuals apply for staff or line positions. This fact represents a major obstacle, especially when hotels and restaurants need a large percentage of semi-skilled employees to perform certain housekeeping or kitchen tasks.

In recent years, as customers have become more sophisticated in their service expectations, more emphasis has been placed on employee training. Lebanon's high literacy rate has made corporate training quite easy. However, the hospitality and tourism industry is hindered by the limited availability of education and training institutions. Presently, there are two universities and five vocational schools offering a hospitality and tourism curriculum. The number of graduates from these schools barely meet expected demand, though, and most of them are able to find attractive offers and relocate to neighboring countries. Existing hospitality and tourism operators are trying to attract more people and retain them by offering higher starting wages, more orientation and training, regular job evaluation, flexible schedules, transportation allowances, and child-care programs. Tourism education and training has become a priority for our government.

Conclusion

Issues limiting employees' entry into the Lebanese hospitality labor force should be tackled and overcome. The migration of what is left from our skilled labor supply must be stopped. Lebanese hospitality operators must offer competitive wages, fair working conditions, and better career development programs. The attraction of new candidates into the industry may not solve the problem unless it is accompanied by solid HR development and planning strategies, which will help ensure that the appropriate number of employees with the required skills are available when needed.

The development of Lebanon's human resources requires the offering of ongoing training and educational programs. The limited availability of vocational/academic institutions offering hospitality education is affecting the quantity and quality of the available labor supply. Although the Lebanese government has taken some steps toward rehabilitating the country's hotel schools, government actions are still shy in this respect. More schools are needed throughout the five provinces of the country. Additionally, active measures should be taken to absorb the young, the unskilled, and immigrant groups into the core of employment. Part-time employment and employee leasing should become more popular and accessible; using part-time employees will fill the worker vacuum and introduce more people to careers in hospitality. The industry as a whole must enhance its image by informing people about the job opportunities and advancement potential in this field. Hotels should invite people to look behind the scenes.

Changing attitudes and societal values is a long-term process. To influence change, government and industry should unite their efforts. The human resource crisis in Lebanon is not insurmountable. Change is possible.

Endnotes

1. D. Daher, "The Touristic Season Shaped by Summering," *Al Hayat* (22 October 1994), p. 26.

2. S. M. Ladki and A. Dah, "Challenges Facing Post-War Tourism Development: The Case of Lebanon," *Journal of International Hospitality Leisure and Tourism Management* 1, no. 2 (1997): 35–43.

3. *Lebanon Tourism Strategic Plan 1996–2010* (Beirut: Lebanese Ministry of Tourism, 1996).

4. "Survey of Economic and Social Development in the ESCWA Region 1996–1997," *Tourism and the Eco of ESCWA Member Countries* (Beirut: Economic & Social Commission for Western Asia, 1997).

5. *Industry Growth Partnerships: Achieving Lebanon's True Economic Potentials: Tourism Cluster Strategy* (United States Agency for International Development/Lebanon, Stanford Research Institute, and the Lebanese American University, 1999), p. 36.

6. L. Shabaan, interview by author, Le Vendôme Inter-Continental Beirut, Lebanon, 1999.

7. B. Cabana, "The Labor Worries of a Successful Emigré," *Lodging Hospitality* (May 1998), p. 13.

8. "The Current Living Situation of Families in Lebanon—1997," *Center for Statistical Studies and Information* 9 (February 1998).

9. United Nations Population Fund, "United Nations Development Program, 1998" (Paper delivered at the UNDP Third Regular Session, New York, NY, 14–16 September and 21–22 September, 1998).

 # Discussion Questions

1. How has the Lebanese civil war affected employment in hospitality?
2. What Lebanese societal values affect employment in hospitality?

3. Do religious practices affect employment in hospitality? How?

4. How has people's perception of the hospitality industry affected employment?

5. According to Lebanese labor laws, what are the jobs that foreign laborers could undertake?

6. How has the presence of foreign labor affected the employee-management relationship?

7. What are some of the occupational choice factors that are in favor of Lebanese hospitality operators? How could the choice factors be influenced in a way to recruit more people into the hospitality labor force?

8. What are some of the techniques and strategies that Lebanese operators are using to recruit more people into the work force and to change negative cultural perceptions associated with employment in hospitality?

Internet Sites

For more information, visit the following Internet sites. Remember that Internet addresses can change without notice.

An-Nahar (Lebanon's daily newspaper, Arabic)
http://www.annahar.com.lb/index.html

Arab World Online—Lebanon
http://www.awo.net/country/ministry/lebanon.asp

Lebanon.com
http://www.lebanon.com

Lebanon Tourism
http://www.lol.com.lb/tourism/index.shtml

LebNet Resource Center
http://www.lebnet.org

Le Vendôme Inter-Continental Beirut
http://www.interconti.com/lebanon/beirut/hotel_beiven.html

World Tourism Organization
http://www.world-tourism.org/

Chapter 11 Outline

The Human Resource Context
Labor Demographics and Market Issues
    Legal and Political Environment
    Cultural Distinctions and Societal
        Work Values
    Corporate Cultures
Labor Relations
    Recruitment and Selection
    Performance Evaluation Processes
    Career Development Programs

Competencies

1. Discuss the history of human resources in Malta, including labor demographics and market issues. (pp. 183–187)

2. Explain how the legal and political environments, cultural distinctions, societal work values, and the corporate culture affect the industry. (pp. 187–188)

3. Identify recruitment, selection, and performance evaluation processes, including career development programs. (pp. 188–189)

Human Resource Management in Malta: Hospitality Insights from a Small Island Territory

Godfrey Baldacchino

Godfrey Baldacchino, *Ph.D. (Warwick, U.K.), B.A. (Gen.), PCGE, M.A. (The Hague), is a sociologist specializing in labor-management relations at the University of Malta, Malta. An accomplished scholar in the study of small states and islands, he has published various articles in international refereed journals and book chapters on the unfolding of human resource themes in the context of smallness and insularity. He is the author of* Global Tourism and Informal Labour Relations: The Small Scale Syndrome at Work. *He has served as visiting lecturer at the University of the West Indies, Barbados; the University of the South Pacific, Fiji; the Seychelles Institute of Management; the University of Mauritius; and the University of Prince Edward Island, Canada.*

Located in the Mediterranean Sea, just south of Sicily, the Maltese archipelago basically consists of three islands: Malta, Gozo, and Comino. Their total population is about 400,000 (of which 95 percent reside on the main island of Malta). Malta is located approximately 62 miles (100 km) south of Italy and 93 miles (150 km) northeast of Tunisia. The islands have a typically temperate climate offering warm, dry summers averaging 90°F (32°C) and mild winters averaging 57°F (14°C); with little rain, they enjoy some 300 days of sunshine each year.

The island's strategic location and sheltered deepwater harbors have allowed Malta to develop as an important trading post, proving to be a convenient stop for traders, travelers, and seafarers. Over the centuries, they also rendered it an obvious target to ambitious regional and naval powers. With a civilization track record going back to at least 3850 BC, Malta has had its fair share of "visitors," ranging from the religious (St. Paul) to the military (Napoleon) to the political (George

Exhibit 1   Maltese Tourism Figures (1959–1998)

YEAR	HOTELS	BEDS	HOTEL EMPLOYEES	TOURISTS	GROSS INCOME (US$ MILLION)
1959	25	1,218	505	12,583	2
1965	38	2,380	819	47,804	5
1969	101	7,562	2,778	186,084	30
1975	91	9,424	3,672	334,519	80
1979	97	10,507	4,370	618,310	210
1985	116	13,486	4,283	517,864	180
1989	133	19,712	5,602	871,776	450
1995	134	21,815	5,400	1,115,971	750
1998	150	30,000	8,700	1,182,240	960

Source: National Tourism Authority, *The Economic Impact of Tourism in Malta* (Malta: National Tourism Authority, Research and Planning Division, 1999).

Bush and Mikhail Gorbachev, who signed the end of the cold war off Malta in December 1989). A regular military and administrative presence by the colonizing powers ensured a regular traffic of personnel and their families to and from the small islands. Today, the islands are a sovereign state, having achieved political independence from Great Britain in 1964.

Malta positioned itself with a deliberate tourism policy in the late 1950s when its "fortress economy" role was practically shattered overnight by a unilateral change in Britain's assessment of the strategic role of the islands. With its days as a fortress base suddenly numbered, Malta had to very quickly diversify its sources of income away from the servicing of military personnel and installations. In addition to industrialization, the tourism industry was clean and attractive—a natural extension of the island's previous fortress colony role and one of the few plausible options for a resource-poor economy.

The start was most discreet: in 1959, there were only 25 hotels providing 1,218 beds and employing 505 workers; these hotels served 12,583 tourists (the large majority being British), with resulting gross receipts amounting to around US$2 million.[1] Throughout the 1960s and 1970s, tourist arrivals grew rapidly as Malta shared in the jet travel and holiday package boom (see Exhibit 1).[2] The transformation led to the construction of large, isolated hotels in the relatively unspoiled northern Malta and on the smaller islands of Gozo and Comino; desirable suburbs were recast as resort towns where hotels lined the seafront; and the small town of Bugibba, on the northeast coast, was practically built from scratch.

This period of expansion reached a peak in 1980 with the number of hotels and holiday complexes numbering 112, providing some 13,200 beds, and employing 5,159 full-time employees (5 percent of the gainfully employed). These hotels served 730,000 tourist arrivals (75 percent of whom come over in the peak months of May to October) with resulting gross foreign receipts of US$330 million. British visitors continued to dominate the tourist market, constituting almost two-thirds of all 1980 arrivals. When the number of British arrivals dropped by almost 50 percent between 1982 and 1986, the market plummeted.

Since 1987, new vigorous infrastructural investment, aggressive marketing, a preferential rate of exchange for the tourist sterling, and the ever-expanding character of the international tourism industry have collectively helped to see Malta out of its worst recession yet. There are now some 50 four-star and five-star hotels and tourist complexes on the archipelago. The tourist figures have shot through the magical one million barrier yearly since 1992 and are much less dependent on the British market. The industry orientation now caters to higher-spending, more culture-friendly, up-market tourists, while at the same time shifting the pressure away from the hectic summer months.[3]

The Human Resource Context

An ambivalent challenge presents itself to small island territories purporting to behave as tourism destinations. On one hand, they risk coming across as so many similar islands, all fiercely competing with the same assets—sun, sea, and sand—for an increasingly discerning clientele where succeeding in getting a sufficient quantity of tourist arrivals may depend increasingly on low prices. On the other hand, being small islands, they may have started to realize that they possess certain qualities that can render the tourist experience even more unique and attractive in marketing its totality and difference, effectively avoiding the placelessness and anonymity that global tourism often implies.[4] Small multi–island (archipelagic) states can augment these experiences with the opportunity to take in still more self-contained and diverse destinations, with the excitement of traveling from one island to another.[5]

The obvious and compelling attraction of the small and insular, be they warm or cold water locations, has to do with their romantic and sensual associations—a relationship seeped in myth and mystique, but no doubt exploited by the public relations machine of the tourist industry itself.[6] Yet, other, probably more tangible assets have to do with the physical and geographical conditions of the territory; the experience of transition across the sea; its relative compression of features on a small land area; and a native population whose exposure, in time and depth, to external interventions renders it particularly open and welcoming.[7] These features enable tourists to small islands to relish a journey, a totalizing experience, and a "host-guest" encounter—ranging from a simple one-to-one experience to a meeting of cultures—not easily found elsewhere, where tourism is an industry apart.[8] However, the foreign tourist pressure on the small social unit may build up to unbearable proportions, causing resentment and "not in my back yard" attitudes in the public at large, otherwise known as **nimbyism**.[9]

Labor Demographics and Market Issues

The number of jobs in hotels is obviously only the tip of the tourism employment iceberg. Tourism in Malta is credited with being responsible for around 35 percent of the country's gross domestic product. The forward linkages of tourism (the economic spinoffs resulting from the outcomes of tourism, such as transportation, catering, telecommunications, and printing) and its backward linkages (the economic spinoffs which are involved in the generation of tourism, such as air transport and construction) have been significant because, unlike the populations of many other small island destinations, the Maltese have remained strongly in control of tourism capital. The hotel and restaurant infrastructure, as well as air travel, has been wisely developed on the basis of local interests, with foreign concerns brought in either as partners, contracted management, or franchise operators. Air Malta, the national airline since 1974, has done remarkably well in handling a large percentage of both scheduled and charter flights to and from Malta.

The tourism industry has not traditionally attracted the best human resources. Malta's economy has traditionally been geared to a more industrialized vocation; in a country with few status markers, low income differentials, and very transparent wealth patterns, service industries have been wrongly associated with servility. Many find it difficult to deploy their **emotional labor**—not just the service, but the service with a smile—and please the guest.[10] The difficulty is even stronger in the southern and eastern regions of the main island, with their traditional orientation to ship repair and ship-building and—since the early 1960s—to factorywork. A second difficulty is that hospitality work goes against the common notion of the working week. Because the busiest tourist times are associated with entertainment, vacation, and leisure—which the Maltese also hope to enjoy—holidays and weekends end up competing for work commitments.

The hospitality industry in Malta continues to complain about its "people problem." It is claimed that the island does not have the trained staff it needs to cope with the quantity and quality of incoming tourists. As a result, the cost of procuring skilled personnel on both a full-time and part-time basis is mounting. The industry claims that it will be obliged to go for immigrant labor unless the local labor market provides the required solutions.[11]

The changing orientation to the tourism industry is a slow but steady process. Among the younger generation, a targeted approach to hospitality training has been making cultural inroads in attitudes, even though there remains a fairly substantial drain of trained personnel away from the industry, mainly due to the unsocial working hours. The key institutional player in this reform process has been the Institute of Tourism Studies (ITS), the only vocationally-targeted tertiary educational institution in Malta, with hundreds of enrolled youth following a diverse range of three- to four-year full-time courses associated with tourism, catering, and hospitality. The students also benefit from a specially devised stipend scheme that provides them with income while also subsidizing those employers who take up the students for training and placement in their establishments during their courses. High flyers, or top students from the ITS, can also benefit from a special arrangement to continue their studies at the University of Malta and graduate in tourism management.

Conditions of employment in the sprawling tourism industry are somewhat uneven. The country's labor legislation upholds minimum national standards but then delegates specifics to collective bargaining between employer and labor representatives at company level. This leads to a fairly large range of conditions, depending on the firm's ability to pay and the employees' negotiating clout. Conditions are generally less attractive in those workplaces where there are no recognized trade unions (such as most two- and three-star hotels and many small catering establishments). Around 37 percent of the workforce in hotel and catering establishments is unionized in Malta, compared to a national unionization rate of around 55 percent.[12] Regular part-time and casual employment is practiced, with arbitrary hiring and firing practices, which does not generally result in superior levels of service and customer care. Labor turnover is arguably high in the tourism employment market (bottom stratum); as a result, the labor force is not expected to be highly skilled. Furthermore, given the instability of employment and the seasonal nature of most contracts in the low-quality end of the business, those attracted to work therein may do so mainly as a supplementary, part-time endeavor. Indeed, the Maltese labor force is characterized by a dual job phenomenon; most (especially male) adults, hold at least one full-time and one part-time job.[13]

Legal and Political Environment

Maltese legislation is very strongly inspired by its British counterpart. Having served uninterruptedly as a British colony for 160 years prior to independence, Malta has been naturally imitating developments on the social and political front in the mother country. Malta prides itself for having been one of those few British colonies that managed a fairly peaceful and smooth transition to a parliamentary democracy, with a fairly regular interchange of political parties in power, and for having done so without generating problems with oppressed ethnic minorities. Nevertheless, the influence of party politics on the minds and behavior of locals is nearly stifling and totalizing because a significant portion of the electorate believes in maintaining loyalty and allegiance to a particular political party.

Cultural Distinctions and Societal Work Values

Malta is an interesting amalgam of a legal-rational administrative regime. On one hand, there is a well-functioning bureaucratic structure using written Queen's English (the country's second language). On the other hand, this basic business structure is grounded in a Latin and Mediterranean culture that is more at ease with informality, quick-fix deals, and colorful and expressive person-specific communications implemented via spoken Maltese (the country's first language). One result of such a cultural amalgam on work practices is that jobs may be expected to go to those qualified and trained to perform them; however, they may just as well go to "friends of friends" including kinfolk, irrespective of whether these people are qualified or best-suited for the post.

The net effect of this Janus-like culture—one of dual identities—is remarkable, even more so for its existence on such a small place. The condition has been aptly described as the "Mdina defence syndrome."[14] A former capital of Malta, Mdina is a very small, walled fortified city with streets that convey a false sense of direction and security. Because the streets follow no specific pattern, it is extremely easy—especially for foreigners—to get lost. In much the same way, the small-scale culture of insular Malta may appear fairly easy for foreigners to grasp, but it is much more likely for them to get completely lost and to fail to appreciate the culture's ramifications. Maltese culture is unwritten and secretive, and its lifeblood is the Maltese language—unknown to the foreigner. This duality is also manifest in the relations between Maltese employees and expatriate managers—as distinct from relations among the Maltese themselves.

Corporate Cultures

Small island territories are typically open economies and societies: their survival depends considerably on their ability to use political resourcefulness to tap and attract foreign interest, investment, and largesse. This includes multi-national firms and management operators, which typically have their own transnational corporate ethos. This company philosophy seeks to promote a unitarist or familial environment (having one undisputed source of power and authority) with a strong orientation toward positive sanctions (such as rewards, incentives, and bonuses) and well-publicized role-modeling programs for those employees who demonstrate allegiance and loyalty to fundamental company principles.

While structured programs like total quality management have become common throughout the hospitality industry worldwide, the manner in which local behavior patterns dovetail with such global management projects is typically underrated and often unrecognized. Rather than having its way, the global corporate project is more likely to suffer infection by the local cultural fabric, creating in the outcome a unique amalgam of "glocal" (that is, global and local) features, otherwise referred to as **glocalization**.[15] The cumulative effects of working in a socially claustrophobic environment where the same individuals habitually meet over and over again in a variety of role sets and where opportunities for market dominance are enhanced constitutes a **small scale syndrome** that may leave expatriate management perplexed, even disarmed—they may not be able to make sense of what is going on.[16]

Labor Relations

Recruitment and Selection

Recruitment and selection is a key interface between the firm and the external labor market. Word-of-mouth recruitment is widespread and can bring substantial benefits and savings.[17] When existing employees recruit newcomers, management saves on advertising and screening costs. However, such a tacit recommendation process must be seen in the context of **brokerage** functions carried out routinely by individuals in small, isolated territories. People are likely to know a substantial percentage of the total domestic human resource field. Consequently, people get to know—deliberately or incidentally—of the needs of others. The likely cumulative effect of this condition is that the citizens of small states and territories are burdened with heavy claims for obligation as well as with tempting opportunities to favor others—an investment that could be handsomely recouped in the future. One pervasive practice of recruitment and selection is to promote relatives and friends for attractive positions—a policy more vigorously entertained in conditions of high unemployment. If management is immune to these antics, recruitment and selection could serve as the levers to extend the networks of sympathy and antipathy that exist among the locals at large.

Performance Evaluation Processes

An equally difficult situation presents itself in relation to performance evaluation. Relations in small locations are excessively personalized.[18] It is very easy and convenient to associate a task with a particular person and to obtain or offer services without any attempt at institutionalizing the practice. The arrangement is non-bureaucratic and efficient in its own way—but depends on a one-to-one bond. Tensions soar and conflicts erupt when arguably objective procedures are used and where accusations of personal preferences are difficult to avoid.

Two critical areas where such a conflict occurs are those of employee remuneration and career promotion. In both cases, regardless of the pains that management may take to set up a just, objective, and transparent process, the losers of the contest invariably cry foul. In small hospitality establishments run as family concerns, nepotism is a standard and expected practice that is even defended by legislation. So, for example, the "last in, first out" principle does not apply in relation to kin according to Maltese labor law. To avoid bad blood and resentment, the "fall back" option, in situations where there is trade union representation, is to go for equal payment packages and seniority-based promotion. Both of these measures may be highly ineffective in motivating effort and they eliminate managerial discretion—but they at least serve their purpose of quashing accusations of any abuse in the exercise of that discretion.

Career Development Programs

It has already been mentioned that the quality and numbers of staff throughout the industry leaves much to be desired. Some top-notch luxury hotels have started introducing in-house career development programs, often benchmarked on a global level. Otherwise, in-house training is extremely limited and certainly insufficient, considering the neglect in strategic human resource development until the late 1980s. Leadership skills enabling individuals to inspire, motivate, and coordinate the work of subordinates are desperately required. The ability to sell and cost operations—to aggressively market Malta as a tourism destination and to calculate the profits from a particular tourism operation (such as a new hotel)—is also scarce, while there has also been a general concern to upgrade standards of hygiene, food preparation, and production for all employees.[19] The concern belies an often disregarded link between human resources and organizational considerations; employees who are not career oriented—especially part-timers—cannot be expected to exhibit full corporate commitment, to go for exacting standards of service, or to "own" problems. Furthermore, the diversification away from the British market in favor of continental tourism must be accompanied by additional language skills—especially German and French—and knowledge of associated customary habits.[20]

Endnotes

1. J. Inguanez, "The Impact of Tourism in Malta: Cultural Rapture or Continuity?" in R.G. Sultana and G. Baldacchino, eds., *Maltese Society: A Sociological Inquiry* (Malta. Mireva, 1994), pp. 343–352.

2. J. Boissevain, "Tourism and Development in Malta," *Development and Change*, Vol. 8 (1977), pp. 523–538.

3. E.P. Delia, *The State of the Maltese Economy 1994: A Commentary* (Malta Chamber of Commerce, 1995).

4. R.W. Butler, "Tourism Development in Small Islands" in D.G. Lockhart, D. Drakakis-Smith, and P. Schembri, eds., *The Development Process in Small Island States* (London: Routledge, 1993), pp. 71–91.

5. T. Baum, "The Fascination of Islands: A Tourist Perspective" in D.G. Lockhart and D. Drakakis-Smith, eds., *Island Tourism: Problems and Perspectives* (London: Mansell, 1997), pp. 21–35.

6. R. King, "The Geographical Fascination of Islands" in Lockhart, Drakakis-Smith, and Schembri, pp. 13–37 and G. Baldacchino, *Global Tourism and Informal Labor Relations: The Small Scale Syndrome at Work* (London: Mansell, 1997).

7. W.C. Husbands, "The Genesis of Tourism in Barbados: Further Notes on the Welcoming Society," *Caribbean Geography*, Vol.1 (1983), pp. 107–120.

8. V.L. Smith, ed., *Hosts and Guests: An Anthropology of Tourism* (Philadelphia: University of Pennsylvania Press, 1977).

9. G.V. Doxey, "When enough is enough: The Natives are restless in Old Niagara," *Heritage Canada*, Vol. 2 (1976), pp. 26–27.

10. S. Fineman, ed., *Emotion in Organisations* (London: Sage, 1993) and A.R. Hochschild, *The Managed Heart: The Commercialization of Human Feeling* (Berkeley, Calif.: University of California Press, 1983).

11. N. Falzon, "Recruitment and Training Needs in the Hospitality Industry," *Hospitality and Leisure*, Issue No.12 (Malta, 1997), p.6.

12. G. Baldacchino, "Trade Unions in the Maltese Private Sector," *Bank of Valletta Review*, No. 13 (1996), pp. 17–30.

13. E.P. Delia, "A Labor Market in Transition" in Sultana and Baldacchino, pp. 461–481.

14. S. Chircop, "As We Sit Together, Should We Use the Phone? A Research Agenda for the Study of Media in Malta" in Sultana and Baldacchino, pp. 357–369.

15. T.J. Courchene, "Glocalization: The Regional/International Interface," *Canadian Journal of Regional Science*, Vol. 18, No. 1 (1995), pp. 1–20.

16. Baldacchino, *Global Tourism*.

17. M.J. Boella, *Human Resource Management in the Hotel and Catering Industry*, 4th edition (Cheltenham, U.K.: Stanley Thornes, 1988).

18. B. Benedict, "Sociological Characteristics of Small Territories and their Implications for Economic Development" in Michael Banton, ed., *The Social Anthropology of Complex Societies* (London: Tavistock), pp. 22–34.

19. E.P. Delia, *Tourism Manpower Survey 1990: The Accommodation Sector* (Malta: Tourism Secretariat, 1990).

20. E.P. Delia, *The Tourist Sector: Some Facts, Statistics, Problems and possible Remedies* (unpublished document, Malta Council for Economic Development, Tertiary Sector Working Group, 1990).

Key Terms

brokerage—The manner in which individuals in a small scale territory customarily go about doing each other favors and serving as crucial catalysts to vital market deals.

emotional labor—How one does one's job becomes as (or more) important as the job itself. Service-oriented jobs considerably constrain and contour the emotions of these employees while they are at work.

glocalization—A condition where global forces invariably become grounded and disturbed by local forces; formed by the combination of *globalization* and *local*.

nimbyism—The "not in my backyard" attitude held by those who become resentful of the foreign tourist pressure on their country.

small-scale syndrome—The cumulative effects of working in a socially claustrophobic environment where the same individuals habitually meet over and over again in a variety of role sets and where opportunities for monopolistic market dominance are enhanced.

Discussion Questions

1. What has been the main selling point of small island territories in being presented and marketed as tourism destinations?

2. Why was Malta obliged to consider an active tourism policy in the 1950s?

3. What factors helped to nudge Malta out of the recession in the tourism industry that developed in the early 1980s?

4. Why are conditions of employment in Malta's hospitality industry fairly uneven?

5. What is one advantage and one disadvantage of recruitment by word of mouth?

6. In what two areas of human resource management practice are employees most likely to protest and claim foul play?

7. What are the key characteristics of a unitarist (familial) work environment?

Internet Sites

For more information, visit the following Internet sites. Remember that Internet addresses can change without notice.

Institute of Tourism Studies
http://its.mitts.net/

Search Malta
http://www.searchmalta.com

Malta
http://www.malta.co.uk

University of Malta
http://www.um.edu.mt/

Malta Tourism Authority
http://www.visitmalta.com

Case Study

The Problem with Parking

The Palm Beach Resort (PBR) is a large luxury hotel with a top stratum of expatriate management who are on a three-year maximum assignment to the small territory. Management does not understand the local language and is not interested in local customs. The hotel, with over 250 full-time employees, is one of the largest private employers on the island and has been a very important employment provider in the area. With time, employees have managed to recruit most of their close kin into employment—so much so that employees consider PBR to be practically "theirs." Thus, the hotel is deftly embedded into the employees' wider social existence. This is further strengthened by a very low rate of labor turnover.

With relationships that exist vertically, horizontally, and diagonally across the organization chart, the pressure to avoid conflict is intense because, when conflict does occur, it is total and bitter. The organization operates in what is aptly described as a "crab in the barrel" situation: a tightly knit community—with its rigid sense of solidarity, mutual obligations, and scare tactics—acts to dampen expressions of divergence.

A total quality management program, recently introduced by international headquarters, is causing a fresh outburst of tensions among the hotel's workforce.

A major recent problem was a decision by PBR's top management that all employees—with the exception of managerial and supervisory personnel—had to park their vehicles in a parking lot outside the hotel's gate. Previously, all PBR employees had been allowed to park their vehicles on the hotel property. The managers considered the employees' responses in a wider context, drawing in issues which go beyond the strict employment relationship:

Sergio Borg, one of the senior managers, put it this way: "The car park is a big issue. It has now revealed itself as a case of ostracism. The employees feel unjustly marginalized. It's a psychological block and shows to workers a certain degree of hypocrisy by management when the latter preach ownership and commitment. It seems that loyalty is only expected from one player."

Another senior manager, Mary Bartolo, said, "The car park issue has become an expression of class conflict. Supervisors still continue to park inside. There is no declared justification for such a policy yet."

The employees were more emotional and crudely ironic in their comments:

"This unilateral management decision smacks of an effrontery to our natural right to park our cars here, as we have always done."

"So much talk about employee involvement and participation. Here, in one fell swoop, management has revealed its real intentions. This has been a most revealing declaration of the meaning of the company philosophy."

"Why should I suddenly start parking my car outside when my supervisor still enjoys the privilege? This is nothing but an exercise in cold and blatant discrimination."

Martina Smith, the HR director—an expatriate with a stronger sense of the native perspective—has believed all along that the TQM program was just a token gesture to show to the head office that they were complying with its directives—without putting any real effort or spirit into the initiative. The car park issue, she reasoned, was to her a clear indicator of the subdued—yet nevertheless bitter—relations between supervisors and their subordinates. However, Martina felt she could not declare these ideas to her GM, who is a keen believer in TQM and is convinced that it is working effectively.

The trade union steward, who organizes most of the employees at PBR, could not restrain the resentment and anger of his membership. He obtained the necessary support from his leaders to declare official industrial action. The next bargaining round was coming up and the union wanted to send an appropriate signal of increased militancy to the PBR owners.

The general manager, an American, is thoroughly unable to understand why the employees should object to the measure. After all, the internal car park is simply unable to handle both staff and guest vehicles any longer, the outside car park is just as convenient, and is only 50 meters further away. He is prepared to act swiftly to stamp out the rebellion by dismissing any employees who choose to strike.

Discussion Questions

1. What could management have done differently to avoid this escalation of negative employment relations?
2. Should the employees have reacted differently?
3. As the senior manager, how could you react to the industrial action?

Chapter 12 Outline

Competencies

1. Identify the factors that have led to the success of Mauritius as a tourist destination. (pp. 195–196)

2. Describe the complexity of Mauritius's multi–ethnic, multi–lingual society. (pp. 196–204)

3. Evaluate the strengths and possible weaknesses of present government policy for the development of tourism. (pp. 204–208)

4. Identify the ways in which local culture and traditions influence labor relations in the context of the hospitality industry. (pp. 208–211)

5. Determine priority needs for the future development of human resource management in Mauritius. (pp. 211–212)

12

Mauritius: Maintaining the "Mauritian Miracle"

Margaret Boullé and Marc Boullé

Margaret Boullé *holds a Doctorat d'Université from the Sorbonne, Paris, a master's degree from the University of Aix-en-Provence, and B.A. Hons from the University of Melbourne, Australia. She has taught at Monash University (Australia), the Institute of Education (Mauritius), and New York University (USA) and has also been a consultant for United Nations organizations in New York and Geneva. She is currently Executive Admission Counsellor at the Ecole Hôtelière de Lausanne, Switzerland.*

Marc Boullé *is the former owner and manager of two restaurant bars in Grand'Baie, Mauritius: Alchemy and Doc 27. He studied at the University of Santa Cruz in California, USA, and is a graduate of the New York Restaurant School. He is a certified PADI diving instructor and has worked in diving centers in Mauritius, as well as in restaurants in New York, Greece, and Mauritius.*

MAURITIUS IS A faraway destination for most of the world: the nearest land mass is Madagascar, off the eastern coast of Africa, about 1,800 kilometers away. The island itself is small—only 1,865 square kilometers, nearly eleven times the area of Washington, D.C., or roughly the same size as England's county of Surrey. Its distance from standard tourist routes makes the island seem isolated and exotic, even though it is well-served by international long-haul carriers. Mauritius is not anchored to one mainland culture or economy but has developed its own unique character, a blend of the many different ethnic groups that coexist on the island.

195

Mauritius as a Tourist Destination

The word *paradise* appears frequently in the tourist literature on Mauritius, together with photographs of white coral beaches fringed by casuarina trees and the contrasting scarlet of flame-trees, bougainvillea, and hibiscus. The island is surrounded by an almost unbroken coral reef barrier that protects it from the ocean beyond, encircling the blue-green waters of the lagoon and ensuring safe swimming throughout the year. Mauritius is of volcanic origin, and the dramatic, jagged peaks of the mountains thrown up by the lava, or the piles of volcanic rocks rising from the fields of sugar cane that cover most of the island, also contribute to its special beauty. The climate is practically ideal: Mauritius enjoys a sunny subtropical climate for most of the year, with little variation in temperature, although humidity is high in the summer months and cyclones are frequent from December through March. In addition, there is a variety of plant and animal life, with some species unique to Mauritius.

Mauritius is a prime destination for sun-sea-sand tourism and is promoted as such. In addition to swimming and snorkeling in the warm tropical water, visitors can enjoy water-skiing, yachting, and diving (most major beach hotels have their own diving centers), not to mention undersea walks, "blue safaris," and boat trips to tiny off-shore islands. Mauritius is also a well-recognized deep-sea fishing center (the world-record blue marlin catch was made in Mauritian waters).

Mauritius has been called "the most cosmopolitan island in the sun," and Mauritians themselves often refer to their country as "the rainbow island." The population is made up of people from three different continents—Asia, Africa, and Europe—reflecting the settlers who have come to the island since the eighteenth century. This diverse population has lived peaceably for many years, with only rare periods of violence or political unrest; the island is often held up as a remarkable example of peaceful coexistence among many different ethnic communities.

The island has a tradition of democracy, with universal suffrage introduced in 1948 when the island was still under British rule. It is a multi-party system, with elections held every five years. There is no army, which is perhaps one of the reasons for the island's political stability. Mauritian society is one in which the same educational opportunities exist for men and women alike, and women participate fully in business and political life.

Surveys of departing tourists carried out by the Ministry of Tourism and Leisure confirm that the "island under the sun" image, together with the cultural aspects of Mauritius as a multi-ethnic society, are the most important motivating factors for tourists who choose to visit Mauritius. The 1998 survey shows that tourists visit the island for its tropical image (48.2 percent), beaches (26.5 percent), people (10.3 percent), accessibility (6.2 percent), with other reasons accounting for 8.2 percent of visits.

Developing a Unique Society

Mauritius is one of the rare countries to have been uninhabited before being colonized. The first transient visitors were the Arabs and the Portuguese, followed by the Dutch, who briefly settled on the island during the latter half of the seventeenth century before abandoning it for the Cape of Good Hope. The Dutch named the island "Mauritius" after their Prince of Nassau; they are chiefly remembered today for having attacked the indigenous dodo bird (now extinct) and for first planting sugar cane, which was to become the principal source of wealth of the island for many years.

The Dutch were followed by the French in 1715, who renamed the island "Ile de France." The island was captured by the English in 1810, but the French influence remained and is still extremely important today.

During their colonization, the French imported slaves from Eastern Africa to work the plantations; by 1810, the island's population of about 73,000 was 20 percent settlers and 80 percent slaves. The plantation structure, with some of the old French families still at the head of most of the sugar estates, continues today, although the economic wealth of the island is now concentrated in other sectors and, increasingly, in other ethnic communities.

The English captured the island in 1810, and it was officially ceded to them at the Treaty of Paris in 1814. The English renamed the island "Mauritius" and ruled it until independence in 1968. However, in capturing the island, the English wanted mainly to put a stop to pirate attacks on their merchant ships; they were not particularly interested in establishing a colony, so they left most of the French economic and social structure to function as before. French continued to be spoken, French cultural traditions continued, and a French-based creole developed, becoming the lingua franca that today unites the diverse ethnic communities of the island.

The English abolished slavery. However, indentured Indian laborers were brought to the island in massive numbers during the latter part of the nineteenth century, helping to turn Mauritius into an important sugar-producing economy. The Indian population, including both Hindus and Muslims, became the largest on the island, playing an increasingly important part in the commercial development of the island. From the 1930s, Indians have been the group with the most political power, closely identified with the newly created Labor Party, which has been a major force in the development of Mauritius as it is today.

Finally, the Chinese, although small in number, have been an important part of the commercial and industrial development of the island since the beginning of the twentieth century.

Mauritian Society Today

The Mauritian population today numbers 1,182,200 and is one of extraordinary ethnic diversity. The main group is the Indo-Mauritians, who make up 69 percent and include Hindus (52 percent) and Muslims (17 percent). The group known as the "general population" is of African, European, and mixed origin and represents 29 percent of the population, while the Chinese community is about 3 percent. (It should be noted that statistical groupings in Mauritius have been established more on religious than ethnic grounds.)

Within these main groups there are several sub-groups and often several different languages. Hindus, for instance, reflect the diversity of the Indian subcontinent and come from several different castes. The general population includes the "creoles" of African and Malagasy origin (the term *creole* therefore having a narrower and more distinct meaning in Mauritius than it does elsewhere), a mixed African/European group, and a small group of European descendants of French origin.

The main religions are Hinduism (52 percent), Christianity (28 percent, with 26 percent Roman Catholic and 2 percent Protestant), and Islam (17 percent). Spoken languages include French and Creole; Hindi, Urdu, Tamoul, Gujerati, and a local version of Hindi, Bhojpuri; Chinese languages; and English, which is the official language but the mother tongue of very few Mauritians. English is used extensively in government, while French is more common in industrial, professional, and social circles.

From this diversity, however, a strong sense of Mauritian identity has developed, together with pride in Mauritius as a nation. This served the country well when Mauritius became independent in 1968.

Since independence, Mauritius has moved successfully from a low-income, single-crop agricultural economy to a strong industrial export economy and a well-developed tertiary sector, with tourism as the largest constituent. Unemployment, which was over 20 percent in the late 1960s, has dropped dramatically; it still remains comparatively low, at six percent in 1997.[1] Growth in the gross national product has been impressive, averaging five percent per annum over the past 20 years. According to *The Economist*, Mauritius "can fairly claim to have Africa's most successful economy."[2]

At the same time, standards of living have risen continuously. Life expectancy is 70 years, and the overall adult literacy rate is 81 percent, reaching 95 percent for the under-30 age group.[3] Population growth has remained at about 1.5 percent since 1970. Mauritius, together with Singapore and Hong Kong, has been cited as an example of strong economic growth combined with increased human development, with a growth in per capita income accompanying an increase in exports.[4]

This rapid and exemplary development is a remarkable achievement for a small island with no natural resources. Because of it, Mauritius is sometimes referred to as the "African tiger." Others speak of the "Mauritian miracle," an achievement which has arisen from a variety of strengths that include a stable political and social background and democratic institutions, a well-educated work force and a dynamic business community, an increasingly well-developed infrastructure (port, transportation network, airport, communications), capital available for financing from the well-run sugar industry, and a government favorable to private sector enterprise and committed to export-oriented development.[5]

The Export Processing Zone. Economic development took off with the launching of the Export Processing Zone (EPZ) in 1970. Through the EPZ, the government sought to reduce dependence on the sugar industry by importing raw materials on favorable terms and then producing goods for export. To this end, it offered a series of incentives to attract foreign investment, including generous tax incentives and exemption from customs duties on imported materials and equipment. Starting with 664 workers in 1971, EPZ enterprises were employing 80,466 workers by 1995.

At the same time, the government launched a policy of active encouragement and promotion of the tourist industry, which has proved to be almost as important a force for growth as the EPZ.

Recent Economic Initiatives. The EPZ continues to be an important force for growth in the economy, although its concentration on textiles and clothing makes it vulnerable to changing market forces; it now needs to diversify.

The government has continued its proactive development policy. The latest initiatives have included offshore banking and financing services and the development of a free port economic sector, thus transforming Mauritius into a four-pillar economy. However, it is clear that in parallel to these developments, agriculture, manufacturing, and tourism will need to keep momentum. Development policies will have to be redefined in light of the changing conditions of the twenty-first century.

Developing the Tourism and Hospitality Industry

Until independence, tourism was practically nonexistent in Mauritius: in 1963 there were a mere 7,700 visitors to the island.[6] Activities were largely left to the private sector, with little government involvement. After independence, the government defined a new policy for tourism, which was considered a powerful potential force for development.

The first development plan of 1971–1975 included policy guidelines for the promotion and development of tourism. From the beginning, tourism promotion aimed at the upper segment of the market, promoting the island as an exclusive, quality destination and discouraging—and even preventing—mass tourism. This policy sought to maximize tourism earnings and preserve the quality of the environment, which is Mauritius's outstanding attraction. Encouraging elite tourism resulted in the development of the high-level beach hotel model, far from city centers and often part of all-inclusive complexes that focus tourist activities on coastal areas.

The development of the tourism sector has been as spectacular as that of the manufacturing sector—due in part to the democratization of air transport, the increasing number of wide-bodied carriers that made the island more accessible, and the government's far-sighted strategy. The growth of the tourism industry is reflected in the increasing number of tourist arrivals (see Exhibit 1), which have grown at an average annual rate of nine percent over the past two decades. Growth is also reflected in the steadily increasing number of hotels (see Exhibit 2). From 1971 to 1999, the number of registered hotels increased from 22 to 89, and the number of rooms grew from 811 in 1971 to 7,365 as of June 1999. These figures do not include a large number of small hotels and guest houses in the informal sector, which are not officially registered.

Although tourism is not the largest revenue-generating sector of the economy—as it is, for instance, in the Caribbean, where the islands are close to popular routes and potential markets—tourism has become the third largest earner of foreign exchange for Mauritius. Gross earnings for 1998 reached 11.9 billion Mauritian rupees (US$521.9 million).[7] The contribution to the gross domestic product has

Exhibit 1   Tourist Arrivals 1989 to 1998

YEAR	TOURIST ARRIVALS	GROWTH (%)
1989	262,790	9.8
1990	291,550	10.9
1991	300,670	3.1
1992	335,400	11.6
1993	274,360	11.7
1994	400,526	6.9
1995	422,463	5.5
1996	486,867	15.2
1997	563,125	10.1
1998	536,125	4.1

Source: Central Statistical Office, Mauritius

Exhibit 2   Growth in Hotels and Number of Rooms

YEAR	HOTELS	ROOMS
1971	22	811
1975	34	1,499
1981	51	2,201
1985	55	2,630
1991	80	5,064
1995	95	5,977
1999 (as of June)	89	7,365

Source: Mauritius Association of Hoteliers and Restaurateurs

also grown steadily: from 3.2 percent in 1990 to 5 percent in 1999.[8] Today, tourism directly and indirectly accounts for nearly 50,000 jobs. The rapid growth of the tourism industry puts Mauritius ninth in the list of the top 20 tourist destinations in Africa in terms of international arrivals.

However, tourism development is almost at the point of becoming a victim of its own success. Aware of the need to preserve the natural resources of the tiny island—including pristine beaches, unspoiled landscapes, and unpolluted waters—the government published a white paper in 1988 that reiterated its commitment to a policy of low-impact, high-spending tourism designed to limit environmental degradation and social pressures. The white paper set strict limits on the growth in tourist numbers and it proposed environmental controls on hotel construction, allowing no high-rise buildings and limiting the maximum size of each resort hotel complex to 200 rooms.

The white paper recommended that tourist numbers should be limited to 400,000 at the turn of the century. These limits have been largely exceeded. One reason is simply the pressure of market forces: for example, the Mauritian government may restrict charter flights, but charters arrive in the neighboring French island of Reunion, resulting in a rise of Reunion tourists to Mauritius. Another reason for growth is simply that too many hotel development certificates are awarded. It is often hard to reconcile the desire for growth and expansion with the need for long-term constraints.

Today, despite the pressure on the environment, government policy is to allow the industry to expand at an annual average rate of up to ten percent.[9] This is likely to result in a change in tourism profiles and patterns. From now on, the construction of new hotels on the beach front will be strictly limited; in fact, building on the hinterland has already begun. This will affect the image and type of product offered, and in turn will probably affect the type of tourist coming to the island. There are new possibilities of diversification with the development of the island as a business and conference center. However, it is likely that there will be an increase in downscale marketing, which will result in increased environmental and social pressure.

Implications for Human Resources

The changing pattern of jobs in response to the island's development has resulted in rapidly changing social patterns. The development of beach-front hotels far from urban centers has resulted in a male-dominated industry at lower levels of employment; the isolated nature of the resort complexes cuts employees off from family and social participation, with the resulting problem of lack of motivation and commitment.

At the management level, the issues are different. The island's highly educated work force means that Mauritius has had few problems in filling the ranks. However, the requirements for maintaining quality service and support for four- and five-star establishments are considerable. Although qualified Mauritians at this level are generally available, fierce competition and a low unemployment rate have a tendency to force the quality downward.

Rapid development entails new educational and training needs. While the Mauritian work force is noted for its high educational level, language skills, and adaptability, it is difficult to respond adequately to the new technical needs of the rapidly changing market.

The Hospitality Industry in Mauritius ————————

The government's policy of upscale tourist development and resort promotion has determined the kind of tourist who comes to the island. Because charter flights are restricted and air fares are high, there are few groups of young people or backpackers. Most tourists, apart from those from nearby Reunion Island, arrive from long-haul destinations and come prepared for a stay of about two weeks.

The main tourist-generating countries for Mauritius are France and Reunion, followed by South Africa and Germany (see Exhibit 3).

Exhibit 3   Origin of Tourists to Mauritius

Country of Origin	1992	1993	1994	1995
France	74,300	85,120	106,286	116,701
Reunion Island	81,260	84,690	77,035	78,431
South Africa	39,790	42,350	39,762	42,653
German	29,800	38,500	41,824	41,637
United Kingdom	24,150	29,950	33,293	31,324
Italy	14,990	15,290	18,149	17,384
Switzerland	10,150	11,010	11,453	13,815
India	8,200	10,740	10,449	11,225

Source: Central Statistical Office, Mauritius

According to a Ministry of Tourism and Leisure survey released in 1998:

- 75 percent of tourists came on holiday, while 10.7 percent were on honeymoon, 9.1 percent were on business, and 2.4 percent were visiting friends and relatives.

- 61.5 percent came on package arrangements.

- 78 percent of the tourists stayed in hotels, 8.8 percent in private bungalows, 4.1 percent in boarding houses, and 6 percent with friends and relatives.[10]

One group of tourists is different, however, reflected in the numbers who stay in private bungalows and boarding houses or with friends and relatives. These visitors are largely from Reunion and are perceived as neighbors—the island is only a half-hour away by air. Reunion is the only place from which it is relatively cheap to visit Mauritius. The potential of the Reunion/French market segment for tourist revenue could probably be far more readily exploited if the hotel sector were expanded down-market. Requirements in terms of service are not the same as those of honeymooners or retirees; even so, Reunion is a sophisticated market with a standard of living close to that of metropolitan France and requires world-class standards.

While confirming the importance of Mauritius as a holiday resort, surveys also point to a rising percentage of business travelers, conference attendees, and sports enthusiasts. The new Labourdonnais Waterfront Hotel at Port Louis offers 109 luxurious rooms and suites, two restaurants and a piano bar, high-quality conference facilities, and a fully equipped business center. Another interesting initiative is the development of historical and cultural inland tourism facilities close to Port Louis in the *Domaine Les Pailles*, including a group of theme restaurants, gaming houses, and other activities set in a large park.

The Beach Hotel Model

The pattern of hotels has evolved partly in order to create market demand and partly in response to the demand created. Nearly all construction is that of the high-level beach hotels that now dot the coastline.

From the start, the government has encouraged local investment in the tourism industry while at the same time promoting joint ventures with foreign investors, granting development certificates and other fiscal incentives and advantages for foreign groups wishing to invest in the island. The government has made financing available through the Development Bank and has given permission for luxury hotel construction on tracts of government-owned land in prime coastal areas. Private commercial banks have provided most of the loan financing needed for the hotels. Another important factor in the growth of such hotels has been a certain flexibility toward hiring foreign nationals and faster processing of requests for work permits.

The big luxury hotels in Mauritius are generally built as part of a leisure complex, many offering "all-inclusive" packages. Most hotels have several restaurants, boutiques, hairdressers, in-house entertainment every night, a diving center, and a boathouse with boating, water-skiing, and fishing facilities. Many are built on vast tracts of land over which are dispersed individual bungalows; they make up a little self-contained world from which outside forays are limited and even discouraged. Tourists' needs are all met by the hotel.

This concept has considerable impact on employees' way of life. Many middle-level staff live on-premises and receive board and lodging. All big hotels employ full-time musicians, who are usually better paid than other staff and do not live on the premises, although their presence is required during the day for practice in addition to their evening performances. Lower-level staff (bartenders, waitstaff, cooks) usually live in dormitories near the premises and are bussed to their housing. This fairly rigid stratification does not encourage cooperation between employees, and it is likely to be extremely demotivating in terms of lower- and middle-level staff seeking careers within the industry.

The Role of Hotel Groups

Many Mauritian hotels are parts of groups, some wholly local and some partially foreign-owned. The two largest hotel groups are Beachcomber and Sun International. Beachcomber is a Mauritian-owned group with seven hotels, including the Royal Palm, one of the most expensive hotels in the world. Mauritius Sun Resorts, owned in part by Sun International (a South African group), has five hotels, including the well-known five-star Touessrok and Le Saint Géran. These two groups together account for about 2,560 rooms and represent 28 percent of the hotel sector in Mauritius.

Other groups represented in Mauritius include Accor, Illova, Constance Hotel Services, Naiade Resorts, Apavou, and Club Méditerranée. Expansion is continuing at a fast pace. Hilton International and the Oberoi hotel group, among others, are opening properties in Mauritius.

In this luxury hotel bracket, room occupancy is high year-round. There are no real seasons for tourist activity in Mauritius, as holiday periods for tourists from different source countries tend to be staggered. The Ministry for Tourism gives the figures of average occupancy rates for 1997 as 72 percent for all hotels and 78 percent for large hotels, defined as beach establishments with more than 80 rooms.

As a result of global dominance by large hotels and chains, small local establishments are being squeezed out. There is a huge gap between the big four- and five-star hotels and the modest local guest-houses, with very few hotels in between. In direct contrast to the large hotel groups, most locally owned hotels struggle to raise occupancy levels. Room occupancy for these hotels often hovers at 45 percent. Restaurants, too, suffer from the dominance of the chains, the all-inclusive concept, and the limited access of most tourists to urban centers.

A two-tier system has developed, with smaller local initiatives lacking the support given by government to the luxury hotels and chains. This lack of support can be observed in many areas, from the easily granted work permits for luxury chains—which contrasts with the bureaucratic delays experienced by small enterprises—to the flexible attitude toward adhering to regulations at large hotels—which contrasts with the overzealous and selective application of the law in the case of small enterprises. Small hotels and restaurants are generally hampered by a system of local influence and power that often leads to corruption and bribery.

When most smaller enterprises are struggling to survive, there is little incentive to invest in human resources—employment cannot be guaranteed, turnover is high, and there is therefore little interest in training and development.

The Political and Legal Environment

Citing Mauritius as an example of successful growth both in human and economic terms, one report has commented, "The lessons are clear: countries can accelerate growth through trade liberalization if they have sound macroeconomic management, good infrastructure and social services, and strong governance with an appropriate institutional framework."[11]

Mauritius is a parliamentary democracy with a multi-party system. Like many former British colonies, its constitution was drawn up at the time of independence and was based largely on the British model. Power is vested in the Legislative Assembly, which is the supreme law-making body of the land. Despite a complex and lively political climate characterized by frequent conflicts and changing alliances, consensus is usually achieved and the political background is remarkably stable. There was, however, a period of social unrest marked by inter-communal Hindu/Muslim rioting shortly after independence in 1968.

Support Services

The banking, insurance, and accounting industries provide a strong support environment. There is a particularly dense and active banking sector, with an array of commercial banks—including the 150-year-old, privately owned Mauritius Commercial Bank—as well as the government-owned State Commercial Bank and Development Bank of Mauritius, and several private foreign banks. Insurance companies also provide important financial resources for savings and loans. Accounting firms are particularly strong and professional; most are the local representatives of international firms of chartered accountants such as Deloitte Touche Tohmatsu and PricewaterhouseCoopers.

The Government–Private Sector Relationship

The development of the Mauritian economy is largely due to the close relationship that exists between the government and the private sector. Although the existence of a dynamic private sector was the main force behind economic expansion, success would not have been possible without the policy framework determined by the government and without its support for large private-sector initiatives. In addition to working through the ministries concerned, the government has set up several organizations to promote the development of the private sector, including the Mauritius Export Development and Investment Authority, the Small and Medium Industries Development Organization, and a World Bank project to improve competitiveness through technological development.[12]

Nationalizations have not been part of government strategy for many years, and, in fact, there is increasing privatization of government-owned or managed bodies, including plans for the partial privatization of Air Mauritius and Mauritius Telecom. The government is a partner or even a shareholder in many groups, including Air Mauritius, in which it is a majority shareholder. It owns and operates the international airport, handling about 150 flights a week operated by 15 international airlines. It is largely because of government backing that the private sector has become the spearhead of the economy.

Social and Environmental Legislation

Legislation exists concerning several aspects of importance to the hospitality industry: worker protection, health and sanitation, and environmental protection.

Worker Protection. Working conditions are protected to a large extent by the Catering Industry Regulations of 1987. Tasks are defined in detail to avoid exploitation. "Trainee" periods are limited; at the end of the training period, a worker must be employed in the appropriate category. A worker may not be employed as a trainee more than once by the same employer. Workers have a right to 12 days' vacation annually; after 15 years of continuous employment they have a right to two months of overseas leave, to be wholly spent abroad. Maternity benefits consist of 12 weeks' leave with full pay. Uniforms and protective clothing are provided by the employer.

Wages are carefully determined for all workers below management level. A bonus representing one-twelfth of an employee's salary must be paid every year. A national pension fund exists; a gratuity is paid for hospitality workers who retire or who die before the age of 60.

Job security is protected. It is difficult for an employer to fire an employee even during the first year of work. An employer must provide a valid reason for the firing and must first provide three obligatory written warnings. Even if the employee is at fault and has received the official warning as required, compensation payments are still required on the part of the company.

Health. Employees are allowed 21 days of sick leave annually with full pay. It is important to note that health services are free in Mauritius, although they are often inadequate in quality. There is an extensive system of private clinics and facilities for those who can afford them. Legislation concerning sanitation and hygiene within the industry is carefully defined and enforced.

Environmental Legislation. This is an area in which increasingly strong legislation exists, particularly as it concerns the hospitality industry. High-rise buildings and certain types of building materials are prohibited. Land use is also now increasingly regulated, although many measures have come too late to stop creeping coastal development.

The government has recently announced a new series of measures designed to contain damage to the environment. Penalties and surcharges are to be applied to firms that do not comply with standards and recycling regulations. The government has introduced an environmental protection fee of MRs50 (about US$2) per room.

There is a strong awareness of the importance of legislation within the hospitality industry itself, whose very existence depends on the preservation of the environment. Hotels are often proactive in applying protective measures. However, much of the danger for the coast in fact comes from construction and effluents from the industrial zone, which is less closely monitored than the hospitality industry.

Labor Market Issues

Employment Patterns

The number of people employed in tourism has grown considerably. Out of a total labor force estimated at 506,000, employment figures for the tourist industry as a whole rose from 8,902 in 1990 to 16,490 in 1998.[13]

According to the Mauritius Association of Hotels and Restaurants, of those employed in tourism, 11,177 are employed in hotels and 1,389 work in restaurants. There is a marked imbalance between the number of male and female employees, with women making up only about one-fifth of the employed population. This results in a pattern different from that in many other countries, in which unskilled workers in the hospitality industry are mainly women. The situation in Mauritius is undoubtedly the result of the development of luxury beach complexes far from local communities, resulting in a mostly male population at lower skill levels, with the men often living in dormitories and the women unable to leave their families for similar jobs.

In general, there is little gender discrimination in Mauritius, except that, as elsewhere, women tend to fill lower-skilled jobs and there are few in upper management. The male-dominated pattern in the hospitality sector may be attributed to the particular way in which the industry has developed on the island.

Hospitality employees tend to be isolated both from other ethnic groups and from the clientele they serve. Not only are staff bussed to and from their work to dormitories—which means that they cannot work meaningfully within the community—but they are treated as a group apart. For example, staff canteens serve food that is completely different from the food served in the restaurants; servers are likely never to have eaten the kind of food they are serving. It is clear that a situation in which the eating and drinking habits of waiters are so completely different from those of the customers is less likely to result in attentive and knowledgeable service.

Education

Mauritius is known for the high educational level of its population. Government commitment is important: education accounts for 15 percent of the budget and is free through high school. Over 95 percent of primary-school aged children attend school, and around 40 percent go on to the secondary level. In 1997 a compulsory nine-year schooling system was adopted, which will increase to 95 percent the number of those going on to the secondary level.[14]

Education in Mauritius is based on the English system. Students complete their secondary studies by sitting for the Cambridge Syndicate School Certificate and Higher School Certificate examination. For students who wish to continue, there is a University of Mauritius, but a large number of Mauritians choose to study overseas.

Besides the government schools, which range from excellent to poor, there is a sector of fee-paying private schools—Catholic schools, Hindu and Muslim associations, as well as a French lycée. Through schooling in a multicultural context, students are constantly exposed to different values and traditions and become used to interacting at every level with other cultures.

Many of the best Mauritian schools have formal agreements with, and are accredited by, English or French national education systems. Formal ties with many British universities also exist. Therefore, many Mauritian students graduate with recognized English and French academic credentials, even though they have received their schooling in Mauritius. These internationally recognized qualifications provide the opportunity for further study abroad—usually in Europe, India, or, increasingly, the United States. The vast majority of young Mauritians return home after their studies, providing the country with a sophisticated, adaptable, and multilingual work force.

Unlike many other developing countries, Mauritius therefore has its own highly competent lawyers, doctors, accountants, teachers, and managers in key positions throughout the economy. Ironically, the general manager in a Mauritian hotel is most likely an expatriate appointment, yet several groups have sent Mauritian managers abroad to positions of responsibility.[15]

The Mauritian system can create problems for the work force at lower skill levels. One problem is language. Nearly all Mauritian children do their schooling in a language other than their primary tongue. This is not a problem for privileged children whose cognitive development is firmly established in their native language. However, many children who begin to learn to write simultaneously in three foreign languages (English, French, and an oriental language) are likely to encounter major learning difficulties. In addition, school textbooks are often a reflection of foreign cultures and may bear little relation to the everyday reality of Mauritian life.

The government is aware of the need to reform the system. The Mauritius Institute of Education, for example, has been working for many years to redesign curricula for the specific needs of the Mauritian population.

Compensation

The wage level in Mauritius is low by world standards but high by African or Asian standards. Although one index showed Mauritius to have less disparity between high and low wages than many other countries, the gap is beginning to widen. In addition, the widespread use of fringe benefits and payments-in-kind tends to mask the gap between management and workers.

Jobs in the hospitality industry are often perceived as low-prestige and badly paid, affecting motivation. However, as has been seen, the hospitality industry is a service provider for many of its employees, offering transportation, housing, meals, and other advantages. These advantages help to keep salaries low and result in employees at lower skill levels being able to live adequately on minimal wages. At the managerial level, fringe benefits are extensive and may include housing, a car, paid overseas holidays, overseas medical treatment, and other perquisites.

The minimum wage is legally enforced but varies according to position and years of service. A person's exact title and job description are determining factors—for example, a "chef," an "assistant head cook," and an "assistant cook" will not have the same minimum wage. In addition, the exact salary increases are spelled out for each job category over a period of several years. Wages rise, often minimally, according to years of service, and an employer is legally obliged to raise salaries regularly. The system ensures fairness, but job descriptions are sometimes arbitrary and often do not correspond to actual tasks, making classification difficult. They also work against cross-training and can result in employees refusing—or showing great reluctance—to do work that is not part of the official description of tasks.

Labor Relations and Unions

Unions have not played a large part in labor relations. They were forbidden during most of the colonial period, but became active during the 1930s when the Labor Party came to power. Perhaps because the government itself was actively engaged in upgrading and protecting working conditions, unions never played an active role. Today, most staff in the hospitality industry belong to a central union that combines workers from most major enterprises. However, despite the disparities between the different social levels, there are few strikes or social conflicts, and these are usually resolved by negotiation or arbitration.

Cultural Distinctions and Work Values

Mauritius is a complex society with unwritten but strictly observed rules governing relationships among ethnic communities. Balance between the communities in the workplace is achieved not through legislation but through unwritten rules of proportional representation in recruitment and promotion.

Some groups are separate but more or less equal. Sometimes, however, ethnic and social categories coincide, making certain groups particularly vulnerable. This is the case for the African/Malagasy creole group, which occupies the lowest stratum of the labor market. The creole population is becoming increasingly dissatisfied and vocal: a period of rioting marked the first part of 1999, following the death in prison of a popular creole musician, and many are worried that civil unrest will continue if the problems of this community are not taken into account.

Some traditional social patterns exist that need to be recognized in the human resources context. For instance, certain jobs are traditionally done by some ethnic groups and not by others; it is important to be aware of these perceptions. Another social factor influences the way in which workers perceive their jobs. Many employees on low wages live as part of an extended family; this leads to the understanding that the granting of a job to one family member means that the job has been granted to the entire family. While this can result in the replacement of a wage earner by another family member if the former is ill or incapacitated, it also contributes to the oversupply of workers in very similar jobs.

Absenteeism is widespread. Mauritians traditionally take time off for important days of religious observance; with the large number of religions on the island, religious holidays fall practically every week. Official holidays now number only 13; however, many people still continue to take days off for religious observance or for sick leave; physician statements attesting to a person's inability to work are easily obtainable for the price of a packet of cigarettes.

The high rate of absenteeism encourages employers to hire more workers in order to ensure minimal service at all times. This results in a ratio of employees to guests that may be four times more than in other countries. Visitors to Mauritian restaurants, for example, may be surprised to see a vast number of waiters standing at attention, without their tasks being clearly differentiated. The result is often slow and inefficient service, with most of the workers' energy expended in trying to appear busy and useful. Slow service is compounded by antiquated back-of-the-house systems, which have not been updated partly because of the workers' low skill levels. The control system is still usually manual, and three carbon copies are necessary when ordering a beer, for example. There is rarely a direct system by which orders are recorded directly in the cash register.

Even so, the Mauritian population is invariably perceived as friendly and welcoming by visitors to the island. Hotel staff at all levels appear to be eager to please clients as best they can. The comments of a recent visitor to the island are typical: hotel staff are "gentle, tasteful, warm and patient," "kind and hospitable," and actually seem to enjoy making people happy.[16]

Labor Relations and Human Resources

Managing human relationships in the complex Mauritian context is very difficult for managers coming in from the outside. Therefore, it is important for expatriate directors or human resources managers to work closely with local management. However, an outside view is an advantage when dealing with the questions of social hierarchy and empowerment in which local management may perpetuate unconscious stereotypes, including a disdain for some social groups or a disregard for their capabilities. Recruitment, training, and development all need to be undertaken with the double awareness of high international standards and the complex social environment in which they need to be achieved.

Training and Development

Training needs in Mauritius are fairly well covered by a combination of government initiatives at lower skill levels and more comprehensive internal training schemes administered by the large hotels and chains. However, there are important gaps that need to be identified and problems that need to be addressed if the industry is to maintain its high-quality image.

National Approaches to Training. The high level of general education in Mauritius is in itself one of the best prerequisites for an efficient labor force, although it is clear that specialized technical expertise is also essential for the hospitality industry. The government has been increasingly conscious of the need to develop vocational and technical skills.

A tax for professional training was initiated in 1989 and provides reimbursement of 75 percent of training costs; the hospitality industry is largely taking advantage of this.

With government help, a small hotel school recently upgraded and reopened as the Mauritius Government Hotel and Training School. It is under the authority of the Ministry for Education and Training and is entirely subsidized by the government. The school has well-equipped facilities and provides comprehensive one- and two-year courses of basic training in kitchen work, service, housekeeping, and the front office. It also offers ongoing training for hotel employees who are already working in these areas. Several hotels work closely with the school, including the Constance group, which also has its own training school: the Constance Academy.

Future projects include developing a general apprenticeship system for the hospitality industry, with official recognition of qualifications. A two-year apprenticeship scheme is being set up for 17 to 21 year olds in food production, restaurant bar service, housekeeping/front office, and pastry. Apprentices work in a hotel under supervision and obtain a National Trade Certificate at the end of their studies. Certificates in leisure and entertainment and in tourism are also being developed, and there are plans for higher-level training, including a diploma in leisure and entertainment management and a diploma in hotel maintenance. A feasibility study is underway for a training hotel that would be managed by students under the supervision of professionals.

Training at Large Hotels and Hotel Groups. Many of the large hotels have their own training schemes. Some send senior executives overseas as part of their management development programs. Sun International has a development program for middle management that it operates with Cornell University in the United States and which includes modules in information technology, human resources, and marketing. Accor also has extensive internal training programs that benefit from the international resources of the "Académie Accor"; Accor's Sofitel also has a training manager who is responsible for basic training. The Labourdonnais Waterfront Hotel has undertaken an extensive survey of its training needs, which are partly addressed by local consulting and training firms. The latter often work in association with specialized institutions such as the Ecole Hôtelière de Lausanne, Switzerland.

The picture is very different at the smaller hotels, restaurants, and guesthouses, which do not have access to many training opportunities and whose high turnover dampens managerial enthusiasm for training.

Strengths and Weaknesses. At the upper management levels, there is no difficulty in recruiting high-caliber staff both locally and abroad. However, it is considered important to provide ongoing training in areas such as finance management, strategic change and creativity management, and human resources management, as well as in industry-specific areas such as food and beverage management systems or property maintenance for executives.

Many of the main training needs are at mid-management level. In addition to courses on supervision, cost control, or management, there is an overriding need, frequently reiterated by management, for the development of communication, team-building, and leadership skills. There are complaints that at this level there is no "managerial spirit" and that people who "work their way up from the bottom" do not have the requisite capacities.

At the operations level, needs include basic courses in kitchen practices and housekeeping, and intensive sessions on wines and beverages, cheese, buffets, and desserts.

One of the main problems in providing quality service is that of family relationships among employees. The social aspect of human resources is of prime importance. In-service courses conducted by outside experts are probably only part of the answer. Similarly, sending upper-level staff overseas for training or bringing in outside chefs, as is often done, without attempting to integrate their knowledge and skills all the way down the line is insufficient. As one restaurant owner has observed, it is one thing to hire the best international chef to make spectacular food, but if the waiters are describing a dish in terms of, "I don't know, I think it comes with potatoes," half the value of the experience is lost. The cultural divide between the kitchen, the waitstaff, and the clientele needs to be bridged. The best way to do this may be through participatory and mentoring methods that would allow staff to become familiar with the food and wine they are serving.

Career development is a closely linked problem. Large hotels and chains offer both lateral and upward mobility, but only from a certain level of middle management. Less qualified employees are generally treated as a group apart, with little or no prospect of advancement. This is a major problem. Unless the staff feels part of the enterprise and can identify with the corporate mission, there will be problems in maintaining efficiency and a high-quality service image.[17]

Conclusion

The growth of the tourist and hospitality industry over the past 20 or 30 years has been remarkable. Its success is the result of a combination of factors: political stability, a well-educated work force, and the wise strategic decision by the government to target the upscale market, implementing that policy with sufficient incentives and supportive measures.

However, today it is not clear whether the "Mauritian miracle" can be maintained. The new era signals the end of privileged entrée for Mauritius to the European market. This will add to factors such as increasing inflation and the higher cost of labor in Mauritius. (Indeed, some Export Processing Zone industries are relocating to Madagascar, where wages are lower.) Social stability is not as assured as it was in the past. The economy is likely to suffer, and the GDP is not predicted to grow as fast as in the "miracle" years.

Tourism is likely to become even more important over the next few years; it has been suggested that it could become the second largest foreign-exchange earner, even taking first place if the slowdown in other sectors continues. Present plans are to continue expansion at the target rate of ten percent a year, while trying to maintain the exclusive upscale image that until now has ensured successful growth. However, the tourism sector has reached a turning point. Further coastal construction will encroach on the already limited access to the beach. Preserving the natural environment with increasing tourist pressure will be a concern. South African tourists already have complained that Mauritian beaches are not as unspoiled as other pristine destinations, such as the Seychelles. Growth in tourist numbers will almost inevitably lead to a down-market spiral that will change the nature of tourism on the island and is likely to lead to a backlash on Mauritian society.

Tourism has not had the negative impact on Mauritian society that might have been expected, perhaps because most hotel complex are isolated and tourists have little direct contact with the majority of the population. However, this situation is already changing. There is increasing resentment that the beachfront is almost completely closed to ordinary citizens. In addition, many hotels police entry to their beaches, denying access to the local population even though this is illegal. The difference between the luxurious hotels and the lifestyle of the ordinary people is likely to become more visible, fanning social unrest.

In an island with no natural resources, the most important resource is its population. A large part of the success of the industry has been due to its well-educated, adaptable work force. However, there are several major areas of concern in the area of human resources that, if not dealt with, will lead to increasing problems in maintaining the high-quality image of the industry. These include the need to value and give a sense of empowerment to all sections of the labor force, working within the multi-ethnic context of Mauritius to ensure that its many different communities are a source of strength.

Endnotes

1. *EIU Country Profile: Mauritius, Seychelles 1999–2000* (London: The Economist Intelligence Unit, 1999), p. 31. See also the regularly updated *EIU Country Report*.

2. "A Half-African Success Story," *The Economist*, 14 December 1996, pp. 45–47.

3. *EIU Country Profile*, p. 10.

4. United Nations Development Programme, *Human Development Report* (New York: Oxford University Press, 1999), pp. 83–85.

5. Philippe Hein, *L'Economie de l'Ile Maurice* (Paris: L'Harmattan, 1996).

6. Hein.

7. *EIU Country Profile,* p. 24.

8. Mauritius Association of Hoteliers and Restaurateurs.

9. *EIU Country Profile,* p. 24.

10. Regular surveys are conducted by the Ministry of Tourism and Leisure and are now available on its Internet site at http://ncb.intnet.mu/mot/index.htm.

11. Hein, pp. 42–43.

12. United Nations Development Programme, *Human Development Report,* p. 85.

13. *EIU Country Profile,* p. 31.

14. *EIU Country Profile,* pp. 11–12.

15. Hein, p. 49.

16. *The Spectator,* 30 January 1999.

17. Survey conducted by the International Business Development division of Ecole Hôtelière de Lausanne, Switzerland in October 1998.

Discussion Questions

1. What are the main strengths and weaknesses of the labor force in the Mauritian hospitality industry?

2. If you were a hotel director or human resource manager in Mauritius, what steps should you take to deal with weaknesses in the labor force?

3. Which services need to be developed to reach the new "down-market" segment? What would these services entail in terms of employee recruitment and training?

4. What steps should Mauritius's many small and medium-size hospitality enterprises take to improve their businesses?

Internet Sites

For more information, visit the following Internet sites. Remember that Internet addresses can change without notice.

Beachcomber Mauritius
http://www.beachcomber.co.za/index.html

L'Express (French)
http://www.lexpress-net.com

Hotel School of Mauritius
http://www.webltd.com/hotel-school/html/

Ile-Maurice.com
www.ile-maurice.com

Labourdonnais Waterfront Hotel
http://www.labourdonnais.com

Mauritius Island On-Line
http://www.maurinet.com

Le Mauricien (French)
http://www.lemauricien.com/mauricien/index.html

Mauritius News
http://www.mauritius-news.com

Mauritius Association of Hoteliers and Restaurateurs (AHRIM)
http://www.mauritius.net/ahrim/index.htm

Mauritius Tourism Promotion Authority
http://www.mauritius.net

Ministry of Tourism and Leisure
http://ncb.intnet.mu/mot/index.htm

Mauritius Information
http://www.mauritius-info.com

Sun International
http://www.webltd.com/sun/index.html

Mauritius Island
http://www.mauritius-island.com

# Case Study

Watching the Waiter Parade

The restaurant was stunning, a tropical paradise of elegance. There were definitely more staff than customers present, however, as Paul and Catherine Neason made their way from the hotel's lobby into the main dining hall—which was decorated with a maze of ornate Indian wood-carved folding doors, large antique earthenware pots, and brass cauldrons. The couple, native New Yorkers, had come to Mauritius to celebrate their twentieth wedding anniversary.

Seeing no host to seat them, the couple walked past a large group of uniformed waiters standing near the entrance. One of the waiters came from the floor and inquired, "Two?" When the Neasons answered yes, he directed them into the dining room, vaguely pointing to a table before turning away. Within seconds, another waiter appeared and asked them, "Two?" then, "This way, please," and pointed in the same general direction. By the time they arrived at their table, the Neasons had gone through this ritual four times. They were finally seated by the first waiter.

Within seconds, all of the waiters were gone. For several minutes, the couple enjoyed the beauty of their surroundings. But five minutes stretched to ten, and they were beginning to wonder if they had been forgotten. Several minutes later, a new waiter arrived with the menus, and he presented them with a flourish, a gracious "Madame" and "Sir," and an elaborate bow.

Sensing that the waiter was intent on sprinting back to the kitchen after his last bow, Paul Neason quickly spoke up: "Could we order drinks now, please?"

"Yes, sir, I will be right back, sir," the waiter responded. And he left.

Paul looked at his wife. "What could he possibly need to do right at this moment when there are 15 other waiters standing around, and only 10 customers in here?" Catherine shrugged.

A different waiter arrived at the table. "Yes, sir, may I take your order, please, sir?"

"We'll have two glasses of white wine to start," Paul said, "and we'd like a bottle of red wine with our dinner. What white wines do you carry by the glass?"

The waiter looked nonplussed. "What?"

Paul frowned. "We'd like two glasses of white wine, please," he said. "Do you have any Chardonnay?"

"I will look, sir." And he left.

Just then, the first waiter returned. "Yes, sir, may I take your order, please, sir?"

Paul considered saying something sarcastic, but Catherine sent him warning glances. "I would like two glasses of Chardonnay, please," he said, trying his best to sound patient.

"What?"

"Chardonnay. White wine. Two glasses. Please."

"Yes, sir, I will bring the wine list, sir."

"No, I have the wine list. I would just like two glasses of Chardonnay now."

"Yes, sir. Right away, sir." And he left, never to be seen again.

The previous waiter returned.

"We don't have any Chap Monay, sir," he said apologetically.

Paul Neason felt a headache coming on. "It's 'Chardonnay.' Probably one of the most popular white wines in the world. Look. Do you have any wine by the glass?"

"I will look, sir," he said. And he quickly disappeared.

Paul's face was turning red.

"Calm down," said Catherine, "we're on vacation, in a beautiful country, in a lovely restaurant. Try to relax. The waiters are nice, and they're trying hard. We're not rushed, and we don't have to go anywhere. Let's just enjoy ourselves."

Her husband took a deep breath. "You're right," he said. "But, frankly, I'm curious about this place. I think I'm going to try this from the beginning again and see if I can figure out what's going on." So the next time a waiter arrived at their table, Paul ordered a bottle of water and sat back to watch the procedure.

The waiter marched directly in front of a table where other guests were trying to get his attention and went straight for the bar, scribbling furiously on a notepad stuffed with carbon paper. He gave one copy of the order to one of the bartenders and stood there watching him, oblivious to everything else around him. The bartender then scribbled busily on a pad of his own, carbon paper protruding in every direction. One of the copies was given to a second bartender, who opened the refrigerator, took out a bottle of water, and gave it to the waiter. After this elaborate procedure, the bottle made its way to the Neasons' table and was poured with the restaurant's trademark flourish.

At that point, a man stopped by who was dressed differently from the waiters. Paul assumed he was the manager. "How is everything, sir?"

"Well, I'm wondering something. Do you sell white wine by the glass?" Paul asked.

"What?"

"Do you sell one glass of white wine at a time, or just bottles?" "Yes, sir," he replied politely and left.

Paul laughed good-naturedly after the manager was gone. Catherine just shook her head at her husband's persistence. But they were both surprised when the manager returned with two glasses of white wine.

"With our compliments," he said pleasantly.

As they enjoyed their delicious meal, Catherine thought she knew what the trouble was. "It isn't the waiters' fault," she said. "They really are trying their best. But you can tell that they simply have no idea what most of the food and drink items actually are. The woman at the next table asked for an after-dinner liqueur, and they brought her a piña colada. Their systems are outdated and slow—all those carbon-paper forms and all those different people involved in what should really be a straightforward process. You know," she added cheerfully, "I think the hotel decided to solve the problem of poorly trained and inexperienced waiters by just hiring an incredible number of them—and hoping that things would right themselves!"

Discussion Questions

1. What are the main service problems described in this case?

2. Did the manager handle the difficulties appropriately?

3. From a human resources point of view, how do you think some of these problems could be resolved, and by whom?

4. What difficulties might arise in attempts to improve service quality?

Chapter 13 Outline

Competencies

1. Identify the key economic conditions in Mexico. (pp. 219–221)

2. Describe the Mexican labor market. (pp. 221–222)

3. Describe the main laws affecting hospitality operations. (pp. 222–224)

4. Explain standard Mexican human resources business practices. (pp. 225–227)

13

Mexico: Managing Human Resources in a Cultural Mosaic

Armando Sanchez Soto

Armando Sanchez Soto, MA, has served as a consultant to many of Mexico's leading corporations and universities. He is currently professor of human resources at Escuela Superior de Administración de Instituciones and coordinator of undergraduate degrees in the areas of marketing, international business, and finance at Universidad Panamericana. His articles have appeared in ISTMO *and* Administrate Hoy.

MEXICO IS, ABOVE all things, a nation of contrasts. The very wealthy, educated upper class contrasts with a large, poor, and uneducated underclass. European, Mestizo, and Indian cultures collide. Even different Indian groups sometimes carry centuries' old grudges against one another. These collisions and contradictions over the course of Mexico's history have fused the frame of a national character.

If there is one thing that binds Mexico's proud people together, it is history. Mexican history can be divided into three periods: the pre-Hispanic period, the *Virreinato* (Viceroy period), and post-independence Mexico.

After a series of early contacts, the Spanish, led by Hernán Cortés, entered Mexico in force in 1519. By 1521, Cortés had captured Tenochtitlán, the Aztec capital (now Mexico City). From this point on, the Spanish and their way of life filtered into the rest of Mexico through a long process of colonization. Independence was declared by Miguel Hidalgo in 1810 and was finally won in 1821. This led to a series of civil and foreign wars, which engulfed Mexico for most of the century. This period of instability ended in 1877 when war hero General Porfirio Díaz took over the presidency. During his more than 30 years in power, however, his reign declined into tyranny. This led to the Mexican Revolution of 1910, which lasted more than a decade.

Today, the country is a federal democratic republic divided into 31 states and one federal district. There are two houses of Congress, each having representatives who are elected for a three-year term. The president holds a six-year term. Although there are three major parties—the right-wing Partido Acción Nacional (PAN), the centrist Partido Revolucionario Institucional (PRI), and the leftist Partido Revolucionario Democrático (PRD)—Mexico's government is essentially a one-party system led by the PRI.

Social and Economic Statistics

Mexico is the world's fourteenth largest country, with 1,953,162 square kilometers (1,212,914 square miles) of territory. It has over 11,593 kilometers (7,199 miles) of coastline, affording it a privileged situation in global tourism. The climate is mostly dry, though it varies greatly from region to region, going from tropical forests in the south to deserts in the north. The land is mountainous and has many natural resources, the most important of which are petroleum and silver.

Mexico is a young nation and a nation of young people, with nearly half of the total population under the age of 20. The vast majority of the population is literate, yet only a small fraction is currently computer literate.

Mexico is the world's eleventh largest economy; in 1997, it was the second largest destination for foreign investments. The gross domestic product (GDP) for 1998 was US$414.9 billion. Service areas made up 65.5 percent of the GDP, including a 31.9 percent contribution from the category that includes restaurants, hotels, and "commerce" (an unfortunately vague term used by the government that includes most service industries). These three industries employed 2,077,523 workers, which is equivalent to 21.1 percent of the economically active population. There is an official three percent unemployment rate.

The world's seventh most important tourist destination, Mexico holds many natural and cultural attractions. It boasts world-renowned beaches, as well as colonial Spanish towns and impressive archaeological sites. In 1996, tourism to Mexico generated US$6.2 billion. (Curiously enough, Mexican tourists abroad spent slightly more than this, creating a deficit in the tourist industry.) In 1997, the latest date for which there is data, Mexico had 9,184 hotels, representing 382,364 hotel rooms, with 71,230 of those rooms available near beach areas. The average national occupancy rate for hotels was 57.52 percent, but some areas showed significantly better business. For example, Cancun had an occupancy rate of 83.2 percent.

In 1997, there were a total of 380 five-star and luxury hotels, providing 76,136 rooms; 784 four-star hotels with 71,371 rooms; and 1,396 three-star hotels with 65,837 rooms. The rest of the 9,184 hotels includes small hotels that would not be typical stops for tourists. There are relatively few youth hostels, as it is not part of the local culture.

The hotel industry in Mexico is generally in a slump. The areas experiencing growth and high occupancy rates are mainly beach hotels, while inland hotels are currently seeing a drop in their occupancy rates due to the peso crisis. The peso crisis has made Mexico more attractive to foreign tourists, but it has decreased the internal market.

Mexican Culture

Mexico is the product of a cultural melting pot that has given rise to dozens of different customs and personality types, determined largely by a harsh history full of conflict and violence. Mexicans are "realistic romantics" who like to analyze and conform to the external environment, even as they carry within them strong ideals. While they often appear immediately friendly and accepting, it might actually take years for them to develop a true understanding and trust.

Mexican society is macho, yet older women acting as matriarchs control much of Mexican social and family life. The average Mexican does not make long-term plans or save money. This means that every economic crisis leads to large and painful repercussions. Mexicans are also procrastinators who need to be stimulated to achieve results.

Mexicans are extremely conservative, sentimental people. This is followed by a strong nationalist pride. There also is a great amount of importance placed on family and friends.

Language and Religion

Spanish is Mexico's official language. There are, however, 81 different Indian tongues, but these are spoken by relatively few people. Spanish pronunciation varies from one geographic region to the next, providing recognizable speech patterns.

Religion—and, particularly, Roman Catholicism—touches all aspects of Mexican public and private life. The national symbol can truly be said to be the Virgin of Guadalupe, who is believed to have appeared to the Indian Juan Diego in the mid-sixteenth century. In the War of Independence, Father Miguel Hidalgo took a pennant of the Virgin of Guadalupe into battle.

Social Customs

Mexico's many unique customs include such things as a Day of the Dead celebration, held on November 2. Twelve days previous to Christmas, it is common to hold *posadas* or traditional nativity parties.

Women receive a "Sweet 15" party to introduce them to society. This party is the second most important event for Mexican women, after marriage. Mexican women typically marry early.

Mexicans are not bound to the clock, and it is standard practice to wait 15 minutes or more before starting a conference or declaring an appointment a no-show.

Despite many long-standing traditions, Mexican culture is currently in flux. It has been changing greatly due to cultural influences from the United States and from what is rapidly becoming a global culture.

The Hospitality Industry Labor Market

The hospitality market in Mexico is well-developed, and Mexicans have a long history of providing hospitality services. In most cases, though, the service lacks initiative on the part of employees. This is caused in part by a fear of being fired. This situation has created a peculiarly Mexican approach to service in which workers act servile. To remedy this, workers must be shown that they are free to take the initiative in serving the customer. When doing this, it is important to judge the individual capacities of the employee, to make sure he or she has the skills and vision to make good judgment calls. Also, some employees will view guests as people to exploit and will want to pressure them for tips due to the employees' very low wages.

Hospitality workers must be taught to enjoy themselves in their work and be shown that they have the capability for self-improvement. Most of the training in the service industries takes place on-the-job, even though there are 165 upper-level training and job training institutions in Mexico.

Despite these problems, the Mexican style of service can be quite good. When properly motivated, Mexican employees can be committed and outgoing. Most Mexican managers have extraordinary flexibility and, for the most part, use American management styles.

Federal Labor Law

The **Federal Labor Law** dictates all work regulations for the entire nation, including all 31 states and the Federal District. The law was originally drafted in the 1930s and has received only periodic revisions. Although it can be considered outdated, the law continues to regulate employee-employer relations.

The law prohibits racial, sexual, age, religious, social, and political discrimination. It also establishes mandatory training courses for employees. These courses must be administered every year, and the content of the courses must be approved by the Secretaría del Trabajo y Previsión Social (Secretariat of Labor and Social Protection), the regulatory body that enforces and judges labor cases.

Ninety percent of the workers in Mexico must be Mexican nationals. All technicians must be Mexican—unless it is impossible to find qualified candidates, in which case companies may hire foreign technicians, up to ten percent of the total number of employees. (These regulations do not apply to workers who have reached the level of manager or director.) The employer is then required to train the Mexican technicians in the unfamiliar specialization. All company doctors must be Mexican citizens.

In Mexico, employees are legally divided into two groups: "trusted" employees and "syndicated" employees. Trusted employees perform tasks involving direction, inspection, security, and accounting. Trusted employees are presumed to represent the owners of the company, so they are unable to join labor unions. Syndicated employees are those workers who may belong to a union.

The law prohibits the hiring of children under the age of 14, as well as 15 and 16 year olds who have not finished their mandatory education (six years of elementary education and three years of secondary education). In cases of family need, children between 14 and 16 years old may be hired with parental consent and as long as it can be proven that the job does not interfere with their studies.

An employer may fire an employee without any obligations if the employee:

- Fakes educational certificates

- Claims to possess abilities he or she does not have

- Lacks honesty
- Has violent impulses
- Makes threats against the employer or the employer's family
- Is disrespectful
- Commits overtly immoral acts
- Commits acts that endanger co-workers
- Reveals company secrets
- Misses work three times in a 30-day period without justified cause
- Fails to follow safety procedures
- Disobeys
- Arrives intoxicated to work
- Is imprisoned or sentenced to a prolonged jail term

An employee may quit without any legal restrictions if the employer:

- Tricks workers
- Mistreats workers
- Reduces salaries
- Fails to pay on time
- Requires work that is dangerous or unhealthy

The employee-employer relationship may also be terminated due to physical or mental incapacity.

The Mexican work week consists of six eight-hour days. Night shifts last seven hours, and mixed schedules last six-and-a-half hours (at most, three of those hours will be nocturnal). All shifts have one half-hour break.

Workers begin with eight days of paid vacation. The number of vacation days increases one day per year of service, until the employee has been in service four years. From that point on, the employee gains one vacation day for every additional four years of service. During vacations, workers receive their regular pay and a 25 percent vacation bonus. In addition to vacation time, employees receive time off to observe a number of national holidays, including: January 1 and December 25, as well as February 5 (Constitution Day), March 21 (the birthday of Benito Juárez, a national political hero and Mexico's president from 1861 to 1872), May 1 (Labor Day), September 16 (Independence Day), and November 20 (Revolution Day).

There is an established general minimum salary and a series of stratified minimum salaries for different professions. The minimum salary is determined by the Comisión Nacional de los Salarios Mínimos (National Commission for Minimum Salaries) on the basis of workers' basic needs. Workers are also legally entitled to a yearly bonus that must be paid before December 20. This bonus must be at least equivalent to 15 days' salary. Employees are also entitled to a share of the company's profits. The percentage of this share is set by the Comisión Nacional para la Participación de los Trabajadores en las Utilidades de las Empresas (National Commission for the Participation of Workers in Company Profits). Profits are distributed at the end of the fiscal year.

Companies are legally obligated to provide training and development opportunities for their workers. Companies, in coordination with unions and employees, must develop yearly training and development programs, and these programs must be approved by the Secretaría del Trabajo y Previsión Social (Secretariat of Labor and Social Protection). These programs must seek to develop the capabilities of the employees, teach them new skills and technologies, prevent work hazards, increase productivity, and prepare workers to occupy higher-ranking positions.

Women are legally guaranteed equal rights. They have the same obligations as men, except for maternity privileges, which include six weeks of paid leave prior to the birth of the child and six weeks of paid leave after giving birth. After they return to the workplace, women are entitled to two half-hour breaks daily to breastfeed their children.

All companies are required to have an **internal regulations manual**, which must include:

- Entry and departure hours for the facility

- Place and time when work must commence and finish

- Dates and times established for facility and equipment cleaning

- Dates and times established for the paying of salaries and wages

- Safety guidelines and first-aid procedures

- Health guidelines

- Information regarding the company's permits and licenses

- Disciplinary guidelines

- All other relevant guidelines needed to run the business

The regulation manual must be put together by a joint commission of labor and company representatives. Once it is agreed upon, it must be presented to the Junta de Conciliación y Arbitraje (Conciliation and Arbitration Board).

The Role of Unions

Workers are free to associate, form labor unions, and strike. Unions may negotiate labor contracts. In many companies, workers are expected to enter into a union before they will be permitted to work. Until recently, labor unions were powerful, heavily centralized institutions. The current economic and political crisis has greatly weakened the existing unions.

Union relationships are incredibly complex and, unfortunately, often full of corruption. Incoming professionals should seek advice regarding unions as soon upon their arrival as possible. They should also work to quickly affiliate their workers with an honest union.

Human Resources in Mexico

There is no uniform human resource management system. The complexity of individual systems is often proportional to the size, resources, and corporate culture of the hospitality enterprise. The main factor operating here is the quality of the administrators who carry out the process. These administrators are responsible for providing adequate personnel for the company, but they may lack the information they need to do an effective job; for example, many restaurant managers have surprisingly little information about their waiters.

Job Descriptions and Requirements

It is essential to have a clear, well-thought-out analysis of job descriptions. This is many times missing in Mexican organizations, which causes distortions in service, especially in smaller companies.

Most companies do not have job requirement analyses. This means that there are no guides to the profiles required for the post, making it hard to fill vacancies adequately. This also implies that there is no way to provide equitable remuneration for the jobs done. Evaluations, then, are largely subjective and unfair, and they often lead to a subsequent drop in productivity. This problem, in turn, also affects training programs. The lack of standards means there is no clear way of finding out what employees should improve upon.

These factors make it extremely difficult for a company to know what human resources it actually possesses or needs. Indeed, many companies act as ships without a compass, unable to find harbor. According to research conducted by Mexico's Secretariat of Labor and Social Protection, the few companies that do have adequate human resource systems work more efficiently and are more successful.

Recruitment and Selection

Mexican companies recruit using a wide variety of means, including: recommendations (extremely important), bulletins, local chambers of commerce (which, in Mexico, work as trade associations that also represent industry interests), newspaper ads, and, on rare occasions, through headhunters. The method used depends largely on the size of the company and the vacancy to be filled.

One more method must be mentioned: interchange groups. These are large groups of similar companies, which ally themselves to share information databases on personnel. These groups are very well-organized and have in-depth knowledge of their needs and their personnel resources. Typically, recruiters from the individual companies meet informally once a month to discuss their employment needs and inquire about the possibility of another recruiter having information about a useful candidate. By sharing their databases, group members can easily find adequate candidates to fill specific vacancies. The companies that form these groups can greatly lower their recruitment costs without lowering the quality of their applicants.

The actual selection process begins with an application form, which places much emphasis on the applicant's work experience. The educational background must be thoroughly checked. In some cases psychometric tests may be applied. It is important to follow up with background checks, even though it is forbidden by law for past employers to give bad references about their former employees.

Most Mexican companies attempt to verify the applicant's socio-economic level, for they all wish to acquire employees with a "good upbringing." While discrimination is against Mexican law, the law is neither enforced nor openly broken. However, the term *good upbringing* is usually used to justify racial discrimination on the grounds that poor Mexicans do not have the social skills to interact at certain social levels—and poor Mexicans are thought more likely to have dark skin. Of course, this is not necessarily true. Mexico, though, is a racist society, and many managers and clients will not empathize with—and, therefore, will not hire or work with—someone whom they do not consider their equal.

The Work Contract and Induction

Before a candidate can be hired, it is necessary to make sure all of the worker's papers are in order. It is of special importance to make sure he or she is registered with the Instituto Mexico del Seguro Social (Mexican Institute for Social Welfare); if not, registration must be done immediately or the company may face a heavy fine. It is also important to make sure the candidate is registered with the Secretariat of the Treasury.

After this is done, the company may draft the employment contract. It must contain the length of the work day, the salary, the dates employees are paid, the location of the work, and a description of the worker's duties.

At the biggest companies, **induction** eases the new worker into the work environment, clarifying the company rules and regulations and helping the employee begin to socialize with peers. Most service industries, however, skip this step. There, workers tend to learn the rules and corporate culture as they go, gaining very little in-depth knowledge about the company along the way. As a result, employees develop little loyalty toward the institution.

Training and Development

Companies are obligated to implement training and development courses. These must be carried out by an accepted institution, such as the appropriate chamber of commerce, or at a specialized institute. Most of Mexico's training centers are low-level institutions. However, some top-notch institutions teach local and international service management and produce dynamic leaders capable of managing complex service institutions. This is the case with the Escuela Superior de Administración de Instituciones (School of Upper Management for Institutions), a part of the Universidad Panamericana. This institution provides professional degrees and development courses for companies that wish to improve the professionalism of top managers. Its services and alumni are currently in demand, as there is a deficit of trained professionals in Mexico.

Performance Evaluation

After working through the hiring and training process, it is necessary to measure the employee's performance. A clear job description makes it possible to judge the employee's ability to conform to what is expected. The lack of a job description makes it necessary to use subjective and unfair evaluations.

Subjective evaluations are common in Mexican culture. Mexicans tend to be highly emotional people and cannot fully separate themselves from their personal feelings for the people they are evaluating. This becomes a problem when a supervisor is asked to evaluate friends, enemies, or people of the opposite sex. This is especially true for female employees, who often unduly benefit from or are unfairly punished by the evaluation process. This has its origin in Mexico's conservative macho society. Attempts have been made to eliminate these distortions by having the person evaluated participate in the process, and then having the evaluation justified to a superior. Yet even this method is not without distortions, due to the close relationship that often exists between the supervisor and his or her boss.

Ideally, evaluations should lead to career planning and development courses. But it is impossible to make career plans with bad evaluation techniques. Few companies have the advantage of complete development career plans. Those that do are better prepared to succeed in the future. They are more likely to develop loyalty, have well-trained upper management, and experience less job rotation or turnover.

Safety, Health, and Social Planning

Mexican law establishes safety and health standards. The Instituto Mexicano del Seguro Social provides quite acceptable health care for the general population.

Mexico recently introduced a new retirement system known as the *Sistema de Ahorro para el Retiro,* which is intended to provide additional social security. Automatically depositing a percentage of the employee's salary into a savings account, this system increases the country's low internal savings index and provides security for Mexicans who might have failed to save for their retirement. The savings account can only be touched when the worker retires at the age of 65.

Key Terms

Federal Labor Law—Legislation drafted in the 1930s that dictates all work regulations for Mexico. It regulates every facet of employee-employer relations, including such areas as discrimination, training requirements, and termination practices.

induction—A process, typically in place at larger companies, that helps new employees adjust to a new work environment. For example, it may focus on clearly presenting company rules and regulations and helping new staff socialize with their peers.

internal regulations manual—A legally mandated manual of company guidelines that all companies in Mexico are required to develop using a joint commission of labor and company representatives. Once finalized, the manual must be presented to Mexico's Conciliation and Arbitration Board.

Discussion Questions

1. Briefly describe Mexican diversity. What methods could deal with the negative effects of this diversity in a constructive manner?

2. How would you rate Mexico's tourist industry?

3. What would you do to increase training and development in Mexico?

4. Describe basic Mexican labor law. What are the advantages and disadvantages of these laws? Do they help the worker?

5. How can managers develop a culture of service when facing adverse economic situations? How can they utilize non-monetary incentives?

6. Why is Mexico such an attractive tourist destination? What combination of factors influence this? How much is service responsible for the attractiveness of a tourist destination?

Internet Sites

For more information, visit the following Internet sites. Remember that Internet addresses can change without notice.

Instituto Panamerico de Alta Direccion de Empressa (English)
http://cibs.tamu.edu/mba-ms/ipade.html

Mexico Net Guide
(English, Spanish, French)
http://www.mexguide.net/index-i.html

Mexico Web
http://mexico.web.com.mx/english

North American Human Resource Management Association
http://www.shrm.org/nahrma/intro.htm

Secretaría de Comercio y Fomento Industrial (Spanish)
http://www.secofi.gob.mx

Secretaría de Hacienda y Crédito Público (English, Spanish)
http://shcp.gob.mx

Secretaría del Trabajo y Previsión Social (Spanish)
http://www.stps.gob.mx

Statistical and Geographical Information (English, Spanish)
http://www.inegi.gob.mx/difusion/ingles/portadai.html

Universidad Panamericana (Spanish)
http://www.upmx.mx/newup/

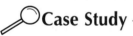

Case Study

"Los Danzantes"

Gustavo Muñoz-Castillo Mendoza opened Los Danzantes restaurant in early 1995 in the historical plaza of Coyoacán. It began as a small business with little capital, run by a young founder who had no prior experience in restaurant management. However, thanks to a process of innovation and total quality management, this company would become a leader in its field within a matter of years.

Muñoz-Castillo began his business with the vision of making it the best restaurant serving modern Mexican cuisine. This required a radically different work philosophy than that of other Mexican restaurants.

The first obstacle the new restaurant faced was finding the adequate personnel to provide the service that had been envisioned. This style of service required motivated and intelligent people who would be willing to be waiters and who would enjoy their jobs. In Mexican culture, however, "waitering" is seen as dishonorable and is certainly not a good career move. This problem was solved by hiring almost exclusively university students, who as waiters earned almost twice what they would make as interns in an office environment.

There were additional obstacles. The restaurant's first chef turned out to be a bad cook, and he left the restaurant after less than four months. He was replaced by a chef who had drinking problems and also lasted a mere four months. The second chef was followed by a well-qualified chef who had taken courses in France. However, he insisted on giving the restaurant a distinctive French taste. This contradicted the restaurant's vision of producing modern *Mexican* dishes. Eventually, the restaurant had to let him go.

This is when the restaurant decided to change strategies. Assistant chefs were given the liberty to create their own innovative dishes, which they presented to the sub-chef who would make recommendations for improving the dish. The kitchen was handled entirely by the sub-chef and an advisory chef. They coordinated the kitchen staff and helped the assistants develop their own potential creativity.

Los Danzantes evolved through a process of learning by trial and error. The original vision remained the same despite the challenges that were inherent to the service the restaurant gave, and the restaurant was able to survive these challenges and expand. By 1997 the restaurant was hiring its first administrative personnel to help manage the increasingly complex business, which had recently been expanded to include a joint venture with a mescal distillery. The business continued to expand, and the company established a gourmet food store.

This period of expansion demanded a change in the administrative processes. These processes were ordered and formalized, with every attempt made to remain faithful to Muñoz-Castillo's original philosophy. A human resource manager was hired to handle the technical details involving such a large staff.

The restaurant's philosophy brought all of the company members together. There were no barriers or conflicts between departments. Internal promotion was a reality. Promotions were based on performance and the enthusiasm shown for personal improvement. Periodic meetings kept the employees informed of new trends, decisions, courses of action, and objectives.

The corporate culture emphasized that the workers should not be motivated only by money, but also by their work and their own desire for personal development. The departmental barriers were eliminated, which helped to develop a sense of trust and unity throughout the organization.

Discussion Questions

1. What are the risks and benefits of formalizing processes in a restaurant based on innovation?

2. Do you believe it to be prudent for the restaurant to expand into other businesses?

Chapter 14 Outline

Perspectives of the Netherlands
  Culture of Consensus, Hedonism, and
    Diversity
The Development of Tourism
  The Significance of Tourism for the
    Future
The Hospitality Industry Today
  Growth of the Hospitality Industry
  Hotel Classification Structure
The Legal and Political Context
  Liberalization
  Self-Regulation
  Labor Conditions and Costs
  Regulation of Work Stress
Labor Market Issues
  Mobility and Flexibility
  Labor Market Strategies
  Approaches from Human Resource
    Management
Industrial Relations
  The Industrial Institution for
    Hospitality and Catering
  Compass for Future Strategy
Cultural and Societal Distinctions
  The Experience Culture
  Individualization
  The Reflexive Society
Challenges for Human Resource
  Management
  Recruitment and Selection
  Training and Development Tools
  Performance Evaluation and
    Multi-Rater Feedback
  Outcome-Based Human Resource
    Management

Competencies

1. Identify the unique aspects of Dutch
    society that have contributed to the
    development of the Dutch tourism
    industry. (pp. 231–237)

2. Describe the implications of the Dutch
    legal and political environment on the
    situation of hospitality employers and
    employees. (pp. 237–238)

3. Analyze the main labor market issues
    and their consequences on the
    situation of the Dutch hospitality
    industry in the future. (pp. 238–240)

4. Discuss the way in which the aspects
    of Dutch culture will influence
    industrial and labor relations in the
    Netherlands. (pp. 240–244)

5. Reflect on the changing qualifications
    of Dutch hospitality managers needed
    to realize high performance from
    multicultural teams. (pp. 245–248)

Human Resource Management in the Netherlands: Moving Toward People Competencies

Marijke Dieleman and *Paul Leenders*

Marijke Dieleman holds a Master's Degree in Social and Cultural Psychology from Nimwegen University. She has done research for The Institute of Education (Amsterdam) and for the Dutch Foundation for Research on Education (The Hague). She has taught at the Universities of Leiden and Utrecht. She currently is Senior Lecturer in HRM at the Hotel Management School Maastricht and Professor at Maastricht School for Management in the Executive Program for International Hotel Management and Tourism. She is a member of the national board of the Dutch Society of Personnel Management and has been a consultant in the service sector.

Paul Leenders holds a Degree in Personnel Management and has worked as an international HRM consultant with Amoco Corporation and as a senior HRM consultant with KPMG in the Netherlands. In 1998, he started his own advisory firm, Bull's Eye Consultancy. He is a certified Birkman Consultant and is eligible to use methods of Cambridge Interactive. He currently serves on the board of the International Chapter of the Dutch Society for Personnel Management (NVP), is a Member of the Society for Human Resource Management, and is a Guest Professor in HRM at Hotel Management School Maastricht.

Perspectives of the Netherlands

THE NETHERLANDS? WHERE'S THAT? Oh yes, *Holland*. The *Dutch*. The informal name "Holland" is widely known and used as a synonym for the Netherlands, although it actually refers to only one part of the Kingdom of the Netherlands. The

Netherlands is a relatively small country of about 41,000 square kilometers with 15.5 million inhabitants. This makes it one of the most densely populated countries in the world.

Most visitors to the Netherlands today come by air and see a neatly laid out land below. The old approach by sea, however, gives a different and in some ways truer view on the physical nature of the country. Almost one-fifth of the land area is reclaimed from the sea. Large parts of the country are flat, and water is abundant. The country has a great number of lakes and is crossed by many rivers and canals. Together with the well-known tourist attractions like windmills, clogs, fields of flowers, and cheese farms, they have become the stereotypes of Dutch tourism. And they still are, but the attention of the tourist is today more drawn by the numerous watersport opportunities in several parts of the country or by the water-defending constructions of the Delta works. Many historic Dutch cities and museums also have become main features of the Dutch tourism product.

The reputation of Amsterdam is a blend of charm, international mindedness, and relaxed tolerance. It faithfully reflects Dutch society as a whole in the care for its inner city, the ingenious use of cramped spaces, the particular style of houses, the generally urban style of habit and attitude, the disdain for shows of authority, the pragmatic businesslike attitudes of its entrepreneurs, and the general international outlook.

Recreational areas are scattered around the country: the hills in south Limburg, various places in the east, and water regions in Friesland and Zeeland. The large reclamation projects in the IJsselmeer have created many new recreational facilities. Sailing, motorboating, and windsurfing are enjoying an ever-increasing popularity in the whole Netherlands. In the center of the country, there is also the National Park of the Veluwe.

In addition to the natural and cultural resources, a typical Dutch phenomenon is the great density and variety of leisure and theme parks. Apart from Euro Disney near Paris, the Netherlands has the biggest theme park in Europe, the Efteling, receiving about 2.5 million visitors each year. Besides the Efteling, there are a great number of other theme parks, all of which have to invest continuously in new attractions in a highly competitive environment.

The accommodation industry in the Netherlands is characterized by many camp sites and bungalows. The luxury bungalow villas of Center Parcs are well known, offering not only overnight accommodation, but also all kinds of all-weather leisure and sport facilities, like whirlpools, saunas, tennis courts, restaurants, and shopping facilities. Recently, these Center Parcs villages also include theme activities like a jungle room or adventure sports. The formula of Center Parcs has been unexpectedly successful, realizing a 97 percent year-round occupancy rate.

The social life of the Dutch has a well developed attachment to domestic middle-class ways, but it also has an overwhelmingly strong international outlook. Nearly 500 years ago, the Dutchman Desiderius Erasmus was writing exclusively in Latin and managed to build up a popular reputation throughout Europe by putting out books full lively depictions of everyday life. He had a strong international instinct. The Dutch are devoted travelers, with an international outlook following that same cultural pattern.

Culture of Consensus, Hedonism, and Diversity

The Dutch socio-cultural climate has a more or less materialistic character. Much interest is attached to such matters as income, food, and security. Some Dutch research has shown that, in the 1990s, a quarter of the electorate chose material targets. The majority of the electorate dwells in between, of which two-thirds incline to the material and one-third to the post material (described later in this chapter). This situation is a typical Dutch feature: avoiding of extreme opinions in favor of the "golden mean." This also can be considered as an expression of the **consensus culture** that is so characteristic of Dutch pragmatism.

Besides the materialistic attitude, allowing individuals to live their lives according to their own views is probably one of the most predominant features of Dutch culture. Self-realization and freedom of movement are two important concepts within this framework. Hence, the concept of authority has a special connotation within Dutch culture: authority must be earned, not presumed, regardless of one's position in work or private life. Authority is earned through a process that relies greatly on individual characteristics. This fact contributes to a process of individualization that has been developing for quite a time.

This process of individualization encompasses three different major aspects in the Netherlands. In the first place, there is a continuous striving for equality and the reduction of power differentials. Some consequences of this are changing relationships between men and women in the private as well as public realm and an increasing desire for non-hierarchical relations in society. Compared with other Western countries, for a long time a relatively low number of Dutch women worked (55 percent). In the last ten years, women have been increasingly entering the labor market or continuing to work after children are born. In response to this trend, childcare facilities have expanded.

In the second place, there is a wider pluriformity in cultures and lifestyles nowadays. Consequences include: attaching less value to assuming traditional social roles, a wider variety of living styles, and a continuing process of international orientation and acceptance of the cultural identity of minorities. It is of considerable significance that minorities are steadily occupying new places in Dutch society in ways that were unanticipated. At a time when various economic developments are forcing increasing numbers of people from the traditional class of small restaurant keepers out of business, ethnic minorities are stepping into this gap.

In the third place, an increasingly hedonist, consumption-oriented attitude to life, strongly influenced by the increased prosperity, has evolved. Western European countries are among the most prosperous in the world; among them, the Netherlands occupies a top rank. Dutch people spend a lot of money in the hospitality industry. In public debate, there is a growing concern about the consequences on social cohesion of the growing individualization. Recently, public attention is more focused on teaching social values and standards because of increasing social problems as criminality and alcohol and drug abuse.

The Development of Tourism ———————————————————

During the 1980s, the main countries of residence of inbound tourists were Germany, Belgium, and the United Kingdom. The high departure rates for Dutch residents indicated a very significant demand, and the overall balance of payments for (travel) tourism was negative. More than two-thirds of the negative balance was due to tourism expenditures by Dutch travelers in the countries of the European Union. In the Netherlands, tourism receipts from non-residents were three to four times higher than those from residents.

For this reason, the government decided to pursue an active tourism policy aimed at narrowing the gap between imported and exported tourism by improving the quality of the tourism product and by using promotional activities in well chosen foreign markets. This policy was combined with the promotion of the Netherlands Bureau for Tourism and promotion of the Dutch tourist product in the Dutch market by an extensive network of tourism offices at the provincial and local levels spread throughout the country.

The Dutch Ministry of Economic Affairs defined four priority themes for promoting the country as a tourist destination: interior waterways, cultural heritage, the coast, and the urban centers. This policy has had the effect it was aiming for: as a result of the considerable growth in the number of incoming tourists and tourist expenditures, the deficit on the balance of trade in travel has decreased, particularly in the last ten years. The number of non-European foreign visitors is growing each year.

The main reasons that foreigners generally give for visiting the Netherlands are the landscape (46 percent), the coast and sandy beaches (36 percent), the cozy atmosphere and friendly people (34 percent), and the museums and cultural life (33 percent). The four big cities—Amsterdam, Rotterdam, The Hague, and Utrecht—account for about 30 percent of all overnight stays by foreigners, accommodated mainly in hotels. The second main area that foreigners visit is the North Sea coast (nearly 20 percent), the majority accommodated in bungalows or on campsites.

At the same time, expenditures from domestic holidays have been increasing. The two most important destinations are the North Sea coast (receiving 14 percent of all domestic holidays) and the Veluwe (receiving 12 percent), which is a forested area in central Holland. The average length of stay is gradually decreasing, but the number of holidays taken by each holiday maker is increasing. Between 1985 and 1990, the average length of stay for domestic holidays decreased from 12.2 to 10.6 days, while the average number of holidays increased from 1.45 to 1.67.

The Significance of Tourism for the Future

Recently, the most important nationalities to visit the Netherlands are Germans (responsible for 45 percent of all overnight stays by foreigners), British (12 percent), and Belgians and Americans (both seven percent). Nowadays there are a growing number of visitors from other countries like Czechoslovakia, Portugal, Turkey, South Africa, and the countries of Asia. The number of foreign visitors is expected to continue to grow. At the same time, the expenditure of domestic tourists in all segments of the market is still growing.

In 1990, total tourism expenditure in the Netherlands by domestic and incoming tourists was about DGL 31 billion, resulting in 140,000 man-years of direct employment and another 38,500 man-years of indirect employment. Including part-time employees, approximately 230,000 people were employed as a result of tourist expenditure, constituting more than ten percent of total private-sector employment. From 1982-1989, tourist expenditure increased by 33 percent; at the same time, tourism employment increased by ten percent.

It is estimated that the Dutch tourism and hospitality sector represents about 45,000 firms. The majority are small family-owned enterprises, although the number of national and international chains is growing. Employment has grown to about 300,000 people, including indirect employment by the entrepreneurs themselves and their family members. The effect of the tourism industry on the country's economic future will be significant.

On the recreation market, the formula of Center Parcs has been unexpectedly successful. The eight establishments in the Netherlands, with a total supply of 5,000 bungalows (approximately 20 percent of the total bungalow capacity), offer accommodation for almost 40 percent of the Dutch bungalow market. Since 1987, the expansion of Center Parcs has taken place in Belgium, Great Britain, and France because the domestic market was saturated for further expansion.

In terms of holiday intensity (that is, the proportion of the population that takes a holiday at least once a year), the Netherlands ranks very high in Europe, showing a figure of almost 70 percent in the 1990s. If short break holidays are also taken into account, the percentage rises to nearly 75 percent. In addition to the camping facilities, more and more Dutch farmers offer campsites to supplement their decreasing agricultural income. The Netherlands ranks third in the world in camping sites (1.7 million), only slightly behind France and the United States.

The Hospitality Industry Today

In general, the Dutch holiday expenditure of both foreign and domestic tourists still is increasing, with some big differences between the types of accommodation chosen. Also growing is the catering and fast-food industry, where Dutch people are spending more and more. Total revenues in the industry increased by 6.1 percent in 1999 to a total of Dutch Fl. 23.9 billion, and are expected to exceed 25 billion in 2000.

Although the estimates look very favorable, it will not be easy for the industry to cope with this growth in revenues. It will be hard for many companies within the industry to prosper due to a tight labor market and increasing customer demands. About one-third of all companies are already dealing with a severe labor shortage; this number increases to over 50 percent for the larger companies. This is a critical development because qualified employees play a pivotal role in the hospitality process: they provide service in direct contact with customers. At the same time, customers are asking for service, quality, attainability, safety, and personal attention.

Growth of the Hospitality Industry

The hospitality industry in the Netherlands has enormously profited from sustained economic growth. First quarter 2000 revenues for the industry increased by 7.1 percent compared with 1999. The confidence of customers and their intention to spend have stayed at a high level. Spending increases are due to a growth of the customer base; groups with less income benefit from economic growth as well and go out for dinner more often. People visit hospitality companies more often and are willing to pay more for better quality. The fastest growth is occurring in hotels and fast-food restaurants.

The rise of luxury hotels goes on without prejudice in the Netherlands. Between 1998 and 1999, the number of four-star hotels increased by six percent, and the number of five-star hotels increased by seven percent. This growth is expected to continue because luxury hotels tend to profit from increases in economic activity—including the effect of companies sending their high performing employees to luxury hotels, congresses, and seminars as a token of appreciation and incentive.

Also, the mentality of the Dutch is changing. With a demand for higher quality goes the willingness to pay a higher price. Consumer research studies show that more customers are visiting luxury hotels to celebrate family. Sustained economic growth combined with increasing leisure time will probably lead to even higher figures for the luxury hotel segment.

In the Netherlands, there are 49 international hotel and catering organizations, subdivided in 28 hotel and restaurant chains, three recreation outlets, 15 restaurant chains, and three catering companies. Almost four-fifths are either Dutch-, U.S.-, U.K.-, or French-owned. The main part of the total number of 45,000 companies in the hospitality industry are small family-owned companies. Over 51 percent of the total number of companies employs only one to nine employees. About 10 percent of hospitality companies have between 10 and 19 employees and only six percent employs over 20 employees. The remaining 33 percent are single-person businesses. The power of the industry on the national market is to be small-scaled. In essence, these companies are more flexible and more suited to take the advantage of innovation.

For small companies, it is easier to find opportunity in the challenge of new developments. However, small companies also often have the disadvantage of being too small to have enough expertise and knowledge. For instance, administration is often outsourced, financial analysis hardly takes place, new developments in customer demands are not seen or understood, and human resource management is treated simply as a means for allocating the right number of people. Employees are seen as costs. New technology and applications are considered too expensive or time-consuming. Normally, there is too much emphasis on merely delivering the product as itself, without attention to extra service. There is little insight that delivering superior service to customers is of great importance and leads directly to higher revenues and returns on investment.

Because of the increasing complexity of business processes, a lack of professionalism will be a real threat to small companies hoping to operate and survive in a competitive market.

Hotel Classification Structure

Several years ago, the Benelux countries (Belgium, the Netherlands, and Luxembourg) developed a hotel classification system. The Benelux Hotel Classification classifies hotels by using stars in five categories. The Industrial Institution takes primary responsibility for this, and the ANWB is cooperating. (The ANWB is the national organization that intermediates all kinds of travel facilities and organizes all kinds of information about traveling inside and outside the country.) This Benelux Hotel Classification is mandatory for all hotels in the Netherlands.

All hotels are marked by an escutcheon with stars on it. The classification describes the minimum quantitative and (since 1999) qualitative norms for facilities on each star level. The Dutch register has over 2,900 companies, of which 2,200 have one or more stars. Each facility is audited every two years by inspectors from the Industrial Institution to guarantee that their quality is still acceptable and meets the norms.

The Legal and Political Context

During the last few years, there have been many changes in the legal and political context of the Netherlands, partly due to the ongoing process of European Unification and partly due to a change in economic strategy from the Dutch government. The following combination of actions is the most important of these legal and political developments:

- measures taken to stimulate the economy,

- combined with a government that pulls back, and

- a growing European unification process.

Liberalization

The measures have both a positive and negative impact on the hospitality industry. In order to stimulate the economic market, legislation regarding the establishment of new companies became more liberal, which led to new entrants in the market. Stimulating industry improvements will on one hand give extra competition from outside the industry, but will on the other hand force the industry to develop new products and services.

A special law in this area (*Mededingingwet* or Act on Competition) prohibits price agreements and so enables a fiercer competition. The same law makes the market dominance of ongoing mergers and acquisitions by the large concerns more difficult to accomplish. Recent developments and changes in social security legislation lead to a shift of cost from the government to the industry. The new Act on Works Councils increases the control of employees.

Self-Regulation

There is a shift from government regulation to more self-regulation by the industry, with an exception for alcohol abuse, which is regulated in the new Act on Liquor and *Horeca* (a Dutch term referring to hotels, restaurants, and cafes). Also, a new law on labor conditions has been developed and taken effect, but measures to regulate work stress are the responsibility of the industry itself. Due to the unification of Europe, national laws are being harmonized. The Dutch tax legislation is being renewed with less direct and more indirect taxes. The increase in indirect taxes leads to price increases and directly influences the willingness of people to spend money. With greater emphasis on environmental taxes, the industry is forced to work more responsibly with the environment.

Added to these rules is European legislation in the area of hygiene and accountability according to ISO 2000 norms, all meant to protect customers. This all results in additional costs and administrative burdens. At the same time, however, it has become easier to employ people from outside the European Union, which opens up new labor markets. All these new regulations mean more costs for the industry.

Labor Conditions and Costs

The costs of absenteeism include the full salaries of the sick employees during their first year of absence, the additional salary costs for replacement workers, higher illness premiums to insurance companies in some cases, and the cost of the employers' time to arrange replacements. Good labor conditions cause fewer sick employees than poor conditions. Low absenteeism reduces costs. The work atmosphere is important. A good atmosphere increases productivity because employees are better motivated. Employers face obligations under the Labor Conditions Act.

Employers and employees are accountable for health and safety in the work place. To meet their obligations, employers must take care of a risk assessment and evaluation, arrange company relief work, and consult with employees about improvement objectives and activities. Employees need to know of work-related health risks. They need to know the company's risk-solving strategies and they need to know the emergency plans. They are entitled to inform external institutions with their complaints.

Regulation of Work Stress

Too much stress is harmful, especially if the situation continues for a period of time or on a regular basis. It could lead to absenteeism, to a worse work atmosphere, to more mistakes, and eventually to loss of revenues. It is well known that the work stress in the hospitality industry is very often high. It can be reduced by improving the labor conditions in the company. The hospitality industry is the first institution in the Netherlands striving to set an agreement to reduce work stress. In such an agreement, both the government and the Unions deliberate on the approach, the instruments, and the objectives in reducing work-related stress.

Labor Market Issues

Employment opportunities within the hospitality industry have been increasing very rapidly during the last few years. The number of employees increased from 165,000 in 1992 to 221,000 in 1997. Today, the industry employs over 300,000 people, including the entrepreneurs themselves. At this moment, it is rather hard to get enough highly qualified employees. So besides opportunities, there are some severe threats to cope with.

Career opportunities with smaller companies in the industry are and remain limited. Through the use of flexible contracts, job security is diminished. Also, there are fewer people with full-time jobs (28 percent of all people employed in 2000 compared with 47 percent in 1991). The average salary level is not attractive and could best be compared with the cleaning industry or retail. Meanwhile, the industry's working hours are long and irregular and include evenings and public holidays. The work has a high stress level and physical burdens.

There is hardly any challenge in the jobs and little possibility for further qualification or development. The dominant management style is hierarchical, and there is almost no room for empowerment or entrepreneurship. These elements do not motivate and satisfy employees, and they reduce the profitability of the enterprise as well. Employee turnover is expensive. Not only does it take time to get new people up to standard, the workload for other employees increases.

Mobility and Flexibility

Traditionally, the hospitality industry has high employee turnover. The highest rate (21 percent) can be seen in the hotel and restaurant segment. Due to a lack of internal mobility to higher level positions, people with higher education change jobs to boost their careers. Their ability to do this is further enhanced in today's tight labor market. Qualified employees can easily find new jobs, and not only in the hospitality industry.

Despite the ease with which employees can find new jobs, employees find it hard to get *full-time* jobs. Most positions are offered on a temporary basis. To handle situations with a great demand for services, employers are using flexible employees. Ideally, this has a positive effect both on the work stress of full-time employees and on the financial results. However, there are some negative aspects as well—for instance, in the level of service provided. The image of the industry is not quite positive.

Labor Market Strategies

In the future, there will be fewer young people and many more elderly people in the Netherlands. The hospitality industry has traditionally relied on young workers. This problem will be enhanced because it will affect all segments of the labor market. The competition for workers will become acute. One potential source of new young employees is multicultural. The industry needs to prepare itself for the future entrance of these labor forces. The guiding principle is the integration of these people into the traditional organizations. Cultural diversity will become a main issue in the Dutch hospitality industry.

Approaches from Human Resource Management

Effective solutions to these problems will largely have to come from the human resources departments or from managers with HR responsibilities. Additional attention needs to go to effective recruitment and selection campaigns. Using a flexible workforce requires a great commitment to teams and to the day-to-day operations of the company. Full-time employees need to be involved in the recruitment and selection process because they have to work with the new employees.

Qualified employees are not always motivated as well. Temporary employees need to be involved not only in the overall operations of the company, but also in regular meetings, scheduling activities, and other human resource practices like performance evaluation and training. Coaching of temporary people is often the responsibility of the non-temps. This will have an effect on their time, so coaching activities need to be recognized and valued by the employer.

The integration of multicultural employees can be facilitated by paying more attention to cultural differences. Human resource managers have to take care of this cultural diversity.

To reduce high turnover ratios, companies need to offer better labor conditions as well. If career opportunities are not available, employee satisfaction can be improved by empowerment and a broader employability and by involving them in the strategic issues of business performance.

The increasing complexity of business operations calls for continuing education. Employees are responsible for their own development and employability in the future. But companies too will profit from the ongoing development of their staff. In the Netherlands, the need for lifelong learning throughout someone's career has created new educational concepts in which learning and working experiences are combined for current and future managers in the hospitality industry. Hotel Management School of Maastricht, in cooperation with the Stichting Vakopleiding Horeca (Foundation for Hospitality Training) will start in 2000 with the first High Vocational Curriculum that addresses just this.

Industrial Relations

In 1950, the Act for Statutory Trade Organization (*Wet op de Bedrijfsorganisatie*) went into effect. This act enables clusters of the same kind of industry (*bedrijfstakken*) to start Industrial Institutions serving as the principal entity of communication between the government and the companies in that particular industry and with the power to set regulations for the whole industry.

This act is based firstly on the belief that industrial segments have their own responsibility to set regulations in their industry and secondly on the assumption that cooperation between employer unions and labor unions is of evident importance to keep power differences in a good balance. The Industrial Institution for Hospitality and Catering was established in 1955 as a statutory trade organization to serve the interest of the whole industry.

The Industrial Institution for Hospitality and Catering

This Institution is meant for the whole branch of the hospitality industry, the recreation industry, and the catering industry. Members of the board are representatives from both unions. Together and in consensus, they determine the strategy and the policies as well as the necessary activities. They run their own budget for which all companies in the industry have to pay. Part of this financial contribution is a percentage of the overall payroll of each company, another part is fixed.

The Institution serves its members in several ways. The most important is conducting systematic research of activities in the industry and its environment. Opportunities and threats are sketched and solutions provided, for example, by giving advice to members, by meeting with other parties, and by information retrieval. Another important task is stimulating the quality of business processes in the enterprises by developing products and services that can help affiliated companies to improve business performance. The Institution is seen as expert and authoritative with a clear added value for its affiliates.

Since 1998, the Industrial Institution for Hospitality and Catering Industry has reported annually on trends and developments within the branch and on related strategic advice for the future. In 1999, the Institution reported on two major issues:

1. The need for stronger investments required to serve customers in a better way and to capitalize on the growth opportunities. Being reluctant in this area will open the gate for outsiders who either add hospitality activities to their core processes or who are willing to invest in the development of new formulas. The industry should become more innovative.

2. Customers are becoming more individualized, more fickle, more powerful, and more demanding of quality, execution, and originality of products and services. In order to fulfill these increasing customer demands, employers have to invest more in people and in products and services with a shorter life cycle. Also the organization has to be changed.

In June 2000, the industry organized its annual congress in which participants debated the question of who should pay the costs of all of this. Is the customer willing to pay additional money for increasing demands, or should the cost be the concern of the entrepreneurs in the industry themselves (for instance, by exploring new ways to balance costs and revenues, by cooperating with competitors, or by further automating back-office activities)?

The congress also debated on the future position of smaller companies. These companies benefit from their innovative power and personal service as well as direct contact with their customers. But they have to compete against larger hospitality chains that possess all the benefits of economy of scale, purchase power, allocation of people, and marketing. The Industrial Institution serves as the knowledge and expertise center for the whole industry and pleads in favor for founding a digital platform for exchange of knowledge on trends and developments, broad and in depth.

Compass for Future Strategy

In the recently published *Compass for Future Strategy*, the following strategic items have been identified for the future:

- Enhancing human resource management

- Improving overall labor conditions by reducing work stress

- Approaching new target groups on the labor market, like women with second careers, elderly people, and young people with a non-Dutch background

- Addressing actively and very concretely the demands of new customers and new employees with different cultural backgrounds

- Paying more attention for the demands and needs of the customers

- Developing a clearer profile for different companies within the industry in order to become more recognizable for customers

- Improving cooperation with competitors within and outside the industry

- Increasing the level of professionalism of managers

- Paying greater attention to safety and environmental aspects of the industry

- Increasing the return on investment

Cultural and Societal Distinctions

The living environment of the Dutch people has changed drastically during the past decade. The number of possible experiences has vastly increased; many of these involve virtual reality more than material reality. Many people are spending more and more time in the imaginary world of television, movies, computers, and the Internet. In Western Europe, watching television is an important form of leisure. This way, people come into touch with a vast diversity of realities from everywhere in the world.

In this expansion of the world of experience, a liberalization of norms and values has created more freedom of movement. The Dutch people today are much less hindered by do's and don'ts than they were in the past. Many former and often oppressive moral limits to relations, family life, and leisure time have disappeared. Oppressive and needless authority has vanished. Social etiquette has become more informal. The Dutch—especially the younger generations—are more relaxed in socializing. People have more freedom and have become the only ones who decide on their own course of life, in work as well as in private life.

The Experience Culture

In the Netherlands, the emphasis has shifted from more traditional values like family, church, and education toward the immediate experience of events and the valuation of the inner life. Experience and feelings have become central categories in themselves. What counts is not only what one has experienced, but also especially how and what one's feelings were about it. Modern Dutch culture emphasizes how the unique individual perceives and experiences an event.

The new state of mind has generated a broad experience market that is still expanding. This market is a growing segment of our services society and stretches from amusement parks through musical events to dining in oriental tents. With all of these, the goal is a specific inner state that consists not necessarily of only pleasure and enjoyment, but also of other emotions. Essential is the tinkering with one's own experiences. The immediate experience has elevated from being a marginal phenomenon to an objective in itself.

The problem for many people is not scarcity, but abundance. A much smaller proportion of income than in past has to be spent on basic needs; the remainder can be used for less prosaic needs. In Western countries, one can see a shift in recent decades from material to post-material values—that is, to values that concern the quality of existence: self-realization, feeling good, independence, expression, and culture. The younger generations are more dedicated to these values than the older ones.

The Netherlands is taking the lead in this. But with more opportunities and fewer limitations, the individual has to make up his mind about the choices that present themselves. When basic needs are satisfied and new opportunities keep arising, one has to question what other needs should be fulfilled? The answer to this question refers to personal needs and personal emotions and will have to be found time and again. The daily consumption of goods, services, and information can no longer be completed without the compass of one's own emotional needs. Disappointment is never far off because repetition of an experience easily leads to habituation and decreases the intensity.

In the end, the high expectations cannot be lived up to, inviting the individual to look for new and other thrills. The experience market can easily overcome the languishing individual and send him ever further in this search of new sensations. New experiences must be found that can satisfy these emotional needs, over and again. In the Netherlands, there is a growing market of events and all kinds of sensational experiences.

Individualization

Probably no issue draws as much attention in the Netherlands as the movement toward greater and greater individualization. This progressing individualization is generally identified with the diminishing influence of church, family, and education and with the possibilities that Western societies offer to determine one's own course of life to a very large extent. Individual goals in life are becoming more important. The focus of all attention, reflection, care, and efforts is the individual and his personal well-being. Not every individual conforms to this image, but it is the dominant normative personality in the Dutch and most Western societies.

The type of personality that comes to fit in is an autonomous individual with characteristics and capacities that enable him to be independent and self-conscious in all situations. Standing up for oneself and being able to get things done have become important values. Individualization refers to strengthening autonomy, self-consciousness, a belief in one's own capacities, freedom of choice, and having control of one's own position and career.

The forceful nature of individualization creates also ambivalence. This brings us to the second characteristic of the new individualization: the increased reflexivity in professional and personal life, which has led to a great mobility in the labor force of the Dutch industry today.

The Reflexive Society

Since the 1980s, individualization has received a new impulse. Insights from microeconomics have been gaining in influence. Terms like performance, efficiency, strength-weakness analysis, and cost-benefit analysis have come to dominate our daily experiences at work and at school. Today, a process of professionalization of the employee is ongoing. It is directed by modern managerial thinking with regard to the individual and organization. Its viewpoint is that of the *homo economicus.*

The core of this process is the individual who minimizes his efforts and maximizes his benefits and pleasure on the basis of rational consideration. The individual pursuits of benefit maximization take place in a competitive atmosphere. The principles of the current market orchestrate and regulate all these pursuits. Market forces are considered profitable for individual and society. Since the 1980s, this thinking has become very well established, manifesting itself in an abundance of management literature and management courses.

One can distinguish two kinds of renewed individualism. The first is called the *utilitarian* form and here three aspects dominate: firstly, the value that is attached to an unrestricted and individual pursuit of one's own interests; secondly, the emphasis on external, material success; and thirdly, the thought that everyone acts in his own interests, that this is "normal," and that it is not a very intelligent thing if one refuses to do so. The utilitarian individualist focuses on his or her right and opportunity to pursue individual interests without much regard for the consequences for others. Achievement and success, property, hard work, and making much money are foremost and can, in this view, be achieved by an attitude of "everybody for himself." This utilitarian trend is gaining influence among young people in the Netherlands. Their lives are increasingly dominated by having a great time, being totally independent, earning money, and having material success. Should this trend persevere, it is feared that such a businesslike and calculating attitude will also cause young people to go off the social rails.

The second kind of individualism, *expressive* individualism, is characterized by an emphasis on individual autonomy, self-determination, and freedom; the view that an individual must be able to develop his own strengths and capacities; and the importance of personal originality or uniqueness. While a utilitarian individualistic attitude focuses on visible, quantifiable success, usually of a material nature, expressive individualists judge success in terms of authenticity, self-realization, and "feeling good." They often have a self-indulgent, hedonistic attitude and a strong orientation to the here and now. They keep the future open, are consumerists, and do not want to be tied down by marriage and children.

According to international studies, young people in the Netherlands take the lead in showing these post-materialist values. Although these two types of individualism seem to be opposites, they often will manifest themselves within one person: they are variations of the same attitude in which working very hard in training or on the job is combined with exuberant pleasure-seeking in leisure time, leading to a kind of dualism.

All of this affects the hospitality industry. The younger generation does not feel attracted to hospitality because the industry lacks career potential. At the same time, young people take temporary jobs to earn just enough money to be able to travel the world. They easily change from the one temporary job to the other.

Challenges for Human Resource Management

The world of hospitality business has been dramatically changing. Even in a small country like the Netherlands, companies are under great pressure to find new strategies to cope with a rapidly changing environment. When the rate and quality of change exceed a certain threshold, the need for talented people to run the business will become a critical success factor. Hospitality organizations have come to realize that they must invest in their human resources to release true value. In all services, the competitive edge will come as much from the people as from the product.

By strategic planning of human resource management, managers can contribute to release true value by the optimum use of **people competencies** (knowledge, skills, and attitudes). This approach requires that the needs and talents of employees be matched with the organization's goals. People competencies should become the building blocks of successful hospitality organizations of the future. To sustain and develop the people competencies required for future success, an organization needs to have a system with which it can discriminate superior to good from average to poor performers by observation.

Organizations in the future will be different from today. Traditional hierarchical relations will be replaced by networks of empowered workgroups. Information will be at everyone's fingertips. Careers will become a sequence of assignments rather than a logical sequence of different jobs representing a climb to the top. In this context, employees work more in clusters, where people are not tied to a management level by traditional hierarchical lines. Because of the complexity of work and the need for autonomy, teams need a certain amount of freedom to accomplish their task. The performance of these teams is measured on the accomplishment of their mission.

To benefit from the opportunities this new type of organization provides, a new type of human resource management—based on a clear notion of required competencies for future success in new (team) roles—is needed. This will require a much sharper image of the real strengths and weaknesses of people and their possible contribution to the organization and to teamwork. Human resource managers should describe the competencies required for future organizational success. All human resource practices like recruitment, selection, training, development, and performance evaluation and measurement have to be based on these requirements.

Recruitment and Selection

In most organizations, recruitment and selection of employees is a purely numerical process. Instead, recruitment should concentrate on bringing in new members who carry the right professional qualifications and who have values that harmonize well with the values of the organization. The required competencies for *future* organizational success are also important, especially those that are missing in the team in which new hires will start to work. This should form the heart of the recruitment and selection process in the industry.

To ensure that the characteristics sought during the selection process are those that will enable new job holders to deliver the required results, serious research should be done to discover which characteristics will lead to successful performance. In doing so, recruitment and selection will not focus on the content of the job, but rather will concentrate on specifying what it is that the job should deliver as *output* and if candidates are competent to deliver this output. One can only know this more or less for sure from former (similar) performance. This information will not be apparent on a résumé or in an interview.

Assessment centers appear to be a more predictable tool in selection. Most of them use projective tests, in-basket exercises, and leaderless group exercises to assess managerial competencies. An overall evaluation of the participants' performance is made by observers that are looking for leadership traits that will predict the advancement potential of managers-to-be. They have to be familiar with the organizational values and business challenges, as well as with the linked critical tasks of the positions they are recruiting for. Between observers, there must exist a shared understanding of the specific competencies they are looking for.

Training and Development Tools

Human resource management has to promote an organizational culture in which permanent learning and growth are viewed as essential to future business success. In such a learning organization, human resource managers will stimulate people to spend time in refining the competencies they need to meet future business challenges. Because an increasing number of business processes will involve teamwork, the development of individuals and of teams has to take place at the same time. Besides the development of new types of organization, we need to concentrate on the development requirements of teams.

There are many ways to develop teams and individuals: classroom training, training on the job, coaching, job rotation, computerized training, and gaining external experience. Training has been shifted from being a company's responsibility toward a mutual responsibility of company and employee. During the last couple of years, one can see a trend in which education is becoming more and more the responsibility of the individual. Self-development is the new device. Self-assessment will become usual practice.

Some leading companies in the Netherlands already provide their management employees with information about the future direction of the company, the foreseen required knowledge, skills, and experience in that future, and the most likely time scale for when this will happen. Knowing this, it is the responsibility of the individual to get personally at par with the future requirements. When the individual wants to, the company will provide support by offering resources for development and tools for improvement in the desired direction.

Performance Evaluation and Multi-Rater Feedback

In the Netherlands, there is growing use of **multi-rater feedback** instruments because of their ability to assess the performance of managerial behavior. Center Parcs is using this instrument for management development. Multi-rater feedback challenges managers to self-improvement and enables the organization to capture different and important information on managerial performance. The value of multi-rater feedback systems is primarily their ability to yield additional performance data and to initiate a dialogue about performance evaluation of the soft assets in the organization.

Many multi-rater feedback instruments are questionnaire-based and aim to describe numerically a manager's performance. Multi-rater questionnaires ask observers to rate the management behavior in different ways. Some rate in terms of frequency and some in terms of perceived standard (the manager is excellent, competent, poor at displaying certain competencies).

Some multi-rater instruments attempt to gain an understanding of how important various traits or behaviors are to different groups of observers and ask them to rate the importance of each competency statement. The latter will help the organization to check if the traits that were identified as management competencies do indeed tally with the perceptions of employees. If not, they have to take care of this incongruity. The organization will also know the self-ratings and whether the manager is capable of strategically choosing the kind of behavior the situation asks for. For the manager, importance ratings of others will help him to learn the different needs and expectations of observer groups. An example of such an instrument is the management questionnaire developed by Schouten and Nelissen, a leading Dutch training company. Hotel Management School Maastricht uses this instrument as a tool for self-development.

Outcome-Based Human Resource Management

In the Netherlands, one can see a growing tendency to consider instruments like the **Balanced Score Card** to measure different kinds of performance. It helps organizations gather information about needed performance improvement in these areas. The Balanced Score Card measures performance from four different angles: the financial perspective, the customer perspective, the business process perspective, and the learning perspective. It is important that Balanced Score Cards demand non-financial performance outcomes as well as financial ones. A strictly financial perspective will underestimate other sometimes even more important perspectives, like customer orientation, achievement motivation, or strategic capacity.

Although the numbers may look positive at first sight, many hospitality organizations have discovered from experience that a narrow financial view results in poor customer service, shoddy products, unfulfilled and unhappy people in the enterprise, or other negative phenomena, all of which eventually reflect themselves in poor numbers in the future. This is especially true for the hospitality industry, where one needs instruments to make all the critical success factors measurable, including the soft assets. The use of such instruments will help people in the organization to focus on *outcomes* of performance instead of input of performance activities. They help in making crystal clear exactly what the results of their performance should be. In many hospitality organizations, people do the reverse: they concentrate on performance of activities instead of on performance of the desired outcomes. As a result, they rarely achieve the kind and level of performance that really matter.

Throughout the whole organization, human resource managers need to set and achieve smart performance criteria across the spectrum that seems relevant to each function. These criteria will align the specific performance from different individuals on all organizational levels with the required competencies on that specific level. People have to know why their contribution makes a difference and how their activities are linked to the desired performance outcomes. They also have to understand the difference between good and bad performance.

Outcomes must simultaneously benefit the customers, the shareholders, the employees, and the management of the organization to realize true value. Douglas Smith has called this the **cycle of sustainable performance**. This cycle helps managers to come to desired outcomes. The cycle will function as a framework to ensure that the organizational goals are set, met, and balanced in the future hospitality business. All these goals have to be S.M.A.R.T.—that is, specific, measurable, achievable, relevant, and time-bound.

Many executives in the Dutch hotel and catering sector understand that financial indicators are lagging in showing effects caused by other indicators like customer satisfaction and people skills or service attitudes. Whether considering the entire organization, a business unit within the organization, a team, or a single person's contribution, sustainable performance emerges when we move beyond only the financial approach to richer variety of reinforcing performance outcomes and results.

The main challenge for human resource management in the hospitality industry will be to contribute to the business core competencies by the use of performance-based competencies. Human resources manager can help hospitality companies to achieve crucial non-financial outcomes by improving business performance through the development of people.

References

Branchemonitor 1998, Kompas voor beleid. Bedrijfschap Horeca en Catering.

Dieleman, A. J. *When the Future Lies Ahead.* Internal publication, Open University, The Netherlands.

Kompas voor Beleid 1999. Bedrijfschap Horeca en Catering.

De uitdaging. De toekomst van de Nederlandse Hotellerie. Hotel Management Diner. Uitgave Horeca Misset Mei 1999.

Mitrani, A, Dalziel, M. and Fitt, D. *Competency-Based Human Resource Management. Value-Driven Strategies for Recruitment, Development and Reward.* London: Kogan Page, 1996.

Multinationale Horeca- en cateringorganisaties in Nederland 1998. Bedrijfschap Horeca en Catering, Zoetermeer, 1998.

Pompl, W. and Lavery, P. *Tourism in Europe. Structures and Developments.* Oxon: Wallingford, 1993.

Shetter, William Z. *The Netherlands in perspective. The Dutch way of organizing society and its setting.* Meppel: Krips, 1997.

Smith, D. K. *Make Success Measurable! A Mindbook-Workbook for Setting Goals and Taking Action.* New York: Wiley, 1999.

Tourism in Europe. European Commission Eurostat, Luxembourg, 1995.

Key Terms

Balanced Score Card—Instrument for performance measurement from four perspectives: financial, customer, business process, and learning.

consensus culture—A culture requiring a large amount of consultation and discussion, with subsequent adjustment in favor of the golden mean.

cycle of sustainable performance—Cycle of performance outcomes that will simultaneously generate benefits for customers, shareholders, employees, and management.

experience culture—Growing emphasis on the immediate experience of events and the evaluation of the personal inner life.

homo economicus—The individual who minimizes his efforts and maximizes his benefits and pleasure on the basis of rational consideration.

multi-rater feedback—A system of feedback on management performances from different angles of perception within the organization.

people competencies—the unique combination of knowledge, skills, attitude, and behavior that are causally related to superior performance.

Discussion Questions

1. What are the main characteristics of the development of the Dutch tourism industry?

2. In what ways could the small enterprises that dominate the Dutch hospitality industry attract more qualified employees?

3. What are the strengths and weaknesses of the Dutch labor market? What are the implications for human resource management?

4. What are the possible effects of the legal and political context on the Dutch industry?

5. What will be the effect of the experience culture and individualism in the future?

6. What would be the specific qualities needed by hospitality managers to cope with a multi-cultural labor force in the Dutch hospitality industry?

7. What would be the way to guarantee improvement of management performance?

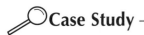

Internet Sites

For more information, visit the following Internet sites. Remember that Internet addresses can change without notice.

Association of Dutch Catering Organizations
http://www.veneca.nl

Association of Dutch Leisure Entrepreneurs
http://www.recron.nl

Center Parcs
http://www.centerparcs.com

Central Bureau of Statistics (Dutch)
http://www.cbs.nl

Dutch Embassy, Washington, D.C.
http://www.netherlandsembassy.org

Dutch Society for Personnel Management
http://www.nvp.plaza

European Union
http://www.europa.eu.int

Eurostat
http://www.statline.cbs.nl

Foundation for Professional Education
http://svh.nl

International Hospitality Net
http://www.hospitalitynet.org

International Hotel Chains in the Netherlands
http://www.hotelselect.nl

International Labor Organization
http://www.ilo.org

Information on management and organization issues
http://www.managementsite.net

Ministry of Economic Affairs
http://minez.nl

National Board for Tourism
http://www.holland.com

The Site of Hotels of Tomorrow
http://www.hotelnet.nl

Trading Organization for Hotel and Catering
http://www.bedr-horeca.nl

Case Study

The Scheveningen Silverman Hotel

Silverman Hotels and Resorts is a national chain of six five-stars hotels. It is a family-owned business that goes back more than 40 years. The Scheveningen Silverman Hotel is a hotel with 200 rooms, three restaurants, 12 meeting rooms, a casino, and an 18-hole golf course.

The general manager, Mr. Steven Van Dam, is a 52-year-old Dutchman with over 30 years of experience in the industry. He was appointed General Manager some months ago by the president of the company, Mrs. Laura Silverman. He has been give the objectives to boost performance of the staff, to attract more guest (especially business people), to organize more international conferences, and—most important—to improve the service excellence of the staff.

In addition to Mr. Van Dam, the management team of the hotel exists consists of three other members. Mrs. Sonja Williams, the finance manager, is a daughter of Karl Williams, who has been an elected Member of Parliament for 35 years and who owns five national job agencies. Sonja is always in her office from 11:00 to 15:00 and pretends to do most of her work from her home office in Amsterdam City. She is single, very beautiful, and dines every evening with her friends in restaurants such as Marriott, Hilton, and Krasnapolsky.

Mr. John Dietrich, the restaurant manager, is an international manager who has held positions with all the large international chains. He started as a cook in Paris, but quickly moved up to more senior positions. He has quite a reputation and is invited all over the world to give seminars and act as chairman of conferences in the hospitality industry. Due to this, he is hardly ever in the hotel, but he is a true believer of management-on-distance. Each time he is leaving for a visit abroad, he appoints a member of his staff to act as his deputy.

Mrs. Myra Danova, the human resource manager, is a Hungarian native with a Ph.D. in psychology. She is just 35 years of age, but already has held various senior positions in international businesses. This, however, is her first assignment in the service industry. She is at daggers drawn with Sonja Williams. She likes the tiny Netherlands, the culture, the atmosphere, and her position. She has decided to have a great time during her four-year assignment. She is the daughter of a business friend of Mrs. Laura Silverman.

The Scheveningen Silverman Hotel employs 185 people, of which 150 are local people from Scheveningen. The other employees are from The Hague, the capital of the monarchy. About 35 percent of the employees have a Mollucan or Surinamese background. They work in housekeeping and stewarding, but also in the sales administration. There are four management trainees from two hotel schools in the country. Morale is low, turnover is extremely high, and most of the temporaries (hired because of sickness and/or maternity leave) are hired through job agencies owned by Mr. Williams.

The people in general believe in Laura Silverman and Steven Van Dam, but they hate the arrogance and patronizing style of Sonja Williams. Myra Danova is seen as a follower and not as a leader. And they like John Dietrich and the freedom of movement he gives them.

Most of the staff, except the management team and four trainees, are moderately educated. They hardly speak foreign languages, are easy going, and just perform their duties.

The occupancy rate of the hotel is a little over 70 percent. The guests are mostly people from countries belonging to the European Community, visiting conferences and meetings, though there are also guests from the United States. Recently, an Asian carrier started a weekend flight with tourists who are attracted by the water-defending systems, the Dutch culture, Rotterdam Harbor, and the different national museums.

There are a lot of complaints about the service delivered. The staff is unfriendly, does not understand questions, is often just too late, and so on. Luggage is missing, invoices are not always correct, and guests sometimes have to wait more than an hour before the shuttle arrives at the airport. Most of the complaints go directly to Steven Van Dam or to his management trainees. As a result of the ongoing developments in IT, however, the hotel has his own web site; complaints arriving at the web site go more and more directly to the desk of Laura Silverman.

In the very early morning of October 5th , Steven Van Dam receives a telephone call from Laura Silverman. She is very angry and wants to know directly from Steven how he plans to handle the situation. Yesterday evening, just after the closing of an international conference (with 140 participants) on human resources and service excellence, she received 25 complaints by e-mail about the lack of service delivered to the attendees. Steven himself did not know anything about this, due to his absence for the last three days.

Steven does not know what to do about it. He decides to call an extra management team meeting to discuss the situation and to decide on a strategy to please Laura Silverman. In an extraordinary move, he also invites Mr. Simon Janssen to the meeting. Janssen presided over the conference. Janssen is a professor in human resource management and just retired from an executive HR position, to become President of a Mystery Guest Research Company.

When the members of the team arrive, Sonja Williams being late and upset as always, they sense that this is serious and that their job is at stake. John Dietrich just arrived from France.

Myra is really upset. Steven wants to know from everyone what they think they have to do.

In the meantime, Laura Silverman has secretly contacted one of the management trainees for a meeting at the airport. She wants to know the trainee's view on the situation and invites him to be very straightforward. After the meeting (which takes several hours), she goes with the trainee to the hotel, where she first visits Mr. Van Dam and asks him for his decisions.

Discussion Questions

1. What would the General Manager of The Silverman Beach Hotel decide to do?

2. Why does Ms. Silverman ask the management trainee to give his opinion to her?

3. What would you think will be the contribution of HRM specialist Professor Janssen?

Chapter 15 Outline

Competencies

1. Identify the historical, geographical, political and socio-economic factors that have affected country development. (pp. 255–258)

2. Describe the challenges facing Romania's labor market. (pp. 258–259)

3. Identify potential areas for development within Romania as a tourist destination and possibilities for international hospitality corporations. (pp. 259–262)

4. Evaluate the challenges facing human resource professionals in an industry that was previously centrally controlled and undervalued as a service enterprise. (pp. 262–263)

15

Romania: En Route to Capitalism

Ray Iunius and *Colin Johnson*

Ray Iunius *is a professor of service operations management at École Hôtelière de Lausanne, Switzerland. He holds a BS and an MS in technical science, and an MBA from the Business School of Lausanne University.*

Colin Johnson, *BA, MBA, is director of the Lausanne Institute for Hospitality Research at École Hôtelière de Lausanne, Switzerland. He is on the editorial board of the* International Journal of Tourism and Hospitality Research *and* Praxis: The Journal of Applied Hospitality Management. *He has contributed articles to various journals specializing in the development of tourism and hospitality in central Eastern Europe. In addition, he has worked in many sectors of the hospitality industry, including airline and contract catering, hotels, and sports and social clubs.*

A Geographical and Historical Perspective

Romania is situated in central eastern Europe in the northern part of the Balkan Peninsula, and its territory is delineated by the Carpathian Mountains, the Danube River, and the Black Sea. It is one of the largest countries in the region, with over 237,500 square kilometers and 22 million inhabitants.

Romanian culture is Latin and Western-based, and it has been preserved in some areas remarkably intact. The country has, by tradition, occupied a crossroads of central Europe, with many different factors exerting influences upon its

255

development. There is a strong folkloric tradition in such areas as art, music, carving, pottery, and architecture.

Following World War I, the country recorded a strong upsurge of development, due in large part to the combination of impressive natural resources and a constitutional regime based on a democratic system. This was the era of the grand hotel, and small segments of the population began to take vacations at the seaside (at Constanta, Mamaia, and Eforie) or in the mountains (at Sinaia and Brasov).

After 1948, Romania entered the network of Soviet satellite countries. Soviet-style nationalization and collectivism followed the communist takeover. But in the 1960s, under the leadership of Gheorghe Gheorghiu-Dej and his successor, Nicolae Ceausescu, the Communist Party of Romania began to implement a foreign policy independent of Soviet goals. During the 1970s, Ceausescu attempted to modernize the Romanian economy further by investing huge amounts of money borrowed from Western credit institutions. It was during this period that many hotels were constructed, and new resorts and villages appeared on the map. More and more foreign tourists were attracted to Romania due to its beautiful countryside, low prices, and the mystique of visiting an eastern European country on the other side of the Iron Curtain.

Due to Ceausescu's grandiose development projects, however, the Romanian people endured rigorous austerity programs. For nearly 25 years, Ceausescu's regime slowly dragged Romania into an economic, social, and moral impasse.

In spite of the substantial capital investment in the hospitality industry in the 1970s, there was no important maintenance activity undertaken during the next 20 years. As a result, the hospitality infrastructure today is in a state of deep disrepair. One of the main reasons for the non-investment in maintenance and renovation was the national centralization of budgets, with hospitality companies having no voice in deciding priorities and policies in investment. As in other socialist countries, the priority was the physical production of goods.

Following popular unrest and the violent overthrow of the dictatorial regime in December 1989, a multiparty parliamentary system, as well as a free press, were reinstated in 1990.

The Legal and Political Environment

Romania, as one of the "economies in transition," has had a troubled journey from communism to modern economy. Although a country of considerable size, it has struggled to lift itself from the decline imposed by Ceausescu's regime. Its neighbors Hungary and Poland have surpassed Romania in most economic indicator terms. Governments have been seen to be ineffective and squabbling when dealing with the mammoth problems of economic and social restructuring, especially in the legal and banking sectors.

Romanian legislation is in a constant process of modification and improvement, with serious efforts being made toward bringing it in line with the legislative standards of the European Union. Legislative changes introduced after 1989 have been profound, and they have affected practically all domains, from common and commercial law to family and criminal law.

In order to accomplish the transition from a centralized economy and omnipresent state ownership to a market economy and private property, a new legal system has had to be created.

Privatization

One of the crucial aspects for all communist states is how to return to a free-market economy. Privatization has been dealt with in various ways by different states in the region, but it is fundamental to the development of a market economy. One of the most basic issues related to hotel development is that of land title. According to Calin Cristescu, director of international relations for the Bucharest city council, "There is a very big problem deciding who owns land that used to belong to the state. Many organizations claim the same piece of land, leaving investors confused and unwilling to invest."[1]

Romania has had a privatization program for the past 10 years, with the State Ownership Fund, an institution of public interest, organized as a special trustee. Its aim is to sell state-owned shares in joint stock companies according to the annual strategies and privatization programs approved by the government. The stated intention of the government was to improve the privatization process—creating a competitive environment, capital market development, transaction transparency, prices based on supply and demand, and environment and investor protection in case of damages due to the economic activities of the company prior to privatization.

Demographic Trends

After Poland, Romania is the most populated country in central eastern Europe. However, as in some other transition countries, its population is declining. One reason is emigration, but death rates and, more importantly, infant mortality rates are relatively high due to increasing poverty, a deterioration of health care, and increased daily stress.

Internal migration flows are an important factor in Romania's regional demographic patterns and are dependent on the degree of economic development and perceived opportunities in larger cities. In 1990, there was substantial rural migration, as large numbers of people began moving from small towns or villages to larger cities.

In relative terms, Romania is ethnically homogeneous. Its 23 distinct minority groups make up only 10.6 percent of the total population. At 7.1 percent, Hungarians represent the largest minority group.

In demographic terms, considerable regional variations are to be observed in Romania. In addition to urban areas, regions with the highest population density also include the hilly areas in the Sub-Carpathians; the lowest densities are found in the mountainous areas and in the Danube Delta. The majority of towns are located in the south, in the center of Transylvania and Moldova. The age structure is relatively well balanced in urban areas but favors the elderly population in rural regions.

Cultural Distinctions and Societal Work Values

In the communist era, everybody had a job assured by the state, and the future was predictable. There were no significant pressures for people to increase or improve the quality of their work. People who performed at different levels received the same salary, regardless. Managers were selected due to their "personal files" and for their links to the Communist Party. Prestige from managing companies derived from the size of production or the number of employees but without consideration for profits. There was practically no possibility of becoming a top manager without being a member of the Party.

Education was considered an essential element on the route to success, which is one of the reasons for the significant number of well-educated Romanians. One element of communism that is often forgotten or ignored is the relative lack of stress and the availability of free time that could be used for cultural pursuits.

The Romanian Labor Market

The process of economic restructuring fundamental to transitional economies has necessitated the introduction of new labor market models. With the onset of political, ideological, and economic reform, the centrally planned model has become redundant; a new model—characterized by a liberalization of the labor market, increasing private-sector employment, and the reduction of the regulatory functions of the state regarding labor—has evolved.

However, the dramatic fall in economic activity, particularly in the initial years of transition, had a corresponding effect on Romania's labor market situation. The active working population has declined as a result of falling production. Unemployment increased to over 10 percent of the active population by the mid-1990s and is expected to increase further due to reform policies. Very high unemployment rates are particularly evident in the regions that were artificially industrialized—for example, Moldova, Oltenia, and North Transylvania. The private sector currently accounts for nearly half of the working population, but many state enterprises still maintain oversized labor forces.

The Active Working Population

Employment in the primary sector has increased following land reform, and there has been a rise in the number of private producers. Exhibit 1 provides a breakdown of employment by Romania's main industries.

Although employment in manufacturing remains high, there have been considerable increases in certain sectors, notably banking, real estate, finance, and insurance. Hotel and restaurant employment accounts only for 1.5 percent. It is also noteworthy that, according to official sources, there has been an increase in overall productivity per hour of 18.2 percent in recent years.[2]

Education. Primary and secondary education is free and guaranteed by the constitution. Schooling is compulsory for children six through 16 in the state schools. Suitably qualified pupils can progress to upper secondary education in general secondary schools, grammar schools, professional schools, or vocational institutes.

Exhibit 1   Employment Statistics by Main Industries

	Numbers of Employees	Structure (in %)
Agriculture	373,000	6.6
Banks and Finance	60,000	1.1
Buildings	495,000	8.7
Education	441,000	7.8
Health Care	310,000	5.5
Hotels and Restaurants	**84,000**	**1.5**
Manufacturing	2,529,000	44.5
Retailing	318,000	5.6
Transportation	370,000	6.6

Source: Romanian National Commission for Statistics, 1998

Romania has both public and private higher-education institutions. Higher education is organized into two types: short-term university education (three years, at a college) and long-term university education (four to five years, provided in universities, academies, and conservatories). The high proportion of universities is the result of a conversion of former "institutes" into universities. In addition, numerous private higher-education institutions have been established since 1990.

Labor Relations and Employment Standards. Labor legislation has been significantly evolving since 1989. Generally, employees work eight hours per day, five days a week. The average monthly salary is approximately equivalent to US$80. Often, employees are paid every two weeks; employment contracts may include a stipulation for a monthly payment. Employees are entitled to a paid annual holiday of at least 18 work days. As a rule, holidays extend over a longer period for people with more years of service or for those working in difficult conditions. Men can request early retirement at 60 years of age; for women, early retirement is available at 55 years of age. Otherwise, the retirement age is 62 for men and 57 for women.

Trade unions are defined by the law as independent organizations intended to defend and promote the professional, economic, social, cultural, and sport interest of their members and their rights provided by labor legislation and collective agreements. Legislation contains provisions related to collective agreements, as well as the way collective bargaining is organized between employers and employees, and the cessation of contracts.

Tourism in Romania

There are evident advantages for international hospitality enterprises doing business in central and eastern Europe in general and Romania in particular, including:

Exhibit 2   Trends of International Tourist Arrivals in Europe

1990 Rank	1995 Rank	1998 Rank	Country	Arrivals (000) 1998	% change 1998/1997	% of total 1998
1	1	1	France	70,000	4.7	18.8
4	5	10	Hungary	14,660	-15.0	3.9
18	6	5	Poland	18,820	-3.6	5.1
11	8	8	Czech Republic	16,325	-3.0	4.4
9	11	12	Greece	11,077	10.0	3.0
19	20	19	Romania	3,075	4.0	0.8

Source: World Tourism Organization, 1999

- Strong prospects for economic growth

- Proximity to major markets

- A relatively cheap and well-educated labor force

- An increasing degree of macroeconomic stability and openness to foreign trade

- Ambitious foreign investment policies to attract foreign investors

- Vast areas of untouched and unspoiled countryside

- Cultural affinity[3]

Exhibit 2 shows developments in certain European countries from 1990 to 1998, allowing a comparison between Romania's performance and that of other central and eastern European nations (Hungary, Poland, the Czech Republic), along with the largest European tourist destination (France) and a southern tourist country (Greece).

Romania is low in the ranking, stagnating at the bottom of the top 20 destinations. Much smaller countries such as Hungary have nearly five times the number of visitors, and Poland, which was in a similar position, climbed into fifth position by 1998. The only positive point from the statistics is the strong growth rate of four percent, which may well indicate that, eventually, there will be signs of improvement. In common with the former Soviet bloc nations, Romania's major barriers to the development to tourism have been economic barriers, mobility constraints, and a low priority given to service industries (regarded as "non-producing" in classic socialist ideology).

Four major changes have stimulated tourism development in other former eastern bloc nations:

- The easing of entry, exit, and currency restrictions

- The changed image of—and more substantial Western media attention given to—the region

- Increasing Western involvement in aspects of tourism development
- Ihe newfound mobility of many East Europeans themselves[4]

As has been mentioned earlier, however, Romania has, to date, not been able to benefit from these changes to any significant degree.

Romania's Tourism Product

Romania had the basis for a modern tourist industry from the start of the twentieth century. Unfortunately, due to economic constraints and political activity, the country was not able to benefit as a destination.[5] It has been argued that central eastern Europe generally missed several golden opportunities from the 1960s to the 1980s to fully exploit tourism's potential, especially in mass tourism. It is also important to note that, principally due to the economic unattractiveness of Romania, there was a reduction of 200 percent in tourist receipts during the 1980s.[6]

In common with other socialist countries, Romania also had the communist form of domestic tourism, whereby almost everyone was permitted to go on holiday in camp-type resorts that were either free or very low cost.

The major reasons for tourists wishing to visit Romania are the variety of landscape, cultural attractions (consisting of rich historical architecture and monuments), the mystique of folklore, an extensive network of health spas and resorts, and also the possibility of practicing winter sports or summer tourism. The most-favored locations are the Black Sea coast (with the resorts of Mamaia, Eforie, and Nord), the Carpathian mountains (especially the Prahova Valley and Poina Brasov), and Bucovina (which has outstanding churches and monasteries dating back to the sixteenth century). In addition, the Ministry of Tourism has acknowledged rural tourism as a potential major growth area. There are also business-related activities that draw travelers, and Romania is used as a main transit route due to its central location.

On a lighter note, there is a worldwide Transylvanian Society of Dracula, an organization concerned with the development of the Dracula myth attractions, including such delights as eating around a bonfire at Vlad the Impaler's castle (home of the real-life model for Dracula), staying at "Castle Hotel Dracula," and sleeping in a coffin.[7]

Structure of the Hospitality Industry

In common with other central eastern European countries, the number of Romania's hospitality establishments declined in the period 1990–1997. The total supply registered with the national tourism authority by 1997 consisted of about 3,000 units, with over 100,000 rooms and 2,888,656 beds. The latter figure gives a ratio of 26 beds per room, which may be due to many of the establishments having dormitories, with many beds per room. The authority itself states that the vast majority of properties are in the one-star category, with 34 percent in the two- or three-star segment, and only eight percent in the four-star bracket. However, there are wide variations in quality within the same star category.

By the middle of the 1990s, private hotels represented just 26 percent of all hotel stock. Forty-five percent of registered units are located on the Black Sea coast, and 17 percent are inland spas. The Black Sea coast was developed from the 1950s to the 1970s and left a formidable legacy of low-quality, unattractive, state-owned properties catering to a price-sensitive clientele. This is not specific to just the Black Sea coast, however.

Training. There are a number of important issues that have to be recognized in analyzing the tourism and hospitality industries in Romania. In common with the rest of industry, all enterprises were previously owned by the state. As a result, managers had no management training, were elected rather than appointed through merit, were often seen to be remote from operational issues, and suffered from low information-technology resources and training. In turn, this situation resulted in deficiencies in staff skills in functional areas such as reception, kitchen, food and beverage outlets, and ancillary services. As a direct result of central planning, everybody was assured a job, which was far removed from the concept of a market-driven, customer-focused organization. Staff needs were seen to be as important as guest requirements in such areas as hours of operation, menus (with the impression that guests ate what staff wanted to cook), and a take-it-or-leave-it attitude.

There have been attempts to improve the situation, with many courses being organized by the National Center for Tourism Education in Bucharest. The center was established in 1974 with the financial assistance of the United Nations Development Programme.

In the future, new and existing small- to medium-size hospitality companies will still need considerable advice in many aspects of business management and operations, especially for training at the basic level through such options as train-the-trainer courses.

Looking to the Future

One of the critical issues for the development of tourism and hospitality will be the degree of financing that Romania can attract from abroad. Romania cannot perform all of the necessary renovations from its own resources.

Three major elements are crucial for future tourism investment:

- competition between central and eastern European countries for inward investment (that is, investment from outside of Romania)

- competition between western companies for central eastern European business

- competition between East and West Europe for multinational tourism investment from North America and Japan

Central eastern Europe in general appears attractive, with a (relatively) cheaper labor force that is well-educated and culturally part of Europe. If countries within the region can continue with market reforms, ensuring stability and dissolving barriers to investment, then the attractiveness for foreign investors looks bright.

Although there have been signs in recent years that international tourist arrivals have declined in Romania, there are exciting possibilities for the future. Rural tourism could well be a mode for a multidimensional tourism model. Examples are given of open-air "village museums" as located on the outskirts of Bucharest, the outstanding scenery in the Carpathians, and the unspoiled nature of the Danube Delta. There is also evidence of international hotel chains' involvement—for example, Hyatt International's 66 percent stake in the Hotel Bucharest, with plans for investment in three more properties in the region.[8] At the other end of the scale, there are signs that North American fast-food companies—responding to relatively low labor costs, low capital investment costs, and market demands—have targeted the Black Sea area for development.

For hotel investors, however, there may be serious problems associated with an over-supply, a short season, and the poor image of Romanian beach tourism. More potential would appear to be offered by the development of mountain resorts that could attract more visitors for winter sports and conferences. Clearly, there must be serious investment to raise the overall infrastructure to international standards. Perhaps even more serious is the necessity of bringing the service quality level up to acceptable standards. This is a long-term challenge, requiring both innovation and intensive training schemes that will have to address nearly a half-century of neglect and will have to turn around a mentality that did not regard the guest as a discerning individual who had choice.

An important element in Romania's success will be the extent to which the government implements its strategy for tourism development. There are obvious needs for education and training in certain areas, not least if tourism is to be developed outside the main cities and alongside the development of magnificent tracts of unspoiled countryside. There is evidence that in certain isolated villages (for example, in the Cabrini mountains in County Maramures), villagers had little experience of tourist behavior and there was the danger of customs and traditions stretching back over 2,000 years being destroyed due to short-term economic exploitation.[9]

As of 2000, the European Union will double its funding to central Europe; Poland and Romania, as the two largest countries in the Union, will receive over half (nearly 400 million euros annually). The majority of the funding is targeted at improving the substandard infrastructure and cleaning up the most heavily polluting industries.

These measures should help to improve both the image and the reality of Romania in terms of cleanliness and in communication via road and rail links, thereby becoming a more attractive tourist destination for all major tourist categories.

Finally, due to all of the tremendous changes as a result of moving from a centrally controlled economy to that of a capitalist state, there is currently a lack of standardization with regard to the different human resources practices. It is expected, however, that the situation will stabilize in the near future and that human resources issues will take greater priority.

Endnotes

1. *Hotel Investment in Central and Eastern Europe,* July–August 1994, p. 6.

2. *Buletin Statistic, Trimestrial 3* (Bucharest: Comisia Nationala Pentru Statistica, 1996).

3. Colin Johnson and Ray Iunius, "Competing in Central Eastern Europe: Perspectives and Developments," *The International Journal of Hospitality Management*, 18 (1999): 245–260.

4. D. R. Hall, "Eastern Europe," in W. Pompl and P. Lavery (eds.), *Tourism in Europe: Structures and Developments* (Wallingford, England: CABI Publishing, 1993), p. 42.

5. D. Turncock, "Sustainable Tourism in the Romanian Carpathians," *The Geographical Journal*, July 1999.

6. D. R. Hall, "Tourism Development and Sustainability Issues in Central and South-Eastern Europe," *Tourism Management* 19, no. 5 (1998): 423–431.

7. *Financial Times*, 31 October 1998.

8. *Finance East Europe*, 29 August 1997, pp. 5–6.

9. *New Orleans Times-Picayune*, 21 September 1997, p. 42.

Discussion Questions

1. What type of guest would find Romania attractive as a tourist leisure destination? What specific problems should a human resource professional consider in meeting these guests' needs in Romania?

2. Is it feasible to change employees' mindsets after nearly 50 years of communism? How might you attempt this process?

3. What are several of the positive and negative effects of the communist Romanian educational system on the supply of appropriate workers for the hospitality industry in Romania?

Internet Sites

For more information, visit the following Internet sites. Remember that Internet addresses can change without notice.

*i*Romania Visitors Guide
(English, French, Romanian)
http://www.1stweb.de/

Romania—General Information
http://home.vicnet.net.au/
~romclub/florin/ro.htm

Romanian Travel Guide
http://www.rotravel.com

Case Study

Helmut's Hotel Dilemma

Helmut Wilke was a 55-year-old Swiss hotel proprietor of a 30-room hotel that he managed with his son in Arborn, Turgovie. In 1987, he began working on an aid program launched by the Swiss in response to the dictator Ceausescu's plan to destroy the national heritage of the Romanian countryside.

Helmut reflected upon the contradictions inherent in Romania. On the one hand, there was the image seen by the outside world: an old-fashioned and cold communist country, with horse-drawn carriages, women wearing head scarves, sick children, and a sad, downtrodden population almost destroyed by dictatorship. Two cult figures were identified with the country: Dracula and Ceausescu. At the same time, there was the wonderful warmth of the people, the beauty of the natural environment, and the richness inherent in the cultural diversity within the nation, with many Romanians famous as international leaders in sport, music, science, and architecture.

In 1990 Helmut was in the first convoy that brought supplies for the Romanian villages from Switzerland. After his first visit, he considered owning a small hotel in a small village in the middle of the country 10 kilometers from Brasov, a town of approximately 300,000 inhabitants. It was, however, too early to be able to do this. The privatization process had not yet been started, and joint ventures were the only form of ownership in hotels in Romania. Helmut wanted to be the sole owner of the business.

After six turbulent years, however, conditions began to improve and Helmut was contacted by a company in Brachove, in the center of the country, that was offering a property for sale—a 34-room hotel with a 50-seat restaurant, public bar, and a spa not far from hotel, but no star classification. The sale was finalized through direct negotiation, with one of the terms of the agreement being that the 20 current full-time employees would be retained for at least two years after the signing of the contract.

At this time, there was an improvement in the foreign investment laws, which provided an advantage in terms of tax incentives and repatriation of profits. One year of difficult renovation followed, with investment that was substantially over budget. The law that gave advantages for foreign investment changed so many times that Helmut began to doubt if he could operate in the long term in such an uncertain business environment. Yet the number of foreign tourists was increasing, which appeared to present attractive possibilities.

Helmut realized that the success of his business would depend ultimately on the people who worked for him. He decided to hire only people with no hospitality experience within the state system. He believed that Romanians with experience in the state hotels had a very different company culture working in a "control and command" environment. They often had no identification with the company, and the most important incentives were tips from customers.

First, he recruited a young doctor. Helmut believed that this person could become an excellent general manager. He paid for his training at the Romanian center for tourist training at Bucharest, and he sent him for a summer course at a Swiss school. He decided to hire an additional two people—one an engineer, another a geography teacher—and to send them for hospitality training as well.

By 1998, the hotel had an occupancy rate of 75 percent, 50 percent of which was made up of foreigners—the majority from Switzerland, Austria, and Germany. There was also a large segment of indigenous business travelers. The hotel had been rated as a three-star property, and it was achieving an average daily rate of US$50. The restaurant became an attraction for the region and turned over three to four times during dinner.

The doctor had become a very successful manager, the geography teacher had developed into an excellent rooms division manager, and the food and beverage operations were thriving under the control of the former engineer. Helmut had also been quite successful in establishing a network for rural tourism with other properties in Romania and Hungary. He had also managed to reduce the work force to 15 full-time employees. During peak production times, he hired 10 students from the local university.

But there was bad news on the horizon. By the end of 1998, the general economic environment in Romania had deteriorated. Substantial changes to legislation led to increased taxation and lower profits. The break-even point forecast for the project by 2005 seemed to be increasingly impossible without serious changes to the law.

In spite of these conditions, Helmut decided to purchase an additional two parcels of land near the hotel, so he could build two additional hotels of a similar capacity. Many friends from Switzerland have advised against it and doubted the wisdom of his decision making.

Discussion Questions

1. What kind of training and management development programs do you believe would be most useful in the short and medium term to help Helmut establish his hotels successfully?

2. One reads much of "employee empowerment" and the hospitality industry. In your view, is employee empowerment possible (or even desirable) under the circumstances in Romania? Explain why or why not.

Chapter 16 Outline

Specific Concerns of the Hospitality Market
   in Russia
Human Resource Regulation
    Political Background
    Employment Regulations
    Socio-Cultural Aspects of Labor Issues
Personnel Development
    Human Resource Management
      Models
    Pitfalls of Human Resource
      Management
    Establishing an Adequate Hospitality
      Educational System

Competencies

1. Identify specific concerns of the
   Russian hospitality market.
   (pp. 270–272)

2. Explain human resource regulations in
   Russia. (pp. 272–275)

3. Describe personnel development
   concerns in Russia. (pp. 275–279)

16

Human Resource Management in Russia

Vladimir Belyansky, Mikhail Laiko, Elena Ilyina, and *Dmitri Chtykhno*

Vladimir Belyansky is a Vice President of the Plekhanov Russian Academy of Economics in Moscow and is a Professor in the Department of Hotel and Tourism Business. He is a specialist in the theory and practice of government regulations and their impact on the national economic and distribution system, and is the author of more than 100 works.

Mikhail Laiko is Vice-Rector of International Affairs for the Plekhanov Russian Academy of Economics and supervises the International Hospitality Management program. He is the author of more than 120 publications concerning the technological and economic aspects of the Russian market.

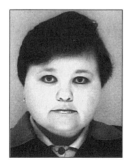

Elena Ilyina is an Associate Professor in the Plekhanov Academy's Department of Hotel and Tourism Business. She is also the director of the International Hospitality Management program and has published 40 scientific works.

Dmitri Chtykhno is a Senior Lecturer for the Plekhanov Academy's International Hospitality Management program. He has written 25 publications and research papers on various aspects of hospitality.

O NLY A FEW YEARS AGO, the Russian hotel market was dominated by state-owned properties that made no effort to meet Western hospitality standards. Today, there are 74 hotels operated by international management or consulting firms among 5,043 lodging properties in Russia. While this is a good start, many problems still must be solved to make the Russian hospitality industry profitable and competitive. This chapter will describe the social and economic background of the situation faced by hotel managers in Russia and give some examples of approaches used by managers to meet international hospitality service standards.

Specific Concerns of the Hospitality Market in Russia ——

Today, hospitality is perceived as one of the most promising businesses in Russia. However, in the former Soviet Union, tourism was never treated as a high-priority industry. According to World Tourism Organization statistics, there were 7.2 million tourist arrivals in the USSR in 1990, and the amount of receipts was $270 million.[1] These figures were much less than for Western Europe and other top tourism areas. At that time, Moscow accumulated 64 percent of hotel properties' total profits and 35 percent of total expenses. The second largest city, Leningrad (now St. Petersburg), was in second position, accumulating 4.64 percent of total profits and 6.95 percent of expenses. These cities later became the first major Russian cities to see the creation of new hotel properties, often with the involvement of Western companies. Exhibit 1 illustrates the scope of the Moscow hotel market in 1998. Due to the development of a market economy in Russia and the involvement of Russian firms in foreign trade, 12 luxurious hotels have opened during the last five years in Moscow, St. Petersburg, Novgorod, Sochi, and other major Russian cities.

Russian hospitality properties fall into two broad types, which we will call "new type" and "old type." **New-type properties** are hotels and restaurants, usually managed by foreigners, that use modern production, marketing, and human resource management techniques. **Old-type properties** are outmoded properties (state-owned in earlier times) offering out-of-date services; these properties are having a hard time adjusting to the need to earn profits and offer competitive services.

Managers of old-type hospitality properties are taking the first steps toward upgrading their businesses by introducing a system of high quality standards. This system is considered to be Western European and consists of three levels:

- Service standards that employees must meet, as well as qualifications (knowledge and skills) that job candidates must possess before they are hired

- Comprehensive human resource management (from job application tests and supervisory methods to salary administration)

- Professional education for employees and employee training and re-training programs

This quality system assumes the use of high-level technology as well as the establishment of a new service-oriented mentality for the staff.

Two new-type Moscow hotels, the Baltchug Kempinski and the Radisson Slavyanskaya, highlight that the solution to the service-quality problem requires

Exhibit 1   Moscow Hotel Market, 1998

Number of hotels:	179
Including:	
Municipal properties	18
State-owned properties	6
Private properties with foreign capital	10
Joint-stock companies	45
Departmental properties*	74
Properties of embassies of CIS# countries	12
Market properties	14
Total profit:	3.5 billion rubles
Including:	
Municipal properties	0.8 billion rubles
Private properties with foreign capital	1.4 billion rubles
Joint-stock companies	0.8 billion rubles
Other properties	0.5 billion rubles
Average occupancy:	55.1%
Number of rooms:	37,811
Number of beds:	64,432
Number of employees:	28,000

*Departmental properties = Hotels owned by state ministries and serving mostly state officials.

#CIS = Community of Independent States (a union of 12 former Soviet republics).

employee education and training; investments in upgrading buildings and technology are useful only if they are supported by changes in the work skills and attitudes of staff members. One of the most effective ways for a hotel or restaurant to meet international hospitality standards is to enter into a franchise agreement. It is quite difficult for Russian employees to quickly change their fundamental understanding of their work responsibilities in the new working conditions of a market economy without help, and franchise operations provide that help. The more franchise hospitality businesses that are established in Russia, the greater the perception that a high quality hospitality industry is being established in Russia.

Globalization and worldwide economic integration have led to the emergence of new demands and expectations for lodging and food service in Russia. Even managers of old-type properties recognize that the main aspect to be changed in the traditional Russian approach to hospitality is how human resources are managed. In Western countries, human resource management is viewed as leading the way in a hospitality company's marketing strategy. Employees are trained to act as company representatives when dealing with guests; this approach is reasonable and efficient. Employees understand that, to guests, they (the employees) *are* the company, and the employees act to handle "moments of truth" with guests correctly. In Russia there is still not a deep understanding of this concept.

Most Russian hospitality employees got their experience in the "Soviet-style" service industry. In many cases, this experience actually undermines or reduces job quality, because the old approach did not pay any attention to personalized service. Many middle-aged Russian applicants looking for a job in international hotels lack courtesy and diligence; for this reason, managers of international hotels prefer to recruit Russians who have little or no previous hospitality experience. Recently, there has been an increase in this type of labor supply, as numerous students graduate from institutes and colleges who have no practical hospitality experience at all. But the problem of hospitality personnel who are not service-minded still exists, because Russian-owned hotels and restaurants still prefer to hire staff members with industry experience, even though often these experienced staff members negatively affect service quality.

Human Resource Regulation

In this section, we will discuss human resource regulations in Russia, beginning with a brief look at the political background of human resource regulation. Then we will examine the three levels of employment regulation for Russian hospitality businesses, and conclude with a discussion of socio-cultural aspects of Russian labor issues.

Political Background

In the 1990s, a demand for good quality lodging accommodations in Russia was recognized by the government and also by some Russian and foreign companies that decided to invest in Russian hospitality businesses. This resulted in several hospitality projects involving the construction of new hotels and reconstruction of old ones. Since 1991, a sharp increase in lodging supply has occurred in Russia, due in part to the government's decision that tourism should become one of its priority industries. The Federal Program of Tourism Development was passed by the Russian government in 1996. This document covered major aspects of national tourism industry development during 1995 and set out development goals and activities for 1996–2005. There are many important points in this program, such as creating up-to-date legislation for the tourism industry and property relations in the tourism area, promoting the growth of the Russian tourist market, and establishing human resources development and educational systems for the Russian hospitality industry.

Employment Regulations

There are three levels of employment regulation for hospitality businesses in Russia. The Labor Codex, federal laws, and other laws make up the first (highest) level of labor regulations. The **Labor Codex** contains 255 articles and is the main labor law in Russia. It regulates all major aspects of employment and consists of the following sections: General Assumptions, Collective Agreement, Labor Contract, Realization of Employment Rights, Working Time, Free Time, Salary, Labor Norms and Wages, Guarantees and Compensations, Labor Discipline, Labor Security, Women's Labor, Youth Labor, Privileges for Employees Combining Work and Study, Labor Disputes, Trade Unions and Employees' Participation in Property Management, Working Collective, Control of Observance of Labor Laws, and Special Cases.

The Labor Codex sets the normal work load per week at 40 hours for adults, less for youths. In most businesses, employees take one or two days off per week. The Codex also requires breaks for food and rest, not longer than two hours per shift. Break time is excluded from working time. An employee's vacation period is equal to 24 working days per year. Sex, age, and race discrimination is prohibited by the Codex.

The second level of labor regulation consists of industry norms and standards regulating lodging and food service activities. Since 1995 it has been necessary to certify hotel and tourist services in accordance with standards established by the State Certification Committee. These standards introduce minimal requirements for technical, fire, sanitation, and personnel conditions. The certificate from this committee is valid for three years and must be reviewed after that period. There are four categories of requirements that cover hotel staff members:

1. *Qualifications.* Each employee must get professional training, corresponding to his or her position, from the hotel where he or she works. At least one staff member at a hotel must have sufficient training to provide security for guests, and at least one hotel staff member must have sufficient training to provide security in food service. There are also special requirements for foreign-language knowledge: at one- or two-star hotels, reception staff members should know at least one foreign language; at three- or four-star hotels, all front office employees should know at least two foreign languages; and at five-star hotels, all front office employees should fluently speak at least three foreign languages.

2. *Behavior.* Hotel personnel should be able to create a friendly and hospitable atmosphere, be ready to respond to guest wishes cheerfully, and demonstrate patience and modesty.

3. *Medical requirements.* All staff members must regularly receive a check-up; this check-up must be confirmed with a certificate.

4. *Uniforms.* All front office employees should wear a uniform; managers should wear a name tag that states their names and positions. All uniforms must be clean and in good condition.

The third and last level of employment regulations is composed of written job descriptions and employee responsibilities for each position. These documents are based on the common duties of each hotel staff position but vary somewhat from property to property.

Socio-Cultural Aspects of Labor Issues

Results of recent sociological investigations show that many factors influence
Russian students to choose to work at and stay with a hospitality property. The
main factors include:

- Good salaries and bonuses
- Career opportunities
- Convenient working times
- Interesting jobs
- Nice working conditions
- Feeling needed
- The need to belong to a group
- Good training programs
- Personal loyalty to the company
- Access to the highest levels of society
- Location

One more factor especially attractive to many Russian employees is the benefit of
receiving free employee meals at their properties. This factor played an important
role after the Russian financial crisis in August 1998 when, despite experts' expectations that many employees would quit their hospitality jobs due to severely
reduced salaries, most employees preferred to stay, in large part because of the free
employee meals and the opportunity to earn tips.

Another labor-relations factor unique to Russia are so-called "black lists" of
people who have discredited themselves at a previous hospitality job; these lists
are used mostly in the restaurant business. There is even a project underway to
make these lists available to all hospitality managers in the form of a computer
database. But there are ethical problems: Who should have the right to use this
database, and what types of activities should get a person put onto the database?
Although this proposed database would seem to be an efficient tool to help managers avoid mistakes in hiring, a special industry committee should be formed to
look into ethical and other problems with the database.

The Role of Trade Unions. In contemporary hospitality businesses in Russia,
social or worker organizations do not participate in the managerial process, and
the role of trade unions is limited. At new-type properties, social programs (benefits) for employees are often well designed, while at old-type properties they
usually do not exist at all. In such conditions, it is more likely that employees at
old-type properties would want to join a trade union. Two factors that influence
Russian employees to establish or join trade unions (these are main factors in why
employees join trade unions in Western countries as well) are feelings of injustice
at how jobs or raises are allocated, and feelings of powerlessness in dealing with
supervisors who use subjective criteria when dealing with employees and act in an

Exhibit 2   Priorities of Russian Managers

Type of Activity	Amount of Responses (%)
1. Working out property's general strategy	83.2
2. Organizational development of property	76.2
3. Budgeting	71.9
4. Current planning	68.0
5. Staff performance evaluation	62.5
6. Performance quality control	62.5
7. Recruiting	59.0
8. Developing motivation systems	53.5
9. Organizing	51.2
10. Creating system of property ethics	46.1
11. Forming system of social guarantees for personnel	44.5
12. Staff training	32.0

unpredictable manner. Trade unions in the Russian hospitality industry, where they exist at all, are the result of poor working conditions and a lack of benefits for employees.

Personnel Development

Personnel development has become a very serious concern for managers of hospitality properties in Russia. This is directly connected with the problem of hiring personnel who are able to meet contemporary international service standards.

Some Russian managers are used to treating their staff members poorly, viewing them as less important than, for instance, the organization's material or financial resources. There is also the tendency, at hospitality properties that pay low wages and salaries, to hire unqualified personnel.

So far, personnel development activities are not high on the list of priorities for Russian managers. According to the results of a survey conducted in the mid-1990s that still hold true today (see Exhibit 2), about 70 to 80 percent of Russian managers are constantly engaged in organizational development (items 1–4), while around 60 percent or less are involved in working with personnel (items 5–12). Examining a specific human resource management function—staff training—reveals that less than a third of Russian managers are engaged in this important activity. The success or failure of any hospitality property strongly depends on its employees, so it is the manager's duty to encourage the staff to be as productive as possible, and the manager should show an active interest in the development of employees and employee programs.

Human Resource Management Models

According to research conducted by the Russian Staff Club (an association of human resource managers established in Moscow in 1995), there are three general models of human resource management employed by hospitality properties in Russia today: the international approach, Soviet approach, and mixed approach.

International Approach. Large foreign companies (hotel and restaurant chains, famous tour operators, etc.) entering the Russian hospitality market have stable organizational structures and human resource policies that have been forming for decades. These companies are willing to invest a considerable amount of money into searching for and hiring highly qualified employees. Such companies thoroughly screen candidates and conduct special interviews with them. International companies spend a lot of time and energy on each job applicant, since they consider it better to spend money on selecting the right employee than to hire the wrong person and have to spend time and money amending mistakes from his or her improper performance.

International companies do their best to hang on to good employees after hiring them. They use rational supervisory methods, modern evaluation systems, and efficient motivational programs to keep their employees. In contrast, many Russian-owned hospitality properties hire employees—even for very specialized jobs—and then do nothing to keep them and end up losing them a short time later.

Soviet Approach. A different human resource picture can be seen at Russian-owned hospitality properties—especially small ones. As a rule, because of their financial status, these properties can't afford to select and hire experienced and qualified personnel, so they hire young and inexperienced workers, or non-professionals in the sphere of hospitality. Gradually these people acquire work experience and frequently move on to jobs at other properties as qualified employees.

Very often the organizational structures of Russian hotels and restaurants were formed chaotically during the day-to-day process of doing business, without special planning on how to use the staff most efficiently. While the international approach to human resource management includes the entire complex of staffing functions—selecting, orienting, directing, training, promoting, etc.—the Soviet approach simply focuses on the problems of compensating employees and complying with the Labor Codex.

Mixed Approach. Some managers of old-type hospitality properties use a mixed approach to human resource management, in which they try to rationalize their properties' inefficient organizational structures by borrowing elements from the international approach. These managers must put together job descriptions, set up communication channels among property departments, and address other fundamental workplace issues that were not addressed at old-type properties during the Soviet era. This process can be described as adapting the Western hospitality model to Russian conditions. It is a slow process, made more difficult by the fact that the Russian work force and legal system are still undergoing the sometimes painful adjustments necessary to shift from a planned economy to a market economy.

Human Resource Strategies. Generally speaking, there are two main human resource strategies used by Russian hospitality properties today.

The first strategy is based on the **steady-personnel concept**. Managers using this concept devote their efforts to keeping employee turnover to a minimum. They put special career planning programs in place to raise the professional status of their employees. This approach results not only in helping employees reach their personal potential and maximize their professionalism, but in raising their morale. The steady-personnel approach to staff management helps ensure that employees will be motivated, loyal to the property and its business goals, and take an interest in the property's market performance. This strategy is usually employed by new-type properties.

The second strategy is based on the **staff-rotation concept**. Its main features are long probationary periods for employees, minimal salaries (and even the absence of a salary during an employee's probationary period), a system of fines, and a constant threat of firing. Managers using this approach to human resource management do not spend time and money on staff training, since employees might leave at any moment. Such an approach to human resource management relies on negative motivation and results in an absence of team spirit and loyalty to the company. The staff-rotation concept provides a property with a short-term financial benefit (because of the low cost of salaries), but can't ensure a long-term competitive advantage for the property (because of the high employee turnover). This strategy is often employed by old-type properties.

Pitfalls of Human Resource Management

When international hospitality companies entered Russia, a very important result was that the rest of the Russian hospitality industry began to implement high international service standards and change employee attitudes toward guests. However, Russian managers face several pitfalls or obstacles to reaching the goal of matching international service standards.

Sources of Personnel. There are two sources of personnel at hospitality properties: internal and external. Internal sources of employees represent a property's current staff. External sources are recruitment agencies, databases listing employees, competitors, business partners, and so on.

A third way of finding new hospitality employees in Russia is called the "mixed way." If there are no suitable candidates to be hired for a given job, company managers ask employees to recommend relatives or friends. This method of selecting employees is quite cheap, but not reliable. Experience has proved that such recommendations are subjective and usually don't take into consideration important professional requirements.

Incomplete Selection Criteria. One of the keys to efficient recruitment is defining selection criteria. The list of candidate requirements shouldn't be too long or too vague. In most cases in Russia, an employer's candidate requirements relate to sex, age, education, some special skills (foreign language proficiency, for instance), industry experience, psychological features, medical conditions, and social characteristics.

Unfortunately, in Russia it is very hard to find a candidate requirement that says "should be friendly and solicitous," or something along those lines. This is counter-productive. If Russian managers want guests of their properties to be served by friendly and polite employees, then they should be looking for friendly and polite job applicants.

Inability to Meet High Service Standards. Another pitfall Russian managers face when selecting employees is that most candidates are not ready to meet the strong discipline requirements and high performance levels demanded by high service standards. Hired on a probationary basis, many newly hired Russian hospitality employees leave after three or four days because of their inability to comply with strict requirements. To combat this problem, human resource managers in Russia should be sure to give job applicants, during the interviewing and hiring phase, a thorough explanation of what will be expected of them once they are on the job.

Unqualified Employees. The hospitality industry in Russia contains a unique paradox: while the number of personnel employed by hospitality properties is large, there is a serious shortage of qualified employees. The socialist goal of full employment has led to the present situation, in which the number of staff members in Russian hotels and restaurants is considerably larger than in their Western counterparts, but the qualifications of these staff members are extremely low and, consequently, employee performance is poor. Since tourism was not given a priority as a separate industry under the old Soviet system, hospitality education was conducted by only a few institutions located in large cities. Consequently, the rapid growth of the hospitality sector in Russia in the 1990s exposed a shortage of qualified personnel.

Lack of a Professional Service Attitude. International hospitality companies are faced with serious problems when they try to employ staff members who have worked for Soviet hotels and restaurants in the past. The problem, when seen in the light of international service standards, is the substandard attitude of these staff members toward guests. This fact has influenced the creation of special training programs by the international hospitality companies in Russia (for example, Marriott and Sofitel Iris have launched special training programs for local staff). Sometimes foreign managers prefer to hire people without any hospitality experience rather than employ former staff members from the Soviet-era hospitality industry. It is taken for granted that educating an employee from the very beginning is easier than trying to teach an experienced person to follow the company's work system while at the same time attempting to change his or her unprofessional service attitude.

Establishing an Adequate Hospitality Educational System

As a recent seminar with the general managers of Moscow hotels revealed, there is a serious lack of qualified hospitality educators in Russia. Most educators deliver lectures based not on their own industry experience but on the theoretical background of translated foreign textbooks. Sometimes students have no opportunity to learn practical skills in a work-like setting because lab facilities at institutions and colleges are obsolete or nonexistent.

Hospitality education in Russia must be reorganized so that future employees of the Russian hospitality industry are prepared properly. Hospitality education should not only teach technical skills and knowledge, but also more theoretical concepts such as marketing and management. Hospitality education programs in Russia should build from the experience of leading hospitality schools worldwide, and teach the modern practices of the international hospitality industry. One obligatory component of the Russian hospitality educational system ought to be instruction on developing a proper professional attitude.

Contemporary Russian higher education in hospitality to some extent suffers from redundant scholasticism and isolation from reality. This trait makes most Russian hospitality educational programs of little value. International hotels and tourist firms are not eager to hire Russian graduates because they lack practical skills and overestimate the value of their education. Many graduates cannot hold managerial positions when they are fresh out of school. There is a gap between the skills hospitality properties are demanding from hospitality graduates and the skills educational institutions are teaching them. Thus there is much room for improvement in Russian hospitality education, in terms of familiarizing students with their future careers and equipping them to be successful.

 Endnotes _____

1. World Tourism Organization, *Yearbook of Tourism Statistics,* Volumes 1 and 2 (WTO, 1992).

 **Key Terms** _____

CIS (Community of Independent States)—A union of 12 former Soviet republics—Azerbaijan, Armenia, Belarus, Georgia, Kazakhstan, Kirghizia, Moldova, Russia, Tajikistan, Turmenia, Uzbekistan, and Ukraine—that cooperates in trade and border issues.

departmental properties—Hotels owned by state ministries and serving mostly state officials.

Labor Codex—The main labor law that regulates all major aspects of employment in Russia.

new-type properties—Hotels and restaurants, usually managed by foreigners, that use modern production, marketing, and human resource management techniques. Most new-type properties belong to international hospitality chains.

old-type properties—Hotels and restaurants that are run by Russian managers and combine outmoded properties (state-owned in earlier times) with out-of-date services.

staff-rotation concept—A human resource management strategy based on long (and sometimes unpaid) probationary periods for employees, minimal salaries, a system of fines, and the constant threat of firing.

steady-personnel concept—A human resource management strategy devoted to keeping employee turnover to a minimum.

Discussion Questions

1. What are the differences between a new-type property and an old-type property?

2. What are the three levels of employment regulation for hospitality businesses in Russia?

3. Why do Russian students choose to work at and stay with hospitality properties?

4. What are three human resource management models used in Russia today?

5. What are the differences between the steady-personnel concept and the staff-rotation concept?

6. What are some of the pitfalls of human resource management in Russia?

Internet Sites

For more information, visit the following Internet sites. Remember that Internet addresses can change without notice.

http://www.visitmoscow.com
VisitMoscow.com is the best source for travel information about Moscow. VisitMoscow.com will help you plan your business and leisure schedule while in Moscow by providing information on transportation, special events, activities, attractions, and more.

http://www.wtcmo.ru/en/index.htm
Site of the Centre for International Trade, Scientific and Technical Cooperation with Foreign Countries (Sovincentr Inc.).

http://www.national.ru
Royal Meridien Hotel National Moscow: Virtual Tour of the Hotel National.

http://www.tourinfo.ru/english_pg.html
Tourinfo is the leading national newspaper serving the Russian travel market. The newspaper publishes news about international and Russian travel exhibitions, transport operators, hotels, visa and customs regulations, analytic surveys, travel statistics, and information about incoming and outgoing travel.

http://all-hotels.ru/
This Web site has the largest database of Russian hotels.

http://www.allexperts.com/travel/russia.shtml
Allexperts Russia: Volunteer experts answer questions about tourism in Russia.

http://www.hotelkaterina.com
The Swedish company Sweagent LTD has recently opened the Hotel Katerina in the heart of Moscow. With 30 rooms and under Swedish management, this charming hotel is the first in what will be a chain of small "personal" hotels in Russia.

http://www.kempinski-moscow.com
The Kempinski Hotel Baltschug Moscow Kempinski was one of the first international concerns to establish a presence in post-Soviet Russia. This hotel's grand design, refined comfort, and Old-World elegance is complemented by state-of-the-art facilities and flawless service.

http://www.russia-travel.com/moscac01.htm
Moscow Accommodations: Official Site of the Russian National Tourist Office.

http://www.moscowcity.com
The Moscow City Tourist Office On-Line.

http://www.moscowtimes.ru
The *Moscow Times* newspaper. The foreign community and Russian businesspeople depend a great deal on this English-language newspaper for up-to-the-minute news on Moscow, Russia, and the world.

Chapter 17 Outline

The Structure of the Hospitality Industry
The Human Resources Context
    The Scottish Political Environment
    The Tourism Economy and Markets
    Employment in the Hospitality
        Industry
    Demographic and Labor Market
        Trends
Labor Relations
    Legislative Responses
    Low Level of Unionism
Education and Training
    Secondary School Curriculum
    Vocational Qualifications
    University-Level Qualifications
    Public Sector Organizations

Competencies

1. Identify the prominent business characteristics of the Scottish hospitality industry. (pp. 283–284)

2. Describe the evolution of the Scottish tourism product, including the political environment and employment trends. (pp. 285–288)

3. Identify the demographic issues, labor market trends, and legislative responses that affect the Scottish hospitality industry. (pp. 288–292)

4. Outline major hospitality education and training practices and their effectiveness. (pp. 292–298)

17

Scotland: Removing the Boundaries

Tom Baum and *Lois Farquharson*

Tom Baum, *Ph.D., is Professor of International Hospitality Management and Head of Department, The Scottish Hotel School, University of Strathclyde, Glasgow. He is a specialist in strategic human resource management for hospitality and tourism and has published three books and numerous scientific papers in this area. He has worked, researched, and consulted in Africa, Asia, the Caribbean, Europe, the Middle East, and North America.*

Lois Farquharson *is a Ph.D. Researcher in The Scottish Hotel School and a tutor in the Strathclyde Business School, University of Strathclyde, Glasgow. Her Ph.D. research concerns the substance and implementation of empowerment initiatives in the travel and tourism industry. She also has an active research interest in education, training, and development initiatives for hospitality and tourism.*

SCOTLAND IS CHARACTERIZED by diversity in terms of its geography, history, and culture, and this variety is one of the most significant features and strengths affecting both the tourism and hospitality product. The country covers an area of approximately 30,000 square miles (77,700 square kilometers), constitutes around 34 percent of Britain's land mass, and is roughly two-thirds the size of England. Mainland Scotland is divided into three geographical areas: the Highlands account for about half the land area of Scotland; the Central Lowlands or "central belt" have the highest population density; and the Lowlands encompass the boundary with England. Glasgow is the largest city, with a population of around 660,000; the capital, Edinburgh, has a population of around 400,000. There are also various isles situated mainly around the Highlands, such a Shetland and Orkney.

It is estimated that the tourism industry in the Highlands and Islands of Scotland generates £373 million of revenue annually, which accounts for approximately 20 percent of the gross domestic product. The tourism industry in the Highlands and Islands alone supports around 13,300 jobs [1] Accommodation is undoubtedly the backbone of the tourism industry and boasts a wide range of provision types that are complemented by over 100 visitor attractions and many hundreds of restaurants, sports and leisure facilities, and entertainment facilities. The vast majority of businesses are small and family-run and accordingly there are around 3,000 businesses that employ fewer than 10 people.[2]

The Structure of the Hospitality Industry

The hospitality industry in Scotland, comprising accommodation, restaurants, and catering, is one of the major components of the Scottish tourism industry. Within the tourism and hospitality sector, as in many other countries, there exists an amalgam of sectors carrying out different business activities, all with a common goal of meeting business and service objectives by satisfying tourist needs. Businesses are primarily in the private domain, although public sector provision for hospitality businesses cannot be ignored.

Scottish tourism accommodation covers a myriad of provision types in diverse locations, serving a large range of market segments. Categories include hotels, guesthouses and bed and breakfasts, self-catering (tourists choose accommodation in which they have sleeping and living facilities, but are responsible for their own food provision and preparation), caravan and camping parks, hostels and educational establishments, and bunkhouse and bothy (temporary shelters, i.e., a place to sleep for the night). There are also the limited number of timeshare and second home accommodations, usually within the luxury bracket. There are 22,314 lodging operations registered with the Scottish Tourist Board, including hotels (2,508), guesthouses (1,420), bed and breakfasts (5,693), self-catering units (12,116), and caravanning and camping (503) which are dominated by local ownership and the small operator.[3] Educational establishments account for the remaining 74 operations.

The dominance of the small, family-run business can be attributed to three main factors evident in the Scottish business environment: low capital, specialist and knowledge barriers to entry; highly segmented market demand best served by a wide range of business services; and economic viability in a local or specialized marketplace where profit is not high enough for corporate gains.[4]

It is also important to note that corporate ownership is most representative in urban and suburban areas, as in the case of the Glasgow Hilton and Stakis Hotels. Mergers and takeovers are common in the competitive city center environment; accordingly, in March 1999, the Stakis hotel group became part of the Hilton group allowing Hilton to offer a stronger Scottish portfolio. However, the key growth area in the accommodation sector in Scotland is represented by chain budget products such as Travel Inn and Holiday Inn Express. This corporate activity continues to challenge the business performance of the small operator.

The Human Resources Context

The Scottish Political Environment

Until recently, Scotland had traditionally been governed by the central body of the U.K. Parliament at Westminster. However, there has always been a bone of contention concerning the Union of Scotland within the U.K., which has led to the Scottish people's ambition to pursue their own destiny: independence from Westminster governance. This was manifest in 1997 when the Scottish people voted to establish their own parliament and government based in Edinburgh and led by a First Minister.

Subsequent to elections on May 1, 1999, the Scottish Parliament was formed, pushing Scotland through radical constitutional change. Elected on May 6, 1999, the Scottish Parliament has 129 members comprised of diverse of political parties. The Queen handed over legislative and executive powers to the Scottish Parliament on July 1, 1999.

The advent of the Scottish parliament will, of course, have widespread implications for many areas of Scottish life. However, the tourism and hospitality environment is of vital importance. There has been much "political evangelizing" concerning the merits of the hospitality and tourism sectors as a major contributor to the country's well-being. Therefore, the influence that the Scottish Parliament holds over these sectors becomes vital to the continued endorsement of the sector. Tourism and distinct but related powers in the areas of transport, the environment, the arts, and local government are the responsibility of the Scottish Parliament. The Parliament will also have an impact on the fiscal environment in which tourism businesses operate. Therefore, the Parliament will have full legislative and budgetary control over the Scottish tourism portfolio that suggests the need for the facilitation and sustainability of an effective operating environment for Scottish tourism. The most significant impact that Scottish tourism policy can make in the short to medium term is to focus on the consolidation of the framework of existing tourism products and services, thus ensuring their quality. This can only be completed through the constant development of tourism's key enhancer—the human resource.

The Tourism Economy and Markets

The tourism industry in Scotland continues to evolve as a major and expanding multiplier of wealth and employment. Recent statistics show that tourism contributes about five percent of the gross domestic product of the Scottish economy, compared to manufacturing and financial and business services (around 20 percent) and agriculture, hunting, forestry, and fishing (under three percent). It is therefore a substantial sector of the national economy in its own right. The most significant targets for all tourist spending are, not surprisingly, mainly within the hospitality industry: accommodation, travel, eating, and drinking.

The attraction that Scotland holds for visitors lies in its varied tourism base. A host of "pull" factors are evident in destination choice decisions about Scotland, including romantic and turbulent history; dramatic scenery; a green, open, and uncrowded natural environment; friendly but independent and feisty people; and rich cultural heritage. The only thing that the country lacks is a temperate climate. Scotland's weather patterns are very varied—and can have four seasons in one day! Generally, the east is characterized by cool, dry weather and the west is characterized by milder and wetter weather. These proverbially Scottish factors provide the key to the divergence of attractions for visitors of various types.

The two major long-term growth areas in the Scottish tourism economy are independent holidays and activity holidays. This is linked with the rise in personal mobility and the growth in discerning visitors who require greater freedom and flexibility. The geography of Scotland is suitable for easy independent traveling (mainly by car) and also lends itself to a variety of pursuits such as sporting and outdoor activities (skiing, climbing, hill-walking, field sports), natural history (wildlife, bird-watching, geology, botany), and attractions varying from historical castles to safari parks. There has also been a notable increase in attendance at festival events, such as Glasgow's Mayfest or The Edinburgh Festival Fringe.

Visitors come to Scotland for a variety of reasons. The predominant motive has traditionally been that of holiday-making, which has been declining in significance, followed by business and VFR (visiting friends and relatives). Expenditure by overseas tourists represents a major input into the Scottish economy and is spread over a variety of businesses. Over two million overseas tourists visited Scotland in 1997 (an increase of 5.8 percent per year over the past 10 years) providing a significant contribution to foreign exchange earnings of almost £1 billion. The largest sources of foreign exchange and trips are visitors from the United States (£189 million) followed by Germany (£102 million) and the Irish Republic (£71 million).[5]

In contrast, in the domestic tourism arena, the expenditure of British tourists in Scotland fell significantly in the 1980s and remains below its 1989 level. This decline is part of a restructuring of the composition of visitors to Scotland. A primary reason for the decline has been the availability of cheaper international airfares, which has reduced the overall cost of overseas holidays and thus rerouted long-stay holidays by domestic tourists to foreign destinations. This is supplemented by the comparatively high costs (both in terms of time and money) of traveling to Scotland, despite the improvement of transport infrastructure.

However, British tourists still account for most trips (11.1 million) and expenditure (£1.69 billion). These domestic trips are mainly for holiday purposes (49 percent) followed by VFR (32 percent) and then business (14 percent). Short breaks have increased in market share substantially during the 1990s with expenditure on 1–7 night breaks increasing by 10 percent (accounting for inflation).[6]

Employment in the Hospitality Industry

Recent estimates by the Scottish Tourist Board show that, in general, tourism employs around 180,000 people (including self-employed) which accounts for approximately eight percent of the working population in Scotland.[7] The hospitality industry itself is one of the few industries that can create employment opportunities throughout Scotland and accordingly, there are over 129,000 people employed in hotels and restaurants.[8]

A major factor that affects hospitality employment throughout Scotland is that of the seasonality of tourism. Tourism remains highly seasonal with 39 percent of holiday trips taking place between July and September which inevitably affects the number of bed nights in Scottish hotels. Currently, attempts are being made to extend the season through marketing "Autumn Gold" breaks. This should improve the year-round viability of small- and medium-sized enterprises and thereby convert the jobs they support from part-time to full-time. This is of particular significance in the more remote areas of Scotland where traditional industries have declined and tourism is the main source of employment.

In relative terms, tourism is more important to the economy in more remote rural areas than in the large cities of Edinburgh and Glasgow, for example. In the Highlands of Scotland, tourism alone accounts for 14.6 percent of all employment[9] in comparison with 7.7 percent of employment in Edinburgh and 7.2 percent of employment in Greater Glasgow and Clyde Valley. In particular, transient labor is an important feature of employment in many Highland and Island destinations and this labor is drawn from elsewhere in Scotland, the U.K., and further afield. Such labor is attracted to seasonal employment by the perceived attractiveness of the destination and its lifestyle attributes. Salaries, including accommodation, are quoted net and, as a result, are unattractive to the local labor market who have no accommodation requirement.[10] Furthermore, those in the local community who are in seasonal employment may choose that particular working lifestyle for sound pragmatic reasons—opting for work in excess of six months per year may end entitlement benefits under the Welfare to Work and New Deal programs.

New Deal is part of the British government's Welfare to Work strategy that aims to reduce the overall unemployment figures. New Deal is a program that prepares individuals for work and then finds them a job for a six-month period (it is expected but not guaranteed that the work will continue after six months), during which their employment with a particular company will be subsidized by the government. After six months, the individual receives a certificate to show what he or she has achieved during his or her employment, plus a work reference to take to potential employers. If the employee remains employed by the company after the six-month period, any benefits received under the New Deal program cease because the individual receives wages in the form of a salary as a normal employee would. The benefits that the employees lose may include travel expenses, Housing Benefit, or Council Tax Benefit, for example. Therefore, it may be more beneficial for the individual to only work for six months per year under the New Deal program and remain unemployed for the rest of the year so that they may continue to claim government benefits.

An issue linked with the seasonality is the culture that exists in remote highland areas and the effect that it has upon tourism and hospitality employment. A 1997 study of seasonal unemployment in the Highlands and Islands noted that,

> In Ullapool, research findings suggest that a proportion of unemployed or temporary employees exist, specifically as a result of the downturn in fishing activity related to the area. For these people, most of who are male, there is a perception that the tourism sector does not hold any appeal. Their traditional fishing employment is viewed as "macho" and

is the culturally accepted and expected mode of employment. The tourism sector is not perceived to represent a suitable alternative to these people (it may take a generation or so for this view to change).[11]

Therefore, the effective utilization of human resources are vital to the predominantly small business characteristics of the hospitality industry in this area.

These factors, coupled with the prevailing characteristics of low pay, long hours, and lack of skills development have produced an image that may deter potential employees from entering the hospitality industry. Therefore, it is fundamental that both public and private sector enterprises address this through human resource policies and practices that identify future labor requirements, recognize skills gaps, assess terms and conditions, and evaluate staff recruitment and development in the industry,

Demographic and Labor Market Trends

The key issue facing the Scottish tourism and hospitality industry in terms of demographic and labor market trends centers on the continuing decrease in the volume of young people available to the major growth industry of the millennium. Figures for the U.K. show that between 1995 and 2001 there will be a decrease of 0.9 million in those under 35[12], and proportionally similar effects will be seen in Scotland. This encompasses the prime recruitment cohort for the hospitality industry.

Pressures are being placed on young people to remain in school longer in order to bring Scotland in line with the European Community (EC) and other developed economies and to increase the intellectual competitiveness of the economy. This constricts the pool of relatively unskilled labor upon which the hospitality industry has traditionally relied. Paradoxically, however, changes in funding arrangements for higher education now mean that more students, like their American counterparts, have to work their way through college or university. This should increase the availability of part-time employees to hospitality businesses in urban areas. These labor shortages will inevitably affect various vocational areas and skills levels in differing ways, but the key shortages which are more than likely to persist are those of the semi-skilled and skilled craft designations in all sectors.

An important consideration in Scotland is the relationship between employment decline within traditional economic sectors and employment growth in new areas of the service sector. In Scotland's transition economy, this is most evident in the industrial areas of the central belt where the decline has been seen in heavy industries such as mining, ship-building, and manufacturing. The growth in services, including tourism, creates new work opportunities, although these do not necessarily match the available unemployed labor pool in terms of skills or aspirations.

The corollary of the declining youth population is an increasing average age within the industry as a whole. Thus the number between 35–60 will increase by around 1.8 million between 1995 and 2001.[13] Likewise, the proportion of the population over retirement age will rise further during the millennium, due to both the falling birth rate and improved healthcare factors. These trends have considerable significance for labor recruitment and the need for Scotland to actively pursue the accommodation of so-called "non-traditional" recruits into the workforce, especially women workers, older workers, and ethnic minorities. This will involve consideration of a wide range of alternative work-related structures and initiatives, including changes in working time (flexible working and job share), provision of support facilities (childcare), renewed prominence of training strategies, and the development of new perceptions of hospitality industry workplaces as examples of excellence that offer superior quality products and services.

Labor Relations

These changes in labor market trends have sparked the introduction of three major inter-linked legislative responses in the U.K. that aim to regulate the often transient workforce. The introduction of the working time regulations (stemming from the EC Working Time Directive) preceded and laid the foundation for the National Minimum Wage and the Fairness at Work legislation. The Directive, which came into effect in the U.K. in October 1998, is one of the most extensive pieces of employment legislation ever to deal with working time and holiday provision.

Legislative Responses

The basic aims of the Working Time Directive are to safeguard the health and safety of workers by providing a flexible framework to address excessively long working hours, together with the provision of appropriate rest breaks, particularly in the case of shift and night working. The Directive includes limits on the number of hours that may be worked on a daily and weekly basis, the hours of work for night and shift workers, minimum daily and weekly rest breaks, and minimum annual paid holiday entitlements. However, it also provides for a range of exemptions and a number of exceptions of certain types of employees (doctors, for example).

The introduction of the **National Minimum Wage (NMW)** in 1999 may influence the prevalence of **in-work poverty** in the hospitality industry. In an industry dogged by a low pay and small business culture, the introduction of NMW has caused some hostility as both large and small businesses find it difficult to apportion funds specifically to meet the provisions of the minimum wage. From a hospitality employee's perspective, the NMW suggests the protection of their rights to a decent wage. The dispersion of gratuities or incentives, however, has been modified in line with the NMW causing contention. Whereas previously the trend was for each individual to pocket their gratuities/incentive payments, these now count toward the minimum wage. Therefore, businesses are now operating a pooling system where all gratuities are gathered and paid through the payroll. While the NMW asserts the positive aspects of worker protection through wage regulation, the major outcomes of the minimum wage for industry businesses may be consolidated in employment cuts, a decrease in individual working hours, and in potential small business failure.

Pay and conditions in Scotland reflect the wider U.K. situation with the important qualification that Scotland has traditionally had lower average weekly wages than the rest of the U.K., leading low pay campaigners to point out that in industries such as hospitality, employers are tempted to pay lower average hourly rates than elsewhere in their U.K. operations (because Scotland has traditionally had lower rates of pay and therefore lower pay may go unnoticed by employees). This practice sustains a low(er) pay culture. The most significant study found that whereas there was widespread compliance by employers with the then prevailing hourly rates, this applied only to the contracted working week and substantial pay avoidance was achieved by refusing to pay premium overtime rates (in some cases overtime was not paid for at all, in others the standard hourly rate was applied). Qualitative data on workers' attitudes and experiences of their work confirmed previous research that revealed a largely unmotivated, transient working population, many of whom took hotel and catering jobs because of the lack of alternative employment opportunities.[14]

The Fairness at Work legislation promotes a partnership between employer and employee in the workplace that reflects a new, supportive relationship between work and family life. The hospitality industry has, over an extended period of time, employed women (and men) returnees to work in order to utilize their flexibility and cost effectiveness. The returnees are considered flexible because they are usually part-time/seasonal workers who can make themselves available to work various hours/shifts. The legislation introduces family-friendly policies that consolidate the need to protect these workers through the regulation of their rights. Some policies include flexibility of hours to allow more time to be spent with family; the provision of time off for family crises; the provision of, or funding for, childcare facilities; and parental and maternity leave (parental leave gives a male or female employee the right to take three months leave as a parent of a baby and maternity leave gives women the right to take 14 weeks maternity leave; in the case of a woman, the employer will normally offer either type of leave, but not both). Although conceptually impressive in the realm of human resource management, such arrangements are at present not widely available since they cost employers both time and money. However, there should be a gradual implementation of these policies in the future.

A 1998 British Hospitality Association survey found that of the 1.3 million employed in hotels, bars, and restaurants, about 15 percent regularly worked more than the 48 hours per week laid down in the Directive. Thus, one of the key features of the working time regulations causing contention for many businesses is the use, or abuse, of derogations (the "opt-out" clause for employees that allows them to work more then 48 hours per week). Derogations can be positively utilized to assist businesses to deal with seasonal problems and continuity of service. However, it has been highlighted that there is the potential for businesses to pressure employees into signing derogations in order to curtail the effect of the working time regulations, especially in an industry with little bargaining power.

The complexity of the regulations (Working Time Directive, National Minimum Wage, and Fairness at Work legislation) will affect both large and small operators in the hospitality industry. While small hotels in the Highlands and Islands will find the Working Time Directive a great burden as pressure mounts to improve and complete basic time sheet systems (as well as to account for statutory paid leave), the larger operations such as Hilton Hotels, which employ around

5,500 staff in the U.K., have introduced expensive computerized time and attendance systems in line with the regulations.

Low Level of Unionism

The level of unionization in hospitality organizations has always been low due to
the inherent characteristics of the industry. Four main reasons are suggested for
low union density in the Scottish hospitality industry:[15]

- *The ethos of hotel and catering work.* Hotel and catering workers have been isolated from mainstream industrial trade unionism and have tended to develop
  individualistic work ethics which have resulted in the view that trade union
  member ship is incompatible with service employment.

- *The structure of the workforce.* The hotel and catering industry employs many
  part-time workers who are often difficult to organize because they work shifts
  and are isolated from contact with other employees. This can diminish the
  workplace cohesion that is often necessary for effective union organization.

- *Hostile employers.* Employers and managers are generally averse to trade
  unions in hospitality services and frequently argue that they are incompatible
  with the ethos of the industry. Employers and managers view their role in the
  organization as that of looking after the employee needs and consider that
  unions will bully management and tell them how to treat their employees.

- *The role of trade unions.* Unions face several obstacles in recruiting members in
  the industry because the union administrative structures are not generally
  suitable to the accommodation of hospitality employees. This highlights the
  inadequacies of the knowledge of trade unions about the hospitality industry.

The results of the research concerning the attitudes and expectations of hospitality
workers toward unions compounds the above complexity of factors contributing
to the low level of union density in the industry. More than half of the Scottish sam-
ple (53 percent) were unaware of union activity in the hospitality industry and
only five percent were members of trade unions (most had retained union membership from a previous job). However, it is important to note that when respondents were asked if they would join a union, around 63 percent replied
positively—this would suggest that, in Scotland, employees are not unsympathetic
to the concept of unions. Over 80 percent of respondents expressed positive views
of trade unions including the support of workers rights, and their defense against
exploitation and unscrupulous employers.[16]

Despite the generally positive views concerning trade unionism, there seems
little prospect of such perceptions producing action. This would suggest that there
is a lack of knowledge concerning the role of unions and that the hotel and catering
unions adopt too low a profile. However, with the "triple whammy" of the Working Time Directive, National Minimum Wage, and the Fairness at Work legislation,
unions could have a much stronger position. If a hospitality employer requires
negotiation of collective agreements (which make use of the working time derogations with a central body of employees), there may be new roles created for
unions. It may be much more efficient to recognize a trade union than go through a

nebulous recruitment structure in order to identify representatives of a non-union organization. Therefore, this may be a prime opportunity for unions to make their mark in non-union workplaces, providing that they show an acceptable face of unionism—i.e. understanding the hospitality culture.

Education and Training

Scotland's system for training and education for hospitality operates at a variety of levels and through a diversity of agencies in the public and private sector. It is comprehensive in the levels that are addressed (from basic skills to senior management), and increasingly geographically distributed. Participation is high—and growing. The following are contributing factors to the evolution of a sustainable training and education culture in the Scottish hospitality industry.

Secondary School Curriculum

The position of hospitality and tourism in a vocational context within the Scottish school system is probably less developed than is the case in a number of key competing destination environments and, indeed, within a wider international context. In part, this is a reflection of differing educational structures and traditions in Scotland. In particular, Scotland has a significantly higher participation rate in higher education and this can act to reduce the vocational focus within the school curriculum.

Higher education takes place at universities where the individuals are allowed to enter at age 17; the qualifications involve undergraduate/postgraduate degree courses. Further education is of a more vocational nature and is offered at further education colleges; individuals can enter at age 16. The qualifications of further education can involve **Scottish Vocational Qualifications (SVQs)**, Higher National Diplomas, and Higher National Certificates. There are also further education colleges that offer university level qualifications.

The *Seasonal Hospitality Employment Programme* **(SHEP)** is designed for secondary schools in highly seasonal areas. The program recognizes the important role that secondary school students play in the labor market and, by offering specific training, can enhance the basic skills base of this seasonal workforce. The program has been operating in some parts of rural Scotland since 1996. The model is also applicable as a pre-seasonal training initiative for tourism employers, especially in the accommodation and food service sector, with seasonal staff already in employment. SHEP is a three-day course designed to be easily accessible and affordable and includes two industry recognized certificates. On a day-by-day basis, the program consists of:

1. Welcome Host—customer awareness, customer care, complaints, a general introduction to tourism

2. Elementary Food Hygiene—health and safety in the workplace, safe systems for food handling and storage

3. Food service and housekeeping with a focus on practical skills

SHEP also introduces one of the main and often unrecognized challenges that seasonal tourism destinations face in seeking to extend their tourist season beyond September: incompatibility with the Scottish school year which commences in late August and withdraws a major source of local tourism employees from the labor market.

Vocational Qualifications

Education and training for hospitality ranges from basic skills development in schools and further education colleges through industry-based programs to a wide range of undergraduate and postgraduate education courses. The SVQ system—geared to meet the needs of a full-time, school-leaver population—is structured to provide formal recognition of skills acquired in the workplace. It is therefore more effective in providing certified recognition of capabilities acquired early in the person's career through contact with a college. Some employees complete them at the beginning of their career by going one day or more per week to college with the support of their employer. Other people register for SVQs at college and are sent on a temporary placement in which they get experience of the things they have learned at college.

The formal system in Scotland is generic and designed to give graduates broad career opportunities within the hospitality sector. At the vocational level, the Scottish Qualifications Association (SQA, formerly Scotvec) has a close liaison and advisory relationship with the hospitality sector. Limited sectoral specific exceptions can be found—the University of Strathclyde's enterprise and small business development programs are a recognition of the dominant business structure in Scottish tourism and hospitality. Likewise, the ongoing or life-long learning needs of those already employed within the sector are not targeted through dedicated provision.

University-Level Qualifications

In Scotland, nine university-level institutions and the majority of further education colleges currently offer university qualifications in tourism-related areas (including hospitality), graduating in excess of 500 students per year. As in the rest of the U.K., academic qualifications in hospitality are not formally tied to professional recognition except in a loose and non-statutory way through voluntary professional bodies such as Hotel and Catering International Management Association (HCIMA). Thus, academic qualifications in hospitality make no necessary formal contribution to the development or enhancement of managerial effectiveness in the tourism sector. This points to the generally weak labor market characteristics which affect hospitality. There are few obstacles, and none based on academic qualifications, to managerial or ownership entry into the hospitality industry in Scotland.

Private Sector Education and Training Provision

It is becoming apparent that hospitality businesses within the industry are no longer satisfied with the education and training products being delivered by public sector further/higher education. As a consequence, they have been moved to provide a private sector education and training provision. An example of this approach is the Drambuie Scottish Chefs Centre. The Scottish Chefs Association, with the backing of most of Scotland's leading chefs, established the center in Glasgow in March 1998. The venture is aimed at both professional chefs and amateur cooks. Courses range from two-hour cookery demonstrations to residential courses and placements providing in-depth training on new techniques, trends, and business skills. Originally, Drambuie agreed to sponsor the initiative for £150,000 over a three-year period, and American Express has since also committed £75,000 to the project.

Public Sector Organizations

In the Scottish context, support for in-company training continues to be dominated by public sector organizations. They work collaboratively with industry with the aim of creating a vibrant training culture that will enhance professional standards; generally improve the access to, and quality of, training; and promote career opportunities to young persons with potential to add value to the industry in the long-term. This is achieved through the provision of training initiatives, training support resources, media activities and events, and the general dissemination of illustrations of best practices and resultant benefits. In addition, the private sector recognizes the commercial opportunity presented in the provision of in-company training support and is active in this area.

Tourism Training Scotland. The key public sector training organization represented in Scotland is **Tourism Training Scotland (TTS)**. It was set up in 1992 under the auspices of the Scottish Tourism Coordinating Group. It is a joint industry/public sector forum and was established to lead a new effort to promote effective training and career development in the tourism industry, inclusive of hospitality. TTS's original strategy, launched in 1993, focused on three key objectives: creating a training culture, enhancing professional standards, and improving access to quality training. TTS has addressed these objectives through:

- the development of an extensive range of tourism specific courses and materials

- raising industry awareness of the importance of training through its publications, media activity, and participation in industry conferences and events

- promoting business benefits of effective training and staff development through case studies and the Scottish Thistle Awards (one of which is Student of the Year, sponsored by the Bank of Scotland)

- encouraging uptake of Investors in People by tourism businesses

- promoting careers in the tourism industry

TTS's programs have been developed and made available to industry through the **Scottish Enterprise** and **Highlands and Islands Enterprise (HIE)** networks. The Area Tourist Boards, schools, colleges and universities, and industry associations have also had important roles to play in disseminating the importance of industry

Exhibit 1   Tourism Training Scotland: Initiatives

INITIATIVES	FOCUS
Welcome Host	Basic customer care
Scotland's Best	Service quality program
Natural Cooking	Promoting awareness of Scottish produce
Tourism Business Success	Management skills
Staff Development Guides	Staff recruitment and development
Service Quality Guides	Training and advice for tourism retailers
SVQs	Occupational standards
Investors in People	Linking skills to business objectives

skills and promoting uptake of the various initiatives. It is possible to tailor these initiatives to the different sectoral needs of, for example, visitor attractions and art organizations. Each initiative and its focus is presented in Exhibit 1.

The Hospitality Training Foundation (HtF) Scotland team is actively involved in the work of TTS and deals with the specific needs of employers and the educational system in Scotland. It is instrumental in helping employers implement SVQs and focus on lifelong learning for employees. HtF projects include:

- raising awareness of Skillseekers Modern Apprenticeships across the industry

- providing a model of good practice on how small businesses can benefit from using the occupational standards and SVQs as a lifelong learning project

- developing case studies of SVQs at work in a range of establishments

In addition, there is an increasing trend of in-company training support in educational institutes participating in the provision. For example, Thistle Hotels has set up a partnership with Borders College Training and Consultancy in Edinburgh to run the Modern Apprenticeship Scheme in all 96 Thistle and Mount Charlotte hotels. The scheme is a structured professional training program for 16- to 24-year-olds and generally takes three to four years to complete.

HIE developed a training support model for the tourism and hospitality industry in their area. The focus of this has been on training for middle managers, with an emphasis on "train the trainer" and vocational qualification assessor development. Local collaboration can also be the key to successful training initiatives as with the majority of Nairn hoteliers who have cooperated to finance and run a vocational qualifications center in the community for their mutual benefit.

In addition, the small Loch Ness-side Drumnadrochit Hotel has put all their staff through the *Welcome Host* training program run by Inverness and Nairn Enterprise. The majority have also completed *Scotland's Best* course, four chefs have taken the *Natural Cooking* course, and the hotel is working towards achieving the Investors in People standard. This is a key example of the correlation between skills development and company success through an education/industry integrative approach that enhances the training culture in small tourism enterprises.

Headline initiatives such as *Welcome Host* and *Scotland's Best* are undoubt-edly important in raising skills and awareness at the critical front-line, but such programs are of limited long-term value within the stable labor markets of remote locations. After the majority of the local tourism labor market has completed the program, it does not offer an obvious progressive route into further training. Investing in longer-term cultural change within the Scottish hospitality sector needs to be the prime objective, but this represents a long-term commitment and not one that can be achieved on the basis of short-term and changing initiatives.

Investors In People. The **Investors in People (IIP)** U.K. national standard is a key initiative which, since its inception in 1993, has been a catalyst driving both small and large businesses toward organizational achievement in training. Unlike pre-vious government training initiatives, IIP has proven successful in generating and sustaining organizational attention. In the U.K., some 4,000 companies have attained the IIP standard, with around another 20,600 organizations, representing more than 25 percent of the U.K.'s working population, committed to gaining the award.[17] Currently, 170 Scottish tourism businesses have achieved IIP and 280 are working towards recognition. Scottish tourism businesses, including hospitality operations, now account for 15 percent of total IIP recognitions with an estimated 14,000 people working in IIP recognized companies.[18]

The appeal of the IIP standard to these businesses extends beyond the initial goal of developing a sustainable training culture. The framework provides a planned approach to setting and communicating business objectives and develop-ing employees to achieve these objectives. The standard is a branding that encour-ages "organizational flag-flying" (both literally and metaphorically) and recognizes the key tenets of change management, people development, individual ownership, communication, flexibility, and the team. IIP requires the organization to evaluate the above against four main benchmarks:

- *Commitment* to invest in people to achieve business goals

- *Planning* how skills, individuals, and teams are to be developed to achieve these goals

- *Action* to develop and use the necessary skills in a well-defined and continu-ing program directly tied to business objectives

- *Evaluating* outcomes of training and development for individuals' progress toward goals, the value achieved, and future needs

A portfolio of evidence showing how companies measure up is then produced and plans for improvement formalized. The process is cyclical and should engender a process of continuous improvement until and after recognition as an Investor in People is achieved.

The accrued benefits include improved business performance and competi-tiveness, enhanced employee attitudes, improved employee performance, and customer satisfaction. The cases of hospitality businesses seen in Exhibit 2 exem-plify the benefits of IIP for both small and large businesses.

One of the key measurements of the success of any IIP recognized establish-ment is in customer satisfaction. Research has found that tourism and hospitality

Exhibit 2   Benefits of Investors in People (IIP) Standard

Rufflets Country House Hotel

Rufflets Country House Hotel is a 25 bedroom deluxe hotel on the outskirts of St. Andrews. The hotel has been family-owned since 1952 when it opened as a seven bedroom private hotel. Today it boasts an award-winning restaurant which seats 80 and a bar catering comfortably for 70 guests.

Training and development has been granted increased prominence since the business' involvement with IIP. It was in 1994 that the management team began to take responsibility for achieving business results by ensuring that staff are able to carry out their roles effectively. Thus, formal training priorities were laid down in the form of a training and development plan. In addition, managers carry out appraisals of all staff for discussion and communication with growing staff numbers. This has resulted in staff who feel valued, effectively trained, and encouraged to develop and progress within the careers structure.

The tangible business benefits are numerous. Between 1994 and 1998, sales increased by 67 percent, with profits increasing by 124 percent. In addition, Rufflets was awarded the Customer Care Scotland Award in 1997. In terms of training development, today Rufflets is one of the few approved vocational qualifications (VQ) centers in Scotland. Approximately 25 percent of the staff have successfully completed or are working towards SVQs.

Source: R. Georgeson, "Case Studies: Investors in People—Rufflets Country House Hotel, St. Andrews," *The Hospitality Review* (January 1999).

The Willow Tea Rooms

The Willow Tea Rooms, now a landmark on Glasgow's famous Sauchiehall Street, was established in 1983 by Ann Mulhern, as a 40-cover tea-room employing eight staff. It is themed to represent the design work of famous Glasgow designer and architect, Charles Rennie McIntosh.

In early 1999, the Willow Tea Rooms were awarded IIP status, demonstrating that staff are a priority, both within the written plan for the business as well as on a day-to-day basis. Induction, on-job training, employee development through SVQs, and appraisals now play key roles in the development of an atmosphere of openness and teamwork in which individuals can express their opinions and ideas to the extent of implementation.

This is, of course, time consuming, even for the largest of businesses. However, over the past eight years the financial turnover has improved dramatically (increased tenfold) and the processes and high standards which are in place also mean that aspirations for future expansion and development are made more realistic.

Source: R. Georgeson, "Case Studies: Investors in People—The Willow Team Rooms," *The Hospitality Review* (January 1999).

operations which are IIP recognized could potentially increase their bookings through the promotion of the IIP standard to customers.[19] With knowledge of the Investors in People standard, customers overwhelmingly expect positive quality of service and hold the establishment in higher esteem. Therefore, that maintenance of high standards of service and repeat business relies on customer reaction and satisfaction.

Therefore, there is a convincing case that credible investment in people will yield tangible business benefits. However, in order to sustain competitiveness and improved customer service, the IIP standard must become more than compliance to basic framework to merely achieve the standard. In reality it should become the entire *modus operandi* of the activities and objectives of the whole business—a philosophy of working life.

Endnotes

1. "Investigation of Seasonal Tourism Unemployment," Highlands and Islands Enterprise, 1997.

2. "Investigation of Seasonal Tourism Unemployment."

3. "Scottish Tourism Market—Structure, Characteristics and performance," The Scottish Tourism Research Unit and The Fraser of Allander Institute (Edinburgh: Scottish Tourist Board, 1999).

4. A. Morrison, "The Tourist Accommodation Sector in Scotland" in R. MacLellan and R. Smith, *Tourism in Scotland* (Cambridge, Mass.: International Thomson Publishing,1998), pp. 135–153.

5. Scottish Tourist Board Research Newsletter, 11 January 1997.

6. Scottish Tourist Board Research Newsletter.

7. "Regional Trends," Central Statistics Office (London: HMSO, 1995) and Scottish Tourist Board Research Newsletter.

8. National Statistics Summary, Office for National Statistics (London: HMSO, 1996).

9. "Scottish Tourism Employment Statistics Summary" (Edinburgh: Scottish Tourist Board, 1995).

10. "Investigation of Seasonal Tourism Unemployment"

11. "Investigation of Seasonal Tourism Unemployment"

12. "A Summary of Labour Market and Skill Trends 1996/97," Department for Education and Employment (Sheffield: Department for Education and Employment, 1997).

13. "A Summary of Labour Market and Skill Trends 1996/97."

14. I.R. Macaulay and R.C. Wood, *Hard Cheese: A Study of Hotel and Catering Employment in Scotland* (Glasgow: Scottish Low Pay Unit, 1992).

15. Macaulay and Wood.

16. Macaulay and Wood.

17. T. Alberga, "Time for a Check-up," *People Management*, 3/2 (1997), pp. 30–32.

18. "Scottish Tourism Strategic Plan: Interim Review" (Edinburgh: Scottish Tourist Board, 1999).

19. G. Maxwell, et al., "Customer Perceptions of Investors in People: Market Research in Scottish Hotels and Visitor Attractions—Summary Findings" (Glasgow: Department of Hospitality, Tourism and Leisure, Glasgow Caledonian University, 1998).

Key Terms

Highlands and Islands Enterprise (HIE)—Established under the Enterprise and New Towns (Scotland) Act 1990. Its remit is economic and social development, training, and environmental renewal in the Highlands and Islands which covers half the area of Scotland.

in-work poverty—Employees who are in employment, but are not paid a wage in agreement with the National Minimum Wage due to employer refusal to pay a decent wage or through decreases in hours to assist in employer cost effectiveness.

Investors in People (IIP)—The national standard for effective staff development linked to business objectives aimed at tourism and hospitality businesses.

National Minimum Wage—The NMW guarantees workers a rate of £3.60 per hour for those over 21 years old; £3.00 per hour for those 18–21 years; and £3.20 for those 22 and over for six months after starting a new job with a new employer if they are receiving accredited training.

Scottish Enterprise—The central body which leads the development of the network of 13 Local Enterprise Companies (LECs) in terms of strategy and tackles key issues such as exports, inward investment, and skills and training at national and international levels.

Scottish Vocational Qualifications (SVQs)—Qualifications that provide formal certified recognition of skills acquired in the workplace.

Seasonal Hospitality Employment Programme (SHEP)—Designed for secondary schools in highly seasonal areas in order to enhance their basic skills base.

Tourism Training Scotland (TTS)—A private and public sector partnership which promotes the business benefits of effective training and career development.

Discussion Questions

1. What are the implications of (a) the small business structure of the hospitality sector and (b) the seasonal nature of the industry for the management of human resources in Scotland?

2. Why does the public sector play an important role in the direction of HR for hospitality in Scotland?

3. What are the main features of hospitality education and training in Scotland?

Internet Sites

For more information, visit the following Internet sites. Remember that Internet addresses can change without notice.

Highlands and Islands Enterprise
(HIE)
http://www.hie.co.uk/

Hospitality Training Foundation (HtF)
http://www.htf.org.uk/

Investors in People
http://www.iipuk.co.uk/

Scottish Enterprise
http://www.scottish-enterprise.com/

The Scottish Hotel School
http://www.shs.strath.ac.uk/

Tourism Training Scotland (TTS)
http://www.gateway-media.co.uk/
tourism/home.cfm

Tourism Training Scotland
Programmes and Initiatives
http://www.gateway-media.co.uk/
tourism/progs.htm

Chapter 18 Outline

The Cradle of Modern Tourism
    The Size and Scope of Swiss Tourism
    Hotel Industry Structure
    A Multicultural Hospitality Work
        Force
Labor Demographics and Labor Market
    Issues
    Hospitality Labor
Political and Legal Considerations
    European Political Integration
    Legal Aspects of Swiss Hospitality
        Labor
Cultural Distinctions and Societal Work
    Values
    Swiss Quality
    Education and Technical Skills
Labor Relations within the HR Context
    Recruitment and Selection
    Evaluation, Training, and
        Development
    Women in Hospitality
Looking Ahead

Competencies

1. List historical aspects in the development of the Swiss hospitality industry. (pp. 303–307)

2. Describe current labor demographics and key labor issues for the Swiss hospitality work force. (pp. 307–310)

3. Identify the special challenges Swiss managers face in maintaining the quality and image of their industry in the face of globalization and the internationalization of the industry. (pp. 310–311)

4. Describe the unique aspects of HR practice in Swiss hospitality. (pp. 311–313)

18

Switzerland: Balancing Traditions with Change

Reinhard Kunz and *Colin Johnson*

Reinhard Kunz, *MA, CHE, is currently senior lecturer in hospitality marketing and human resource management at the DCT Center of Hotel Management in Lucerne, Switzerland. He also guest lectures at European University and has contributed papers and articles to HSMAI EuroCHRIE as well as to the* Journal of International Hospitality Management.

Colin Johnson, *BA, MBA, is director of the Lausanne Institute for Hospitality Research at Ecole Hôtelière de Lausanne, Switzerland. He is on the editorial board of the* International Journal of Tourism and Hospitality Research *and* Praxis: The Journal of Applied Hospitality Management. *He has contributed articles to various journals specializing in the development of tourism and hospitality in central eastern Europe. In addition, he has worked in many sectors of the hospitality industry, including airline and contract catering, hotels, and sports and social clubs.*

The Cradle of Modern Tourism

Switzerland has been described as the cradle of modern tourism, and its long tradition of travel and hospitality reaches back centuries.

If you were a traveler around 1250, you may well have turned for advice on available hostelries to *The Pilgrims Guide,* which mentions the hospice of Great St. Bernard Pass as "one of the three great religious establishments founded to give support to the poor, comfort to the pilgrims, rest to the penniless, consolation to the sick, salvation to the dying, and succour to the living."[1] This tradition of Christian lodging was widespread and is still in evidence today. There were other forms of accommodation as well, the most popular being farm houses and smaller professional inns and hotels; by 1800, such businesses had an established reputation among travelers as renowned as Ruskin, Goethe, Voltaire, Byron, and Dumas.

This early tourism industry developed mainly to cater to the wealthy English who, on their grand peregrination, took in the Pilatus and Rigi at Lucerne, the Chateau Chillon at Montreux, and other magnificent natural mountain and lake sights. To cater to these increasing numbers, a series of grand or palace hotels sprang up, which resulted in the *Baedeker* guidebook asserting that "without a doubt, Switzerland possesses the finest hotels in the world."[2]

More professional management and care were required to cope with the growing number of tourists, so schools of hotel management, such as Ecole Hôtelière de Lausanne, and Alpine schools for mountain guides were established. Subsequent phases of growth in hospitality occurred after World War II with the large-scale development of winter sports, which created an entirely new market for the winter resort regions.

The reputation for high quality has also continued to grow. The Victoria Jungfrau in Interlaken, the Beau Rivage in Lausanne, and the Baur au Lac in Zurich—to name but a few internationally known properties—continue to command respect from peers throughout the world.

The Size and Scope of Swiss Tourism

Swiss tourism benefits from a natural comparative advantage based on the country's central location in western Europe, as well as its spectacular landscape and a topography that lends itself to sports and outdoor activities throughout the year.

Over the past 25 years, there has been considerable diversification in the industry beyond the common distinction of urban and resort travel. Today, Swiss tourism consists of a broad mix of leisure, group, sport, cultural, business, nature, and luxury travel; in recent times, hospitality providers have taken considerable measures to extend their offerings to the various needs of these more specialized segments. In the mountain regions, for example, one can find a wide range of activities, including snow boarding, downhill skiing, cross-country skiing, mountain biking, hang gliding, tours for seniors, and recreation centers for families. In the cities, there are business hotels, "aparthotels" (similar to extended-stay establishments), and airport hotels.

In addition to its various lodging establishments, Switzerland has a heavy concentration of food service outlets, with 34,230 businesses generating revenue of CH22 billion in 1998. This amounts to one establishment for every 207 inhabitants, in contrast to Austria, which has 125, and Sweden, which has 920 inhabitants for every food service outlet.[3]

As a subset of the tourism industry, Swiss hospitality is inextricably tied to the larger developments in global travel and tourism. In terms of international tourist arrivals, Switzerland has slipped from eighth in 1990 to thirteenth in 1998, with 11 million arrivals.[4] (This shift in relative standing among destinations may be attributed largely to growth in other regions, most notably central and eastern Europe, and does not to a significant degree imply an actual downturn in the quality or scope of what is offered in Switzerland.) Despite the inevitable global shifts in travel, tourism is still the third largest industry in the country and achieved gross revenue of 20 billion Swiss francs in 1998 through hosting a total of 68.1 million overnight stays.[5] While there was some decline in the relative share that tourism contributes toward overall GDP, revenues from tourism both foreign and domestic amounted to 5.3 percent of overall GDP in 1998.[6]

During the ealy 1990s, tourism remained static, with a near "bunker mentality" in the industry as macroeconomic and microeconomic pressures converged. The most significant problems were the high exchange rate of the Swiss franc (which appreciated by more than a third from 1990–1996), European economic stagnation, and increasing global competition. Additionally, operational problems inherent within Swiss hotels—inadequately trained personnel, poor marketing and financial management, and a failure to reinvest in hotel stock—continued to plague both quality and occupancy levels.[7] Only since 1997 have there been modest gains in overnight bookings among both domestic and foreign guests. There are also signs of an imminent upturn in the industry coming from the food service sector.

Both local and federal governments strongly recognize the cultural and economic benefits that arise through tourism and participate in a powerful network of support to private businesses. Infrastructure in the form of transport and communication networks is generally of very high quality throughout the country and provides a direct benefit to the entire hospitality industry; for example, a guest staying in a hotel in Basel may receive a complimentary pass for the public transport system. Additionally, organizations such as Schweiz Tourismus (National Tourism Board), Schweizer Hotel Verein (National Hotel Association), and Gastro-Suisse offer comprehensive support, establish standards, and coordinate recruitment, training, and assistance to individual hospitality businesses.

Hotel Industry Structure

While Swiss hospitality has an image of full-service luxury hotels, the heaviest concentration of stock is in the mid-market range of three- and four-star properties. The five-star, full-service sector however is centered in the financial and international communities of Zürich and Geneva, as well as in resorts such as Zermatt, St. Moritz, and Davos.

In terms of ownership, the industry consists largely of small proprietorships; in 1998, there were only 143 hotels (2.4 percent of total stock) that offered more than one hundred rooms.[8] Exhibit 1 shows that although marketing consortia such as Best Western and The Leading Hotels of the World have reasonable representation in Switzerland, there is little international chain penetration *per se*.

Industry experts have been forecasting consolidation in the European hotel market for a number of years. In view of this, the small, family-owned property is at a clear competitive disadvantage due to the lack of economies of scale and scope in virtually every form, ranging from finance to marketing and production. The impact of this has recently become apparent in the decline in productivity among

Exhibit 1   International Chain Presence in the Swiss Hospitality Market

NAME	NUMBER OF PROPERTIES
Leading Hotels	22
Best Western	72
Top International	87
Marriott	2
Hilton	3
Kempinski	2
Preferred Hotels	4
Mövenpick Hotels	10
Swisshotel	4

these properties, as well as in the disproportionate pricing of the product relative to competitive regions in neighboring countries.

A Multicultural Hospitality Work Force

Switzerland has four distinct regions, each with distinct cultural traits—reflected in language, attitude, and work ethics—that characterize the service product: the strongly industrial, German-speaking North; the Romanche-speaking Grisson in the East, featuring the renowned resorts of Arosa, St. Moritz, and Davos; the Italian-speaking South, with its quasi-Mediterranean lifestyle concentrated around the cities of Lugano, Locarno, and Ascona; and, finally, the French-speaking West, with its truly cosmopolitan lifestyle, which may be observed in Geneva and Lausanne. These diverse cultures blend together and give shape to the final hospitality experience that guests receive.

Furthermore, due to the peculiar nature of the Swiss labor market, large numbers of foreign workers also are present in the work force. Nineteen percent of the overall Swiss population is made up of foreigners, compared with 8.8 percent in Germany and 1.2 percent in Italy.[9] While one out of five residents in Switzerland is of foreign origin, in the hospitality work force the ratio of foreign to Swiss workers is nearly one to one. While labor diversity is often quoted as a generally positive thing in business, the cumulative effect of this wide range of skills, knowledge, and abilities in the Swiss hospitality work force is often problematic. It is difficult to establish consistent standards and service levels in a patchwork of small businesses with limited resources and numerous competing cultures.

There are also signs that structural changes in the labor market are beginning to have serious effects on supply. According to the job index from the Swiss Bureau of Statistics, there was a 25 percent increase in the number of job postings from 1998 to 1999. In the first three months of 2000, there was a 59 percent increase in the number of jobs posted in newspapers for positions in restaurant and hotel service.

Switzerland is no longer considered so attractive by guest workers coming from the traditional source countries of Portugal, Spain, and Austria, due primarily to improved economic conditions in the home countries. One response that is seriously being considered is recruitment from eastern European countries. This raises political issues, because agreements with the European Union (EU) demand that Switzerland give priority to the EU when recruiting abroad. Qualified people looking for work in the EU have also become rare, however. GastroSuisse supports the principle of bilateral agreements between Switzerland and the EU that would ease work permits for EU employees.

Labor Demographics and Labor Market Issues

Employment levels in Switzerland are considerably above the European Union average (at only one-third of the total European unemployment rate) and are higher even than the extremely high levels achieved by the United States through-out the 1990s. This may be attributed to the relative economic strength and produc-tivity levels in many Swiss industries.

With the monthly average wage of CH4,988 equivalent to US$3,325 in 1999, Swiss workers enjoy among the highest wages in the world, as well as high levels of job security, stability, benefits, and a positive work environment. The Swiss labor market, therefore, is attractive to foreign workers who can often greatly benefit from favorable exchange rates when sending part of their wages to their home countries.

Hospitality Labor

In 1998, there were 239,000 workers in hospitality. A great many of these workers are foreign-born employees who work in lower-paid jobs, carrying out duties that native Swiss are generally reluctant to do.

As in many other countries, hospitality jobs in Switzerland suffer the com-mon image problems of long and odd hours, hard work, and low pay—the aver-age monthly salary in hospitality is CH3,475.[10] As Exhibit 2 shows, there is dissatisfaction among Swiss hospitality workers with their wage levels, with the feeling especially high among female workers; 40 percent of the women surveyed stated that their salaries were either "very bad" or "bad" in comparison with other sectors.[11]

Exhibit 3 compares statistics for three categories of employees—unskilled, semi-skilled and managerial—in manufacturing, services, and hospitality. Income for manufacturing and services is generally evenly balanced. Unskilled and semi-skilled workers in manufacturing, however, earn slightly more, and managerial staff in services are better paid due to the inclusion of the high-value sectors of information technology, banking, and insurance. Equally evident, however, is that in all three categories, hospitality workers lag behind the leader by an average of 30 percent, which is largely due to the strong presence of part-time and seasonal workers.[12]

Despite current wage dissatisfaction, there clearly have been positive changes in the entire remuneration package that hospitality service workers have received over the past 25 years. While this indicates an overall improvement in the labor picture from the point of view of the employee, employers have seen declining hourly productivity. As a result, Swiss hourly labor costs rose by almost 12 percent

Exhibit 2 Salary Satisfaction

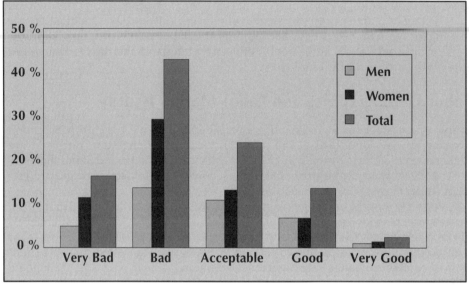

Source: Manfred Ritschard, HSW, Lucerne, 1999.

Exhibit 3 Relative Employee Income

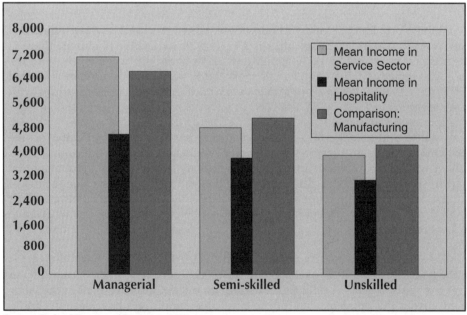

Source: Federal Bureau of Statistics, 1996.

from 1990–1995, compared to six percent increases in France and Austria. Italy, on the other hand, actually reduced the labor portion of its production costs.

Political and Legal Considerations

Although Switzerland is centrally located in Europe, its political orientation has historically been neutral and isolationist. For example, Switzerland is still not a member of the United Nations, as it is believed that membership would threaten its traditional neutrality. With the integration of the European Union trading bloc becoming a reality in all surrounding countries, Switzerland is reassessing its place in Europe and revising both its domestic and foreign policy.

European Political Integration

Seven bilateral trade agreements with the EU were signed in 2000, and they will fundamentally affect the increasing liberalization of the movement of people, research, agriculture, technical barriers to trade, government purchasing, and air and road transport.[13] The EU issue has become a strongly polarized political debate, with membership seen as both a threat and a boost to the current standard of living. Conservatives are calling for additional measures to protect the country from foreign influences, while liberals are turning toward the EU in the hope that economic and political integration will bring long-term benefits and growth. A yes or no to Europe will have significant long-term influence on the flow of labor—both inbound and outbound—and on the end result of what visitors experience.

Legal Aspects of Swiss Hospitality Labor

The Swiss labor market, in common with other European countries, is highly structured, with systematic practices determined by detailed labor laws. Labor practice in all Swiss industries is strongly regulated through the national labor law (*Obligationsrecht*), and hospitality labor has its own branch of labor laws called the *Landes-Gesamtarbeitsvertrag (L-GAV)*. Hospitality labor specifically enjoys the support of three umbrella organizations: the National Tourism Board; Gastro-Suisse, which has 20,000 members and includes 80 percent of all catering outlets; and the Swiss Hotel Association, with 3,685 members. These organizations offer a comprehensive set of support services ranging from recruiting apprentices from the hotel schools to training, job information, and government lobbying.

A unique characteristic of Swiss labor practice is the strongly decentralized nature of government, whereby each of the 26 cantons or districts has its own jurisdiction over labor and other issues. Organizations such as Schweiz Tourismus and GastroSuisse therefore have a wide network of offices that adapt their services to the idiosyncrasies of individual cantons.

Swiss labor practice in hospitality is spelled out in the *L-GAV*, which sets clear parameters for labor practices nationally in order to achieve fairness and stability in the labor market. The labor laws are updated every four years to make adjustments in wages and benefits. The basic labor issues of wages, salaries, work hours, pensions, vacations, maternity leave, insurance, and deductions are systematically organized on the national level and provide a basis from which employees can negotiate individually. Although there are fierce negotiations, strikes and labor actions—for example, strikes and boycotts—are virtually unheard of.

Cultural Distinctions and Societal Work Values

The industry found itself in a crisis in terms of both service quality and productivity during the late 1980s and early 1990s. The crisis was compounded by the high exchange rate of the Swiss franc and by the stagnation of the Swiss economy, which had virtually zero growth from 1991–1996. Furthermore, much of this decline in productivity was passed onto customers in the form of higher prices, this during a time of already dwindling demand. While the national Consumer Price Index rose by roughly four percent during those five years, hotels increased their prices on average by 11 percent.

Swiss Quality

Swiss goods and services continue to enjoy a remarkable reputation for quality. While consistent, efficient management has been a formula for success in the past, global competition demands that industry practice also encompass innovation and flexibility and be responsive to change. Swiss management has gained a reputation over the years for being somewhat military in work practices—especially in the area of human resource management. Historically, this was due to the fact that in many companies, successful business careers were often dependent upon advancement as an officer in the Swiss army. Many organizations have been making strenuous attempts to shed this image in recent years.[14]

The increasingly standardized expectations by growing numbers of international guests often give rise to service problems when providers engage in strongly local practice and are restrained by local laws and traditional customs. In Switzerland, retail opening hours, for example, might appear to a visitor to be a random matter, with a variety of lunchtime and evening schedules posted from one town to the next.

Research has shown that the natural environment and infrastructure are clear tourism industry strengths, while the price-value relationship, service friendliness, and a spirit of innovation achieve average-to-weak ratings.[15] In the wake of the problems of the early 1990s, there is recognition of a need for change toward more professional management, including sound and comprehensive marketing, financial, and human resource practices. The challenge to hospitality managers is to develop service quality that merits the Swiss label and focuses on the "soft" side of the service encounter, especially in terms of genuine warmth of welcome and flexibility in meeting guest needs.

Education and Technical Skills

Like the legal system, national education is a decentralized matter, with each of the cantons having considerable freedom in formulating its own public-education mix of subjects. Swiss education emphasizes developing skills that are useful for business, management, and operations. In Zürich, for example, English, which is not an official national language, is now being taught as a standard subject in first grade, while French, which is the second official national language in that canton, is introduced only in grade five. This decision is based on the belief that an overall strength in English will bring additional long-term advantages to the Swiss labor market and, hence, to industry.

In the Swiss system, vocational and business education involve apprenticeship. In hospitality, as in other industries, students undertake industry training for a period of at least one year, and their performance at a training job is evaluated as an integral part of their studies. This practice brings a number of benefits to the trainee, the school, and the industry. Apprentices experience a smoother transition between school and work experience, whereby learning and the following life in the workplace become fully integrated. Employers benefit by being provided with a focused and publicly funded form of recruitment; society as a whole benefits when education and industry practice stay consistently aligned.

Labor Relations within the HR Context

While labor practices in Switzerland are well-structured, the fragmented nature of the hospitality industry shows some significant contrasts. Due to the relatively small scale of Swiss hospitality firms, labor practice is less formal and structured than might be found in large chain operations in other parts of the world. Formal job analyses and job descriptions are the exception rather than the rule. However, this is not necessarily a deficiency. Small operations often are able to use informal communication channels in a remarkably flexible and efficient way, which may be more effective than the systematic mapping out of labor flow that is commonly found in formal job analyses.

Recruitment and Selection

Recruitment and selection in hospitality are both systematic and random. Systematic recruitment takes place through the collaboration between hotels and the various hotel schools that place their students in apprenticeships. Random recruitment occurs primarily when single properties recruit workers from virtually any source according to the urgency of need. Vacancies are posted in professional journals such as the *Hotel Review,* as well as on the various Web sites of hotels and public organizations.

The selection process can range from being very simple to highly complex. Operational workers in back-of-the-house positions are often hired without a thorough screening, depending on the urgency of the situation, while management positions involve a more formal and systematic selection process.

Evaluation, Training, and Development

According to one hospitality consultancy, "The long-term benefits to a business through systematic training substantially outweigh the costs incurred."[16] This is illustrated by the success of several properties in being able to increase revenues and profits despite the downturn in the industry during the early 1990s. Yet, despite numerous examples that endorse the case for training, systematic training

Exhibit 4   The Distribution of Work among Men and Women

MAIN ACTIVITY	MEN	WOMEN
Direct Sales	31.3	68.7
Administration	34.0	66.0
Customer Service	32.1	67.9
Marketing	47.3	52.7
Team Leaders	47.4	52.7
Executive/Strategic Decisions	71.6	28.4
Training, Personnel	45.5	54.5
Accounting	40.9	59.1
Production, Kitchen, Service	45.9	54.1

Source: M. Ritschard, *Lohn un Qualifikation im Tourismus* (Lucerne, Switzerland: Fachhochschule Zentralschweiz, 1999).

programs are not the norm in Swiss hospitality. Many properties are unable to dedicate the required resources, fail to recognize the link between training and service quality, and are reluctant to spend money on training workers who are unlikely to stay with the organization beyond a single season. Therefore, consistent quality standards do not become embedded in the organizational culture, guests are less likely to return, and resources remain scarce. This is a pattern by no means limited to small, family-owned properties; it applies across the board. There are some notable exceptions: the Victoria Jungfrau Hotel in Interlaken and the Palace Hotel in Lucerne, as well as the famed Il-Giardino in Ascona. These, among others, are luxury properties that are able to provide consistent, innovative, world-class service.

Women in Hospitality

The gender issue is strongly present in the Swiss hospitality labor market. Women play a key role in providing service in guest contact situations such as catering, front desk, telephone, and sales. As seen in Exhibit 4, there is a dramatic decline in the percentage of women as one moves up the organization to the executive and strategic decision-making levels. In common with the service sector in many other economies, women hold the great majority of part-time jobs in the industry.[17]

Looking Ahead

Industry experts are optimistic that the overall positive economic outlook will also reach the hospitality industry. An anticipated increase in arrivals of four percent, slightly above the European average, is projected for the coming decade. The long-term outcome of the crisis of the mid-1980s and early 1990s is likely to have provided an awakening and triggered change toward a more competitive stance in the form of higher productivity through better-trained workers and a more innovative range of guest products. Whatever the eventual outcome, however, it is clear that human resource managers in Swiss hotels will find the next decade very challenging.

In the increasingly competitive world order, there are many issues that human resource managers will have to face if the Swiss hotel industry is to regain the mantle of leadership and innovation in hotel best practices. Not least among these issues is the quality of service provided by front-line employees. Managers must ensure that guests feel welcomed, are convinced that they receive good value for their money, and make plans to return. Sound human resource practices in recruitment, selection, training, and retention of key personnel are also essential to long-term viability. The International Hotel and Restaurant Association, in their recent think tanks on organizational challenges for the twenty-first century, stressed the need for hotel corporations to develop flexible strategies when attempting to attract the increasingly diverse work force of tomorrow. The industry needs to change its predominantly male mindset and image, become more sensitive to the needs of ethnic minorities and women, and provide the quality of work and life experiences demanded by the current generation of 20–30 year olds.[18] The Swiss hotel industry may see more consolidation as the smaller and older hotel stock is closed down or, in some cases, taken over and converted to new operations.

The challenge for the future is to ensure—through good human resource practices—that employees are motivated and professional, evidencing a sensible mix of good technical and social skills. Such skills will help to develop a sense of loyalty in the customer that extends both to the individual establishment and to the region or country as a whole.

Endnotes

1. L. Gaulis and R. Creux, *Swiss Hotel Pioneers* (Paudex, Switzerland: Editions de Fontainemore, 1976), p. 12.

2. Gaulis and Creux, p. 37.

3. KATAG Lucerne, Research and Consultancy for Hospitality, 1999.

4. *Tourism Market Trends* (Madrid: World Tourism Organization, 1999).

5. Federal Bureau of Statistics (Bundesamt für Statistik), 1998.

6. Federal Bureau of Statistics, 1999.

7. M. Marvel and C. Johnson, "A crisis of currency or creativity? Problems and prospects for the Swiss hospitality industry," *The International Journal of Hospitality Management* 16, no. 3 (1997): 279–288.

8. Swiss Tourism Board, 1998.

9. Federal Bureau of Statistics, 1998.

10. KATAG Lucerne.

11. Manfred Ritschard, *Lohn und Qualifikation im Tourismus* (Lucerne, Switzerland: Fachhochchule Zentralschweiz, 1999).

12. KATAG Lucerne.

13. *Eurocity Survey 1999* (London: Pannell Kerr Forster, 1999), p. 83.

14. Sheila M. Puffer, *Management Across Cultures: Insights from Fiction and Practice* (Malden, Mass.: Blackwell Publishers, 1996), p. 263.

15. *Tourism Industry Report 1996* (Switzerland: United Bank of Switzerland Economic Research, 1996), p. 13.

16. MaederZanetti & Partner, Lucerne, Switzerland, 1999.

17. Ritschard.

18. "Visioning the Future," International Hotel and Restaurant Association, Holland, 1999.

 # Discussion Questions

1. What recruitment strategies could Swiss hotel managers adopt in order to compete successfully in the labor market against firms in other industries that offer substantially higher wages and benefits?

2. How can Swiss hotel managers maintain the unique Swiss characteristic of their properties while at the same time aligning their products with developing customer trends in the global market?

3. What measures could a luxury resort hotel in the mountain regions of Switzerland take in order to attract qualified seasonal staff and ensure that the quality of service is maintained to the level expected by the guest?

4. How could Swiss hotels make themselves appear more "employee-friendly" to older employees and mothers who are returning to employment?

 # Internet Sites

For more information, visit the following Internet sites. Remember that Internet addresses can change without notice.

DCT International Hotel and
Business Management School
http://www.hotelschool.ch/

Ecole Hôtelière de Lausanne
(English, French)
http://www.ehl.ch/

Federal Statistical Office
(English, French, German)
http://www.statistik.admin.ch/
eindex.htm

GastroLine (German)
http://www.union-helvetia.ch/
main_set.htm

GastroSuisse (German, French, Italian)
http://www.gastrosuisse.ch

hotel+tourismus revue (German)
http://www.htr.ch/

Mövenpick Group (English, German)
http://www.moevenpick.
ch/e/default.htm

Research Institute for
Leisure and Tourism
http://www.cx.unibe.ch/fif (German)
http://www.cx.unibe.ch/fif/institut/
english.htm (English)

Swiss Hotel Association
(English, French, German)
http://www.swisshotels.ch/
e/default.htm

Case Study

A Place with a Heart

"The building and facilities, no matter how unique in character, can all be copied and mean nothing to a guest if the service is off. The only way for a restaurant or hotel to survive and grow is by continuously developing its staff." So says Robert Hauser, the owner of Waldheim Hotel. The property, which might best be called a country inn and restaurant, is situated on the side of a highway in a busy industrial region just 18 kilometers southeast of the city of Basel. As a graduate of a nearby hotel school, Hauser has a lengthy bond to the Waldheim property. He was assistant manager for six years, worked as GM for six more years, and recently acquired ownership of the company. Being relatively young, well-trained, and experienced, he places the performance and development of his staff at the center of his decision making.

Hauser describes his restaurant's product as *Erlebnisgastronomie*—experiential gastronomy—a concept that aims to integrate service, environment, and menu items into a cohesive experience of tastes, sights, textures, and sounds. In contrast to the strongly industrial character of the surrounding region, the Waldheim experience is an answer to a very real need by guests to get away from the harsh world of industry.

The building dates to 1742 and is a registered national landmark with quintessentially Swiss characteristics. The place stands out through its distinctive steep-slanting red tile roof, flags in front, painted emblems lining the edges of arched ceilings, wooden carvings of carts and cows, antique pictures, lamps, ornaments, and various memorabilia from the more recent era of rustic country life. By Swiss standards, it is a very large property with six dining rooms, the largest one serving 100 covers. Above the dining rooms, 28 bedrooms are spread out over three floors; however, many of these rooms are old and in need of renovation. Outside is a large garden restaurant with 300 seats and a well with a small pond. Additionally, there is a large parking lot and a playground. The property has its own bus and tram stop in front.

Hauser believes in total quality management as a means of differentiating his property through service quality, and he invests resources for training and staff development in quantities that are above the norm for the industry. Staff are encouraged to attend external courses of their choice for three days each year, and the company invests, on average, CH1,800 per worker per year in training and development. External consultants analyze the service delivery process and conduct training seminars.

One day per month there is a formal team meeting for each department. The staff has formulated its own "Ten Points of Quality" standard, of which the final point is: *All female guests receive a rose when leaving the property. Saying good-bye should have the same genuine friendliness as the original greeting: "Thank you very much for your visit!"* Besides the ten quality standards, there are six points of conduct determined by management that guide staff performance. All employees are thoroughly familiar with these points, and applicants receive them by mail before any interview is scheduled.

Six Points of Conduct

1. The guest is at the center of all of our actions. All staff members are hosts who need to project an attitude of genuine warmth and friendliness to all guests at all times.

2. We only employ cheerful, flexible, and capable staff members who like to work. Trust, friendship, and mutual understanding are the basis of our teamwork.

3. All staff members make decisions from the point of view of the guest and never lose sight of his or her well-being.

4. The success of the business is the direct result of the work of the staff. Through their personal commitment, staff members can directly influence and then also benefit from the success that the business has.

5. All staff members use their skills and abilities to develop better solutions. We require active participation in making improvements. Even things that are very good can be improved upon.

6. Serving comes before earning. The better we serve our guests, the greater also will be the benefits that we receive in return. All employees need to understand that performance is what counts, and that you can count on returns stemming from good performance.

As a result, service is detailed, consistent, and genuine. All guests are called by name whenever possible. Names are read off credit cards and the payee is thanked by name when signing. When a guest asks for a phonebook, it is brought along with a slip of paper and a pencil. All staff members announce themselves by name and carry their own business cards. In a place that positions itself as authentically Swiss, language is critical for guest contact positions; therefore, all telephone calls—as well as all service in the restaurant and banquet rooms—are carried out in native Swiss German.

Due to the overall success of the property, staff members receive wages and benefits that are above average. The basis for all salary decisions is the Swiss standard set by GastroSuisse, the umbrella organization for hospitality workers, yet employees are able to negotiate their own compensation package based on the following criteria:

- The position
- Performance and conduct
- Qualifications
- Work experience
- Age and tenure on the job
- Conditions in the labor market

Indirect rewards in the form of a pleasant and positive work environment also play an important role in the life of the property and are characterized as:

- Accurate and open information regarding the workplace
- Regular and systematic training for all employees
- An interesting/motivating workplace
- Loyalty between co-workers and supervisors
- High-quality food

Discussion Questions

1. What are the critical success factors for the Waldheim property? List them in order of importance.

2. Which aspects of human resource management at the Waldheim Hotel are transferable to similar properties in other regions? Which are not?

3. What points might you add to the "Six Points of Conduct"? Are any of the current points unnecessary?

4. From a management point of view, discuss the value in having employees design quality standards for service products.

Chapter 19 Outline

Competencies

19

Human Resource Management in Turkey

Teoman Alemdar

Teoman Alemdar is the chairman of the Tourism and Hotel Management Department and the Tourism and Hotel Services Department in the School of Tourism and Hotel Management, Bilkent University. He oversaw the construction phase and grand opening of a five-star hotel in Alanya, a city in the Antalya province of Turkey, and managed the hotel for two years before joining Bilkent University in 1991. His other hospitality experience includes jobs with the Maçka Hotel and Etap İstanbul in İstanbul and, in the United States, jobs with Holiday Inn, ITT Sheraton, and Don Cesar Beach Resort. He is a graduate of Florida International University's School of Hospitality Management.

"THE GATEWAY BETWEEN EUROPE AND ASIA"; "the crossroads of civilization"; these and similar phrases are typically applied to Turkey, and no wonder. Turkey is located where three continents making up the Old World—Asia, Africa, and Europe—come closest to each other: The Asia Minor.

Turkey has also been called "the cradle of civilization." Çatalhöyük, a Neolithic city thought to be one of the world's first, dates back to 6,500 B.C. From the days of Çatalhöyük up to the present, Turkey boasts a rich culture that has made a lasting impression on modern civilization. Hattis, Hittites, Phrygians, Urartians, Lycians, Lydians, Ionians, Persians, Macedonians, Romans, Byzantines, Seljuks, and Ottomans have all made important contributions to Turkish history.

Turkey has a total area of 780,580 square kilometers. The main area of Turkey, Anatolia, is in Asia between the Mediterranean and Black Seas (see Exhibit 1). Thrace, the European region of the country, lies to the northwest of the Sea of Marmara and makes up just three percent of the country's territory. The country is bordered in the east by Georgia, Armenia, and Iran, and in the south by Iraq, Syria, and the Mediterranean Sea. The Aegean Sea, Greece, and Bulgaria are to the west, and the Black Sea forms the northern border. Almost surrounded by seas, Turkey's coastline is more than 8,333 kilometers long. İstanbul is the largest city in Turkey; Ankara is the capital.

Exhibit 1   Map of Turkey

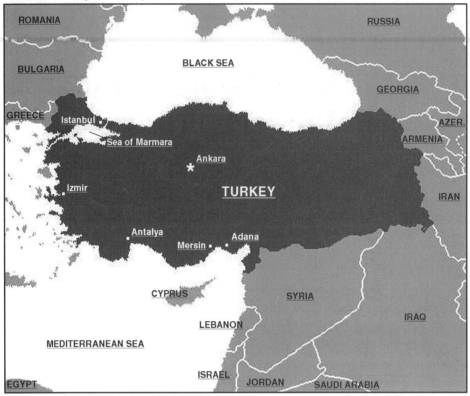

Turkey is a paradise of sun, sea, mountains, and lakes that offers tourists a complete change from the routine of everyday life. It enjoys a variety of climates, from the temperate climate of the Black Sea region, to the continental climate of the interior, to the Mediterranean climate of the Aegean and Mediterranean coastal regions.

In this chapter, we will take a brief look at Turkey's economy in general and the Turkish tourism industry in particular. We will explore human resource issues in Turkey, including demographics, cultural influences on the Turkish work force, and the status of working women in Turkey. Next we will discuss expatriate managers, in Turkish companies as well as international companies, and identify the biggest difference between Turkish and international corporate cultures. The chapter concludes with a glimpse of near-future trends for the country.

Turkey: A Brief Overview

Turkey has been a secular and democratic republic since 1923. The Republic of Turkey is based on a pluralistic and parliamentary system, where human rights are protected by law. The 550-member National Assembly is elected by popular vote.

The nation is governed by the Council of Ministers, which is headed by the prime minister, who represents the majority party or coalition in the assembly; when necessary, the prime minister consults with Turkey's president. The president is chosen by the assembly and serves a seven-year term. Assembly members serve five-year terms.

Turkey is a founding member of the United Nations, the Organization for Economic Co-Operation and Development, and the Black Sea Economic Cooperation Organization, and is a member of:

- NATO (North Atlantic Treaty Organization)
- GATT (General Agreement on Tariffs and Trade)
- WTO (World Trade Organization)
- IMF (International Monetary Fund)
- UNESCO (United Nations Educational, Scientific and Cultural Organization)
- FAO (Food and Agriculture Organization of the United Nations)
- INTERPOL (International Criminal Police Organization)
- IDB (Islamic Development Bank)
- The European Council
- The European Parliament

Turkey is also an associate member of the European Union.

Although 98 percent of its population is Muslim, Turkey also has citizens who practice the Jewish, Catholic, Orthodox, Protestant, and Gregorian faiths. State and religious affairs are considered two separate domains. People enjoy the right and freedom to worship according to the faith of their choice.

The political structure of Turkey is complex, with several political parties on the right and left wings and liberals in between. The political parties and their aims and ambitions are considered reasonable by a majority of the public, with one exception; a religion-based right-wing party that seeks to rebuild the Turkish Republic under Islamic rules. The supporters of this party have also invested in tourism, building and operating a few hotels where Islamic rules are carried out, such as no alcoholic drinks on the premises and separate beaches for men and women.

The Turkish Economy

Turkey has achieved a remarkable transformation from an inward-looking economy based on import substitution—that is, creating Turkish substitutes for imported essentials—to an outward-looking economy that is integrated with the rest of the world in almost all sectors.

The government has a great deal of influence over the Turkish economy and owns several important industries, such as the railroad industry (run by the Turkish Republic State Railways). The government also operates four national radio networks and five television channels. Five-Year Development Plans are prepared by the State Planning Organization and are put in effect when a bill is passed by the

National Assembly. These Five-Year Development Plans drive the public sector and provide guidelines for the private sector.

Turkey is among the world's leaders in the production of chromium ore, extracting 1.7 million metric tons in 1996.[1] Principal exports are textiles, iron and steel, dried fruits, leather garments, tobacco, and petroleum products. Chief imports are machinery, crude petroleum, transportation vehicles, and chemical products. The government's liberalization of foreign trade policies played an important role in transforming Turkey from an agricultural commodities exporter, trading mainly with its neighbors, to a worldwide trader, exporting mainly industrial goods. The volume of trade, exports plus imports, rose from $11 billion in 1980—15 percent of the Gross National Product (GNP)—to $68 billion in 1996 (40 percent of GNP). Turkey has become one of the seven countries in the Organization for Economic Co-Operation and Development that has the least number of restrictions on capital account transactions.

Similar to most other countries in the world, the economic policies of all Turkish governments have been based on a **mixed-economy system,** but it is natural that over the years successive governments have adopted varying economic policies, due to the changing economic conditions at home and in the rest of the world. However, most Turkish administrations have shared a basic aim: increase the market share of Turkey's private sector and reduce the public sector's commercial ventures in the Turkish economy.

Tourism in Turkey

Turkey has experienced major improvements in its tourism industry, in part due to efforts by the Turkish government. Turkey's Ministry of Tourism was established by Law No. 265 in 1963. This was followed by the Travel Agencies and Union of Travel Agencies Law No. 1618, put in effect on September 29, 1972. The Tourism Encouragement Frame Decree was passed by the National Assembly in 1980. Finally, the Tourism Encouragement Law No. 2634 was passed on March 12, 1982.

However, prior to 1985, tourism growth stayed below expectations despite these legal changes. In 1985, the government benchmarked other leading countries' tourism performances and identified major deficiencies with Turkey's tourism effort. The government then introduced monetary incentives such as grants and allowances for tourism businesses, following the example of countries that had implemented similar incentives. Turkey has enjoyed steady progress and a great deal of achievement in the tourism industry since these and other tourism-friendly measures were undertaken. In fact, Turkey's tremendous tourism success has drawn notice in the international arena, because so many countries are interested in the positive economic impact that can be created by foreign visitors. International tourism is now a big business in Turkey; it generated approximately $7 billion in foreign travel receipts in 1997, which is almost 26 percent of Turkey's Foreign Exchange and Export revenues.

The basic concept of 1982's Tourism Encouragement Law was to build up a new, modern tourist industry with an emphasis on the lodging sector. Under this law, hospitality properties that conform to the terms and regulations of the law are given licenses by the Turkish government. Properties that do not meet these standards remain under the control of local authorities, such as municipalities. Currently, Turkey has 3,319 hotels and **holiday villages** licensed by the Ministry of Tourism, with a 563,340-bed capacity; 7,975 hotels are under the control of municipalities, with a total capacity of 344,551 beds. The area with the greatest density of lodging properties lies from Balikesir province, throughout the coastal strip of the Aegean and Mediterranean shores, to the Mersin province. The Antalya province has been considered the capital of Turkey's tourism industry. The Kemer and Belek regions are the prime resort development locations in Antalya, with properly designed, environmentally sound, and highly popular resorts. There is a 140,000-bed capacity in Antalya province alone.

İstanbul, a world city of fascinating museums, churches, palaces, mosques, bazaars, and sights of inexhaustible natural beauty, is considered the pearl of Turkey's tourism industry. Most of the national and international five-star deluxe hotels, the majority of Turkey's travel agencies, and the headquarters of many national and private airline companies are found in İstanbul.

In order to ease tourist pressure on the coastal areas of the country, Turkey's tourism industry has adapted diversification policies. Mountaineering, scuba diving, hiking, golfing, horseback riding, winter holidays and sports, cultural and other tours, spas, meetings and conferences, and incentive travel have been promoted in order to better utilize the wide range of Turkey's diverse resources.

In 1998, a total of 9,752,697 foreign tourists visited Turkey (see Exhibit 2), mostly for holiday purposes (56 percent), followed by cultural reasons (11 percent), business (6 percent), and shopping (6 percent). Turkey enjoyed tremendous progress in the 1990s in tourism, but, for any country in the world, it is not realistic to expect tourism trends to increase all the time, because competition in the international tourism market is intense. Economic crises and social unrest in Asia, devaluation of currencies, reduction of value-added taxes and airport taxes in competitor countries, the revitalization of the Croatian and Egyptian hospitality industries, the financial crisis in Russia, uncertainties concerning Euromoney, and acts of terrorism—all have affected Turkey's tourism industry in recent years. From January to October of 1998, total visitor arrivals to Turkey decreased 1.2 percent over the same period in 1997. Though it was a minor drop, the government is considering adopting measures to head off further declines.

Human Resource Issues

In the following sections, we will discuss several human resource issues:

- Labor demographics
- Labor market issues
- Cultural factors
- Recruitment and selection practices
- Training and development practices
- Performance evaluation practices
- Working women in Turkey

Exhibit 2   Foreign Arrivals by Nationalities

Nationality	1998
Germany	2,233,740
CIS	1,311,357
U.K.	996,512
Romania	505,766
USA	439,885
France	436,932
Netherlands	328,002
Iran	304,924
Italy	259,483
Bulgaria	244,741
Israel	238,298
Austria	235,120
Sweden	156,116
Others	2,061,821
Total	**9,752,697**

Source: Ministry of Tourism.

Exhibit 3   Profile of Tourism Personnel

Sex	Accommodation	Restaurants	Travel Agencies
Male	81%	93%	64%
Female	19%	7%	36%
Total	100%	100%	100%

Source: 1993 Manpower Survey of the Tourism Industry by the Ministry of Tourism and the International Labour Organization.

Labor Demographics and Labor Market Issues

The population of Turkey is estimated to be around 65,311,000 by Turkey's State Institute of Statistics (SIS).[2] According to the Women's Indicators and Statistics of SIS, women make up almost half of the population (49.5 percent). However, this percentage does not hold true in the hospitality workplace. The staffs of hotels, restaurants, and travel agencies are still dominated by men (see Exhibit 3).

The most noteworthy fact in the Percentage of Turkey's Population by Age Group statistics is that 55.6 percent of the population is under the age of 25 (see Exhibit 4), making Turkey a country dominated by the young. Having such a large

Exhibit 4   Percentage of Turkey's Population by Age Group

Age Group	Percentage
0–24	55.6
25–44	27.0
45–64	13.5
65 +	3.8
Unknown	.10
Total	100.00

Source: State Institute of Statistics, 1990.

percentage of the country's population in this age group puts a tremendous strain on Turkey's educational system. It will also be difficult to find jobs for all of these people when their schooling is finished.

Turkish Labor Law No. 1475 was put in effect on August 25, 1971. It was designed to secure the working conditions of all employees, as well as give employers legal recourse when worker abuses take place. The law dictates that an employee's normal working day is 7.5 hours. Article No. 35 of the law sets an employee's daily overtime at a maximum of three hours, and an employee cannot lawfully have more than 90 overtime days in a year. Overtime pay is one and a half times the regular hourly wage; all work on public holidays is considered overtime. Despite Labor Law No. 1475, many hotel companies—most of them in the resort cities along Turkey's Aegean and Mediterranean coasts—force employees to work ten to twelve hours per day, six days a week, with no overtime pay.

All employees have the right to join a union but they don't have to. Turkish employers must have a good reason to fire an employee; if they do not have a good reason and they fire an employee anyway, they must, by law, compensate the employee by paying him or her what amounts to a "separation fee." Because of these and other worker-friendly policies passed by the government in the past decade, many labor organizations have declined almost to the point of extinction.

There are three social security systems for Turkey's working citizens: Emekli Sandiği (ES)—the social security system for government officials; Sosyal Sigortalar Kurumu (SSK)—the social security system for public- and private-sector employees; and Bağ-Kur (BK)—the social security system for small business owners. These systems are facing the prospect of reorganization and possible consolidation by the Turkish government under a new umbrella institution. All employers are obliged to register all of their employees with the SSK and to pay part of the employer's social-security contribution fee in the names of their employees. The SSK, which covers almost all employees working in the tourism industry, has 5,500,000 registered employees. Based on the 1995 census, the SIS surveys show that 460,000 individuals are directly employed by the hotel and restaurant industries. Today, almost 2.5 million people in Turkey make their living directly or indirectly, or earn at least a part of their income, from the tourism industry.

Turkey's tourism industry is heavily dependent on Turkish employees who can properly speak such foreign languages as English, German, French, Italian, Spanish, Russian, and Arabic. The most crucial requirement for a worker to be employed by a tourist company in Turkey is his ability to communicate in at least one of the languages spoken by that company's major tourist groups. A person who speaks German fluently has a better chance to get a job offer from a resort property on Turkey's Mediterranean coast than a new Vocational School of Tourism graduate who has a basic knowledge of the hotel and restaurant business but can't speak German. English is mostly preferred in large metropolitan cities where international hotel companies are located, such as İstanbul, Ankara, and İzmir, and on the Aegean coast of Turkey, where some of the resort hotels and holiday villages are linked to British tour operators. The tendency of Turkish hospitality companies is to pass over university graduates who only speak Turkish to recruit less educated people who are fluent in a foreign language.

Because of the seasonal nature of most resort jobs, university graduates also tend to be passed over by hotel companies operating in the Aegean and Mediterranean resort areas. For these resort properties, the tourist season lasts around seven to eight months, starting in the middle of March and going until the beginning of November. Therefore, these properties employ seasonal staff and only keep necessary personnel, such as top management staff and security and engineering department personnel, during the winter season when the resorts are closed down. Even though the top managers of these resorts prefer to work with graduates of tourism and hotel management schools, they hesitate to recruit them because they can only offer seasonal jobs with no job security and low salaries.

Foreign tour operators offer low package tour rates to their clients traveling to Turkey, which forces hotel companies in Turkey to employ mostly low-cost personnel in order to make some profit at the end of the season. Market factors weaken the bargaining power of individual employees to increase their wages. Unions are very much concerned with these problems and attempt to establish themselves in such an environment. Although it would seem that hotels and resorts in the Aegean and Mediterranean regions would be the best places for unions to increase their numbers and therefore augment their power, two of the leading labor confederations—Türk-İş' TOLEYİS (which began in 1977), with 37,000 members, and DİSK's OLEYİS (started in 1947), with 25,000 members—represent employees working in metropolitan destinations such as İstanbul, Ankara, and İzmir.

In many cases, educational preparation in the tourism field is necessary to enable personnel to perform the duties required of them. However, many hotels and restaurants find themselves obliged to fill entry-level positions with individuals who barely meet the job specifications, and pay them the minimum wage, which is currently the equivalent of $200 per month (including taxes). This kind of hiring leads to high turnover rates and quality problems regarding service levels—major headaches for hospitality human resource departments. With high turnover, human resource departments struggle to train employees and improve their job performance, only to lose them and have to start over with newly hired employees.

Currently, Turkey has 48 universities offering 12 bachelor's and 36 associate programs leading to degrees in the field of tourism and hotel management. As you

Exhibit 5   Distribution of Personnel According to Level of Formal Education

Level of Education	Accommodation	Restaurants	Travel Agencies
None	1%	2%	1%
Primary	41%	49%	10%
Secondary	16%	22%	6%
High School	31%	22%	46%
University	11%	5%	37%
Total	100%	100%	100%

Source: 1993 Manpower Survey of the Tourism Industry by the Ministry of Tourism and the International Labour Organization.

can see from Exhibit 5, primary school and high school graduates form most of the lodging and restaurant personnel, while travel agencies have more high school and university graduates on their staffs. A graduate of a primary education program can attend a vocational high school of tourism where concentrated practical training is combined with theoretical knowledge. The Ministry of Tourism also contributes to tourism education by owning and operating 12 **TUREM schools** ("TUREM" stands for "Tourism Education Center"). These schools—which are also operating, three-star hotels—educate and train almost 1,000 young people each year.

In addition to tourism educational programs run by Turkish universities, educational programs from the American Hotel & Motel Association of the United States and the City & Guilds organization from the United Kingdom are also available for many young people seeking entry-level positions with hotels, airlines, and travel agencies. Turkish hotel companies such as Bilkent Holding Company and Eresin Corporation also offer educational services to their employees.

Cultural Factors

As mentioned earlier, most Turks are Muslim and follow the rules of Islam. This affects the working relationship between Turkish citizens and the international companies they work for. For example, most of the Turkish people would like to visit mosques at noon on Friday—the holy day of the week—to pray. As a result, many companies have built their own **masjid**—a small temple—on their premises for the convenience of their employees. The thinking of these companies is that it is better from an efficiency standpoint to provide a place for employees to pray at work than to have them leave the premises every Friday to go to an off-site temple.

Today, approximately 18 percent of women in Turkey wear head scarves as a proof of their Islamic belief and never take them off, at home or at work. This creates a problem in some situations, and many hospitality companies avoid employing women from this segment of society.

There are two major religious holidays on the Islamic calendar each year: Ramadan and the Greater Bairam. Ramadan is the ninth month of the Muslim calendar, during which Muslims observe the Fast of Ramadan; throughout the month they fast during the day and in the evening eat small meals and visit with friends and family. It is a time of worship and contemplation, a time to strengthen family and community ties.The Greater Bairam is a feast that commemorates Abraham's sacrifice of Isaac. Most Turkish companies are closed during these holidays; however, hotels and restaurants are an exception, due to the nature of their businesses.

Islam bans the consumption of pork and wine. Pork has never been part of any dishes in Turkish cuisine, and pig-breeding has never been carried out by Turks. You should never suggest pork to a Turk. However, Turks do consume wine, which is in keeping with the history of their mainland, Anatolia, where wine was made for the first time in the world, at the time of the Hattian culture during the Bronze Age and during the succeeding Hittite Empire.

Tasty food of good quality is an important part of the Turkish culture. A decent breakfast with tea, a hearty lunch, afternoon tea or coffee time, and a proper dinner are all part of daily work life. At all Turkish hotels, resorts, and holiday villages, half-hour breakfast, lunch, and dinner breaks are customary for employees, with 15 minutes for tea time in the afternoon, and all of the food and beverages employees consume are provided free of charge by their employers. This adds up to an appreciable expense, considering that a mid-size hotel, for example, might have 50 to 100 employees.

Turks are creative, dedicated, hard workers and firm believers in group solidarity. Turks expect to be individually appreciated but motivated as part of a group. The group will recognize the authority of its supervisor if the person in charge is older than the group members he oversees, has more work experience, or is better educated than the employees in the group. While the performance of employees working for the government is typically low, employees in the better-managed private sector reach higher efficiency rates.

One should never question the nationalistic feelings of Turks; they are aggressively proud of their country. Also, the act of marriage is regarded as highly sacred by Turkish society.

As part of their custom, Turks are keen to help out people and are well known for the hospitality they show visitors to their homes. The hospitality of the Turkish people is also displayed at the companies where they work, contributing to the quality of services rendered. In the last few years, Turkish companies such as Koç and Sabanci Holdings have won worldwide quality awards.

Recruitment and Selection Practices

The tourism and hospitality industries are people-intensive and encompass a wide range of services. Therefore, they employ labor from a diverse spread of occupations. The basic recruiting principle, of course, is to select the right person for the right job. Recruitment has long been considered one of the major human resource issues in Turkey, because of the nepotism that is prevalent throughout the country.

Although the National Recruitment Agency for Workers is the official source for getting a job in Turkey, it is not preferred by most unemployed citizens, due to its low placement rate. But it may begin receiving more attention from the public because of the introduction of the new social security law passed by the National Assembly on August 24, 1999, granting unemployed citizens the right to receive unemployment pay, backed by the unemployment insurance guarantee—both of which involve the agency.

Currently, the tourism and hospitality industries depend on teenagers to fill most front-line positions. Vocational high schools of tourism, vocational schools of tourism, and tourism management schools at the universities are the major employee sources for the tourism industry in Turkey. Although Law No. 3308 dictates that employers must pay three-quarters of the minimum wage to interns coming from vocational tourism high schools, there is no equivalent law to protect the rights of university students who seek to complete their student internships with a tourism or hospitality company. Therefore, companies can and do employ university interns without paying them, usually for three or four months during the peak tourist season. In most hotel companies, 20 percent of the staff is made up of interns, excluding the banquet department's part-time, on-call staff.

Graduates of Turkey's hospitality programs, as well as graduates from other disciplines (finance, accounting, humanities, and so on) who try to enter the tourism and hospitality job market, find it difficult to be hired on the merits of their education; they are often hired on the basis of who they know. Even international hotel companies that, in their own countries, readily hire college graduates on their own merits do not do so in Turkey; they too follow local customs, which means that applicants with relatives or friends within a company's current work force or who are backed by influential people get preferred over deserving applicants with no such support. This raises an ethical issue for the international hospitality companies. Favoritism in hiring damages the public faith in the fairness of these companies.

Another source of labor for hospitality companies in Turkey is experienced employees currently working in the tourism field. This is the most expensive way to recruit employees, and is only done when a company wants to hire an employee away from a competitor or when it has no other option.

An alternative source of labor is experienced employees who have worked in other service sectors or in other, non-tourist-related industries. When these people are hired over graduates of university tourism or management programs, it causes university graduates to lose their confidence and the public to wonder about the value of a university diploma.

Non-traditional sources of labor, including senior citizens and people with disabilities, are also available for employment. However, few senior citizens look for a job, due to the social and cultural mores of Turks. Labor Law No. 1475, Statute 18, Article 4, asks all employers employing more than 50 full-time employees to have at least two percent of their staffs made up of disabled people.

As mentioned earlier, most Turkish people try to get a job with the help of their relatives, which leads to nepotism. Companies also hire new personnel on the recommendations of their current staff. Turkish companies hardly ever put ads in newspapers or in human resource magazines. The new strategy is to share information on the human resource Web sites in Turkey.

Training and Development Practices

The amount of training employees receive varies from company to company, depending on the quality of the company, the company's financial restrictions, and top management's philosophies. Large international companies and some mid-size hotel properties carry out good employee training programs. These programs might be provided by the employers themselves, by Turkish universities, or by national or international consulting firms. Turkey's Ministry of Tourism continues to work with the International Labor Organization to create written materials—such as job descriptions, job specifications, and detailed, step-by-step how-to manuals—for entry-level positions in hotels, restaurants, and travel agencies.

Training helps employees improve their ability to provide guest service; however, human resource departments must always consider if the training investment generates a return in terms of increased profits for the company. In properties with high turnover rates, training has been targeted as a way to decrease turnover, but training can still be a money-losing activity if trained employees quickly leave their jobs for better offers at competing properties.

Unions have a particular interest in training programs because these programs allow their members to attain better positions and achieve a measure of job security. Unions provide union training halls on work premises to provide employees with job-related training and training on general subject areas.

Performance Evaluation Practices

Employees are evaluated periodically within the scope of the training programs developed and directed by the human resource departments of hospitality companies. Scientific evaluation criteria have been adopted by most of the leading hospitality organizations. Employee performance evaluation methods vary from company to company and include the rating-scale method, peer-appraisal method, self-appraisal method, and appraisal-by-subordinates method. One of the best indicators of employee performance at resort properties is believed to be the employee's contribution to encouraging guests to stay longer this year or return next year.

Many managers in small- and mid-size properties depend on their intuition when evaluating employees, which can leave employees faced with unfair performance evaluations. Most of the criteria these bosses use are subjective; they do not rely on any scientifically approved evaluation method. When business is good, these bosses claim the credit; when business is down, they blame their employees.

Working Women in Turkey

The number of women who own or manage large hotels in Turkey—five-star properties and the like—is very low. However, a much higher number of women own or manage travel agencies (see Exhibit 6). In fact, Turkish women working in the tourism and hospitality industries have made substantial progress over the last 15 years. However, research shows that management jobs in Turkey are still dominated by men; Turkish organizations still prefer to hire or promote men into managerial and administrative positions.[3]

Exhibit 6 Percentage of Female Personnel at Each Level for Accommodation, Restaurants, and Travel Agencies

Level	Accommodation	Restaurants	Travel Agencies
Top/General Management	9%	8%	17%
Managerial	24%	9%	43%
Supervisor	16%	4%	42%
Broad-Skill Worker	15%	4%	53%
Skilled Worker	34%	11%	27%
Limited-Skill Worker	5%	13%	23%

Source: 1993 Manpower Survey of the Tourism Industry by the Ministry of Tourism and the International Labour Organization.

The number of working women in Turkey tends to increase faster than the working population as a whole, as more Turkish women receive vocational education and have more opportunities to work. However, this increase has not resulted in a parallel increase in the number of female managers in the workplace.[4] There are several potential reasons for this.

First, occupationalists argue that gender inequalities in management selection stem from the gender composition of jobs, in the sense that some lower-level jobs with limited opportunities for promotion, like teaching and secretarial work, are supposed to be more suitable for female personnel.

Another reason is the socialization of women, which leads many women to not aspire to high managerial positions and to be drawn to jobs traditionally staffed by women, such as nursing. Such socialization may lead working women to accept or prefer non-management jobs or jobs at low managerial levels, either because they feel less competent than men or because they lack motivation or fear success.

Last but certainly not least, family considerations and responsibilities tend to keep women from achieving high positions in the workplace. Factors such as raising children and a lack of mobility (women stay home to raise their children, and fewer women than men own cars or have access to cars) seem to be important reasons for women's absence from senior management positions.

The Expatriate Manager

Encounters of Turks with expatriate managers go back to the development of the Bosphorus Hotel, now called the Pera Palas, built in 1892 in İstanbul during the Ottoman Empire years by the Compagnie Internationale des Wagon-Lits, the owner of the famous Orient Express train. After two world wars and their aftermath interrupted international ventures, another early introduction of expatriate managers occurred in 1955, when the Hilton Hotel Company won a bid to operate a hotel in İstanbul that the Turkish government built with Hilton's assistance—this hotel was Hilton's third overseas investment and only its second hotel management venture in Europe, after the Hilton Castillana in Madrid, Spain.

Expatriate managers work in Turk-owned companies as well as international companies. In this section we will take a brief look at some of the problems and opportunities expatriate managers face in Turkey.

In Turkish Companies

While there are a number of expatriate managers working for international tourism companies in Turkey, few work for tourism companies owned by Turks. Those few expatriate managers who do work for Turk-owned hospitality companies are well known, experienced managers who formerly worked for international hospitality chains in Turkey and have proven track records in Turkey. These managers are very familiar with the Turkish culture and know how to comport themselves in Turkish society. Moreover, they are able to reach out to new, foreign market segments for the benefit of the Turkish companies they work for. Turkish hospitality companies looking to hire expatriate managers typically have good reputations in the international-trade arena and sound relationships with and high respect from foreign businessmen.

In International Companies

Four Seasons, Hyatt, Renaissance, Hilton International, Conrad, Ceasar's, Holiday Inn, Sheraton, Swissotel, Kempinski, Intercontinental, Mercure, Ramada, SAS, Corinthia, Club Med, Sol Group, Robinson, Iberotel, and Aldiana are the major international hotel companies currently operating hotels, resorts, and holiday villages in Turkey, mostly in such major metropolitan cities as İstanbul, Ankara, İzmir, Adana, and Mersin, and at resort destinations on the Aegean and Mediterranean coasts. Most of these companies prefer to have expatriate managers in the top management positions of their Turkish operations. Notable exceptions are the Holiday Inn company and the Mersin Hilton SA Hotel in Mersin.

The internationalization of production affects the human resource function in a number of ways and makes management more difficult.[5] First, the management task becomes increasingly complex; for example, the business becomes involved in international compensation, taxation, and insurance issues. Second, managers must cope with expatriate staff members who have (or whose families have) more than the ordinary financial, health, or schooling difficulties in their new country; the scope of these types of problems typically is much less in companies staffed entirely by natives.

The current international business environment is increasing the incentive for international companies to transfer managers to operations outside their native countries for reasons of personnel and organizational development. With the growth of international mergers and acquisitions, joint ventures, and alliances, the value of having international management teams able to operate across a range of cultures is considerable indeed.

The growing importance of international experience means that companies are paying considerable attention to expatriate-manager selection and are looking for ways to minimize the problem of expatriate-manager failure. There are three main reasons for expatriate-manager failure:[6]

1. *Inappropriate selection of expatriate managers.* They were selected simply because they were successful in the company's domestic market, so it was assumed they would be successful overseas.

2. *Inadequate preparation and training.* They were not given the proper training they would need to be successful in a new country.

3. *Stress associated with expatriation.* Their job performance suffered because of the stress associated with learning about a new culture and working in a different work environment—even from the stress associated with worries about possible repatriation problems when the managers were eventually sent back home.

Because of these and other reasons, some international companies think that the best strategy is to recruit and develop home-country managers for their international operations. This is hard to do, however, because the international companies usually have a poor knowledge of the labor markets and educational standards outside the country from which they are based. Cultural and linguistic problems can also crop up when selecting home-country managers for foreign operations, and international companies may use, unknowingly, inappropriate recruitment methods.[7] However, these problems are minimized in Turkey, because it has a large number of properly educated and experienced staff members ready to take over responsible positions with international companies.

Corporate Cultures

Turkish Corporate Cultures

The administrative structures of Turkish tourism and hospitality companies are very similar to international companies' structures, with one major exception: the general manager's ability to manage the company. In Turkey, most of the single owners or the families that possess a majority of a company's shares claim the right to have the final word on all company issues, without considering the advice of their companies' top management professionals. Top managers of Turkish companies are not given by their companies' boards of trustees the responsibility and authority commensurate with the positions they hold. Many general managers in Turk-owned hotels cannot even sign a check of a few thousand dollars on their own. Certainly, this discourages these managers and lowers the job satisfaction they can achieve from working for such a company.

Professional managers usually resign as soon as they can from companies run by such independent owners. These owners then look for other top-level managers and will hire one who might not be as qualified as the previous manager but who is willing to carry out the owners' bidding without question.

This approach prevents the implementation of contemporary, scientific management methods to overcome company problems. The unsuccessful promotional efforts by Turk-owned hotels, resorts, and holiday villages on the Aegean and

Mediterranean coasts point to the fact that the Turkish owners of these properties cannot get together to support their common product through their local trade association, or band together to lobby for higher tour-package prices from the world's largest tour operators (**TUI, NUR, Thompson, DER,** etc.). In the absence of professional managers on their staffs (because the owners are overbearing), hotels, resorts, and holiday villages in the newest and most beautiful destinations on Turkey's Mediterranean coast stay poorly promoted and do not receive their fair share of the market.

International Corporate Cultures

The advantage international hospitality companies have in Turkey over Turkish companies is that they have better organizational structures and give their top managers the responsibility and authority they need to oversee daily operations. The expatriate managers of international companies bring with them the required education and training. At the same time, ideally, these managers must have the ability to understand and work in the local culture. The successful expatriate managers of international companies can help develop middle managers recruited from the local labor force.

International companies have also made mistakes from time to time, such as transferring to Turkey human resource directors who do not speak Turkish and have little or no knowledge of the legal framework or the personnel issues in Turkey. Without understanding Turkish rules and regulations, these expatriate human resource directors are forced to call the human resource directors of competing hotels, often English-speaking Turks, every time they have to make a decision. This helps explain why Turkish natives within the industry are puzzled by such appointments.

Trends in the Near Future

The expansion of multinational corporations is a major—perhaps the major—phenomenon of the international economy today. Tourism and hospitality companies play a big part in this expansion. International hotel chains penetrate new markets in China, Central Asia, and Eastern Europe. Airlines fly to new and more remote destinations, and tour packages are put together even for such far-off places as the North Pole and the lonely steppes of Mongolia. The world is getting smaller and cultures are coming into closer contact with each other.

More foreign investments are expected to enter the Turkish economy. As the number of international companies in Turkey grows, more expatriate managers are expected to come to Turkey to take charge of these companies, and more workers from foreign countries are expected to come to Turkey. International companies, bringing to Turkey more expatriate staff members, should help improve the working standards of the Turkish work force. Turkish businesses and personnel will also benefit from the technological breakthroughs and organizational innovations of these international companies. At the same time, the expatriate staffs of these international companies will learn about Turkish culture.

For this new wave of expatriate managers, there will be no clear-cut guidelines. Success will come through the adaptation and integration of prior experience with local realities. These managers will develop new management approaches based on local advice and their best judgment.

Endnotes

1. "Turkey," MSN Encarta Learning Zone (2000), available at http://encarta.msn.com/find/Concise.asp?ti=05D7D000.

2. State Institute of Statistics (2000). "Economic and Financial Data for Turkey" (on-line). Available: http://www.die.gov.tr/TURCAT/turcat.html#Population.

3. Terry C. Blum, Dail L. Fields, and Jodi S. Goodman, "Organizational-Level Determinants of Women in Management," *Academy of Management Journal*, 37 (2): 241–268.

4. Meryem Akoğlan and Öznur Yüksel, "Managerial Behavior and Effectiveness: Perceptions of Female Managers in the Hospitality Industry," *Anatolia*, 9, no. 1 (Summer 1998).

5. P. J. Dowling, "International and Domestic Personnel/Human Resource Management: Similarities and Differences," in R. S. Shuler et al, eds., *Readings in Personnel and Human Resource Management* (St. Paul, Minn.: West Publishing, 1988), 456–462; and P. Enderwick, "International Human Resource Management," in P. J. Buckley and M. Brooke, eds., *International Business Studies: An Overview* (Oxford: Basil Blackwell, 1992), 523–539.

6. W. Holmes and F. K. Piker, "Expatriate Failure: Prevention Rather than Cure," *Personnel Management*, 12 (1980), 30–33; and M. Mendenhall and G. Oddou, "The Dimensions of Expatriate Acculturation: A Review," *Academy of Management Review*, 10 (1985), 34–37.

7. H. Scullion, "Attracting Management Globetrotters," *Personnel Management*, 24 (1992), 28–32.

 # Key Terms

DER—The second largest German tour operator.

holiday village—A type of hotel, usually located at a resort destination, that offers simple accommodations but emphasizes food and beverage service, recreational facilities, and entertainment activities.

masjid—A very small mosque, in terms of available area to pray, with no minaret.

mixed-economy system—A system where public and private sectors co-exist in the country's economic activities and ownership of resources. Some business and economic decisions are made by individual businesspeople and private-sector firms, some by government.

NUR—One of the largest and most influential German tour operators.

TUREM schools—"TUREM" stands for Tourism Education Centers. These are schools, which are also operating, three-star hotels, owned and managed by the Turkish Ministry of Tourism, where students study theoretical hospitality knowledge and practice job skills on the spot.

TUI—The top German tour operator, created by the unification of several travel agencies.

Thompson—One of the largest British tour operators.

Discussion Questions

1. What sorts of problems may Turkey be faced with in the near future, as a result of having 55.6 percent of its population under the age of 25?

2. What are the three social security systems for Turkey's working citizens?

3. Why are hotels, resorts, and holiday villages on the Aegean and Mediterranean coasts of Turkey obliged to pay low salaries to their employees?

4. What is Ramadan and the Greater Bairam?

5. What are the major sources of labor in the Turkish tourism and hospitality industry?

6. What are three major reasons for expatriate-manager failure?

Internet Sites

For more information, visit the following Internet sites. Remember that Internet addresses can change without notice.

Turkey: MSN Encarta Learning Zone
http://encarta.msn.com/find/
Concise.asp?ti=05D7D000

Republic of Turkey, Prime Ministry,
State Institute of Statistics (SIS)
http://www.die.gov.tr/ENGLISH/

Republic of Turkey Website
http://www.turkey.org/start.html

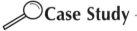

Case Study

A Tale of Two Dreams

Jasmin and Bora are two university seniors studying at a highly renowned Turkish university's school of tourism and hotel management. During the fall semester of their senior year, both must complete an internship program, working 15 weeks in a hotel on a full-time basis. With the help of the school's placement office, both have landed an internship with different leading international hotels. Jasmin has been asked to work in Hotel A's highly acclaimed fitness center, while Bora has been assigned to Hotel B's public relations department.

They both work hard at their jobs, to prove to their hotels' managers that they are good students who deserve to be hired upon their graduations. During their internships, they know that they won't be paid, as is the custom in Turkey, because there is no law that protects the employment rights of university interns. They consider their unpaid internships as opportunities to earn job offers from their hotels for jobs after graduation.

Jasmin's hard work is noticed by her department manager and the general manager of the property, and toward the end of her first month at the hotel she is given the opportunity to manage the property's fitness center on her own when the department manager is absent. On these occasions, she is in charge of six full-time staff members. Near the end of the fall semester, while he is at the university as a guest lecturer, Hotel A's fitness center manager tells the tourism and hotel school's department chairman that he'd like to have Jasmin work at the hotel during the spring semester as well. Since Jasmin has been helping to manage the department, he explains, there has been an increase in the number of return guests and in the income generated by the department. He says that he is sure the hotel will offer her a full-time position after she graduates. Back at the hotel, he tells Jasmin this good news; the hotel's general manager also tells Jasmin that the hotel will hire her when she has completed her studies.

Meanwhile, Bora also has been working to the best of his abilities to prove to Hotel B's management that he is worthy of a full-time job. He was given the responsibility to organize the hotel's "Halloween Night" promotion, and his promotion actually turned a profit—the first time a promotion has been profitable in the history of the public relations department. The property's general manager and public relations department manager are both happy to have Bora as an intern, and they tell Bora that he will have a full-time job with the hotel after he graduates. During a visit to the university's tourism and hotel management school, Hotel B's general manager also tells the department chairman that he'd like to hire Bora on a full-time basis after he graduates, and he would like to see Bora continue his hotel internship during the spring semester as well.

Both students are very happy to have jobs promised to them by the managers of two well-known international hotel companies, and feel that all their efforts at school and on the job during their internships are paying off. Both do their best to keep working hard at their hotels during the spring semester.

Upon their graduations, Jasmin and Bora meet with the general manager, their department manager, and director of human resources at their separate properties. At Hotel A, Jasmin is told that the hotel is unable to hire her on a full-time basis, but, if she wishes, she can continue to work with no pay, just as she has during the last eight months (the two school semesters) until a job opening arises. She isn't given a guarantee that a job will eventually be given to her, however. In contrast, over at Hotel B, Bora's dream has come true! He is given a full-time job with the hotel, and he thanks the hotel's managers for honoring their pledge to hire him after his graduation. At Hotel A, on the other hand, Jasmin is quite sad and is wondering if something is wrong with her or her work performance. Since she was counting on having a job with Hotel A, she did not look into any other job possibilities during her last year at school, and now she has graduated from college but has no job lined up.

Discussion Question

1. Did Jasmin do anything wrong during her internship with Hotel A? If so, what was it?

Chapter 20 Outline

A Brief Overview of the U.S. Travel and
  Tourism Industry
The Organizational Structure of the HR
  Function
The U.S. Labor Market
    The Legal Environment
    Labor Relations
    Recruiting Employees
    Retaining Employees
A Look into the Future

Competencies

1. Describe the economic impact of the
   travel and tourism industry in the
   United States. (p. 340)

2. Discuss how the human resource
   function fits into the organizational
   structures of hospitality businesses.
   (pp. 340–341)

3. Describe the U.S. labor market in
   terms of diversity issues, the legal
   environment, and labor relations.
   (pp. 341–346)

4. Summarize the efforts today's
   hospitality businesses are making to
   recruit and retain employees.
   (pp. 346–350)

Hospitality Human Resources in the United States

Debra F. Cannon

Debra F. Cannon *is an Associate Professor in the Cecil B. Day School of Hospitality Administration at Georgia State University and has taught full-time in its hospitality program since 1991. She has more than 11 years of hospitality industry experience in human resources with The Ritz-Carlton Hotel Company and Hyatt Hotels. She is the executive director of* Praxis—The Journal of Applied Hospitality Management. *A Certified Hospitality Educator (CHE), she also teaches CHE courses worldwide.*

IN THE EXTREMELY competitive environment of the hospitality industry in the United States, service is the key differentiating factor between companies that lead and those that do not survive. Providing good service to employees—"**internal customers**"—in order to encourage them to, in turn, provide good service to guests—"**external customers**"—has become a philosophical foundation for hospitality companies committed to the highest level of guest service. As one human resources director expressed it, "Why shouldn't employees have a one-hundred-percent satisfaction guarantee just like their guests?"[1] Guided by criteria from sources such as the United States' Malcolm Baldrige National Quality Award and the work of W. Edwards Deming, a founder of the modern quality movement, U.S. hospitality companies have learned that quality results are keenly dependent on each individual employee.

Hospitality businesses in the United States are quite varied, from small, independent bed-and-breakfast inns or sole-ownership restaurants to huge corporate structures. This chapter will focus on human resource issues and practices that are applicable to a wide range of hospitality operations. First, we will take a brief look at the U.S. travel and tourism industry as a whole, then discuss how the human resources function fits into the organizational structures of hospitality businesses. The next section will present information about the U.S. labor market, including the legal environment, labor relations, and strategies for recruiting and retaining employees. The chapter concludes with a glimpse of what the future might hold for human resources personnel struggling to cope with the current labor shortage in the United States.

A Brief Overview of the U.S. Travel and Tourism Industry

As we enter a new millennium, the U.S. travel and tourism industry is the largest service export of the U.S. economy, the third largest industry in terms of employment, and the third largest retail or service industry segment. The industry generated approximately $482 billion in tourism expenditures in 1997 and had a payroll of almost $128 billion. Tax revenues amounted to over $71 billion.[2]

The largest segment of the U.S. travel and tourism industry, food service, employs more than 10.2 million people, with employment projected to be 12 million by 2006. Total annual wages and benefits equal $40 billion for full-service restaurants and $32 billion for limited-service (quick-service or fast-food) establishments. One-third of all adults in the United States have worked in food service at some time during their lives.[3]

The hotel industry employs 1.16 million people, including full-time and part-time employees, and paid, in 1998, $20.2 billion in wages. The lodging industry, in total, directly supports 7.6 million jobs in related areas.[4] The meetings, conventions, and exposition segment of the hospitality industry supports 1.5 million jobs in the United States[5] and the U.S. casino and gaming industry directly employs more than 46,000.[6]

Approximately one out of every 17 workers in the United States is employed in the travel and tourism industry.[7] Employment in major travel industry sectors has outperformed other major U.S. industries, with growth between 1994 and 2005 forecasted to exceed 18 percent.[8]

The demand for managers in the hospitality segments of food service and lodging is projected to grow 33 percent from 1994 to 2005—more than twice the growth rate of the total work force. During that same time period, it is projected that there will be 192,000 new management positions and a total, considering turnover, of 313,000 management openings.[9]

The Organizational Structure of the HR Function

The support available for managers, supervisors, and employees through some type of human resources department varies considerably in the United States, depending on the size of the business in question and its organizational hierarchy. Small hospitality organizations typically do not have a human resources department at all; human resource responsibilities are totally in the hands of **line managers** and supervisors. Large operations have human resource departments that range from a department of one—a generalist human resources manager—to larger departments with specialists in various human resource areas, such as employment, benefits administration, training, and employee relations. These specialists typically report to an assistant director of human resources or a director of human resources. In most of the large, branded hotel and restaurant companies in the United States, property-level human resource departments are supported by human resource divisions at the corporate level.

In the more successful, service-oriented hospitality organizations, human resources is increasingly considered a "business partner," with a recognizable impact on the bottom line. Though considered a support department, not a revenue-generating one, there are numerous ways that human resources can positively contribute to an operation's success, some of which are:

- Effectively recruiting, selecting, orienting, and training new employees

- Providing ongoing training and career development for current employees

- Building progressive employee relations throughout the company

- Providing guidance to line managers on how to continually build a positive work environment

With the increased use of computerized **human resources information systems,** human resource personnel can also provide extremely valuable data to their organizations in an efficient, timely way to further support operational areas of the business.[10]

The heads of human resources in large hospitality organizations are typically given Vice President or Senior Vice President titles and serve on high-level decision-making teams or the executive committees of their organizations. This indicates the vital role the human resource function plays in today's business world. Having human resource managers on decision-making teams puts them in a better position to partner more effectively with line managers and help them meet corporate objectives.[11]

The U.S. Labor Market

The vital need to attract and retain workers is the most critical issue facing U.S. hospitality operations today. With unemployment in the United States at a 30-year low, hospitality operations are sometimes forced to curtail plans for expansion—and, in some cases, even daily operations—because of worker shortages.[12]

In addition to coping with the labor squeeze in the United States, hospitality companies must also adjust to the changing demographics of the labor market. The U.S. labor market is becoming more diverse, a trend that will continue throughout the twenty-first century.

There are many types of diversity present in the U.S. work force. More women are working than ever before, for example. While women represented 42.1 percent of the civilian labor force in 1979, this percentage had increased to 46 percent in 1994 and is expected to increase to 47.8 percent by 2005. Approximately two-thirds of single mothers (separated, divorced, widowed, or never married) are in the labor force; almost 45 percent of mothers with children under the age of three years old are working.[13]

The U.S. labor force is getting older. By the end of the year 2000, one in every three workers will be 45 or older.[14] The median age of the labor force was 34.7 years in 1979; in 1995, the median had hit 37.8 years, and it is expected to be 40.5 years by 2005.[15] The aging of the work force has had a big impact on the U.S. hospitality industry, particularly in segments such as food service, where the primary labor

Exhibit 1   The Diverse U.S. Population

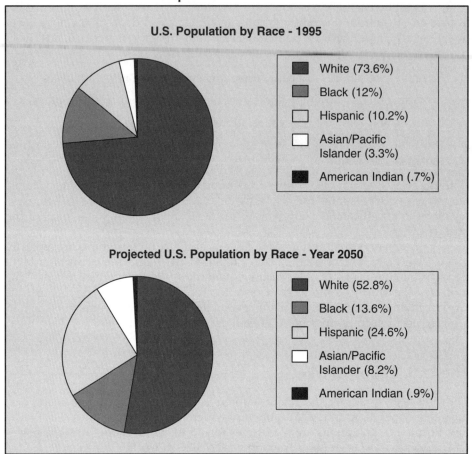

U.S. Population by Race - 1995

- White (73.6%)
- Black (12%)
- Hispanic (10.2%)
- Asian/Pacific Islander (3.3%)
- American Indian (.7%)

Projected U.S. Population by Race - Year 2050

- White (52.8%)
- Black (13.6%)
- Hispanic (24.6%)
- Asian/Pacific Islander (8.2%)
- American Indian (.9%)

Source: U.S. Department of Labor, 1999, www.dol.gov.

pool traditionally has come from the 16- to 24-year-old population. According to the U.S. Bureau of Labor Statistics, the number of workers within the 16-to-34 age bracket will have dropped from 50 percent in 1985 to 38 percent in 2000.[16]

Another type of labor diversity in the United States involves race and ethnic background. In 1995, Hispanics represented 10.2 percent of the civilian labor force; by 2005, they are expected to reach 12.6 percent. Asian-Americans will grow from 3.3 percent of the labor force in 1995 to 4.4 percent in 2005. The African-American presence in the workplace will also increase slightly, from 12 percent of the labor force in 1995 to 12.4 percent in 2005. On the decline is the percentage of Caucasian workers. While representing 73.6 percent of the work force in 1995, Caucasian workers are expected to decline to 69.9 percent by 2005.[17] Exhibit 1 shows how the trend toward a more diversified U.S. population is projected to continue through the year 2050.

The work force found in the U.S. hospitality industry reflects this diversity. For example, minority employees constitute 31.5 percent of the U.S. food service work force today; that figure is expected to increase to 33.5 percent by the year 2005. Of this projected 33.5 percent, it is expected that Hispanics will be the largest group, with 15.5 percent of the labor force for this segment, followed by 11.7 percent for African-Americans and 6.3 percent for Asian-Americans.[18]

The diverse and limited labor market found in most areas of the United States necessitates creative recruiting and selection approaches on the part of hospitality businesses. They must also place a high priority on employee retention. The diverse labor force also has legal implications for the industry.

The Legal Environment

Laws regarding employment in the United States are found on two levels—federal and state. Federal laws come from the U.S. government and are in force throughout the nation; state laws are in force only in their particular state. While there are limited exemptions from the federal laws, most private businesses—including hospitality companies—must comply with the mandatory federal employment laws. Laws on the state level must meet federal standards, at minimum, but may also exceed the federal standards. Therefore, owners and managers of hospitality businesses must not only have a comprehensive knowledge of federal legislation; they must also be aware of applicable laws in the particular state or states in which their businesses are located.

The laws presented in this section are provided to give you an idea of the number and variety of regulations that must be followed by the typical U.S. hospitality business. Although the list is not exhaustive, the laws that are described include the major areas of employment legislation on the federal level affecting most U.S. hospitality companies.

Equal Employment Opportunity Laws. On the federal level, a fundamental group of laws known as equal employment opportunity laws prohibits job discrimination on the basis of a wide range of reasons. The first of these laws, the Equal Pay Act of 1963, protects men and women who perform substantially equal work in the same establishment from sex-based wage discrimination. This legislation was followed by the Civil Rights Act of 1964. Title VII of this major federal law prohibits employment discrimination based on race, color, religion, sex, or national origin. Court decisions later extended the Civil Rights Act to include protection from sexual harassment.

In 1967, the Age Discrimination in Employment Act was passed. This law protects individuals who are 40 years or older from employment discrimination based on age. In 1978, the Pregnancy Discrimination Act was passed, which protects pregnant job applicants and employees from discrimination if they can perform essential job duties; it also protects pregnant employees from mandated maternity leave determined by the employer. Another far-reaching federal employment law was Title I of the Americans with Disabilities Act of 1990. Employment discrimination against qualified individuals with disabilities, mental or physical, is prohibited under this law, which includes private sector employers as well as federal, state, and local governments. The Civil Rights Act of 1991 allows both compensatory and punitive damages in cases of intentional illegal employment discrimination and provides workers with the opportunity to seek jury trials.[19]

All of these equal employment opportunity laws, administered on the federal level by the **Equal Employment Opportunity Commission (EEOC),** prohibit discriminatory practices in any area of employment, including hiring and firing; compensation; assignment or classification of employees; transfer, promotion, layoff, or recall of employees; job advertisements and recruitment; testing and training of employees; benefits; and other terms and conditions of employment. Employers are required to post notices to all employees, advising them of their rights under the law and how to contact the EEOC. These notices also state that employees have the right to be free from any type of retaliation for filing a complaint or lawsuit.[20]

Other Employment Laws. In addition to the equal employment opportunity legislation, there are many federal laws—more than 180, in fact—concerning the workplace that are administered by the United States **Department of Labor.** One of the most far-reaching laws in this group is the Fair Labor Standards Act of 1938, which is administered by the Wage and Hour Division of the department. This legislation requires employers to pay certain classifications of employees (such as non-management workers) the federal minimum wage and overtime of one-and-one-half times the regular wage. This law also restricts the hours that children under 16 can work and forbids their employment in certain jobs that are considered hazardous. In addition, the Department of Labor administers the Family and Medical Leave Act. Passed in 1993, this law requires employers of 50 or more employees to give up to 12 weeks of unpaid leave to eligible employees for the birth or adoption of a child or the serious illness of the employee or of an immediate family member.[21]

An additional group of laws important to the workplace are those administered and enforced by the U.S. government's **Occupational Safety and Health Administration (OSHA),** an agency created by the Occupational Safety and Health Act of 1970. The goal of OSHA is to help U.S. businesses maintain safe and healthful work environments and avoid occurrences of serious workplace accidents.

Other major federal employment laws include the Immigration Reform and Control Act of 1986. This law requires employers to obtain verification that the individuals they want to hire or have hired have the legal status to work in the United States and are not illegal aliens. Penalties for violations of this law include fines levied against the employer, probable deportation of the illegal aliens, and—for employers with repeated serious offenses—possible criminal charges. The law is applicable to employers of any size.

In the area of employee terminations, one of the major legal concerns is **wrongful discharge.** Wrongful discharge claims can involve employers of any size and are not limited to groups protected by civil rights legislation. In addition to wrongful discharge lawsuits alleging illegal discrimination, there are two other basic types of wrongful discharge lawsuits. One type, a "contract theory"-based lawsuit, alleges that a contractual relationship, stated or implied, existed between the employer and employee via the employer's employment application forms, employee manuals or handbooks, offer letters, and other documents. Wrongful discharge cases based on this theory allege that these documents constitute a con-tract that was broken when the employee was terminated. The second type of wrongful discharge lawsuit is based on violation of public policy. These lawsuits allege that the employee was terminated because he or she refused to break the law or insisted on obeying the law.

In the U.S. work force, it is estimated that there are 50,000 to 200,000 unfair employee dismissals each year. Because a sizable number of these unfair dismiss-als result in lawsuits involving large jury awards that can reach $1 million or even more, many small to medium-size organizations are trying to protect themselves by purchasing employment-practice liability insurance specifically written for wrongful discharge lawsuits.[22]

Litigation of all types is a growing concern for hospitality businesses. In the United States, the number of employment discrimination cases brought to federal courts doubled in three years, to 23,000 in 1996, with the number of attorneys specializing in the field having tripled since 1990.[23] In 1997, the EEOC handled 15,889 sexual harassment complaints and won $49.4 million for victims.[24] These figures do not give an accurate picture of the number of sexual harassment law-suits filed nationally, because it is estimated that 95 percent of such cases are settled out of court.[25]

In an attempt to avoid legal problems, many hospitality organizations train their managers and supervisors on the complex legalities of doing business in the United States. Because of the diversity and scope of federal and state laws, this training must be regularly updated and reinforced. The hope is that this legal knowledge will help managers ward off legal difficulties in the workplace and maintain a positive image for their companies.

Labor Relations

Another complex legal area in the United States concerns labor relations. The National Labor Relations Act of 1935 (also known as the Wagner Act) established the right of employees to organize and engage in collective bargaining—that is, form unions. Today, approximately 14 percent of the non-agricultural U.S. labor force is unionized. This figure has fallen from 20.1 percent in 1983 and the record high of 35.8 percent in 1945.[26] The primary reason for this decline is due to the United States' shift from a manufacturing economy to a service economy.[27]

Labor laws in the United States vary from state to state. Some states, labeled **right-to-work states,** do not allow labor contracts that make union membership a condition for keeping one's job. In all other states, unions may set up "union shops" or "agency shops." In a **union shop,** employees must join the union where they work after a prescribed period of time and pay dues to the union; in an **agency shop,** employees may choose not to belong to the union, but they still must pay union dues. The differences in labor laws among the states explain in part the great variances in union membership among the states. For example, 26.8 percent of the work force in New York is unionized—one of the highest percentages among the 50 states. In contrast, only 3.7 percent of South Carolina's work force is organized.[28]

The largest and most active union in the hospitality industry, the **Hotel Employees and Restaurant Employees International Union (HERE),** represents more than 300,000 hospitality employees through more than 120 local unions in the United States and Canada. The local unions range in size from a few hundred members to more than 40,000 members (in Las Vegas, Nevada). Their members come from a variety of hospitality segments, such as lodging establishments, restaurants, cafeterias, clubs, casinos, contract food services, in-flight food preparation businesses, and concession businesses.[29]

Even though the percentage of U.S. workers belonging to unions has dramatically declined over the past half century, union organizing attempts still occur throughout the United States, including those involving the hospitality industry. In fact, the President of the American Federation of Labor has predicted that more service-sector workers will be turning to unions in the years to come, and unions are putting more resources into organizing workers in service sectors. Unions today are using new strategies and tactics in their organizing efforts. One strategy, termed **"corporate campaigns,"** involves intense anti-business or anti-owner publicity that might be done "on the Internet, in the media, or with investors, guests, employees, local citizenry, and so forth."[30] Specific examples of these tactics include "sending alarming alerts to potential investors, staging rallies during peak business hours, intruding on a company's efforts to secure loans, forwarding letters to charitable groups claiming hypocrisy among the company's executives, and leafleting customers about alleged safety and health code violations of the company."[31] The number-one reason for employees wanting to join a union, however, remains dissatisfaction with the way they are managed, dissatisfaction that may be linked to a number of factors: lack of control over work, lack of respect, inconsistent policy enforcement, unfair treatment, poor communication, lack of security, and unacceptable handling of grievances.

Recruiting Employees

Because of the labor shortage, hospitality companies in the United States have found that multiple and varied approaches must be used to recruit new employees. The traditional approach—placing classified advertisements in major newspapers—does not work in reaching diverse labor markets in most communities. (Ads in smaller, ethnic newspapers can be effective, however.) Companies must now, more than ever, think of creative ways to expand the number of potential employees they reach.

Some hospitality companies have found partnerships helpful and have joined with city and county governments, social service agencies, and schools in order to attract new workers. Hospitality businesses in some areas of the country have discovered that outreach programs to potential applicants must include such services as translators and transportation options. Some hospitality businesses have even partnered with other hospitality businesses. In some locales, hotels and restaurants are joining forces in events such as city-wide job fairs and are finding strength in their united numbers.[32]

Another recruiting strategy for hospitality businesses is to expand benefits thought to be particularly meaningful to potential employees. "Lifestyle benefits" are increasingly becoming important in organizations that are trying to attract and maintain a committed work force. Lifestyle benefits address a number of personal needs, from child care to elder care to legal assistance, as companies develop competitive packages for their employees. For example, the Inn for Children in Atlanta, Georgia, is a $5 million collaboration among the Hyatt, Marriott, Omni, and Hilton hotel companies. The Inn is managed by AmeriCare Early Learning Centers and offers 250 child-care slots to low-income workers, including people from the community at large as well as employees from the collaborating hotels, with very competitive rates for qualifying parents/guardians. The Inn is open from 5:30 A.M. to 1:00 A.M., to accommodate hotel employees from all work shifts. The Inn for Children has become a full-service family center, offering benefits such as influenza shots and income tax preparation assistance. Marriott has expanded this model in the Washington, D.C., area.[33]

Other recruiting strategies have involved paying higher wages and offering flexible work schedules. Employees are often paid "recruiting bonuses" for referring applicants who are hired and remain in their jobs for a stipulated period of time, usually 90 days. In areas with extremely limited labor markets, applicants—particularly for management or other jobs requiring multiple or specialized skills—are offered signing bonuses (typically lump-sum payments) for joining a company.

Many communities have implemented "School to Hospitality Career" programs in their high schools. Specialized classes in food service, lodging, and tourism are offered to students who also gain hospitality work experience during after-school hours. Many of these programs are supplemented with mentoring opportunities with industry professionals. The goal is to interest high school students in the hospitality industry and give them work experience prior to graduation. It is hoped that, with this head start, many of these students will go on to long-term careers in the hospitality industry.

Expanding into new labor markets will continue to be vital for hospitality companies as they seek to recruit and hire the most qualified employees. For many hospitality companies, a significant number of new employees will come from the ranks of older workers, disabled people, high school students, non-English-speaking applicants, and college students recruited to serve internships. Those hospitality companies that can remain flexible in addressing varied employee needs and fulfill expectations for career satisfaction and development will have a better chance of finding good workers.

Retaining Employees

Hospitality companies, after expending considerable time and energy recruiting potential employees, must follow up their efforts with effective employee selection tools, training processes, and approaches to retaining their new hires. Otherwise, the people they worked so hard to find may walk out the door.

With the use of employee selection techniques ranging from **behavioral interviewing** to psychological testing, hospitality organizations strive to hire the best applicants (see Exhibit 2). With more awareness of the legal pitfalls of negligent hiring and negligent training, employers in the United States are under increased pressure to adequately screen applicants, conduct reference checks,

Exhibit 2   Examples of Behavioral Interview Questions

Qualification being evaluated: customer interpersonal skills.

Questions:

1. "What was the most difficult time you ever had with a customer, and how did you handle it?"
2. "Have you ever had to make an angry customer happy? If so, tell me how you did it."

Qualification being evaluated: interpersonal skills with co-workers.

Questions:

1. "What have you found most difficult in working with other people? Describe a specific challenge with a co-worker, and how you handled it. What was the outcome?"
2. "Describe a situation in which you disagreed with a co-worker. How did you handle it, and what was the result?"
3. "What were the characteristics of a supervisor or manager with whom you worked with effectively?"

Qualification being evaluated: the ability to effectively manage stress.

Question:

1. "What was the most stressful day you ever had at work? How did you handle it, and what did you learn from this experience?"

Behavioral interview questions are based on the premise that the past experiences of a job candidate can help an interviewer predict the future behavior of the candidate. These are open-ended, probing questions that require the candidate to reflect on specific prior work and life experiences.

obtain criminal background reports, and document and evaluate training to determine its effectiveness.

Retaining employees is crucial to maximizing quality, and the hospitality industry must do a better job in the retention area. For example, the American Hotel Foundation conducted a comprehensive study which found that the national turnover of line-level hotel employees (hourly employees without supervisory responsibilities) was 83 percent in 1995, 75 percent in 1996, and 92 percent for the partial-year data collected in 1997.[34] A survey conducted by the National Restaurant Association (NRA) found that full-service restaurants averaged 84 percent turnover in 1996; quick-service restaurants reported 116 percent turnover.[35]

Recently, the American Hotel & Motel Association's Blue Ribbon Task Force established the goal of "attracting and retaining the 'best of the best' in the labor force for the hospitality industry." To do this, it recommended to the association's members that they:

- Improve the workplace environment through upgraded wage and benefit packages, more career development opportunities, increased employee recognition, and mentoring.

- Improve their connections with their local communities through outreach programs, educational efforts, and youth mentoring.

- Improve the image of the hospitality industry by communicating the many opportunities it offers as a great place to work, with numerous career options.[36]

In its 1999 Restaurant Industry Forecast of Management Trends, the NRA indicated that many food service employers are concentrating on increasing the job satisfaction among their current employees by creating a caring, supportive work environment. This type of environment requires an interactive style of management built on open communication, collaborative relationships, and recognition of staff achievements. In a recent survey conducted by the NRA, approximately two-thirds of table-service restaurant operators reported providing bonuses to salaried employees for superior performance; a majority of quick-service restaurants also reported paying performance bonuses to salaried employees. Recognition on the hourly employee level seems to be largely limited to publicizing superior employee performance through various awards, such as "Employee of the Month."[37]

Providing career opportunities for all groups of employees is another important strategy in the struggle to retain workers, and one in which the industry must do better than in the past. According to an American Hotel Foundation study, there is twice the percentage of racial and ethnic minorities in line-level hotel positions than in the general population, but this percentage does not hold true for supervisory and management ranks. While minorities accounted for 55.2 percent of line-level hotel jobs, minorities held 38.4 percent of supervisory positions and only 21.5 percent of management positions. In contrast, Caucasian employees accounted for 45.6 percent of line-level positions, 53.9 percent of supervisory positions, and 75.8 percent of management positions.[38]

Many hospitality companies are realizing, as they move into the twenty-first century, that their management styles and organizational structures will not work in the future. Employee empowerment, meaningful work, and challenging career opportunities are all key considerations as hospitality companies strive to become "employers of choice." A study of job factors considered most important by employees from various industries identified "responsibility for work and the results it produces" as having the top priority. This factor was followed by acknowledgment for their contributions and having work tasks matched to their strengths.[39]

Numerous examples of how hospitality companies are changing to retain workers and maximize success were identified in a recent study of best practices in the U.S. lodging industry.[40] For example, Accor North America has implemented a "booster program for employee empowerment" that takes decision-making down to lower levels in each property. Accor also implemented a **multi-directional performance review** process for managers, in which managers are reviewed by subordinates and peers as well as superiors; employees were given training in how to conduct these reviews. Each Accor North America hotel also has employee roundtables to facilitate discussions with the hotel's executive team. The Boulders resort has initiated self-directed, three-person housekeeping teams that are responsible for everything from assigning room duties and work areas to achieving room quality and conducting room inspections. Each team is required to be multi-cultural, in order to create the greatest degree of employee interaction and help employees learn English who don't speak it. Marriott International has established a management framework for senior managers to develop future talent for leadership positions within the company. With the development of its Benchstrength Management System, Marriott helps managers focus on the core management capabilities that are keys to the company's growth as a global organization. The Ritz-Carlton Tysons Corner reorganized its staff into self-directed work teams involving job enrichment and employee empowerment. The results? A reduction in employee turnover, lower payroll costs, greater employee development, and heightened employee and guest satisfaction levels.[41]

Improving the workplace for managers so that they, too, will stay on the job is also of concern to hospitality organizations, as evidenced by recent changes made by major restaurant chains. Olive Garden was one of the first chains to reduce the work week of managers (to 50 hours) and give them two days off per week. Outback Steakhouse helps managers balance their work and personal lives by being open only for dinner, thus reducing the length of work shifts. In addition, the company's compensation structure allows managers to buy into the units in which they work. This gives them a genuine ownership stake in the company. The hope is that managers who are given more reasonable work schedules and monetary incentives above and beyond their salaries will be less likely to leave.[42]

A Look into the Future

Picture this scenario: At a downtown hotel, a woman is met in the parking lot by a hotel staff member, warmly greeted by name, and personally escorted into the lobby. She is then taken to a "club lounge" area, where she is served coffee and a continental breakfast. Afterwards she is taken on a tour of the property, during which she notices and admires the financial planning facilities, the business center, and the fully staffed concierge department that is available to run a variety of personal errands. Upon departure, she realizes that her car was washed during her visit, and the next day she receives a note of appreciation from the hotel.

If you thought this scenario described a wonderful experience for one of the hotel's most valuable clients, you were wrong! It was an applicant's visit to discuss one of the many job openings in the hotel. (By the way, in case you haven't guessed by now, the financial planning facilities, business center, and concierge department in this example are for the hotel's employees.)

Is this a picture of the future? In many areas of the United States, treating applicants as "clients" might soon become standard operating procedure for hospitality "employers of choice." According to Al Church, Vice President of Human Resources for Hilton Hotels Corporation, this scenario is already occurring in cities such as Las Vegas, where unemployment is extremely low, growth is astronomical, and the hospitality industry is extraordinarily competitive.[43]

Human resource strategies for finding, hiring, and retaining workers are certainly changing throughout the United States, as more and more businesses begin treating employees as valued "internal customers." J. Willard Marriott, Jr., Chairman of the Marriott Corporation, put it this way when speaking about employees: "Motivate them, train them, care about them, and make winners out of them. If we treat our employees correctly, they'll treat the customers right. And if the customers are treated right, they'll come back."[44]

Endnotes

1. Kirby D. Payne, "Leadership, Motivation Can Stem from Human Resources," *Hotel & Motel Management,* (3 November 1997), 44–45.

2. Travel Industry Association of America (1999). "Travel Economic Impact Model" (on-line). Available: www.tia.org.

3. National Restaurant Association (2000). "2000 Restaurant Industry Pocket Factbook" (on-line). Available: www.restaurant.org

4. *The 1998 Lodging Industry Profile* (Washington, D.C.: American Hotel & Motel Association, 1999).

5. C. Love and E. Polivka, "Meetings, Conventions, and Exposition Industries," in R. Brymer (ed.), *Hospitality and Tourism: An Introduction to the Industry* (Dubuque, Iowa: Kendall/Hunt, 2000 [in press]).

6. American Gaming Association (1999). "Casino Gaming Industry Employees" (on-line). Available: www.americangaming.org.

7. *The 1997 Lodging Industry Profile* (Washington, D.C.: American Hotel & Motel Association, 1997).

8. Travel Industry Association of America (1999). "Travel Economic Impact Model" (on-line). Available: www.tia.org.

9. Tom Powers and Clayton Barrows, *Introduction to Management in the Hospitality Industry* (New York: Wiley, 1999).

10. Robert H. Woods, *Managing Hospitality Human Resources,* Second Edition (Lansing, Michigan: Educational Institute of the American Hotel & Motel Association, 1997).

11. P. Buhler, "Managing in the 90s: The Changing Role of HR: Partnering with Managers," *Supervision* 60, no. 6: 16–18.

12. American Hotel & Motel Association (1999). "Curtis Nelson to Help Launch AH&MA Historic Leadership Task Force to Attract Workers to the Lodging Industry" (on-line). Available: http://list.ahma.com.

13. G. Dessler, *Human Resource Management,* Eighth Edition (Upper Saddle River, N.J.: Prentice-Hall, 2000).

14. P. Marshall-Mims, "Aging Work Force Creates New Challenges for Restaurant Industry," *Nation's Restaurant News,* 26 July 1999.

15. Dessler.

16. K. D. Rutledge-Jones, "Restaurants Find It's Hard to Put Food on the Table," *Nashville Business Journal*, 8 June 1998, 6–8.

17. Multicultural Foodservice & Hospitality Alliance, *1999 Report to Industry: Multicultural Diversity—A Profitable Business Strategy* (Minneapolis: Multicultural Foodservice & Hospitality Alliance, 1999).

18. Multicultural Foodservice & Hospitality Alliance, *1999 Report to Industry.*

19. EEOC (1999). "Federal Laws Prohibiting Job Discrimination—Questions and Answers" (on-line). Available: www.eeoc.gov.

20. EEOC (1999). "Federal Laws Prohibiting Job Discrimination."

21. Department of Labor (1999). "Fair Labor Standards Act of 1938, As Amended" (on-line). Available: www.dol.gov.

22. A. Sherman, G. Bohlander, and S. Snell, *Managing Human Resources* (Cincinnati, Oh.: South-Western College Publishing, 1998).

23. Dessler.

24. "United States: The Perils of Flirtation," *Economist* 346 (8055): 25–26.

25. "Inappropriate Sexual Conduct Named Top Risk of the 90s," *Internal Auditor* 54, no. 6 (1997): 14–15.

26. Bureau of Labor Statistics (1999). "Union Members Summary" (on-line). Available: http://stats.bls.gov; and Woods.

27. Woods.

28. Dessler.

29. Hotel Employees and Restaurant Employees Union (1999). "HERE History" (on-line). Available: www.hereunion.org.

30. A. Stokes, "HERE Is Here Again!" *Praxis—The Journal of Applied Hospitality Management* 2, no. 1 (Spring/Summer 1999): 30–33.

31. M. Prewitt, "Unions Embrace New Tactics vs. Operators," *Nation's Restaurant News* 31, no. 19 (1997): 1, 4.

32. J. Higley, "San Francisco Job Fair Manages to Hit It Big," *Hotel & Motel Management*, 10 August 1998, 30.

33. S. Balzar, "Hotels Consider Child Care Benefits Program," *The Business Journal Phoenix*, 14 September 1998, 9, 14.

34. American Hotel & Motel Association, "Turnover and Diversity in the Lodging Industry," 1998 American Hotel Foundation study.

35. "Foodservice Trends," *Restaurants USA*, February 1998, 39–46.

36. American Hotel & Motel Association (1999). "Curtis Nelson to Help Launch AH&MA Historic Leadership Task Force to Attract Workers to the Lodging Industry" (on-line). Available: http://list.ahma.com.

37. National Restaurant Association (1999). "1999 Restaurant Industry Forecast—Management Trends" (on-line). Available: www.restaurant.org.

38. Marty Whitford, "Study Confirms There's a Lack of Minorities in Management," *Hotel & Motel Management*, 10 August 1998, 1, 138.

39. R. E. Herman and J. L. Gioia, "Making Work Meaningful: Secrets of the Future-Focused Corporation," *Futurist* 32, no. 9 (1998): 24–26.

40. Laurette Dubé et al., *American Lodging Excellence—The Key to Best Practices in the U.S. Lodging Industry* (Washington, D.C.: The American Hotel Foundation, 1999).

41. Dubé et al.

42. M. Coeyman, "Lighten Up!" *Restaurant Business* 96, no. 4 (1997): 46–52.

43. Al Church, panel presentation on "Recruiting Out of the Box," Atlanta, Georgia, 2 September 1999.

44. C. Bernstein and R. Paul, *Winning the Chain Restaurant Game: Eight Key Strategies* (New York: Wiley, 1994).

Key Terms

agency shop—A business in which employees who do not belong to the union are still required to pay union dues.

behavioral interviewing—An employee selection technique using interview questions that ask applicants to describe specific situations from their backgrounds, how the applicants handled the situations, and the results of their actions. The technique is based on the theory that past actions are good predictors of how the candidate might perform on the job.

corporate campaign—An organizing strategy or tactic used by unions that involves intense anti-business and/or anti-owner publicity efforts; corporate campaigns might use the media, the Internet, and other outlets to get the union's message to guests, investors, employees, and local citizens.

Department of Labor—A major U.S. government agency that administers and enforces more than 180 federal employment laws, including wage and hour laws, worker safety and health laws, laws concerning pension and welfare benefits, and others.

Equal Employment Opportunity Commission (EEOC)—The U.S. government's administrative agency that oversees and enforces all civil rights legislation prohibiting employment discrimination based on race, religion, color, national origin, gender, age, or disability.

external customer—A guest or patron of a business.

Hotel Employees and Restaurant Employees International Union (HERE)—The largest union representing hospitality workers in the United States.

human resources information system—A computerized system that is used for collecting, maintaining, updating, and analyzing a variety of applicant and employee-related information.

internal customer—An employee of an organization; this term is part of the quality-oriented philosophy which holds that employees must be treated positively so that they, in turn, will be more likely to provide excellent service to guests, the "external customers."

line manager—A manager with decision-making authority within a department or work area that directly provides services or products to guests, as opposed to a staff manager, who advises line managers but has no decision-making authority within their departments.

multi-directional performance review—A performance appraisal for supervisory and management personnel that is conducted with feedback from subordinates and peers as well as superiors.

Occupational Safety and Health Administration (OSHA)—An agency of the United States Department of Labor that develops and enforces mandatory job safety and health standards.

right-to-work state—A state that does not allow labor contracts that make union membership a condition for keeping one's job.

union shop—A business in which employees are mandated to join the union and pay union dues.

wrongful discharge—Terminating an employee for an illegal reason, in violation of an express or implied contractual agreement, or in violation of public policy (for example, because the employee refused to break the law or insisted on obeying the law).

Discussion Questions

1. What is the connection between the satisfaction of a company's "internal customers" and the level of guest service provided at that company?

2. What is the impact of the travel and tourism industry on the economy of the United States?

3. How is the work force in the United States becoming more diversified?

4. What are some of the major U.S. federal employment laws?

5. How do state laws vary regarding union organizing and labor relations?

6. How are hospitality companies in the United States recruiting employees in very limited labor markets?

7. How are U.S. hospitality companies dealing with legal concerns in the employment process, such as negligent hiring and negligent training?

8. What type of turnover among hourly employees has been experienced by lodging and restaurant employers?

9. What types of initiatives have been taken by the American Hotel & Motel Association and the National Restaurant Association to reduce turnover and retain quality employees?

10. How have major U.S. hospitality companies made major organizational changes to create a more positive workplace and increase employee retention?

Internet Sites

For more information, visit the following Internet sites. Remember that Internet addresses can change without notice.

American Gaming Association
http://www.americangaming.org

American Hotel & Motel Association
http://www.ahma.com

Club Managers Association of
America
http://www.cmaa.org

Equal Employment Opportunity
Commission
http://www.eeoc.gov

Hotel Employees and Restaurant
Employees Union
http://www.hereunion.org

National Restaurant Association
http://www.restaurant.org

Society of Human Resources
Management
http://www.shrm.org

Travel Industry Association of
America
http://www.tia.org

United States Bureau of Labor
Statistics
http://stats.bls.gov

United States Department of Labor
http://www.dol.gov

Case Study

Challenges in Housekeeping

Your latest promotion with a leading hotel company provides a wonderful career opportunity. Having started with this company as a management trainee shortly after graduating from college with a hospitality degree, you plan to one day be a general manager of a large convention hotel. With your most recent promotion to the position of director of housekeeping, you face many challenges. You are now located in what the company considers to be its flagship hotel. Having recently been renovated, this property is expected to set the standards in cleanliness and guest service for the entire company. As you review what has preceded your arrival in housekeeping, you notice several areas to prioritize—all involving human resources. Turnover has been high in this department—25 percent more than in housekeeping departments in comparable company properties. Guest comments regarding room cleanliness dropped to an 85 percent satisfaction rate for the preceding year; the company frowns on guest comments dropping below a 95 percent satisfaction rate. You also notice that housekeeping had the highest number of work-related accidents for the past two quarters in this hotel, and three employees are still out of work with injuries involving back strains. As you look at the hotel's current staffing guides, you realize that the ten openings you currently have in the department equates to 20 percent of the department's full complement of 50 employees. A very busy season is about to begin in about two months and you want to be fully staffed with trained employees. In looking at the demographics of the housekeeping department, you notice that the hourly employees are from diverse racial and ethnic backgrounds, reflective of the diversity found in the surrounding community. As you have been told by the hotel's general manager, your ability to "turn this department around" is important to you, the hotel, and the company.

Discussion Question

1. As you sit at your desk to develop your "game plan" for your first quarter in this position, what should you do? Delineate the top five to eight activities that you will spend most of your time and energy on as the new director of housekeeping. What are the general goals that you hope to accomplish through these activities? Also consider:

   • What are obstacles that you can envision encountering?

   • As the director of this department, what skills and knowledge areas will be important to use as you work to achieve these goals?